WAYNE MUTZA

THE US AIR FORCE

AIR RESCUE SERVICE

AN ILLUSTRATED HISTORY

SCHIFFER MILITARY

4880 Lower Valley Road · Atglen, PA 19310

Library of Congress Control Number: 2022932098

Designed by Justin Watkinson
Type set in Impact/Minion Pro/Univers LT Std

ISBN: 978-0-7643-6480-8
Printed in India

Published by Schiffer Publishing, Ltd.
4880 Lower Valley Road
Atglen, PA 19310
Phone: (610) 593-1777; Fax: (610) 593-2002
Email: Info@schifferbooks.com
Web: www.schifferbooks.com

For our complete selection of fine books on this and related subjects, please visit
our website at www.schifferbooks.com. You may also write for a free catalog.

Schiffer Publishing's titles are available at special discounts for bulk purchases
for sales promotions or premiums. Special editions, including personalized covers,
corporate imprints, and excerpts, can be created in large quantities for special
needs. For more information, contact the publisher.

We are always looking for people to write books on new and related subjects.
If you have an idea for a book, please contact us at proposals@schifferbooks.com.

CONTENTS

ACKNOWLEDGMENTS

Numerous persons assisted in the research of this study, many of whom participated in the events that shaped the proud heritage of USAAF/USAF (US Army Air Force/US Air Force) Air Rescue. I am especially grateful to veterans who resurrected memories to pen narratives about their firsthand experiences—they are the core source of information. Special thanks go to the gurus of particular subjects; they include Felix McLarney and his son, Kelly McLarney, who preserves the history of Grumman's "Albatross" amphibian. Who hasn't heard of the "Huey" helicopter, the history of which is well known by Dr. Ray Wilhite, who maintains a vast library of material and information. When it comes to Kaman's Huskie helicopter, Johan Ragay is the go-to expert, while Stephen Mock oversaw the superb Huskie website. Others shared insight they gained while researching and writing their insightful works: Terry Love, the "L Planes"; Karl Hayes, the Douglas SC-54 "Strato-Rescuer"; Darrel Whitcomb, the Sikorsky "Super Jolly Green Giant"; Nicholas Williams, the Military Air Transport Service; Robert LaPointe, pararescuemen in Vietnam; and Lennart Lundh, the Sikorsky H-34 helicopter. Neil Aird maintains the most comprehensive holding of material about de Havilland's Beaver airplane. Always willing to provide scads of photo assistance and information were Joe E. Ballinger, Bruce Ware, Sid Nanson, Thomas Hansen, David Hansen, Stephen Miller, John Lindgren, Carlton Damonte, Ronald Thurlow, Robert F. Dorr, William T. Larkins, Erik Roelof, Donald Brabec, William "Don" Eastman, John E. "Jay" Merz III, John Ratliff, Ronald Milam, Robert Brackenhoff, and Lori Nye, Selfridge Military Air Museum.

Special thanks are due Richard T. Kight, colonel (USAF, ret.), ARS commander 1946 to 1952; Byron "Hook" Hukee, who managed the Skyraider Association website and authored *USAF and VNAF A-1 Skyraider Units of the Vietnam War*; my brother Dale Mutza; Steven Southiere; David Wendt; Larry Wielgoscz; Dave Menard; Raymond L. Robb; Damon Blair; James E. Atwater; Jack Stoops; David Stoops; Jim Anderson; Stanton Nelson; John Grasser; Ron Angelly; Merle Olmsted; Jim Burns; Terry Kiss, librarian, Air Force Historical Studies Office; Richard Reinsch; Gary Phillips; Bill Streicher; William Kratch; James Hedderly; Larry Ford; Ed Arva; Stamford Robertson; Herb Hardin; Joel A. Harper; Timothy Dring; Terill Aitken; Karen L. Green, curator, National Atomic Testing Museum; Michael Allen; Leo Kohn; David Bergemann; Jeffrey Bright; John W. Caldwell; Michael Holloway; Denise Vavra Myers; Robert Jones; Jerry Jones; James Mandelblatt, Delaware Aviation Museum Foundation; Jo Stys; Fred Zayas; Stephen Ove, historian, 6th Air Mobility Wing; Gary A. Gault, ANG historian; Peter Purvis; Kerry Brunner; Steve Williams; Ted A. Morris; Paul Regan; Diane D. Revolinski; Ron Loftis; Arthur Brand; Forrest Fenn; Gary L. Bain; Michael LaCasse; Hugh LaCasse; James "Pappy" LaCasse; Hank Fannin; Aubry Johnson; Carl Scargall; Russel Vick; Charles R. Wagner; Baldur Sveinsson; Jim Sullivan; William J. Erickson; Charles H. Isackson Jr.; Charles Rouhier; Charles Halcomb, Lt. Col. USAF; James Moore; Fred Scopinich; Roger Connor; Kyron Hall; Ron Olsen; Bill Bailey; Jonathan Bernstein; and Don Jay.

One of the many colorful characters who climbed aboard my project was William A. "Wild Bill" Lyell. Wild Bill led an interesting life, which included a long association with helicopters. He flew fighter aircraft during World War II and after the war worked for the post office, while pursuing a career as a singer and guitarist. When called to active duty during the Korean War, he instructed pilots in multiengine aircraft and helicopters. During six years as a helicopter instructor, Bill taught General Curtis LeMay to fly helicopters. He was the air training command officer and test pilot for the Kaman H-43 "Huskie" and, through that experience and mutual guitar interest, enjoyed a long-lasting friendship with helicopter pioneer Charlie Kaman.

After commanding the 58th Air Rescue Squadron in Libya, Lyell commanded the presidential "Doomsday Squadron," which he discusses later in this book. He then got his wish to fly the helicopter in combat, commanding the 40th Aerospace

Rescue and Recovery Squadron at Udorn Royal Thai Air Force Base (RTAFB), Thailand. In that capacity, he provided the helicopters and crews for the Son Tay Prison raid, later becoming director of combat operations at Nakhon Phanom RTAFB.

Lyell had taught friend, broadcaster, and entertainer Arthur Godfrey to fly a helicopter; he was a crop duster pilot; he drove race cars; and he flew scenes in the film *Flight from Ashiya*. In retirement, he resumed his love for music, becoming nationally recognized as a fiddle and guitar player. After what he called a "good run," William Lyell "flew west" in 2016 at the age of ninety-three.

I am indebted to the following organizations: A-1 Skyraider Association, American Aviation Historical Society, Air Commando Association, Igor I. Sikorsky Historical Archives Inc., Air-Britain, Vietnam Helicopter Pilots Association, Pararescue Association, USAF Helicopter Pilots Association, Air Rescue Association, Jolly Green Association, and USAF Rotorheads.

Often challenging in writing about an expansive subject with infinite history is establishing a starting point. I chose the preliminary period of World War II to identify the beginning of air rescue, although it goes much further back. We could say that the very concept of rescue by air goes back to Greek mythology, which tells the story of Daedalus and his son, Icarus, fabricating wings of feathers and wax to fly to safety. Icarus was lost in the attempt, foretelling the reality of the danger of attempting to escape death by air.

We could say that the first rescue by air occurred in 1870 during the Franco-Prussian War, when the French used balloons to rescue 164 wounded soldiers from Bismarck's onslaught of Paris.

We know that during World War I the French modified airplanes to evacuate wounded. Although a 1912 recommendation that US Army aircraft be used to transport patients was approved, the idea didn't take hold until 1918, when two army officers converted a Curtiss JN-4 "Jenny" into an air ambulance at Gerstner Field, Lake Charles, Louisiana. The Air Service director then ordered that additional JN-4s be modified with a fuselage stretcher compartment for assignment to each airfield. American forces began converting other aircraft types into flying ambulances, with a number of de Havilland DH-4As modified for crash rescue work. It wasn't until the early years of World War II in Europe that air rescue transformed from unprecedented, even novel, concept to organized effort. But the distinction between medical evacuation and rescue remained ill defined.

History has shown that war, in the most paradoxical sense, brought about advances in fields such as technology and medicine that might not otherwise have been attained. Similarly, amid the slaughter and wantonness of war arose the effort to make good on high regard for human life. Indeed, rescue is one of the great stories of humanity. How do you measure someone's sense of altruism, sometimes so profound that they lose their life in the effort to help another? This psychological dimension of air rescue, rife with humanistic value, is overshadowed by the number of historical accounts written about the air force as an agent of war, while less has been written about its humanitarianism; that of rescue, disaster relief, and providing assistance, not only within US borders but globally, paying dividends in international relations that cannot be overstated.

The mention of the US Army Air Force (USAAF) in the acknowledgments section might prompt skeptics to say, "But the army didn't have an air rescue service." Oh, but indeed it did, and with air, land, and water capability, to boot, under the US Army Air Corps. Army aviation has its roots in the Balloon Corps of the Army of the Potomac, under the guidance of Professor Thaddeus Lowe beginning in 1861. Aviation sections organized with balloons and airplanes followed, leading to congressional establishment of the Air Corps in 1926. With a wary eye toward Hitler's sweep through Europe, President Roosevelt asked Congress during 1939 to shore up what he called "an utterly inadequate military." America's air arm rapidly expanded, formed mainly of groups categorized by function. These groups fell under wings, which were assigned to numbered air forces. The 1st through Fourth Air Forces originated in 1940 and came under the Army Air Force (AAF), formed in June 1941. These remained in the States throughout the war, while the Fifth, Seventh, Tenth, Thirteenth, Fourteenth, and Twentieth Air Forces covered the Asiatic-Pacific theater; the Eighth, Ninth, Twelfth, and Fifteenth operated in the European–African–Middle Eastern theater; the Sixth in the Panama Canal Zone; and the Eleventh in Alaska. Within this ever-changing organizational structure, a hodgepodge of rescue units existed. It was from them that the US Air Force Air Rescue Service evolved, and to which it owes its very existence.

Read on and also discover that *air* rescue didn't always mean rescue from the sky; sometimes rescuers came in special boats or made their way over treacherous terrain to reach those who needed help. Gain insight to the many unique aspects of air force air rescue seldom written about; the techniques, training, and equipment, and the wide variety of aircraft. Enter the world of the super-elite pararescueman. Learn about the air rescue navy, air rescue's role in America's space program, the role of the Civil Air Patrol, and, most importantly, the people who made a living of air rescue, whose proud tradition continues.

The history of air force air rescue is told in the tens of thousands who have been helped and whose lives have been saved by those who came to help. I have endeavored through this book to shine a light on the fortitude of the rescuers, and to pay tribute to their indomitable spirit.

ABOUT THIS BOOK

Books I have had published that cover specific Air Rescue aircraft and operations fueled my goal to have it all come together in one volume. The long and expansive history of Air Rescue can never be complete, nor can it ever be precisely accurate. The very nature of rescue work often precludes participants from documenting their discernment and recollection of events. Even if they could, perceptions differ, and time has a way of erasing or clouding memories. Many facts are lost to history, and in existing references—whether official or otherwise—contradiction abounds. But sometimes, given technology and social media, new and fascinating details surface, particularly if the researcher acts the proverbial bloodhound, diligent and tenacious in the hunt until the trail goes cold. And so, writing history is hardly what some say is mere repetition of previously written material.

Both in wartime and in peacetime, air rescue became an octopus whose far-reaching appendages reached areas previously devoid of "friends in high places" with outstretched arms. When Col. Richard T. Kight—second to command the Air Rescue Service—in 1946 wrote the rescue man's creed, he could not have imagined the sacredness of his words and the level of devotion to which they were held. They were, and remain, the light that guides legions of angels.

Throughout the development and growth of air rescue, often it foundered and even faced extinction, but it survived thanks to the perseverance of those who had rescue in their blood, and the undisputable number of lives saved. More than any facet of air rescue, it is the men and women on whom the light shines. Hardware and the organizational structure aside, the heart of this tome is the achievements of rescuers and the rescued, often told in their own words.

Besides many previously unpublished photos, included here is an exclusive listing of air rescue aircraft. Unit assignments are given successively, based on available information. Aircraft and crew call signs are hyphenated as they were actually used. For example: "Jolly 7-0" was spoken as "Jolly Seven-Zero," not as "Jolly Seventy," as is commonly written. Every effort has been made to identify, locate, and credit photographers of images, often a daunting task, given the age of some images, the absence of accompanying attribution, and their passage through many hands.

ROUGH BEGINNINGS

Before the United States entered World War II, its military leaders had given little thought to planning the search for and rescue of missing or downed aircrew. The umbrella of organized protection that existed for mariners was not found in US air operations. Missing fliers were searched for haphazardly by whatever means could be cobbled from local resources. Agencies that came to help had good intentions but little else when it came to proper training, aircraft, equipment, and an established search-and-rescue plan.

The US prepared for war against an enemy in Europe that, initially, could be reached only by transoceanic flight. The same held true to an even greater extent in the Pacific. Markedly increased aircraft production emphasized the glaring need for a global air-sea rescue net, as did vastly accelerated training in the US, overwater flights to war theaters, ship convoy defense, and ocean patrol. But America had not to worry; the bitterly embattled British, as well as their German adversary, would show the way.

Early in his quest for world domination, Hitler's miscalculations led him quickly to more-expansive fronts than anticipated, which caught him, in some regards, unprepared. One of Germany's strengths, however, was the Luftwaffe, and its strength was versatility, as evidenced by Germany's sea rescue service, the "Seenotdienst." Formed in 1935 as the "Ships and Boats Group," it was first operated as a civilian boat service commanded by a Luftwaffe officer, Konrad Goltz.

Designed as a torpedo bomber and first flown as a landplane in 1931, the He 59 went into limited production. It served most of its service as the He 59C in the air-sea rescue role. The Heinkel carried six dinghies, along with a variety of rescue gear, and was modified to bring survivors aboard. Two 660 hp engines gave the 3-ton aircraft a top speed of 137 mph, with a range of nearly 1,000 miles. Red crosses replaced the "Balkenkreuze" insignia on white livery; however, swastikas remained on tail fins. A rescue ladder extended from a belly hatch.

Beginning in 1931, the US Army Air Corps began air rescue and evacuation with modified Fokker XIV (YC-14) transports, designated YC-15s. Outboard motors packed in straw, and bomb casings filled with emergency supplies, could be dropped by parachute. This is the ninth YC-15 modified by General Aviation. A 575 hp Pratt & Whitney R-1690 Hornet radial engine gave the YC-15 a top speed of 137 mph and a range of nearly 700 miles. Its inability for short-field work led to other types for rescue work.

WORLD WAR II

Goltz first oversaw a handful of coastal boats for rescuing airmen downed over the sea. One of these, the *Krischen*, he rigged with a boom for hoisting small seaplanes, a feature that would become standard both on Allied and Axis rescue boats. He then established six rescue zones in the North Sea and the Baltic, each having a rescue boat assigned. Goltz concurred with Luftwaffe leaders of the certainty of war with Great Britain, which meant intense activity over the English Channel and the North Sea and the subsequent need for rescue aircraft. Fourteen Heinkel He 59 floatplanes were acquired and modified by the firm Walther Bachmann Flugzeugbau KG, in Ribnitz, Mecklenburg. Refitting for air-sea rescue included first-aid gear, electrically heated sleeping bags, and artificial-respiration equipment, along with a floor hatch with collapsible ladder, a hoist, and storage for life belts, signaling devices, and survival gear. The finishing touch was overall white livery with red crosses.

Beginning with the invasion of Poland in 1939, the dominoes fell quickly as Hitler's legions stormed through Europe, relentless in their goal of creating a thousand-year Reich. So rapid and sure was their onslaught that one could barely keep up with territory newly labeled "Occupied Europe," which spread across a world map like a widening puddle. Until the fall of France to the Germans in 1940, British strategists had underestimated the furor of the German war machine and, consequently, did not envision the Luftwaffe poised within easy range in France. And the Low Countries, especially Belgium and the Netherlands, which they assumed would act as buffers as they had in World War I, were now in German hands. Great Britain now faced the realization that she would need every pilot to defend her shores in the battle of Britain. The British Air Ministry knew that the few Royal Air Force (RAF) and Royal Navy (RN) boat stations along the coasts would not suffice in retrieving downed aircrew. Dinghies and life jackets aboard RAF aircraft only prolonged a downed flier's agony if there were no boats or aircraft to pluck him from the unforgiving sea.

Why reinvent the wheel, the British surmised, since the Luftwaffe's Seenotdienst had already made progress in the field of air-sea rescue? In some of its first operations against the British, in fact, the Seenotdienst rescued downed RAF Wellington crews that had been mauled after bombing Wilhemshaven. All Luftwaffe aircraft were equipped with yellow survival rafts, and crews had been trained in ditching their aircraft. The Luftwaffe pioneered the use of fluorescein green dye to make survivors' positions in the water more visible. So intense was battle over the English Channel that

The Supermarine Walrus first flew in 1933 as spotter aircraft catapulted from cruisers or battleships, and later was pressed into rescue service with Great Britain, Australia, and New Zealand. In May 1942, the RAF Walrus of No. 277 Squadron takes aboard a downed flier, while a Lysander orbits. By the time the Eighth Air Force arrived in England, the RAF had established six rescue squadrons flying Walruses. While unglamorous, Walruses were sturdy, often taxiing long distances in stormy seas, unable to take off since they were loaded with survivors. No. 277 Squadron would operate seven aircraft types throughout the war, with Walruses serving the duration.

White cowl bands of P-47Ds of the 5th ERS, Eighth Air Force, were replaced by red, white, and blue bands, seen here on serial no. 42-75855 at Boxted Airfield, which used the call sign "Dogday."

the Germans strategically positioned yellow-painted rescue buoys that could accommodate four men and were stocked with blankets, clothing, food, water, and flares. The RAF followed suit. Both German and British patrol boats checked the buoys periodically, leaving the occupants to guess whether they would be rescued or become prisoners. The overwhelming advantage that the Seenotdienst had over the British was its use of floatplanes, which composed most of its aircraft inventory. The Seenotdienst would operate fourteen types of aircraft throughout the war, some of which were captured French aircraft. Before the old Heinkel He 59s were replaced by the larger and more capable Dornier Do 24 floatplane, their numbers would more than double for the 1940 Battle of Britain. After two He 59s were forced down in July, RAF crews received the order to shoot down the white rescue planes, on the conviction that they were monitoring ship positions and being escorted by Luftwaffe fighters. The Luftwaffe maintained that the fighters and Heinkels constituted an innovative rescue task force. Nevertheless, the weight of the controversial decision lay in British prime minister Churchill's declaration that he no longer wanted German pilots rescued so they could again bomb England. The Luftwaffe responded by camouflaging and arming the planes, and the Seenotdienst gallantly continued to rescue both German and British aircrew, despite the loss of four He 59s by RAF fighters. It is estimated that the battle sent 1,200 airmen into the drink, more than one-third of whom were rescued by the Seenotdienst; of those, one-fifth were British airmen. As the German war machine stayed on the offensive and gained territory, its rescue assets, consisting of boats, aircraft, and submarines, followed.

While savoring victory over Germany's failure to crumble Britain's air defenses, the nation's military leaders weighed heavily the lessons learned, and in January 1941 organized the Air-Sea Rescue Services. By fall, the service combined RAF and Coastal Command squadrons. Development was slow, and it wasn't until late 1941 that air search units were formed along the coasts to dispatch high-speed launches (HSLs) of the RAF and the Royal Navy's larger rescue launches. Initially, it fell upon Westland Lysander aircraft to conduct searches and drop their rubber dinghies. A Supermarine Walrus amphibian or an HSL then picked up survivors, whose position was marked by the Lysander's smoke bombs. While the Walrus, true to its name, would never win a beauty contest, to fliers in the water awaiting rescue it was a thing of beauty. For everything it lacked as a rescue aircraft, the Walrus, designed during the early 1930s as a shipboard reconnaissance platform, made up for in durability, and it was available.

In fall 1941, longer-range Hudsons joined the Lysanders and Walruses, all of which carried droppable dinghy packs, flares, and smoke markers. In January 1942, preparations began for wooden, 20-foot, powered boats for the Hudsons. Usually with fighter escort, pilots worked in close conjunction with rescue launches, with all involved under control of direction-finding, or fixer, stations and Air-Sea Rescue Central Control at Saffron Walden.

When the US entered the war, its Army Air Force was unprepared to meet the demands of rescue at sea. The US Navy shouldered the load, and with the increasing buildup of the US Eighth Air Force in Europe, Great Britain's air-sea rescue service assumed the responsibility for all services. Eighth Air Force command in September 1942 formally agreed

"Tony" was a P-47D of the 5th ERS, seen here carrying centerline fuel tank, dinghy pack, and smoke marker. *Courtesy of Roger Freeman / Boxted Airfield Historical Group*

to the arrangement to avoid duplicating services. The agreement stipulated that the AAF would provide aircraft and assistance to keep pace with operational tempo. To ease the burden borne by British rescue forces and for the AAF to become more self- sufficient, in spring 1943 operational control for air-sea rescue went to the AAF, while British units persevered. Since the matter of overall responsibility for air-sea rescue remained open ended, each command of the AAF assumed responsibility for training and equipping its aircrews, some to the extent of forming their own air-sea rescue units. After three AAF command reorganizations and shuffling responsibility, an Emergency Rescue Branch was established in the Pentagon during August 1943. Just weeks earlier, on the fourth of July, the 52nd Fighter Control Squadron of the Eighth Air Force set up shop in the British control center at Saffron Walden to coordinate air-sea rescue. British rescue units remained on station, and all Allied forces participated in searches and rescues as resources allowed. A typical day had the controllers plotting the routes of Allied aircraft so that rendezvous points in the English Channel and North Sea could be determined for rescue boats and search aircraft. All fixer stations were then alerted. As the war intensified, operating procedures that relied on aircraft and boat teams set the pattern for rescue in other theaters and in the US.

THE ARMY'S AIR RESCUE NAVY

Not all of the friends of airmen in distress came from high places—some came from the sea. A vital yet lesser-recognized element of air rescue during World War II did not consist of aircraft or aircrew, but instead boats and sailors—sailors whose time-honored sailor hats clashed with their army insignia. These dedicated soldiers turned sailors manned special boats to rescue aircrew from the drink.

The use of boats to rescue fliers of downed aircraft is as old as the aircraft industry itself. Thanks to the development of the internal-combustion engine with its high power-to-weight ratio, fast torpedo boats were developed in Great Britain, Italy, and Germany prior to World War I. The US Navy watched with casual interest, more intent on building large ships, while rescue boats continued to be patterned after pleasure craft. The army had operated patrol and rescue vessels since the early days of army aviation. In fact, history records the existence of these vessels as far back as 1918.

In 1927, Hubert Scott-Paine founded the British Power Boat Company to develop a fast boat he had hoped to sell to the Admiralty as a torpedo boat. When that failed, he transformed his V-hull speed boat design into an aircraft rescue boat, earning him credit for the designation "Air Sea Rescue Boat." During the early 1930s, the British stationed marine rescue craft at bombing and air gunnery ranges. In 1935, British Air staff approved construction of an experimental high-speed launch. Tests the following year proved successful, and fifteen of the boats were ordered for Coastal Command's reconnaissance squadrons.

In the years leading up to World War II, the US Navy still had not shown interest in small craft. As the navy's aircraft inventory grew, along with that of the US Army Air Corps, requirements for rescue boats still did not exist. Not only would that change when President Franklin Roosevelt forced the issue in Congress, he would become even more persistent as the war in Europe intensified. In compliance, and in view of the success of British and German air rescue boats, the US Army and Navy got on board, and the development of purpose-built air rescue boats became reality.

Fred Scopinich Jr. of the Hamptons Shipyards Inc. recalls: "[The years] 1938 through 1941 was a development time for air-sea rescue boats, and the final design was adopted by the

One of the first army crash boats, P-19, makes a test run on the Atlantic Ocean in March 1940. Destined for use in gulf waters, it was the first of many to be stationed at army bases flying seaplanes. The twin-screw boat was 40 feet in length with an 11-foot beam. Its forward cabin served as a four-litter emergency hospital. Equipment included ship-to-shore phone, six-man raft, and aft rescue boom.

US Army and US Navy during this period. There was no US Air Force in 1938, so the early boats were developed by the US Army Quartermaster Corps." After having mastered the boatbuilding trade under the flags of Italy and Austria, Scopinich's father, Frederick, and uncle, Mirto, in 1922, immigrated to the US. They set up shop at Long Island, New York, and in 1929 established Freeport Point Shipyard. The brothers' yard had earned a reputation for beating contract deadlines and for turning out high-powered skiffs, which led to an order for US Coast Guard patrol boats to stem the flow of rumrunner boats violating Prohibition. The patrol boats had to be fast because some of the rumrunners' muscled boats had been built in Freeport Point's yard. Unsurprisingly, military planners again came to Freeport Point, this time in 1938 for air rescue boats.

Freeport Point Shipyard's response was three 45-foot air rescue boats powered by a pair of 275-horsepower (hp) Hudson Invader engines; they were designated P-16, P-17, and P-18. In 1939, the yard built the 40-foot P-19 for delivery to the US Army Quartermaster Corps. The vessel had provisions for four litters below deck forward, along with a boom hoist on the aft deck (for preventing downed aircraft from sinking) and a 6-foot life raft. Power was derived from twin 275 hp Hall Scott engines.

Meanwhile, the Navy waded into the rescue boat business in 1940, with five boatbuilders selected from twenty-two that had submitted proposals. Freeport Point was one of those selected, and built two of the experimental 45-foot models, which were powered by twin 650 hp Hall-Scott V-12 marine engines. During this time, the two functions of small army boats—patrol and rescue—were married into the "P" boat,

officially designated the Aircraft Rescue Boat (ARB), commonly called "crash boats." The army was not as rigid as the Navy in classifying vessels, taking what it could early in the war and grouping different hull types according to size and function. Thus, ARBs fell under the general heading of "service craft" among nearly 128,000 ships and watercraft operated by the army during World War II. The ARBs were then loosely categorized as self-sustaining offshore, offshore shore-based, inshore, and shallow-water types.

Composing the ARB fleet were P boats and J boats. The "P," which designated "Rescue," identified wooden, gasoline-powered craft ranging in length from 42 to 104 feet, while motor skiffs or launches up to 50 feet in length were classified as J-type ARBs. More than fifty boat manufacturers from coast to coast are known to have built more than seven hundred P-type ARBs during World War II. Some of these builders also produced J-type ARBs, the identification numbers of which exceed 2,200. Higgins Industries of New Orleans, alone, built more than three hundred J boats. During World War II, J boats were loosely classified as ambulance, rescue, patrol, and firefighting vessels. Three of the boatbuilders produced Swamp Gliders, designated "SG," with 135 of the shallow-water rescue craft built in lengths from 16 to 38 feet. Prigg Boatworks of Miami accounts for 118 of that total. Identifying all P- and J-type air rescue boats proves a daunting task considering the large number of builders and scarcity of both government and manufacturers' documents. Compounding the difficulty is the fact that ARBs did not retain the popularity of other vessels such as PT boats.

A class of 45- and 72-foot ARBs built between 1938 and 1940 served as basis for later types built during the war. The smallest measured 42 feet, while 63- and 85-footers resembled US Navy PT boats; 104-foot models resembled the Navy's 110-foot submarine chaser.

Miami's Fogal Boat Yard, when contracted to build the Navy's first PT boats, filled its contract requirement to employ a recognized naval architect by hiring Dair N. Long, along with Charles David Roach. When in 1940 the Union of South Africa began searching for a boatbuilder that could craft an air rescue boat capable of making 42 knots, Long and Roach went to work designing the largest boat that could reach a speed of 43 knots. Combining PT boat test data with the powerful Kermath 500 bhp (brake horsepower) Sea Raider engine resulted in the 63-foot ARB. The Fogal Boat Yard owners, the Buhler family, meanwhile, had changed the company name to Miami Shipbuilding Corporation, and the 63-footer became known simply as the "Miami." Powered by four Sea Raider engines, the Model 127 Miami, with a full load displacement of 25 tons, had a maximum speed of 42 knots. The firm would build more than five hundred of the high-speed, offshore-capable boats, with more than 140 going to the US Army Air Force as Mk. IIs; Army Air Force Mk. IIs were procured under Navy contract with army funds. In view of the Miami's success, Great Britain placed an order for a modified version powered by two 630 bhp Hall-Scott Defender engines. The first example of the new series was the firm's hull number 152, which resulted in the designation Model 152. Model, or design, numbers of ARBs commonly were derived from a builder's hull number assigned to the first boat of a specific type.

US Army leadership, in its awkward attempt to fit air rescue boats into its organizational chart, got an assist from one of its Air Corps officers, who became responsible for forming the army's first rescue boat unit. The unit's history, in essence, reflects the formative period of the army's navy. Especially watchful of the Royal Air Force's success with small, fast boats to rescue fliers downed during the Battle of Britain was Maj. Everett S. Davis, commander of Alaska's Elmendorf Field. Davis took that extra step by sending Lt. Gordon R. Donley on a fact-finding mission to Ketchikan, Alaska, where the Coast Guard agreed to assist in training small-boat crews. Donley recruited a sufficient number of men, many of who were Alaskans with boat experience, to form a special unit called the "Air Corps Marine Rescue Service." Soon, the group

acquired a pair of 42-foot Owens ARBs (P-30 and P-31). Donley moved the unit from the Ward Lake Civilian Conservation Corps (CCC) camp to Annette Island Army Air Field. When Stephens Brothers Shipyard began construction of the unit's first two 104-foot boats, Donley sent twenty crewmen to San Francisco's Treasure Island for gunnery and navigation training, the Hall Scott factory in Berkeley to learn the engines, and Stockton Field for weather interpretation. The unit operated, besides converted commercial vessels and numerous sizes of ARBs, one of eleven steel HA (Hauling, Auxiliary) aircraft recovery ships built during 1942 and 1943. Named the *Col. Joseph C. Morrow* (HA-2), the ship mounted a 30-ton lift boom.

Despite its supply function, the Army Quartermaster Corps became the parent command of air rescue boat units. Accordingly, in June 1942, Donley's Air Corps Marine Rescue Service was redesignated the 924th Quartermaster Boat Company (Aviation). After all army air rescue boat operations were transferred to the Army Air Force during late 1943, Donley's unit became the 10th Emergency Rescue Boat

For inland waters and calm bays, the army acquired small, open-cockpit craft powered by four-cylinder Gray marine engines. This pair, a wooden 36-foot Higgins and 22-foot Chris-Craft, were among ten boats of the Hamilton Field ARB unit, San Francisco Bay, in 1943.

The army's navy at Langley Field, Virginia in September 1942. The P-25 was one of fourteen 42-foot ARBs built by Owens Yacht Co., Baltimore. The P-16 at left was one of three 40-foot ARBs built in 1938 by Freeport Point Shipyard, Freeport, New York. The master of each Langley boat was a civilian pilot intimately familiar with the region's coastline.

Squadron under the Eleventh Army Air Force at Attu in the Aleutian Islands. Throughout the war, the unit would spawn at least ten detachments throughout Alaska, using more than forty ARBs of all sizes, along with the rescue and recovery vessel *Morrow*.

After the attack on Pearl Harbor, US military planners opened the floodgates, inviting shipbuilders from across the country to submit designs and bids for air rescue boats. After engineering the Miami-class Model 168, Mk. I ARB, for the US Navy, Dair Long started his own business in California designing boats for the Army Transportation Corps. Charlie Roach also left Miami Shipbuilding, signing on with Dooley's in Fort Lauderdale to oversee building of Long's 85-foot ARB. This boat was the answer to the army's quest for an ARB that combined the speed of the 63-footer and the range of the 104-footer. Part of the military specifications for the 85-foot Model 379 stated: "The boat is intended for offshore, long-range operations. The hull is a twin screw, 'V' bottom, stepless hydroplane and shall be capable of being driven at high speeds under severe weather conditions without excessive pounding, yet remaining dry."

The 63-foot Miami had a beam of 15 feet, 6 inches, with a draft of 8 feet, 9 inches. Its full load displacement was just over 25 tons. Thanks to a 2,000-gallon fuel load, it ranged 500 nautical miles. Accommodations included two officer staterooms, a galley, a radio room, and a six-litter dispensary aft, which was formed by concealing the engines below fold-down berths. Engine controls and steering were remotely controlled from the pilothouse. Relocating the engines from aft to amidships to eliminate angle drive, which necessitated changes in general arrangement, resulted in the Model 314.

Sidestepping proprietary issues with Miami Shipbuilding, the War Department pressed the company to provide direct assistance to seven other yards in building the Model 314. The Miami was the most produced, totaling 740 in a dozen models by fifteen different shipbuilders; nearly half the boats were Model 314s.

Each boatyard selected to construct 85-footers was contracted to build about nine boats, with all builders working from the same specifications provided by the War Department. Dair Long's 85-foot Design 379 carried a crew of twelve to fourteen, including a medical technician. Its twin 1,500 hp Packard-Allison engines were fed by a 3,800-gallon supply of avgas. The 50-ton vessel cruised at 24 knots, with a top speed of 35 knots. The designer of the 104-foot Model 235 was Benjamin Dobson of Fairharbor, Massachusetts, who had designed rumrunners during the 1920s. King among the ARB fleet, the 104-footer was powered either by three 625 hp Kermath V-12 engines or by three Hall-Scott 640 hp engines, which allowed cruising at 18 knots; later models were powered by twin Packard engines that gave 20 knots; fuel capacity was 4,000 gallons of avgas. Also standard on 104-footers was a pair of six-cylinder Chrysler Crown engines that allowed a 6-knot slow cruise. Standard armament for both boat types consisted of twin .50-caliber machine guns in barbettes, or "tubs," on each side of the flying bridge, and a 20 mm cannon aft in a recessed well; a machine gun forward was optional. Small arms for the crew consisted of .30 cal. carbines, 12-gauge double-barrel shotguns, and .45 cal. Thompson submachine guns. A typical crew of twelve comprised three warrant officers—skipper, mate, and chief engineer—plus a boatswain, medic, gunner, radio operator, two oilers, and three deck crewmen. The size of the 104-footer inhibited its ability to be transported to global theaters by ship, since deck space was always at a premium. Thus, 63- and 85-footers, being smaller, faster, and more maneuverable, became the favored standard ARBs. A total of 140 Model 379s were built by thirteen different shipbuilders.

The boats of the 10th Emergency Rescue Boat Squadron, along with many others, went from production to two Washington shipyards for ARB outfitting prior to delivery to their units. Barbee Marine Yards of Renton outfitted the vessels during the war years, as did Olsen & Winge Marine at the Lake Washington Ship Canal at Ballard, in the Seattle region. The latter yard, called the "Swede Shipyard," performed extensive outfitting of uncompleted air rescue boats during the war. Since ARBs were built for temperate regions less severe than the Bering Sea and the Aleutians, 10th ERBS crews had an oversized heater installed on the portside deck, and they insulated hull spaces and added skiff hoists and "catfall" rope systems to haul aboard 75- or 100-pound Danforth fluked anchors. To boost the constant demand of small Kohler light plants for the all-electric boats, crewmen rigged a cruise engine to run a belt-driven generator.

In 1938, the USAAC ordered twenty-six Grumman OA-9 "Goose" amphibians for transport and air-sea rescue. These were supplemented in 1942 by five ex-navy JRF-6B navigation trainers redesignated OA-9s. All Goose survivors were designated A-9s in 1948. The Goose was Grumman's first monoplane and its first twin-engine aircraft.

While shipbuilders turned out air rescue boats, units were formed and operational parameters and tactics were discussed. Some Continental air force commands didn't wait for the results of high-level air-sea rescue planning and took the initiative in putting their boats and aircraft to work. Since Third Air Force regularly conducted overwater flights in its coverage of the southeastern states, its leaders began boat rescue operations in 1941. Civilians with experience in small boats were hired to supplement military personnel, and mixed crews often used privately owned pleasure boats, which weren't up to the job. Operations improved late in 1942, when qualified citizens were commissioned as warrant officers. The ARB units commonly were designated quartermaster boat companies (aviation), which in the US were stationed along coastlines and on inland waterways near army airfields. Over

time, ARB units were assigned to all combat theaters. The exact number of ARB units established during the war remains elusive; however, upward of fifteen primary boat companies reportedly were formed, all of which had numerous detachments dispersed within their theaters.

One of the first ARB units formed was the 923rd Quartermaster Boat Company at California's Hamilton Field, along the shores of San Pablo Bay. As headquarters of the US Army Air Corps, a major training base, and an aerial port for troops and equipment destined for the Pacific and China-Burma-India (CBI) theaters, Hamilton's busyness necessitated an ample water rescue presence. Jo Stys, whose father, John George Scheiner, was a crewman aboard the unit's 104-foot ARB P-209, explains: "He answered a call for formation of the rescue squadron being formed. They put together some sort of ad and ran it at the movie theater in Stockton, where he was taking training. They say never volunteer, but he did because he owned a houseboat on the Ohio River and that's what they wanted to hear. He told me stories of how he and some of his crew had to go out to replace targets in the bay for the fighter pilots to practice on. Sometimes communications weren't the greatest, and they were still out there when the fighters came in to strafe with live rounds." Bill Somers, who had mastered boat-handling during his youth on Puget Sound and served as a member of the US Coast Guard Auxiliary, also volunteered for crash boat duty and was assigned to the Hamilton unit. He trained aboard the 104-foot P-218, eventually becoming skipper of three ARBs and later squadron commander. The P-218 operated from Marshall on Tomales Bay near Hamilton Field. The Marshall and San Pablo Bay stations were under Fourth Air Force, which controlled nine stations along the Pacific Coast having a combined total of forty-four ARBs.

Quartermaster Corps vessels were organized into the Army Transport Service, which governed large transport ships, and the Harbor Boat Service, which included all smaller craft.

When the Army Transportation Command assumed the army's water transport operations on July 31, 1942, the two were combined to form the Transportation Corps–Water Division. Since the army felt it important for its air arm to have control of all aviation-related functions, in late 1943 air rescue boat units were transferred to the US Army Air Force. The move resulted in a designation change to "Emergency Rescue Boat Squadron (ERBS)," numbered 1 through 15. This gave overseas theater commanders flexibility in using boats to follow battle fronts and for clandestine work. Training ARB crews initially was left to theater commands; however, at the transfer, the Air Training Command assumed this duty. In February boat crew training had begun at Lake Pontchartrain, New Orleans Army Base, by the 1007th Quartermaster Rescue Boat Overseas Training Unit. The school initially used 110-foot vessels built during World War I, but eventually acquired 104-foot ARBs. One year later the ARB school merged with the Aircrew Training Branch at Keesler Field, Mississippi, with crash boat crews trained at nearby Gulfport as part of the Emergency Rescue School. A significant crash boat presence had been established in the region with activation in

The OS2U-3 "Kingfisher" proved a capable search-and-rescue platform during the war. This Kingfisher of Cruiser Scouting Squadron 1 (VCS-1) launches from the light cruiser USS *Detroit* in the Aleutians in 1943.

Built in 1944 by Allis Chalmers, the M-7 Snow Tractor was equipped with a portable heater and two stretchers. In the background is the AAF SAR Kennel at Presque Isle, Maine. *Courtesy of Glenn Tremble collection*

late 1943 of the Main Crash Boat Base at Ocean Springs, Mississippi. Five ARBs of various sizes covered the Mississippi Sound, while ARBs operated from four subbases at Cameron, Louisiana; Municipal Field, New Orleans; Brookley Field, Alabama; and Gulfport, Mississippi. All were consolidated in fall 1944 at Gulfport AAF, with sixty boats, although one-third

were out of commission. Greater interest in B-17s carrying droppable lifeboats spelled the end of the marine section of the Emergency Rescue School. The school itself was disbanded in April 1946, and all boats went to Brookley Field.

Besides their specialization and basic seamanship training, crewmen were trained in aircraft and ship recognition, swimming, small-boat handling, gunnery, and sanitation and decontamination; they were cross-trained in navigation and emergency medical care. In August 1944, training in smaller boats was discontinued because they could not be used for open-sea rescue. Only crews of 63- and 85-foot ARBs were trained, with seven crewmen assigned to 63-footers and thirteen assigned to 85-footers for operational training. This phase included search operations, rescue procedures, rendezvous missions, and working with aircraft, ending with a three- or four-day sea voyage. Crash boat veterans recall that many crewmen were considered temporarily assigned to the boats, although most served long stints on the boats and their military specialty was recorded as "seaman." Aboard the boats, their clothing was a mix of army and navy uniforms, with most preferring navy bell bottoms and the time-honored white sailor hats because they were most comfortable for boat

Watercraft used for rescue work took many forms, such as this DUKW of the 4th ERS at Bonin Islands, Iwo Jima. Fourteen saves are recorded on the "Duck's" side.

work. When ashore, ARB crewmen were amused by the confused looks given their sailor hats and army insignia.

Later in the war, Miami Shipbuilding became the first to install bullet-sealing fuel tanks in boats. Warplanes were using the tank, and the firm was fortunate to receive assistance from US Rubber Company's Virgil L. Van Dinter, who had devised the tank with Gen. Jimmy Doolittle for his epic Tokyo flight. As in aircraft design, changes often meant compromise, with the added weight of the bullet-sealing tanks decreasing the boat's speed to 35 knots. Crews accepted the trade-off since their boats frequently doubled as gunboats in both theaters. As such, periodically they became part of task groups, which were battle groups formed for particular engagements.

Most boats initially were painted gray, with some units painting deck and pilothouses yellow, along with lifeboats and life rings. Later in the war, a scheme was developed calling for the hull above the waterline to be painted Sea Blue, along with the pilot and after-cabin sides, mast, life raft, and dinghy. Horizontal surfaces, the main deck, and the pilothouse deck, along with exterior steps, deck gear, and fittings, were Deck Blue.

Although air-sea rescue along US shores during World War II was disorganized and had few amphibious and seaplane aircraft assigned, the number of air rescue boats was deemed adequate. In Third Air Force, for example, more than sixty Army Air Force and Coast Guard boats were on hand from Charleston, South Carolina, along the coast to Corpus Christi, Texas, compared to only five aircraft dedicated to open-sea

The OA-10 Catalina was the most common air-sea rescue aircraft in the Southwest Pacific. Others were the L-5, C-47, C-45, AT-11, and B-24. A large teardrop search radar was mounted above the cockpit. A scorecard immediately aft of the navigator's/radioman's/radarman's compartment window records four saves. In the pylon that connected the fuselage with parasol wings was the flight engineer's window.

Stinson L-5 "Sentinels" were abundant, with 3,590 ordered for the US Army between 1942 and 1945. The versatile "Flying Jeep" had short-field capability, making it ideal for rescue work. Modification of the L-5 to accommodate stretchers resulted in the L-5B seen here. Many were transferred to the RAF, many of which were returned to the USAAF after the war. A 190 hp Lycoming engine gave the L-5 a top speed of 130 mph at maximum weight of 2,050 pounds. The Sentinel cruised at 110 mph and had a range of 360 miles.

rescue. Although First Air Force units were present on the Atlantic coast, air-sea rescue was largely the function of navy and coast guard assets. Navy aircraft, including five seaplanes, a helicopter, one blimp, and seventeen air rescue boats, plus forty-one coast guard lifeboat stations, ruled out the need for an extensive Army Air Force presence. Experiments with helicopters pointed to the possibility that they would replace crash boats as well as other aircraft types. Despite the development of helicopters, however, crash boats would serve much longer than expected.

RESPONSIBILITY

Since the age-old question of responsibility for air rescue vexed military leaders, AAF staff in August 1943 acted on their desire to become self-sufficient by drafting plans to form seven air-sea rescue squadrons. Since the 65th Fighter Wing, the first of three wings formed under Eighth Air Force in Great Britain, was tasked with air-sea rescue beginning in May 1944, it spawned Detachment B, Flight Section, to augment the theater's fleet of search, or spotter, aircraft. The newly appointed unit commander, Capt. Robert Gerhart, got the ball rolling by first connecting with famed 56th Fighter Group, commander Hubert A. "Hub" Zemke. The 56th, later called "Zemke's Wolfpack," was first to use the Republic P-47 "Thunderbolt," and Zemke obliged by providing a number of them, along with a portion of Boxted Airfield's real estate. Gerhart then had to cobble together pilots, ground crew, and everything else necessary to get his detachment up and running.

Whenever a bombing mission got underway, a pair of Thunderbolts went aloft, and air rescue boats were launched.

Their pilots monitored a common mayday radio channel, which served as the direct link to the air-sea rescue controller and provided fixer stations with bearing signals. When a distress call went out, one P-47 went low to orbit survivors, dropping dinghies and flares, while the other stayed high for radio relay, to provide location for fixer stations, and to engage any opposition intent on interfering with the rescue. As aircraft ran low on fuel, relief P-47s were sent, ensuring that survivors never were without air cover.

Gerhart's unit acquired twenty-five war-weary Thunderbolts, with the inventory eventually topping out at forty-two P-47s. Most had four of their eight .50 cal. wing guns removed to allow for flares, smoke bombs, and dinghy packs. Since their weight caused balance problems on takeoff, the dinghy packs were divided between underwing stations, with flare racks mounted behind a 150-gallon centerline fuel tank that allowed five-hour flight. Pilots were nicknamed "seagulls" and flew under the aptly named call sign "Teamwork." Detachment B's P-47Ds were identified initially by white cowl bands, which were changed to red, white, and blue, along with a yellow band on the vertical stabilizer. By June 1944, invasion stripes had been added. After relocating to RAF Halesworth in January 1945, P-47Ds appeared in natural-metal finish. Shortly thereafter, "spotter squadron" Detachment B became 5th Emergency Rescue Squadron, having added OA-10s, B-17s, and helicopters to its inventory.

Since most flight operations during World War II occurred overwater, the Consolidated Aircraft Corporation's Catalina flying boat easily qualified as the best choice for water rescue. Contrary to popular belief, the Catalina was not the first amphibian used by US forces for air-sea rescue. Grumman's "Goose" claims that title, having been designed as a flying yacht for the Manhattan wealthy in 1937. Taking its cue from the US Coast Guard and US Navy, the Army Air Corps, in 1938, ordered twenty-six of the type, which were designated OA-9. These were supplemented in 1942 by five JRF-6B navigation trainers redesignated A-9s. Consolidated's "Cat" too had been proven in navy service prior to the war. Although it was destined to become the mainstay of search and rescue (SAR) for AAF and US Navy forces, more fliers were pulled from the drink by surface vessels and submarines. The Catalina's slow 120-knot cruising speed and high-wing design, which allowed it to conduct searches, was offset by its limited range and lack of defensive armament. Its most glaring drawback was its lack of structural strength to withstand repeated water landings and takeoffs. That drawback, however, did not dampen the determination of a Catalina crew in August 1943, when three B-17 bombers ditched. After spotting ten survivors in a raft, the OA-10 landed in seas the crew knew was too rough, tearing off a wing float when they slammed onto the waves. They got the fliers aboard and, with takeoff impossible, began taxiing toward friendly territory. A Spitfire pilot radioed, spotting ten more crewmen in the water, and guided the Catalina to them. With its precious cargo of twenty survivors,

The Northwest Staging Route, consisting of Canadian and Alaskan airfields, allowed transfer flights of Lend-Lease aircraft to the Soviet Union during the war. Along the route was RCAF Station Whitehorse, Yukon, used jointly by the Royal Canadian Air Force and USAAF. Here, among AT-11B and UC-64A aircraft on the Whitehorse flight line, rescue dogs are exercised using a wheeled carriage during summer to keep sled dog teams in condition.

the overloaded Catalina struggled through pounding seas for seven hours, when, finally, a launch arrived and took the battered aircraft in tow.

Although RAF aircraft were rescuing downed aircrew, Catalina amphibians were requested for Eighth Air Force, with six Canadian Vickers-built OA-10As sent from Keesler Airfield in January 1945. In anticipation of the need for larger facilities to accommodate the flying boats, along with six B-17s modified to carry lifeboats added in March 1945, Detachment B, 65th Fighter Wing, relocated to RAF Halesworth, where it was redesignated 5th Emergency Rescue Squadron (ERS). Modifications of the Catalinas to AAF air-sea rescue configuration, done at Neaton, Norfolk's air depot, included the installation of AN/APS-3 sea search radar, heaters, and additional flooring around observation blisters to facilitate water rescue, and replacing Canadian radio equipment with US gear; they were devoid of armor and unarmed, to reduce crew to six and allow for carrying more survivors. The modifications and new all-white paint schemes delayed their operational start to March. Eventually, ten OA-10A Catalinas joined the original six. The 5th ERS worked closely with RAF aircraft and armed motor launches. At war's end, the unit would record 938 men rescued, along with hundreds of crippled aircraft shepherded back to England.

As in Great Britain, in North Africa and throughout the Mediterranean the AAF relied heavily on the RAF for air-sea rescue. The British had paid little attention to air-sea rescue in the region until Italy attacked France in June 1940. However, committed to protection of the homeland, British rescue sources were spread thin. By the time the AAF's first independent air rescue unit became operational in mid-1943, an ample number of British aircraft and rescue boats were in place. Beginning in August, they were augmented by the 5th, 8th, 11th, and 12th Emergency Rescue Boat Squadrons, which were under British control. Initially assigned J-type boats, these units were limited in open-sea and rescue operations. Thus, their primary duty became target towing at African ports, carrying mail, and ferrying passengers between ships and shore. After the units relocated to Naples, Italy, in the spring of 1944, they often served as transport hacks and even carried soldiers on recreational trips to the Isle of Capri. Crew frustration of not being used efficiently was only made worse by long waits for parts and the absence of radios, which crews eventually acquired and installed.

Three USAAF OA-10A Catalinas and crews became part of the 12th Fighter Command, which worked under the Northwest African Air Force Coastal Command. Five Catalinas originally had been dispatched to Malta; however, one was damaged at Puerto Rico, and another developed trouble and had to land in neutral Spanish Morocco, where aircraft and crew were interned. Pilots of the detachment's three crews were among forty AAF pilots trained in the PBY at NAS Pensacola, Florida, beginning in March. The remainder of the crews, which comprised copilots, navigators, engineers, radio operators, and radar observers, also underwent intensive training. Another three crews went to the Fifth Air Force in the South Pacific, and the remainder helped form the 1st ERS in December 1943. In spring 1944, the crews were assigned as instructors to the newly established Emergency Rescue School at Keesler Field. The downing of a general, Nathan Twining, was the impetus behind formation of the rescue school. After their B-17 went down in the Coral Sea on January

THE US AIR FORCE AIR RESCUE SERVICE

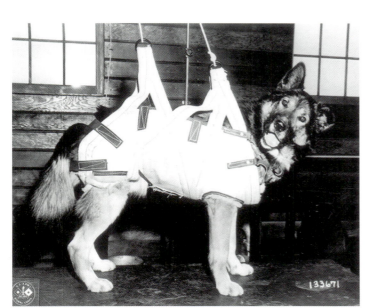

This Alaskan malamute obligingly tries a Rimini dog parachute harness, found to provide dogs the best possible protection during jumps. Camp Rimini cadre chose the paratrooper's 24-foot reserve chute for use with the harness.

27, 1943, Twining and fourteen others spent five days in life rafts while hundreds of aircraft and ships from all services were diverted from combat duty to search the ocean. The much-publicized search and successful rescue underscored the need for greater emphasis on rescue. It also triggered extensive training of aircrews in ditching and survival equipment; the number of airmen recovered rose dramatically. Despite the obvious need for training, less than half the aircraft necessary to qualify crews were available. This was compounded by the Catalina's tendency to sustain damage during water landings. The problem, it was discovered, occurred at the factory, where fewer stringers than were called for in the original plans were built into the rear hull. Although the area could be strengthened, the bow remained weak, prompting a directive forbidding water landings. This didn't deter a Pensacola PBY instructor from making his mark in history and reflecting the altruistic spirit of air rescue. When the Philippines-bound cruiser USS *Indianapolis* was sunk by the Japanese in July 1945, Lt. R. Adrian Marks arrived on scene to see scores of survivors being attacked by sharks. He knew he had to act, so in defiance of orders against landing the Catalina in rough seas, he skillfully put the PBY down in 12-foot waves. His crew took aboard so many sailors—fifty-six in total—that many had to be lashed to the wings. With the engines shut down, Marks's damaged Catalina became a rescue platform until rescue ships arrived.

A similar incident in May 1944 spotlighted not only the rescue capabilities of the navy's Kingfisher seaplane, but the partnership of aircraft and vessel. Lt. j.g. John A. Burns launched in his OS2U from USS *North Carolina* at Truk Atoll in the North Pacific, landing near the island to pick up downed fliers. Overloaded with survivors, whom he had spread out across the wings to balance his wallowing Kingfisher, Burns taxied to the lifeguard submarine *Tang*, waiting in deeper waters to take survivors aboard. It took two trips to get twenty-two grateful airmen to the sub.

With combat operations both in the Pacific and European theaters in full swing, the responsibility for air-sea rescue had to extend beyond traditional parameters. Cooperation between the army and navy usually was achieved at operational levels but fell hopelessly short at command levels. Not having the strong British rescue arm in the Pacific, AAF leaders desired a greater presence there, which fostered only more rivalry with the navy. During bureaucratic stalemate, the spotlight sometimes is diverted onto dedicated individuals who rise above the mire and take the initiative to do what is necessary. Such sensibility was found in Maj. John H. Small, who not only produced a jungle survival book for distribution to aircrews but formed a small air rescue unit designated the Fifth Air Force Rescue Service. Based in New Guinea with four Catalinas, Small's unit saved 455 airmen by the end of April 1944. In September, Small's unit combined the 3rd ERS and the 14th ERBS to become the 5276th Rescue Composite Group, based in the Philippine Islands. By year's end, the group had thirty-five crash boats, ranging in size from 28 to 85 feet, with more than four hundred men assigned. In April 1945, the 6th ERS also joined the 5276th, which became the 5th Emergency Rescue Group. The Morotai-based 15th ERBS, which joined with the 2nd ERS to form the 5230th Rescue Composite Group in October 1944, had twenty-four boats, ranging in size from 63 to 104 feet, with 130 men assigned. For a time, the joint chiefs considered delegating one service responsible for air-sea rescue. It seemed a natural function for the Coast Guard, and Coast Guard commandant Adm. Russell R. Waesche, in July 1943, agreed, citing air-sea rescue as "a most proper function of the Coast Guard." Feeling that

Dropped by an RAF Hudson of No. 279 Squadron, a lifeboat drifts toward dinghies carrying crewmen of a B-17 downed in the North Sea following a raid on Germany on July 25, 1943.

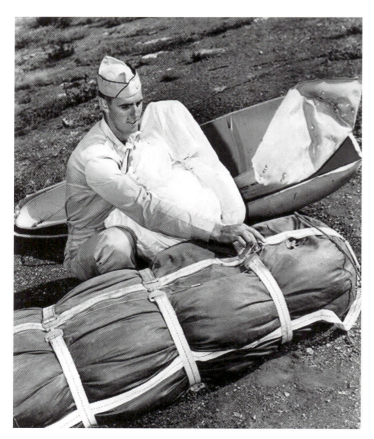

Maj. James B. Tapp of the 78th Fighter Squadron at Iwo Jima devised this emergency rescue kit, using a fuel tank casing that split open on impact after being dropped by P-51 aircraft. One rescue P-51 of the 15th, 21st, and 506th Fighter Groups was designated "Josephine" and carried the rescue kit.

"Old Flaherty" was a North American B-25H of the 10th Air Jungle Rescue Unit in Burma. Some search-and-rescue units were equipped with Mitchells to provide close air support during rescue missions, often doubling as search platforms. The B-25H brought massive firepower to bear in the form of .50 cal. machine guns, a 75 mm cannon, eight rockets, and a 3,000-pound bombload.

global expansion would overwhelm the Coast Guard, the joint chiefs relented and fell back on the decision for each service to assume responsibility, with theater commanders calling the shots. They did, however, recommend that a central coordinating body be established in Washington, which brought about the Air-Sea Rescue Agency early in 1944. By that time, AAF plans for global air-sea rescue prompted AAF commander Gen. Henry H. "Hap" Arnold to direct that two squadrons be immediately activated. Arnold's genuine concern for the need for SAR forces often is cited as the driving force behind the buildup of SAR units.

The original plan to form seven air-sea rescue squadrons gained momentum, although not at the rate that needs dictated. Gen. Dwight D. Eisenhower was still waiting for a response to his request for speedy action in sending rescue squadrons to his theater. Each squadron was to be equipped with twelve Catalinas and four light planes, along with Beech AT-7 or AT-11s for utility duty. Experiments by the army with light airplanes in 1940 at Camp Beauregard, Louisiana, had led to a 1941 purchase of more than six hundred light airplanes. Since their versatility in wartime had already been proven, commanders were quick to adapt them to rescue duty. The standard for rescue units was Stinson's L-5 "Sentinel," nearly 3,600 of which went to the AAF during the war. Based somewhat on Stinson's Model 105 "Voyager," the L-5 served in numerous roles, including rescue in remote areas and flying wounded to rear-area medical facilities. Nicknamed "the Flying Jeep," the L-5 had superior short-field takeoff-and-landing capability. A slightly larger version of the two-place L-5 was produced with an additional door to accommodate stretchers. The Catalina had been a navy stalwart since the late 1930s. Although fifty-six Consolidated PBY-5 flying boats were transferred from the navy to the Army Air Force in 1941, rescue squadron development prompted an order for 230 PBY-5As, an amphibious version built by Canadian Vickers and designated the OA-10 in AAF service. Soldiers were quick to nickname the Catalina "Dumbo" after Disney's flying-elephant caricature. The nickname became so widely used that it identified not only the mission, but succeeding multiengine rescue aircraft as well: SB-17, SB-29, and SA-16A Albatross.

THE HUMP

In the China-Burma-India (CBI) theater, thirteen "Hump" bases were designated base units from which cargo aircraft operated to fly the Hump, which was the Himalayan mountain range between Burma and China. Flying the Hump meant daily supply flights into China to keep Allied forces supplied after the Japanese blocked the Burma Road beginning in April 1942. Steady increases in tonnage and inexperienced aircrew due to shortages took their toll, necessitating search-and-rescue coverage for the treacherous flights. Crewmen who had bailed out or crash-landed in some of the world's highest mountains in horrendous weather found themselves in rugged jungle terrain, not only among the enemy but headhunters

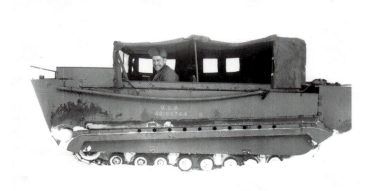

Studebaker, peacetime manufacturer of trucks and autos, made good on its wartime slogan "Give more than you promise" when it added the M29 "Weasel" to its war production. Powered by a Studebaker Champion engine, the M29C seen here was the improved version equipped with rudders, buoyancy chambers, and a reshaped hull for water operations. Studebaker also built Wright Cyclone engines for B-17s and a long line of military trucks.

and predatory creatures ranging from mosquitoes, ants, leeches, and poisonous snakes to tigers. Airmen, who often were injured, struggled for days or even weeks trying to reach safety, their only hope that other Hump aircrew were searching for them. The longest walk out of the jungle made by a survivor lasted ninety-three days. Losses were high, and something had to be done.

Among twenty units of the Air Transport Command's India-China Division (ICD), only one was committed to search and rescue of airmen downed over the Hump. At Assam, India, in July 1943, veteran Hump pilot Capt. John L. "Blackie" Porter grabbed the reins by borrowing two Douglas C-47s from airlift units, along with volunteer crewmen known for their moxie. Eventually L-4s and L-5s were added, which

Vought's OS2U Kingfisher proved its value as an air-sea rescue platform countless times. This view of a Kingfisher speaks for the seaplane's durability in stormy seas. Lt. j.g. John Burns and Radioman Aubrey Gill in their OS2U laden with rescued aircrew await rendezvous with a vessel off Truk, Caroline Islands, on May 1, 1943.

sometimes were able to land on crude short strips prepared by survivors and natives. The ATC indulged Blackie's dedication to rescue by appointing him sector air rescue officer and officially recognizing his ad hoc group in October 1943. The unique, dedicated unit became known as "Blackie's Gang" and moved from Assam, India, to Chabua in eastern India. One of Porter's C-47s bore on its nose the inscription "Somewhere I'll Find You," which became the unit motto. Veterans of the unit stated in interviews that two .30 cal. machine guns were aboard each C-47, along with handheld machine guns fired from the pilot's windows and the rear cargo door. On November 6, 1943, Blackie and crew jubilantly painted a Japanese kill marking on the C-47 after destroying a Zero fighter they discovered had made a forced landing.

In their small fleet of salvaged airplanes, Blackie's Gang accounted for 62 percent of personnel missing from flights over the Hump during 1943; this included news correspondent Eric Sevareid and nineteen others forced to bail out of their C-46 on August 2.

In October, Porter recruited volunteer medics, plus a doctor or two, to parachute into crash sites to aid injured fliers. Some jumpers trained alongside British, Indian, and Gurkha troops of the 50th Parachute Brigade at Imphal, India. Little did wing surgeon Donald Flickinger and Medical Corpsmen William G. MacKenzie and Richard S. Passey realize the impact their parachute jump into the C-46 crash site would have on the pararescue concept. Periodically, messages were received from Burmese villages about Americans who had bailed out over mountainous jungle terrain, prompting volunteer rescuers and medical personnel to jump into the area. In November, Porter added a pair of B-25s that doubled as search and armed-support platforms. On December 10, he was at the controls of one of the Mitchells flying a search mission when it was jumped by Japanese Zero fighters, killing Porter and six crewmen.

Building on Blackie's work, his search-and-rescue unit expanded, becoming the 1333rd Army Air Forces Base Unit (AAFBU) in 1944. When Brig. Gen. William H. Tunner took command of ATC's India-China Division, he was dissatisfied with the SAR arrangement and assigned Hump veteran Major Donald C. Priser to revamp the unit. Blackie's Gang, then officially designated 1352nd AAF Base Unit, used four B-25s, a C-47, and an L-5, all painted yellow and blue for high visibility in the rugged terrain. Occasionally, the unit enlisted aid from an R-4B helicopter based at Myitkyina. By war's end, of 590 aircraft that went missing over the Hump, with nearly 3,000 airmen, 1,171 were saved.

The need for additional search-and-rescue resources in the CBI theater was the impetus for a deal struck between the Office of Strategic Services (OSS) and the ATC, despite the misgivings of Gen. MacArthur and Adm. Nimitz, who saw little use for the OSS in their theater. Early in 1943 the OSS created Detachment 101 to conduct unconventional warfare in the CBI theater. Since the ATC was losing aircraft

Early-model Catalinas were strictly seaplanes until beaching gear was added. "Pick-up" was an OA-10 of the 5th ERS.

over the Hump at the rate of one per day, Det 101 offered an aircrew rescue program and training of aircrew in jungle survival. In return, the ATC would provide Det 101 with an airdrop capability by furnishing planes, parachutes, and parachute instructors. Det 101 took an additional step by offering rewards to natives who would help downed crewmen. The deal paid dividends for ATC when Det 101 parachuted small tactical teams to rescue downed airmen, while pioneering techniques and procedures that helped give birth to pararescue. Similar six-man teams formed by the OSS in Europe were influential too in the development of pararescue concepts. In July 1944, the OSS, in cooperation with the Fifteenth Air Force, established the Aircrew Rescue Unit (ACRU). Known in OSS circles as the "Halyard Mission," the ACRU dropped teams into Yugoslavia to rescue hundreds of airmen who were hidden by civilians. The seeds of a long-lasting partnership between air rescue and special operations were being sown.

Expansion of search and rescue included activation of the 1st Emergency Rescue Squadron on December 1, 1943, at Boca Raton, Florida. When it deployed to Camp John B. Passage, Casablanca, in March 1944, it had eleven Catalinas, only seven of which were flyable for three instructor pilots

on loan from the navy to qualify 1st ERS pilots in the aircraft. The squadron also had two L-5s, a B-25C, and an air rescue boat detachment at Kindley Field, Bermuda. The unit's three flights were dispersed among Corsica and Foggia Main and Grottaglie, Italy. Two weeks later the 2nd ERS opened its doors on the opposite coast at Hamilton Field, California. After training at Gulfport and Keesler Fields, Mississippi, the squadron deployed to New Guinea in July 1944, much to the relief of Maj. Small's unit. Operating sites for the squadron's OA-10As and B-25 included Mokmer Airfield on Biak Island; Oro Bay Airfield; Milne Bay; Middleburg, Indonesia; and Wama Airfield at Morotai. After assignment to the 5320th Rescue Group, and later the 13th Emergency Rescue Group, the squadron moved to Clark Field and Tacloban, Leyte, in the final months of the war. The 2nd ERS, popularly called "Snafu Snatchers," is credited with rescuing more than seven hundred fliers in the South Pacific, having flown the OA-10A, L-5, C-47, C-45, and AT-11. To cover the Philippine Islands, the 3rd ERS was established in mid-February 1944 at Tacloban, Leyte, with Flights B, C, and D positioned at Clark Field, Zambales, and San Jose, Mondoro, respectively. During the final months of the war, Catalinas of the 3rd would be joined by three lifeboat-equipped B-17Hs. When the 4th ERS reported for duty in the Pacific in April 1945, its Catalinas and B-17s at Peleliu and Iwo Jima, along with navy rescue boats and "Lifeguard" submarines, began supporting B-29 bombers of the Twentieth Air Force. The squadron's Flight D was assigned to Angaur Island, Palaus, and Flight E went to Hawaii's Wheeler Field. Not only would the 5th retain its roots in Great Britain, it expanded operations to RAF Thorpe Abbots. Flying OA-10As and B-17Hs, the 6th ERS began operations at Floridablanca Airfield, Luzon, Philippines, and at Ie Shima, Okinawa, in mid-1945. The 6th would also operate from Tacloban, Leyte, in the Philippine Islands.

In the China-Burma-India theater, an AAF detachment of two Catalinas and one crew were attached to the RAF in June 1944 to supplement cover for the increase in long-range bomber missions. The move proved insufficient, so in January 1945 two flights of the 1st ERS were sent to Agartala, India, to form the nucleus of a new unit, the 7th ERS, officially activated on January 25. One month earlier, the War Department had directed that manpower be added to emergency-rescue squadrons and that their aircraft inventories include eight B-17s, four float-equipped L-5s, and four helicopters, in addition to their twelve Catalinas. The B-17s' lifeboats and the L-5 floats were of little consequence since most CBI missions were flown overland. The unit complied with the directive but added, oddly enough, PT-19s, a small low-wing trainer typically found only in the US. The operational period of the 7th ERS was brief, lasting only from March until July, with half its rescues accomplished overland. The unit had been provided helicopters, but they remained unassembled and would end up in the hands of the next unit to arrive in theater. After the end of hostilities, the 7th relocated to Okinawa.

Particularly interesting but scantily covered in historical annals is the use of Douglas A-24B "Banshees" for air-sea rescue scouting. Appearing in a World War II training film is an overall yellow A-24B-1 (S/N 42-54328) wearing air-sea rescue markings and a unit emblem. The Banshee was the army version of the navy's SBD-5 "Dauntless" dive-bomber/scout aircraft. Built as land planes with more-powerful engines for the USAAF, 615 A-24Bs were produced, many of which the army pressed into noncombat roles. Equally elusive is documentation of B-24 bombers, periodically mentioned in accounts as having carried airborne lifeboats and flown search-and-rescue missions. Although difficult to obtain, Liberators were favored for their high-wing construction, which allowed optimum visibility for search, and their load-carrying capacity, speed, and long range.

The 8th ERS was activated at Chanute Field, Illinois, in March 1945 and deployed to China in May, when the Air Search and Rescue Section of the China Air Service Command formed under Fourteenth Air Force. The mix of aircraft used by the 8th to cover missions over "the Hump" into China was unique. Besides being the only rescue unit with R-6 helicopters and C-47 aircraft, it flew four L-5s and two camera-equipped

B-25s from a batch of forty-five B-25Ds that had been converted for photo work and designated F-10s. It's believed that the 8th ERS acquired the unique Mitchells when they were deemed excess to a photomapping squadron based in China. The unit's pair of C-47s was modified for flyby ground retrieval, a technique that had been developed years earlier to snatch items from the ground when landing was ruled out. Operating helicopters in mountainous territory, the squadron proved the value of the helicopter for rescue. Although other emergency-rescue squadrons received helicopters late in the war, only the 8th ERS flew them on combat rescue missions. Helicopters had been delivered to the 7th ERS but went to the 8th ERS to be used for parts, to bypass inadequate supply channels. Despite its short wartime existence, the 8th ERS flew 110 missions and accomplished forty-three rescues, not one of which was overwater. The 9th ERS was established at Keesler Field in 1945 but was disbanded two months later. The 10th ERS continued to write the book on Arctic rescue, and the 11th ERS was established in the Mediterranean in 1943. All units were to have been in place by spring 1944, with most assigned to the Pacific. The navy had other ideas. The Pacific was their turf where they practiced area coverage, assigning rescue units to specific areas. The AAF, on the other hand, for

During a test demonstration at NAS Lakehurst in early October 1944, a TBM Avenger drops a three-unit rescue kit, which included a ten-man raft. The method provided carrier-based aircraft a means of prolonging survival in the water until the arrival of seaplanes or vessels.

flexibility, assigned rescue units to theater air forces. The AAF fell short of its goal, with only two squadrons in operation in summer of 1944; some of the squadrons did not become operational until war's end. Despite delays and the unresolved disparity between services, the number of lives saved rose dramatically. Eventually, the development and procurement of air rescue equipment was given higher priority, and standards for equipment carried by all aircrews, including those of rescue aircraft, were established. Since no single aircraft had been designed purely for rescue, and given the Catalina's spotty record for rough sea landings, more emphasis was placed on maximizing aircrew lifesaving equipment. Aircrews, basically, were being told to think more about escape and survival than rescue. The most logical means of self-survival, then, could come only from delivering a boat to survivors.

AIRBORNE LIFEBOATS

The use of rescue aircraft to deliver lifeboats for self-rescue proved a faster and farther-ranging method than air rescue boats. Dinghies dropped from spotter aircraft since the war's early period sufficed, but tides and winds often overpowered paddling efforts, and survivors were captured. More practical was a durable powered vessel that could be air-dropped to survivors. Credit for the concept goes to the British, who, in 1940, considered a glider-type boat. Its design proved overly complex, so planners focused on a 32-foot motor dinghy; however, plans for that were tabled too. Air Chief Marshal Sir Arthur Harris is said to have resurrected the concept, while, in mid-1941, group captain E. F. Waring developed the plan and yacht designer A. C. Robb designed the boat. Lockheed's Hudson aircraft, a stalwart in the RAF's Coastal Command, would carry the boat. The 20-foot wooden boat, with motor, a sail, and oars, was to be carried within the Hudson's bomb bay so as not to impede the aircraft's aerodynamic properties; however, the arrangement of bomb bay door mechanisms ruled out the package. British naval architect Uffa Fox too had taken up the cause for droppable lifeboats after his stepson was captured following a ditching. Uffa's wooden double-planked boat design was streamlined and sculpted to form-fit to the belly of a Hudson, with no penalty in performance. Ideally, it was dropped from 700 feet altitude at 140 knots and suspended by six parachutes. A 4 hp Britannia Middy engine mounted inboard amidships proved ideal for the boat, allowing 6 knots; however, it was no longer in production. So the call went out to private boat owners to turn in their Middy engines for the war effort. Designated the Mk. I, Uffa's boat featured buoyancy chambers to prevent capsizing. The chambers were filled by carbon dioxide cartridges, the seals of which were released by opening parachutes. The chutes were blown away by a charge on splashdown, and rockets fired 200-foot floating lines outward. The 27-foot boat was ordered into production in November 1942, with the first examples in service by February 1943.

British planners again eyed the 32-foot, 1,700-pound Mk. II, which entered service in 1944 and was carried by Vickers Warwick aircraft. Mindful of the British experience, in late 1943 the Sea Rescue Unit of US Army Air Force Material Command Equipment Laboratory came up with a design for an all-wood airborne lifeboat. Their intent was to mate the boat with the B-17, although serious consideration was also given the B-29, C-46, and C-54, given their ground clearance. But the B-17 was the obvious choice; they were proven, they were armed, they were in abundance, and they had twice the range of the Catalina. Since the B-17G was the definitive, final version of the bomber for the USAAF, plans were made to convert about 130 of them to air-sea rescue aircraft. Sources conflict as to the actual number converted during the war, but a smaller number was converted with A-1 lifeboats and a search radar in place of the chin turret, resulting in the designation B-17H; all other defensive armament was retained during the conversion.

Meanwhile, American industrialist Andrew Higgins was certain that he could improve on the Fox design with his 27-foot, 3,000-pound A-1 lifeboat, which was nicknamed "Flying Dutchman." The moniker would also identify the B-17s carrying the boat. To develop the boat, Higgins teamed with Major Robert Rizon, who had been named commandant of the rescue school at Keesler after serving as a B-17 instructor.

The boat was tailored to the B-17, which, ideally, dropped the vessel at 1,500 feet in altitude at 120 mph airspeed. Faired to the fuselage, the boat incurred only an 8 mph penalty on the B-17's speed. A smoke pot attached to the boat was ignited by the static line that opened three 48-foot-diameter parachutes, or a single 100-foot-diameter chute. Removable stabilizers at the boat's stern assured a bow-down attitude so that the boat entered the water bow first to absorb landing shock. Like their British counterparts, on splashdown, rockets

The first-generation Sikorsky R-4 was demanding to fly and maintain, but it paved the way for further helicopter development during the war. Here, Lt. Robert Cowgill of the 2nd ERS poses with his R-4B (serial no. 43-46532) at Leyte in 1945.

Wearing both army chevrons and a sailor hat, a crewman of a 22-foot Chris-Craft J boat of the Hamilton Field Air Rescue Boat unit rescues persons from San Francisco Bay in 1943.

with switches triggered by salt water fired floating lifelines outward from both sides.

To carry the boat, the B-17's bomb bay doors were removed and the bomb hoist was used to pull up the boat, which was held by cables attached to bomb shackles. Initial tests with a dummy boat damaged the aircraft when the wind stream hurled the boat into the fuselage, necessitating that a catapult be installed to "kick" the boat clear. Problems persisted when the first engine-equipped boat tore away from its chutes when test-dropped.

Painted yellow, Higgins's A-1 was stocked with supplies to sustain ten to sixteen survivors for about one week. A 20-foot mast and 145-square-foot sail were included, along with basic instructions for its use, a map drawn by the rescue aircraft's crew, and a Gibson Girl radio. Although US-manufactured, the Gibson Girl emergency transmitter was born of the German air-sea rescue experience. In 1941, the Luftwaffe introduced an ingenious emergency transmitter, designed by Fiesecke and Hopfner. The self-contained unit was buoyant, waterproof, and compact and was powered by an internal hand-cranked generator. Designated Notsender NS2 or NSG2, the unit had a sea range of 200 miles. Units captured by the British stirred a plan to jointly produce an Allied dinghy transmitter. The first sets, which were produced by Bendix, were delivered in May 1942. Designated the SCR-578, the curvy-shaped unit got its nickname from the narrow-waist female drawings of 1890s fashion artist Charles Gibson. Improved units had ranges exceeding 1,000 miles, if the antenna could be kept aloft by kite or balloon. The SCR-578 was modified in spring 1945 to broadcast distress signals automatically on two frequencies, and during the last months of the war it was replaced by the AN/ERT-3, which was sent to Pacific units. Gibson Girls remained in use long after World War II, eventually being replaced by improved UHF and VHF devices of US and British manufacture.

The boats had twin 5 hp engines fed by 11 gallons of gasoline, allowing for a top speed of 8 mph and a range of 400 miles; a range of 1,500 miles was possible with the use of both engines and sail. Engines also operated two saltwater stills, and their manifolds served as stoves to cook food. Tests were conducted at Keesler Field's rescue-training facility in September 1944, and by mid-December, thirteen lifeboats were on hand, although without carbon dioxide cartridges. The delay pushed training to January 1945, and by the end of February, eight B-17 crews had completed training. One dozen OA-10A crewmen completed training simultaneously, and both groups formed the new 6th Emergency Rescue Squadron.

The first rescue with an A-1 occurred at the end of March 1945 in the North Sea, when a B-17 dropped a lifeboat to the crew of a rescue PBY Catalina that was damaged while landing to rescue a P-51 pilot. Andrew Higgins's belief that Fox's lifeboat didn't hold up to his A-1 proved valid when four Fox boats dropped to the scene were lost. The Mustang pilot, meanwhile, had drifted a considerable distance and was captured. For four days, six crewmen rode out a fierce storm in the A-1 until rescued by rescue boats. Their A-1 had to be sunk by gunfire. Just minutes before the B-17 crew at Halesworth had gotten the message that the Catalina was down at sea, the boat had merely been suspended below a B-17 for inspection by Generals Doolittle and Spaatz. Holes were quickly cut in the bomb bay doors to mount the boat for flight. The second rescue occurred on May 1, when a 1st Rescue Squadron B-17H dropped its lifeboat to a fighter pilot found drifting near the harbor of Trieste. Mines ruled out landing an amphibian. The survivor clambered aboard and easily made his way to shore, where rescuers joked that it appeared he had done this before. He told them he had; this was the third mission he completed in an airborne lifeboat. The first two had been dropped by British aircraft.

Despite its scant operational use, the Higgins airborne lifeboat not only would remain in service but would serve in the next war. Nor would Uffa Fox's success be forgotten. For all of his accomplishments, the one considered most worthy is etched onto his gravestone: an airborne lifeboat.

EXPANSION OF SEARCH AND RESCUE

As the war dragged on, expansion of search and rescue became necessary to keep pace with constantly changing fronts. More coverage was provided along mission routes in combat theaters, and along routes used by aircraft transiting great distances to reach theater assignments. Major ferry routes were the North and South Atlantic, the South Pacific, the Northwest Staging Route, and the Crimson (Canadian) Route. To better organize AAF Air Transport Command units in the continental US, in mid-1944 they were realigned as base units (AAFBUs), with all units at one base merged under control of the base commander. The proven concept had expanded globally, with primary airfields along the five major ATC ferry routes having air base units that incorporated air rescue sections.

FLING-WING RESCUERS

Much like the air rescue boat, the helicopter was a vital but historically overlooked element of air rescue during World War II. When a downed flier was spotted by 8th ERS aircraft, the difficult part of the mission became rescuing him from jungle and mountainous terrain; the job fell to a land rescue unit that had been formed at Chabua in 1943. It could take weeks in enemy territory and treacherous terrain to reach survivors and get them to an area where an L-5 could land and take off. There had to be a faster, safer means of rescue by air. Little did a few visionaries know that their work would come together to provide the answer, not only saving lives but changing the course of military history.

When the time was right and the technology available, Igor I. Sikorsky invented the helicopter and controlled vertical flight, justifiably earning him the title of "the father of the helicopter." A true humanitarian, Sikorsky continually stressed that the best use of his designs was saving lives: "It would be right to say that the helicopter's role in saving lives represents one of the most glorious pages in the history of human flight." Germany, as it had in the field of air-sea rescue, was first to take the stage in the development of the first successful helicopter. The US Army Air Corps' first helicopter was the Platt-LePage XR-1A, based on Germany's Fa 61, but it was Sikorsky's R-4 design that premiered in April 1942, to become the world's first production helicopter. The two-place helicopter with fabric-covered rotor blades was powered by a 200 hp Warner radial engine, giving it a top speed of 81 mph. Deliveries of the first fifteen R-4As to the army began in July 1943. Coincidentally, one month later at the Quebec Conference, President Roosevelt made a commitment to Winston Churchill for US forces to team with the British to break the Japanese hold on Burma. With President Roosevelt's blessings and General Arnold's uncompromising authority, army lieutenant colonels Philip Cochran and John Alison quietly selected about five hundred skilled volunteers to form an elite outfit. They also shaped a small but formidable air force consisting of thirty P-51A fighters, thirteen C-47s, twelve UC-64 Norsemans as intermediate aircraft, 100 CG-4A gliders, and twenty-five TG-5 gliders, which were training gliders modified from Aeronca's L-3. Since availability of Vultee L-1 Reliants fell short of meeting their goal of a hundred planes to evacuate the wounded, L-5s filled the gap. The L-1 was the light plane of choice since it could carry two stretchers, and three in a pinch; the L-5 carried one. When the acquisition from the RAF of one dozen B-25H medium bombers for close air support fell through, heavily armed Mitchells were diverted from Fourteenth Air Force deliveries. And they requested from Wright Field six Sikorsky YR-4B helicopters to test them in combat. There now was an added measure of hope for fliers who went down in the CBI theater's forbidding land. Cochran and Alison's secret, unorthodox unit was first designated the 5318th Provisional Unit (Air), which Arnold insisted be changed to 1st Air Commando Group. British general Orde

C. Wingate's Long Range Penetration Group, or "Project 9," now had the air arm Roosevelt promised. Only four R-4s survived the trip to India, which was made in C-46s early in 1944. Although intended to support Wingate's raiders, the choppers and their handful of Sikorsky-trained pilots rescued downed aircrews flying the Hump. Shortly after the helicopters were assembled, the detachment suffered its first loss when Lt. Burt Powell crashed in an R-4B on March 21, making him the first person to die in a US helicopter in a combat zone.

The 1st Air Commandos secretly trained at Hailakandi and Lalaghat, India, during late 1943. On March 5, 1944, Project 9 made its move, flying over the surprised Japanese and landing hordes of commando-laden gliders in the enemy's backyard. They cut a fortified airstrip out of the jungle and named it "Broadway." Thousands of Wingate's troops, called "Chindits," then were landed on Broadway to systematically dismantle Japanese operations; additional glider assaults opened strongholds named "Chowringhee" and "Aberdeen." The small band of helicopter pilots was at Aberdeen. The strip was also home for Air Commando pilot TSgt. Ed "Murphy" Hladovcak and his Vultee L-1. Stamford Robertson, also a light-plane pilot at Aberdeen, tells why that is noteworthy:

> We had 30 P-51s, a dozen B-25s, C-47s, UC-64s, and 100 light planes that were either L-1s or L-5s. We also had three R-4s that had just completed tests and had never been flown in combat. The reason for the formation of the group was to have light planes as a means of evacuating the wounded that would take part in the second invasion of Burma under General Wingate. In the first invasion, those who were wounded and couldn't walk had to be left behind. Now, morale went sky high when it became known that light planes and helicopters were able to land on roads and rice paddies and also in jungle clearings. The R-4 was so underpowered that pilots had to weigh under 150 pounds. It didn't have much of a range or ceiling and not too fast a cruise.

In May 1943, Capt. John L. "Blackie" Porter acquired two B-25s, which his ground crew modified for air rescue by replacing bomb bay racks with a platform for paradropping survival supplies. Later, the unit's B-25s were painted yellow and blue, as were unit C-47s.

Murphy was flying an L-1 when he was hit by ground fire and forced to land. He was able to make a safe landing, and the three wounded British soldiers he had aboard were carried to what was thought to be a safe place. They discovered that the place they had picked was close to a path used by the Japanese, and they heard them talking most of the night. When he didn't return from his flight, we went looking for him and found him and the three men on the top of a hill. A message was dropped to him informing him that he would be rescued and to stay there. One of the jokers in the outfit flew over him and dropped a three-day pass. Murphy didn't find it funny as he was afraid they might be discovered. It was five days before the rescue was made on April 25th; Murphy and the men subsisted on two containers of bullion.

The helicopter was called in to make the rescue. The radio was removed to save weight, and an extra gas tank installed to increase range. The area of rescue was 150 miles deep in enemy territory. Carter Harman was the pilot and James Phelan the crew chief. I was selected to lead the chopper to the site and also to fly Bill Vandergrift from *Life* magazine to take pictures of the rescue.

The weather was so hot that it was a problem to get the helicopter to fly. Harman discovered that by overrevving the engine 15 to 20 percent and then doing the equivalent of popping the clutch, it would leap off the ground and, with forward motion, would fly. We flew to the site and Harman was able to spot the first man and fly him to a nearby light-plane strip. Eventually the engine overheated and the chopper had to be left there overnight, and in the cool of the next morning, the rest of the men were flown out. Murphy, like a true captain of his ship, was last to leave and said that it was then that he knew the true meaning of being alone.

All aircraft flown by Blackie's Gang eventually were painted yellow and blue for high visibility over "the Hump." Capt. John "Blackie" Porter's search-and-rescue unit in 1945 became the 1352nd AAF Base Unit of ATC India-China Division, based at Mohanbari, Assam, India. This C-47A (serial no. 43-15991) wore the Latin legend "UTVIRIVIVANT" below the star emblem on its nose, which translated means "That Men May Live." The C-47 went into storage at Davis-Monthan AFB in 1946 and the following year was sold to a private owner. *Courtesy of Lt. Col. Frank Schirmer / David Menard collection*

From his grandstand seat, Robertson didn't realize that he was watching history being made: the first combat rescue by helicopter. Robertson added, "To us it was just another type of aircraft that would help us win the war. All of us had a tremendous sense of satisfaction when we were flying out the wounded, and that is hard to beat." Only Igor Sikorsky could have felt a greater sense of satisfaction, and he would draw from the experience to give the helicopter an even larger role in air rescue.

When the R-4 was introduced to the AAF, it was an unknown, and officials preferred to keep it that way. As the 1st Air Commandos trained in secrecy, so too did the first airmen who learned how to fly and fix the aircraft. The assignment of six pilots and six mechanics to the Sikorsky plant at Bridgeport, Connecticut, in April 1944 was kept low profile. They were to learn the R-4 and then form the cadre of the Flying Training Command's helicopter school at Freeman Army Airfield, Seymour, Indiana. In December the school moved to Chanute Field, Illinois. Thirty-nine pilots were trained by year's end. When the school relocated with its seventeen helicopters to Sheppard Field, Texas, in June 1945, nearly a hundred pilots had been trained. In the meantime, the three YR-4Bs undergoing service testing with the 1st Air Commandos in the CBI theater succumbed to parts issues, but not before they accounted for twenty-one saves and paved the way for further helicopter deployment.

The CBI theater would be without helicopters until January 1945, when an R-6A was urgently requested by General Arnold to rescue a B-25 crew that had been downed in Burma. Instead, a YR-4B at Wright Field was dismantled and loaded onto a

C-54 for the long flight, accompanied by three experienced helicopter officers, one a twenty-one-year-old Wright Field helicopter test pilot. At Myitkyina, Burma, the YR-4B was assembled with help from personnel of the Tenth Air Force Air Jungle Rescue Unit, which had become operational in 1943. The B-25 crew had evaded the Japanese and reached safety, but on the twenty-ninth, the helicopter, escorted by two L-5s of the jungle rescue unit, was airborne and headed to a mountaintop to rescue a soldier who had been shot in the hand. After rescuing the soldier, the YR-4B was used to familiarize members of the 10th AF Air Jungle Rescue Unit with the helicopter. Besides rescue duty, the helicopter was put to use locating the many aircraft wrecks, removing valuable equipment, and marking the wreck with a yellow "X." Missions with the single helicopter lasted four months, and in May the 8th ERS arrived in the CBI theater with five R-6A helicopters for field trials. So substantial was the rescue business in the theater that within twenty-four hours of their arrival at

Five 85-foot air rescue boats undergo outfitting at Olson & Winge Marine at Lake Washington Ship Canal during the early 1940s. All wear on their wheelhouse sideboard the emblem of the 10th Emergency Rescue Boat Squadron. Mounted in the afterdeck well was an Oerlikon Mk. 12 mount for a 20 mm cannon. A collapsible canvas awning covered the well. Mounted on both sides of the wheelhouse were .50 cal. machine gun tubs. Olson & Winge outfitted numerous boat types, such as the minesweeper YMS-127 in the background, which was sunk in the Aleutians on January 10, 1944.

All branches of the US military used Catalinas for search and rescue. After this test with the new AR-8 airborne rescue boat mounted to a US Coast Guard PBY-5A in July 1945, a number of coast guard and navy Catalinas carried the boat. Designed to form-fit to the PBY's wing, the 18-foot, 1,500-pound plywood boat was attached with a folding frame, which kicked the boat away and automatically opened its eight parachutes. The first USCG PBY was assigned to San Francisco, where this test was conducted.

PHOTO — COURTESY OF HUBBARD'S SOUTH COAST CO.

First Aid
for Fliers . . .
forced down at sea!

The lives of many of our Airmen are saved by the high-speed, able handling, and reliable performance of the Aircraft Rescue Boats we are building for the Army Air Forces. Never before has the traditional Herreshoff craftsmanship served a finer purpose.

Herreshoff
SHIPYARD
BRISTOL, RHODE ISLAND

Kunming, China, helicopters of the 8th ERS chalked up their first rescue by saving twelve crew and passengers from a crashed C-46.

Nearly lost to history over the years was another operation that capitalized on the helicopter's ability to perform rescues when fixed-wing aircraft could not. Code-named Project Ivory Soap, in October 1944 the first of six liberty ships converted to aircraft maintenance facilities dropped anchor in the Pacific. By February 1945 all six were in theater to serve off coasts of airfields to ensure the tempo of air operations in the offensive island-hopping campaign. Designated aircraft repair units (floating), or ARU(F), the 3rd, 5th, and 6th ARU(F) went to work in the Philippines, while remaining units supported the Twentieth Air Force in the Marianas. A total of eighteen smaller aircraft maintenance units (floating), or AMU(F), also were deployed. Unique to each ARU(F) was the assignment of four R-4B helicopters, which flew from a 40-by-72-foot deck to fly parts between ships and island airfields. The concept of using ships as offshore aircraft repair facilities had been tried in the Mediterranean with navy LST

vessels. Since LSTs were more in demand in the Pacific, lower-priority liberty ships were used, manned by Merchant Marine crews and commanded by an army colonel. Almost immediately, the support role of the helicopters became one of air rescue. Word spread and calls went out for pickups of wounded soldiers and airmen. Although the ARUs arrived during the final months of the war, they are known to have evacuated 150 wounded, more than half of whom were rescued during Luzon operations. The job of flying the temperamental R-4B was made more difficult when trying to fit patients into the cramped two-place cockpit. Although external stretcher mounts were used in trials, none were aboard the ships, sending mechanics to the onboard machine shop to fabricate mounts. One of Sikorsky's two follow-on helicopter models, the R-6A, sent to the theater in June 1945 was also without stretcher mounts.

Concurrent with development of its next-generation helicopter, the R-5A, Sikorsky engineers used the feedback from R-4 pilots to create an improved version designated the R-6A. The R-6 was basically an all-metal, streamlined R-4

An R-4 helicopter of Project Ivory Soap is secured aboard a Liberty ship. In the foreground is the ship's main armament, a stern-mounted 4-inch antiaircraft gun. Liberty Ships were disbanded in October 1948.

using the same transmission and rotor system, but having a more powerful 245 hp engine. Since the military was immediately sold on the R-6A, and the R-5A was experiencing developmental problems, Gen. Arnold pushed for procurement of nine hundred R-6As. Since Sikorsky was partnered with Vought Aircraft, with both under the parent United Aircraft and Transportation Corporation, Gen. Arnold allowed R-6A production only if it did not interfere with priority production of the navy's Vought F-4U Corsair. But Arnold's decision alone did not sell Sikorsky on the idea. The firm's production of R-4 and R-5 helicopters was at peak, prompting the USAAF Production Division at Wright-Patterson Field to direct that the R-6 be license-built by Nash-Kelvinator at Kenosha, Wisconsin. The company already was license-building Hamilton-Standard propellers and Pratt & Whitney Wasp engines for United Aircraft Corporation. Industrial competition was fierce, and Sikorsky was reluctant to pass along engineering and design data but eventually complied. A total of twenty-six prototype R-6As, followed by nine hundred production machines, were to be built at the Kenosha plant; however, labor shortages led the War Production Board to direct that the R-6 line be opened at Michigan facilities, with Sikorsky oversight. Continual changes in the R-6's design by engineers, and subsequent delays in submitting updated drawings to Nash-Kelvinator, resulted in R-5 production eventually superseding that of the R-6. Before production was halted at war's end, more than two hundred R-6s had been produced.

Pilots didn't find the R-6A much of an improvement over the R-4B, but aircrew made the best of them, and survivors were grateful. After their arrival in the CBI theater in June 1945, R-6As of the 1st Air Commando Group sometimes performed rescues from elevations reaching 8,000 feet. The R-6As shared cramped deck space aboard floating aircraft repair ships, the navy put them to work in the Pacific, and emergency-rescue squadrons joined the 8th ERS in adding them to their stable of aircraft.

PICKUP

In view of the success of the pioneer 1st Air Commando Group, additional units were formed in 1944: the 2nd Air Commando Group in India and the 3rd Air Commando Group in the Philippines and later New Guinea. Among their mix of aircraft, all three groups were well stocked with Stinson L-5s for search and rescue, P-51 fighters, C-47s, and Waco CG-4 gliders. Capable of carrying a 2-ton load, including wheeled equipment loaded through a hinged nose section, the CG-4 could be towed at 125 mph, usually by a C-47. Like some aircraft, the glider's value as an air rescue platform was underrated. Usually thought to be a one-way ride in, gliders also became the ride out to safety. A pioneer in aerial retrieval systems, All American Aviation had tackled the development of glider pickup. Tests to enhance the glider's flexibility began at Wilmington, Ohio, in 1943, with a Douglas B-23, C-47s,

Operating helicopters from Liberty ships had its downside. This R-4B (serial no. 43-46573) of the 5th ARU(F) was a total loss when it went into the water on May 1, 1945. Months earlier, Lt. Jack Zimmerman's R-4 got caught in the ship's downdraft on takeoff and crashed into the water. Zimmerman, who became a noted helicopter test pilot and record holder, saved the life of his passenger, Pvt. William K. Troche.

and, ultimately, B-17s. The ability to snatch a glider from the ground was first demonstrated in Burma in February 1944, when a Tenth Air Force glider, after offloading cargo, was picked up for the return flight to India. Six gliders were then used to evacuate wounded in Burma, and the following year in Europe they regularly transported wounded from the Remagen bridgehead on the Rhine to field hospitals. The most extraordinary glider rescue occurred after a C-47 with twenty-five souls aboard crashed into a deep mountain valley of New Guinea on May 13, 1945. Only three of the military exploration team aboard survived. Three Filipino medics who had jumped into the site tended to the trio until June 28, when a C-46 flew down into the valley to hook a line strung between two posts, snatching a glider flown down to them.

Since air rescue boats were built by different boatyards, they were identified by length and P number. The 85-foot P-73 was built by Ventnor. It had a 20-foot beam; drafted 4 feet, 8 inches; and was powered by twin Hall-Scott Defender engines fed by a fuel capacity of 3,840 gallons of gasoline. Fully loaded, she displaced 46 long tons. Bell-mouth ventilators were above and below deck. Foredeck ventilators were spray-proof, and some used suction blowers.

The P-106 ARB was a 104-footer powered by triple Hall-Scott V-12 engines. Largest of the ARBs, the 104-footer had a crew of fourteen and featured a dispensary that could accommodate eight patients, twenty-three if necessary. The 2-ton-capacity boom hoist was used to secure aircraft, tow targets, or assist deep-sea divers. Bell-mouth ventilators were vital over the dispensary, engine room, galley, and crew quarters. An extensive framework allowed a weather canopy.

All American's long success with mail pickup service and glider retrieval had engineers seriously considering adapting the company's equipment to rescue humans from the ground. On September 5, 1943, at Wright Field, volunteer Alexis Doster became the first human to be snatched from the ground by an aircraft pickup system. Being a paratrooper, Doster wore a parachute and strapped on a knife to cut himself free should anything go wrong. Although interest in human air retrieval waned in lieu of the preference for helicopters, those early tests foreshadowed the human pickup system that would long be a standard feature on air force C-130 rescue aircraft.

FRIGID FIRSTS

The number and type of aircraft assigned to rescue units usually were determined by the geography of the region in which they operated. That was especially true in Arctic regions, where the demands of air rescue differed vastly from that in other theaters. Alaska, the only US soil other than Hawaii to see fighting, became a major campaign in the war, although overshadowed by the concurrent Battle of Midway. After the Japanese attacked Dutch Harbor in June 1942 and seized Attu and Kiska Islands in the Aleutian chain, bitter fighting one year later would place Attu back in American hands. Their ranks decimated, the Japanese withdrew from Kiska before Americans and Canadians stormed ashore. Never again could America let down her guard in the region.

Although the hazards of flying in Alaska and the North Pacific warranted a rescue capability, Army Air Force rescue units initially were only lightly committed, since the US Navy's Patrol Wing 4 (later redesignated Fleet Air Wing 4) shouldered the load of search and rescue in the Aleutians. Equipped with PBY-5A Catalinas and later PV-1 Venturas, the wing was moved from Seattle to the North Pacific in May 1942. With thirty PBYs on hand, the wing's presence was deemed adequate. However, since SAR was an added duty of patrol squadrons, searches for lost fliers were augmented by ship-launched OS2U Kingfishers, and aircraft of AAF transport squadrons; even bomber squadrons and aircraft assigned to the Cold Weather Test Station at Ladd Field sometimes joined the effort.

Bolstering the military presence in Alaska was necessary not only to prevent the enemy from gaining a foothold, but to keep open the Allied corridor to Russia, through which thousands of US aircraft passed under the Lend-Lease Act to sustain Russian airpower. Thus, the Northwest Staging Route was established, which stretched across the US northern tier, Alaska, and Canada and incorporated the Alaska Highway. More than seventy airfields, many of which were hastily built, were positioned about every 100 miles along the route, with air base units at primary fields incorporating air rescue sections. Before air rescue in Alaska was organized, rescue missions had been organized on the spot with any aircraft available, with the expected results. This led to the Air Transport Command's formation of the Alaska Wing Search and Rescue Squadron in mid-December 1943. Although begun with few

Built by Owens Yacht Co. of Baltimore in 1943, the 42-foot P-195 was powered by twin 250 hp Kermath Sea-Raider or Hudson engines. Design 221 was a V bottom with twin screws. The after-cabin served as a dispensary, above which was a .50 cal. machine gun.

aircraft, the squadron eventually had eight UC-64s, two C-47s, L-5s, and two OA-10As dispersed among three flights in Canada and two in Alaska. Since Arctic terrain and climate dictated the need for durable aircraft, air rescue boats, and land rescue vehicles, the squadron was equipped accordingly, receiving sled dogs and snow vehicles in spring 1944; rescue boats finally reached the unit in spring 1944. Despite growth of the unit's boat fleet, which comprised a mix of more than thirty vessels ranging from 6-foot skiffs to a cabin cruiser, it saw little use due to the presence of the Elmendorf-based 10th Emergency Rescue Boat Squadron. When an 85-foot ARB finally arrived from outfitting at Seattle, the Bering Sea had frozen over. The 10th ERBS wrote the book on air rescue boat operations in brutal Arctic conditions. The lack of speed of the squadron's 104-foot ARBs was offset by their endurance and durability in rough seas, which accounted for the lion's share of open-sea rescues. The enthusiasm of squadron personnel over the arrival of new 63-foot ARBs in mid-1944 soon dimmed when they discovered that the boats were difficult to manage in heavy seas, and the unseasoned lumber used to form their hulls warped and leaked.

Specialized equipment too was necessary to carry out search and rescue in eastern Canada's rugged, cold regions of Newfoundland and Labrador, in Iceland, and at the top of the world, where bases were established in Greenland to support thousands of planes departing Presque Isle, Maine, for Europe along ATC's North Atlantic Division "Snowball Route." Eventually, fourteen support sites dotted the route in Greenland. Key among the bases, which were named "Bluie," which was military code for Greenland, was Bluie West 1 (BW1) on the southwestern coast at Narsarsuag (Narsarssauk). Under the army's Arctic Training Command, the 1st Arctic Search and Rescue Squadron was formed and trained at

Army Air Force "sailors" manned this swamp glider, which was powered by a 65 hp Lycoming aircraft engine and steered by a rudder in the prop wash. Later models used a 75 hp Continental engine. This swamp glider responded to aircraft crashes off the shores of San Pablo Bay surrounding Hamilton Field, near San Francisco. A litter was kept in the bow.

Buckley Field, Denver, Colorado, and deployed to Bluie West 1 in October 1943. The 2nd Arctic Search and Rescue Squadron followed, and the 3rd Arctic Search and Rescue Squadron was established in Newfoundland in February 1944, remaining in service for only two months before it was disbanded.

Vital to SAR operations in Arctic regions were aircraft with proven abilities to operate not only on water, but on ice and snow. It was in such harsh climes that Noorduyn's UC-64 "Norseman" and Grumman's amphibious OA-9 "Goose" made names for themselves; OA-10As, B-17s with airborne lifeboats, and C-47s filled out the inventories of both squadrons. Particular care of electronic and mechanical equipment, including survival gear, was never more important, lest crewmen find themselves marooned on ice or snow, battered by gale-force winds and subzero temperatures and without food or water. Equally as important as aircraft were durable and reliable land vehicles for overland treks to reach crashes in areas that ruled out aircraft landings. Those favored by SAR teams were Studebaker's M29 "Weasel" and the Allis Chalmers M7 snow tractor. The Weasel too was designed for operation in snow, and it was amphibious, although marginally. The improved M29C was fully amphibious, thanks to rudders and a bow with float tanks. Both air and boat crew and ground rescuers required special training to operate in some of the most brutal conditions on earth.

FOUR-LEGGED RESCUERS

For air operations, Arctic rescuers adapted to the region by drawing from the experience of skilled, courageous bush pilots flying small planes over inhospitable terrain. For ground operations they did likewise, learning from skilled explorers and natives. Their tracked vehicles often succumbed to torturous weather, as did aircraft. But there was one item in their inventory on which they could rely completely—the sled dog. Unaffected by mechanical woes from weather that immobilized machinery, sled dogs performed. Shortly after "war dogs" were introduced in 1942, search and rescue became a priority use of dogs. Each base along the "Snowball Route" had a SAR squadron, with three flights of thirty-six dogs each to form four dog sled rescue teams; teams were also used in Alaska's interior.

After downed airmen were located by air, sled dog teams were sent, while survival gear was dropped to sustain survivors. The decision to parachute dogs to the site had the shops and test facilities at Camp Rimini, Montana, hard at work developing harnesses and erecting jump towers. Some dogs were accomplished parachutists, joining early parajumpers who faithfully relied on their four-legged partners to help carry equipment and follow trails. These dogs, like their handlers, earned their jump wings after five jumps. Tail wagging was observed during SAR dogs' "silk letdowns," and seasoned dogs often became excited when strapped into their parachute harness. So highly trained were some dogs that they knew upon landing to jump into their billowing parachutes to spill air and collapse them.

Favored among the breeds was the Alaskan malamute, followed by other "northern dogs" such as huskies, wolf mixes, and Labradors. Developed in the Alaskan wilderness, the malamute is considered the oldest Arctic sled dog and a herculean worker. In Greenland, search-and-rescue sled teams often were combinations of huskies for speed and malamutes for strength. Army dogs came into official use at Colorado's Camp Hale in 1942. After the foundation had been laid, all phases of K-9 operations were shifted to Camp Rimini, which was labeled the War Dog Reception and Training Center. Located near the abandoned mining town of Rimini, the area's ample snow and cold, plus timberland and wide-open spaces, proved ideal for training dog teams and drivers. When Camp Rimini closed in March 1944, dog operations at San Carlos, California, and Cat Island, Gulfport, Mississippi, were consolidated at Fort Robinson, Nebraska. Upon completion of training, drivers and teams then were sent to fill requirements in the Arctic and eastern Canada.

Sled dogs would make the difference in two highly publicized search-and-rescue missions on Greenland's ice cap in 1942. In July, when the "Lost Squadron" comprising six P-38s and two B-17s went down, rescuers made their way to the survivors by dog sled. When a C-53 transport with five men went missing in November, one of the 120 aircraft involved in the search was a B-17 with nine crewmen. The Fortress departed Bluie West 1 and never returned, having slammed into a blizzard, stranding more men on the ice. The months-long search echoed the chilling, unofficial motto of the Coast Guard: "You have to go out, but you don't have to come back," when one of their Grumman J2F-4 "Ducks" launched from

the cutter *Northland*. The Duck, after having rescued two injured survivors of the B-17, crashed into a mountain. One of two land motor sledges (the precursor to modern snowmobiles) plunged into a crevasse a mere 100 yards from the wreck, killing its driver. After a Catalina that landed on the ice on its bow proved too heavy for takeoff, rescuers and survivors set out with an experienced AAF nine-dog sled team an aircraft had dropped 5 miles away. After two weeks in winds approaching 150 miles per hour, the group reached the coast, where they were picked up by Catalinas, ending a saga of endurance, suffering, and sacrifice.

The survivors were among a group estimated to number about a hundred who owed their lives to Norman Vaughan, an adventurer and explorer who made dog mushing his life. Vaughan's affinity for driving dog sleds began during the 1920s and led to his position as dog driver on Admiral Byrd's historic Antarctic expedition. During World War II, the Army Air Force held Vaughan's expertise in such high regard that he was employed as a major and managed more than four hundred dogs for polar missions. Famous among them is his lone retrieval of a classified Norden bombsight from a B-17 of the "Lost Squadron." His dog teams led by navy lieutenant j.g. Freddy Crocket (also one of Byrd's dog drivers) rescued the squadron's twenty-six fliers. Vaughan quickly rose to the rank of colonel in 1943, to train and equip ATC North Atlantic Division's search-and-rescue sled dog units.

THE POWER OF VOLUNTEERISM: CIVIL AIR PATROL

In the continental US, then called the Zone of the Interior (ZI), AAF Headquarters attempted to define areas of responsibility that included the navy, coast guard, and civilian agencies. Guidelines often were subject to revision, but a February 1945 AAF regulation aligned specialized search-and-rescue units of the Second, Third, and Fourth Air Forces, along with ATC's Alaskan Division. The Northeast required little air-sea rescue involvement by the First Air Force, since the navy and coast guard had the region well covered with PBY, PBM, and JRF

Armed with a depth charge, this 1931 Stinson JR-S (NC11168) operated from Civil Air Patrol's Base 11 at Pascagoula, Mississippi. The sub hunter was painted red overall and wore the phrase "Yucatan or Bust" on its forward fuselage.

seaworthy aircraft, nearly twenty air rescue boats, a blimp, helicopters, and more than forty coast guard lifeboat stations. Prior to the regulation, no Fourth Air Force aircraft were assigned to air rescue; however, eight Pacific coast detachments were in place. Air rescue boats were in abundance along the Atlantic coast, while the number of rescue aircraft fell short.

Important to search and rescue in the ZI, as well as to the overall war effort, was the Civil Air Patrol (CAP). In 1940, gathering war clouds were a clear indication that civil aviation, unorganized, might be grounded for the duration. Unrestricted use of private airplanes was viewed as cluttering what would become busy airways, thus becoming a menace to military traffic. A handful of leaders knew that the only hope of continued flying was to organize civilians to make them useful to the extent of outweighing objections. On December 1, 1941, just one week before the attack on Pearl Harbor, the Civil Air Patrol was formally created. The similarity between CAP's prop-and-triangle emblem and that of the Office of Civil Defense (OCD) is no coincidence, since CAP was established under the Office of Civil Defense, which had been formed six months earlier. President Roosevelt had named New York mayor Fiorello La Guardia as OCD director, and it was he who signed the bill activating CAP. The two organizations would share the common purpose of mobilizing the civilian population to assist the war effort and prepare for emergencies. In every state, pilots and aviation-inclined men and women signed applications and went through FBI checks to be entrusted with wartime duties. Thousands of pilots, student pilots, former pilots, and skilled citizens—a cross section of America—mobilized in the patriotic common defense of their country. The CAP proved a boon to the military, since not only did members perform innumerable home-front duties, but the organization became a pipeline adding to the ranks of the armed services.

Later transferred from the OCD to the War Department, CAP maintained a countrywide radio net; flew border patrol; performed searchlight tracking service, forest fire patrol, and courier service; towed targets for antiaircraft batteries; conducted

This Sikorsky R-4 was experimentally fit with a cold-weather patient enclosure. Bleed air piped from the engine heated the enclosure.

Since the Sikorsky R-6A experienced developmental problems, only a few saw service during the war, including this example, serial no. 43-45330 of the 8th ERS, in 1945. This pair of R-6As is seen at a field in the CBI theater used by the 1st Air Commando Squadron. In the background are 1st ACS P-51s.

search-and-rescue missions; and responded to natural disasters, to name a few. Lacking the resources to counter relentless submarine attacks on shipping in coastal waters, military leaders had no choice but to honor the requests of CAP leaders that they be put to use. The light planes, at first, were unarmed, a secret well kept from submarine commanders who dove when spotted. Civil Air Patrol pilots could summon attack aircraft, but since they often were unavailable, CAP was authorized bombs and depth charges. Besides nearly two hundred sub sightings throughout the war, CAP crews are credited with sinking two. Flying from specially built coastal bases, they spotted floating mines, airmen downed at sea, and victims of ship sinkings. From the beginning, CAP knew no gender boundaries, with women sharing nearly equal status with men. Ironic, however, was that they were later restricted from flying hazardous coastal patrols, while they did fly over Alaska's equally hazardous terrain. Women in CAP also formed a pipeline that fed the ranks of female units in the armed services: WACs, WAVES, Women Marines, Spars, and flying WASPs. A cadet program added in October 1942 introduced teens to a military setting and provided education in various aviation fields.

Civil Air Patrol aircraft initially were a mix of privately owned light land and amphibian aircraft built during the prewar "golden era of aviation." Beginning in 1942 the Army Air Force began issuing CAP units training gliders, L-4 and L-5 light planes, and twin-engine Beech C-45s. A total of sixty-four CAP volunteers lost their lives during World War II, nearly half of them flying coastal patrols.

Since the Hawaiian Islands were stepping-stones for aircraft crossing the Pacific, the importance of a strong rescue presence couldn't be overstated. Initially, the waters off Hawaii were served by the 927th Quartermaster Boat Company. It was necessary that rescue be available as far west as Midway and Johnson Atolls, so the navy and AAF shared the responsibility. Based in San Francisco, the 13th Emergency Rescue Boat Squadron was assigned to the Hawaiian Islands in December 1944; however, the navy's Hawaiian Sea Frontier Air-Sea Rescue Task Group quickly overshadowed the unit, even adding three plane-guard vessels to make the Hawaii mainland route safer. Regions such as the North Atlantic, Panama Canal, Alaskan coastal waters, and Caribbean received little attention with regard to a sweeping air rescue organization. These areas were either covered by the navy, saw significant shipping activity, or were covered by air rescue boat units. The latter was the case in the Caribbean, where ARBs were in abundance, and the only aircraft assigned to ATC's Caribbean Rescue Division were two OA-10As, an OA-9, and an obsolete B-18 bomber. The first step the ATC Caribbean Division had taken to become rescue capable was the February 1943 acquisition of the 1005th Quartermaster Boat Company (Aviation), which had been formed in 1941 at Morrison Field, West Palm Beach, Florida. The 1005th stationed boats at key Bahama islands Cat Cay, Great Exuma, Mayaguana, and South Caicos. The unit's inventory included eight 63-foot ARBs, one 45-footer, and two 22-footers. The 104-footers initially assigned proved too large for the shallow waters of the Bahamas and were exchanged for 63-footers. A futile attempt to use carrier pigeons to guide air and water rescue crews to downed aircraft during the first half of 1944 gave way to direction-finding (DF) installations at numerous sites in the Caribbean. Four pigeons were to be carried on aircraft transiting the region, and they were to be released with messages giving the plane's position. Despite the RAF's use of pigeons early in the war, US aircrew were not convinced, often refusing to take pigeons aboard.

Likewise, the South Atlantic was low on the air rescue totem pole until after VE-day, when thousands of troops and aircraft were to be sent back to the US from Europe and the Mediterranean along the South Atlantic route. Rescue coverage for the massive move, called simply Project Green, brought US Navy destroyers and blimps, along with Army Air Force OA-10As, B-17s, and air rescue boats stationed along Brazilian coastlines. These bolstered a force of one 63-foot and four 104-foot ARBs, five B-17s, and four OA-10As that had been partnered for rescue in the South Atlantic during 1943. On the Pacific side of the Isthmus of Panama, in June 1944, rescue duty was assumed by the 12th ERBS, whose personnel found it necessary to trade 104-foot ARBs for 63- and 85-foot boats, which were better suited to the region.

Arguably, the most significant addition to the rescuers' inventory late in the war was the helicopter. Validating Igor Sikorsky's belief in the helicopter's highest calling, the machine's humanitarian age dawned on January 3, 1944, after the destroyer USS *Turner Joy* exploded off Sandy Hook, New Jersey, killing 139 sailors. Flying a Sikorsky R-4, US Coast Guard commander Frank Erickson delivered a load of life-saving plasma from New York to the site to treat sixty-five wounded crewmen. Besides the AAF, the US Navy and Coast Guard, along with the British Royal Navy, found Sikorsky's R-4 and R-6 worthy of further development. Concurrent with the YR-4B helicopter sent to the CBI theater for service tests in 1944, another had been shipped to Alaska to monitor its performance in frigid extremes. The results were the same. In August 1944, the navy developed an electric hoist for its YR-4Bs (HNS-1s) to replace rope ladders. The first rescue by helicopter in the Arctic occurred on May 2, 1945, when a US Coast Guard HNS-1 brought out eleven Royal Canadian Air

Force fliers in northern Labrador, marooned when spring melting prevented fixed-wing aircraft from landing.

Other than the helicopter, never during World War II was serious consideration given to designing an aircraft specifically for air-sea rescue; only the Catalina came closest despite its bow weakness when landing on rough seas. For searches of downed aircraft in the great expanse of the Eastern Air Command, rescue units found the B-24 Liberator bomber the best available for its long range and dependability. When the long-range, heavily armed B-29 bomber dominated the skies of the Pacific, it was deemed a natural for the air-sea rescue role. Carrying extra fuel and equipped with droppable rescue equipment, plus additional radio gear and operators, standard B-29 bombers initially assumed the rescue role to escort long-range missions; 21st Bomber Command assigned two on missions to Japan. Conversion to a rescue configuration called "Superdumbo," complete with large, powered airborne lifeboats, got under way in 1945, but refinement of the system came too late for its use in the war. In the final months of the war, a small number of early rescue-type B-29s joined airborne lifeboat-equipped B-17s on B-29 missions, along with a small number of Catalinas of the 4th Emergency Rescue Squadron. Since B-29s far out-ranged Catalinas and B-17s, they, along with submarines, were positioned closest to enemy shores. To avoid surfacing, thereby revealing their position, subs often were directed to survivors, who attached themselves to the sub's periscope for a harrowing ride to safer waters where the sub could surface and take them aboard. The bulk of support came from the navy's Air-Sea Rescue Task Group, which coordinated with AAF Bomber Command to position surface craft along B-29 strike routes, with submarines along routes serving as lifeguard stations. Escort and continual orbits flown by rescue aircraft during long-range strikes were called "Duckbutt" missions, a term that lasted through future conflicts.

A conference in Manila on August 5, 1945, brought together representatives of Army Air Force Headquarters and its Fifth, Seventh, Thirteenth, and Twentieth Air Forces, along with US Navy leaders to discuss responsibility for air rescue operations during the planned invasion of Japan. The outcome would prove irrelevant when the next day a mushroom cloud covered Hiroshima.

Despite the valiant efforts of Allied air-sea rescue crews during most of the war, the odds were against those who flew in harm's way and found themselves in a doomed aircraft. Eventually, the tables were turned, with rescue no longer taking a back seat to combat. Staggering accident rates both in the US and abroad due to hastily and marginally trained pilots lowered. By war's end, numerous rescue units were stationed in the Pacific and European theaters, their achievements standing as tribute to the pioneers of rescue. The most significant contribution of those who made rescue their business was instilling in aircrews the assurance that someone cared and would do whatever was humanly possible to come to their rescue. Some facts—such as the partnership of airplane and surface craft—remained constant throughout the war: in Europe the Army Air Force depended on the British for air-sea rescue; in the Pacific the US Navy dominated air-sea rescue, while in the Southwest Pacific, the Army Air Force ran the show. Through trial and error, the techniques the services employed in a wide variety of wartime situations helped pave the long road to modern rescue. At war's end came the realization that an organized, adequately equipped, and fully trained combat-ready rescue service was needed worldwide. And the question of responsibility loomed even larger—which service would do what? Answers had to be forthcoming, because a few years later America would again be embroiled in conflict.

Although ill-fitting and cumbersome, rubber one-piece "zoot suits" were worn by Civil Air Patrol air crew flying US coastal patrol. Largely unpopular, the suits were designed to keep a flyer alive for a few hours in the frigid Atlantic. These CAP aviators pose with a Fairchild 24R and one of its bombs.

At the end of World War II, America welcomed peace and a return to a sense of normalcy. That meant rapid demobilization of military forces, which worked well for combat units but proved problematic for continuation of rescue service. The concept and potentiality of air rescue had been proven during the war. Such successes, especially during the latter part of the conflict, had leaders of all services agreeing that global air-land-sea rescue coverage was needed and should remain, but that's where accord ended. The Air Sea Rescue Agency, established in 1944, remained intact; however, it was governed mainly by the coast guard, which protected America's ports and offshore waters. The First through Fourth Air Forces covered land areas of the US, while rescue in overseas theaters was entrusted to US Army Air Force and US Navy commanders. The ATC was responsible for regions covered by global air lanes.

The viewpoints of military leaders concerning rescue were worlds apart. The army felt that the coast guard was ill suited to take on global rescue, contending that only army aviation was sufficiently flexible and mobile to handle national emergencies. The navy, which never came to terms with the army over the issue of joint air rescue, was content to let the coast guard take over. The Civil Air Patrol, its future uncertain since its scope of operations narrowed during the final months of the war, had intentions of formulating a plan for rescue in the US.

A 1944 statement by the assistant chief of Air Staff, Gen. Laurence S. Kuter, to Gen. Arnold reinforcing the established function of air-sea rescue in the AAF lent credence to the formation of a single rescue agency. This led to a plan for placing responsibility for rescue with the AAF not only within that period, but in the postwar era. However, ATC commander Gen. Harold L. George felt that his organization was ill prepared to take on the responsibility for rescue over the world's oceans, insisting that only the navy was best suited for the monumental task.

The navy brass had other ideas, however, and began dismantling rescue units while backing the coast guard, which was poised for the takeover; the Army Air Force held firm, despite opposition from its own Air Transport Command, which became taciturn lest it lose air rescue completely. Finally, Gen. Hoyt S. Vandenberg, assistant chief of Air Staff for operations, broke the stalemate by delegating responsibility for global land-air search and rescue to the ATC. As the army began planning to establish rescue units throughout the world, the navy maintained control of the oceans, and the coast guard reinforced its vigil over waters of the US and its possessions, and along transoceanic routes. Vandenberg's conclusions placed little value on air rescue boats, a view seen by many as a flawed assessment of the boats' wartime service. His mention that the boats were successful only in the English Channel likely was based on their limited range in comparison to navy ships. Vandenberg declared that all air rescue boats over 45 feet were excess; however, smaller craft were to be retained for rescue operations in waters near airfields. Abroad, some boats were turned over to governments in regions where boats operated, such as ARBs of the Thirteenth Air Force that remained in the Philippines. Many became supply vessels or were converted to gunboats, or even hacks, especially in the Pacific. Others served as gunnery targets and were sunk, and some were sold to private concerns.

After the 14th ERBS was deactivated in March 1946, some of the unit's boats and crews were assigned to 5th Fighter Command at Itazuke Air Base to provide crash boat coverage, and at Ashiya AB. Between fifty and sixty air rescue boats of all sizes went into storage in Yokohama Harbor, sharing storage space with numerous army watercraft. The US Air Force in May 1949 boasted having its own fleet, although small, comprising three 42-foot ARBs modified to accommodate twenty-five passengers for scheduled shuttle service between the Pentagon and Bolling Field. Each boat of the Air Force Marine Boat Shuttle Service was manned by a master, engineer, and mate, whose training included courses in how to treat generals, congressmen, and cabinet members.

In 1945, eighty-two 63-footers were transferred to the coast guard for coastal patrol and rescue throughout the US.

SHORT YEARS

Personnel and budget cutbacks, plus the boats' reputation for being "gas hogs" and, therefore, expensive to operate forced their removal from coast guard service by 1947. More valid than Vandenberg's opinion of the boats was development of the helicopter as a vital rescue tool to replace air rescue boats. But development of the helicopter was slow and only added to the myriad problems facing air rescue; they included personnel shortages, lack of funds, antiquated aircraft and equipment, and the near extinction of a nationwide communications net. One solution to postwar austerity lay in the all-volunteer Civil Air Patrol, which in August 1945 had come under the Army Air Force's Air Defense Command. Recognizing the opportunity to secure CAP's future beyond hope, its leaders expanded operations to alleviate shortcomings imposed on army air rescue. Free of wartime duties, CAP personnel could place more emphasis on emergency services during natural disasters and on conducting nationwide search-and-rescue efforts. To meet these demands, upward of three

This SC-47D (serial no. 45-894) seen over Alaska in postwar markings had "blister" windows for observers at waist positions. An MA-1 air rescue kit was carried in the rear fuselage. *Courtesy of David Menard collection*

For more than two decades, beginning in 1949, Grumman's Albatross served as the backbone of air rescue. The first production SA-16A (serial no. 48-588) undergoes open-sea tests to prove that its triphibian gear did not affect handling characteristics on water. The air force ordered 145 SA-16As with triphibian gear, which incorporated a two-section, keel-mounted skid, the aft portion of which retracted. Swivel skids were attached to wing floats. On the nose of no. 588 is the name "Arctic Albatross." *Courtesy of Harold G. Martin*

hundred "L" planes were loaned by the air force to CAP, with the air force retaining responsibility for their support.

The inevitable downsizing of the military at war's end meant abrupt closure of the rescue school at Keesler. At the school's helm when it closed on April 22, 1946, was Maj. Robert Rizon, who often was called "Mr. Air Rescue," and for good reason. Rizon had been in the rescue business long before anyone else. Rescue was in his blood. He started flying airplanes in 1925 at thirteen years old and, before he was fifteen, had parachuted from airplanes more than thirty times. With the closing of the rescue school, Rizon lamented, "They felt that we had trained enough squadrons and that it was not necessary to maintain a school strictly for that purpose. That was not my point of view. I envisioned that there would be

An OA-10A (serial no. 44-33999) at Goose AFB sheds its blue paint, revealing its wartime high-visibility white livery. "OB" was postwar code for the OA-10. A total of 105 OA-10s were built; fifty-eight survivors were redesignated A-10s in 1948.

vastly increased air travel after the war, and there would be a much-greater need for rescue than ever." He continues, "As far as we were concerned, the military pilots, the amount of flying we had to do overwater gave us a lot to think about. We were always concerned as to what would happen should we go down. When I was on coast patrol in conventional-type aircraft, I expended a lot of time wondering what would happen if I had to ditch." Rizon embodied the concept and history of air rescue, and his visions would be realized.

Rizon's sense of dedication took him in February 1947 to Bolivia, where the Mamore River had burst its banks and flooded a 100-square-mile region. Finding an elevated airstrip at Trinidad covered by only a few inches of water, he radioed back to Panama for C-47s, eight of which arrived at La Paz by nightfall. In five days, Rizon and his crews evacuated 2,300 natives who were brought to the submerged strip. On return trips, they flew in 15 tons of food and medical supplies. On one of these trips, Red Cross workers counted ninety-seven people helped from Rizon's C-47, a world's record for the number of passengers carried on a C-47. A grinning Rizon downplayed the feat, stating that most of them were babies.

Faced with the monumental task of building a rescue organization that covered the US and along air transport routes, the ATC waded in slowly, first gaining a foothold in the US. Its first step was designating on December 5, 1945, the 62nd AAF Base Unit (Search and Rescue), with activation begun at Andrews Field, Maryland, on January 23, 1946. Personnel were drawn from continental air force search-and-rescue base units, which the new unit was to replace. On March 13, its designation became Headquarters, Air Rescue Service, which is recognized as the birth of air rescue. On May 21, 1946, the 5th Emergency Rescue Squadron, which months earlier had returned from overseas to Keesler Field, Mississippi, was then assigned to the Air Rescue Service. On May 29, the same day that headquarters shifted to Washington National Airport, Col. Wallace S. Ford replaced 62nd Base Unit commander Lt. Col. Joseph F. Westover to take command of the new service. Joel A. Harper, who served as intelligence officer of the 13th Emergency Rescue Group during World War II, said the following in a 1994 interview with the author:

The 13th Emergency Rescue Group was commanded by Col. Wallace S. Ford, with Col. Joseph H. Batjer the intelligence chief of staff. After their return from overseas, both Ford and Batjer were at the Pentagon, where they wrote the policy on rescue for the air force and wrote the regulations establishing the Air Rescue Service. I joined Headquarters, Air Rescue Service, at Morrison Field 5 July 1946 under the command of Ford, and I have a copy of the order dated 8 July 1947 moving headquarters from West Palm Beach to MacDill Field, Tampa, Florida.

Headquarters had been moved to West Palm Beach one year earlier to bring it closer to the 5th Emergency Rescue Squadron.

An OA-10A (serial no. 440-33939) in its striking postwar scheme at Hamilton AFB in late 1948. A typical crew comprised two pilots, radar operator, navigator, radio operator, engineer, and surgical technician. Large observation blisters originally designed for .50 cal. machine gun positions facilitated the recovery of survivors. *Courtesy of William T. Larkins*

In keeping with the medical function of newly founded Air Rescue, four medical officers assigned in September 1946 were quickly replaced by three lieutenants who were graduates of the School of Aviation Medicine at Randolph Field, Texas, and had become airborne qualified at Ft. Benning. Lt. Albert G. Lewis was assigned to ARS headquarters, Lt. Randolph W. Briggs to Squadron "B" at Hamilton Field, and Lt. Truett V. Bennett to Squadron "A" at Andrews Field. The following month, one dozen medical enlisted men were assigned to Air Rescue, foreshadowing the future structure of pararescue.

As fast as the Emergency Rescue School closed its doors, the Army Air Force stopped taking delivery of R-6A and R-5A helicopters after VJ-day, and helicopter training had all but disappeared by the end of 1945. Development of Sikorsky's R-5, however, reaffirmed the value of the helicopter, and the helicopter pilot training program was resurrected in May 1946 at San Marcos, Texas, with R-6As and R-5s.

Dedicated rescue men were as resistive to shutting down the Army's sled dog program as they were to curtailing development of the helicopter. Although the dog program was officially terminated at the end of the war, Army Air Force rescue dogs remained in use until the helicopter reached its full potential during the 1950s. As an army function, sled dog teams for search and rescue had been overlooked in transition to Air Force Air Rescue. Helping to fill the gap caused by dog

attrition during the postwar period was Joe Redington, who became the "father of the Iditarod." Redington worked as a civilian for the air force in Alaska from 1949 to 1957, using his dog teams for rescue missions, many of which became aircraft salvage or body recovery missions.

Many of the skilled rescue men left the military at war's end, leaving Ford challenged to build from scratch; his foundation blocks were 1,100 men, 116 obsolete aircraft, and a lean budget. Thus began a dizzying shell game of unit relocations and redesignations throughout 1946. Some moves enhanced efficiency, while others were the result of base closings. Control centers across the country were established only to be combined with others, moved, or eliminated; rescue units would be subject to the same schedule, while intermittently labeled as squadrons or detachments.

A similar shell game was being played out overseas; the 2nd, 3rd, 4th, 6th, and 7th Emergency Rescue Squadrons were in the Pacific at war's end. The 2nd shifted from Morotai to Luzon, Philippines, until March 1947, when it moved to Okinawa and absorbed the 6th ERS, which was then inactivated. The 3rd and the 5th moved to Japan. The 4th remained in the Pacific until it was absorbed into the Air Rescue Service. The 7th, which had shifted from the Pacific to the CBI in late 1945, relinquished its assets to the 6th, moved to Hawaii, and was inactivated on May 15, 1947. The 1st returned to the US

Less than two weeks after Adm. Richard Byrd left his base camp during his fourth expedition to the polar ice cap, on February 4, 1947, this dog sled team transferred a survivor to an R-5A helicopter.

early in 1946, to be inactivated at the end of March. Major Rizon was elated when he was directed to gather the men from the first squadron he had trained at Keesler who were still in uniform. In September, they became reactivated in the 1st Rescue Squadron and were sent to the Caribbean. The 8th Emergency Rescue Squadron had been inactivated in spring 1945. Other rescue veterans were sought and formed into small units called detachments, which became add-ons to larger units throughout the US.

In Alaska at the end of the war, all rescue activities were consolidated into the 10th Air Rescue Squadron, which was activated at Elmendorf Field on April 1, 1946, under the command of Lt. Col. Edward E. Cunningham, who succeeded Maj. Charles E. Mosse, the first commander of Alaskan Air Command's Air-Sea Rescue, as the unit had been known. Detachments were established at Elmendorf AFB, Ladd AFB, Adak Naval Station, Nome, Cold Bay, and Shemya.

Despite the strain of personnel and aircraft shortages, during the second half of 1946 the Air Rescue Service conducted searches for 107 aircraft, both military and civilian, along with numerous ocean searches and humanitarian missions. Taxing rescue's meager resources were directives to participate in activities having little or nothing to do with its mission. During the summer of 1946, air rescue assisted the US Forest Service's Project Container Missile for drop tests of fire-extinguishing agents. Even more unrelated to the mission was the use of air rescue helicopters, albeit on trial basis, to haul mail from large municipal airports to downtown main post offices. Eight helicopters were tasked with the project at Los Angeles and Chicago. Some California-based R-5s flew over cherry orchards during spring rains, with the hope that their rotors would dry the fruit.

In December 1946, Col. Richard T. Kight took command of the Air Rescue Service. Kight, formerly of ATC's Pacific Division, had been advised by ATC deputy commander Gen. Gordon Saville to give the organization a hard look and then decide if it should be strengthened or disbanded. Kight's hard look revealed about eight hundred men and an aircraft inventory that comprised thirty-three C-47s, thirteen B-17s, a dozen OA-10 Catalinas, thirty-two L-5s, nine AT-11s, and seventeen helicopters, a meager force expected to cover the entire US. It appeared obvious to Kight that Rescue had become a collection point for unwanted equipment, not to mention a handful of individuals who lacked motivation. On a personal tour of rescue units in the field, Kight found that what stood out most were men who were enthusiastic and dedicated. "I couldn't understand it," Kight remarked. "They were ready to whip the world with nothing." It became crystal clear when a young lieutenant said to Kight, "Sir, I'd rather save people than kill them." Buoyed by his men's confidence and armed with conviction, Kight's mission was clear: to train personnel and to acquire aircraft suited for rescue. In a 1999 interview with the author, Kight stated:

> I wrote the code of an air rescue man and had it printed up on small cards so the members of Air Rescue Service could carry it in their wallets: "It is my duty as a member of the Air Rescue Service to save life and to aid the injured. I will be prepared at all times to perform my assigned duties quickly and efficiently, placing the duties before personal desires and comforts. These things I do that others may live." This last line became our motto.

By late spring 1947 a stable organizational framework was in place, with emergency rescue squadrons now designated rescue squadrons. Besides units at Morrison Field, nine detachments fell under two squadrons: Detachment 2, Westover Field, Massachusetts; Detachment 4, Selfridge Field, Michigan; Detachment 5, Scott Field, Illinois; and Detachment 6, Biggs Field, Texas, came under Air Rescue Squadron A, relocated to Pope Field, Fort Bragg, North Carolina, while Detachment 8, McChord Field, Washington; Detachment 9, March Field, California; Detachment 10, Hill Field, Utah; Detachment 11, Great Falls Army Air Base, Montana; and Detachment 12, Lowry Field, Colorado, came under Air Rescue Squadron B at Hamilton Field, California.

Reorganization during the late 1940s seemed endless; however, no change in the organizational table would have as much impact as formation of the US Air Force as a separate branch on September 18, 1947. The Army Air Force Air Transport Command, which had been in limbo since the end of the war, now had to fight for its very existence. But leaders of the newly formed Department of Defense (DoD) had a better idea: forming the Military Air Transport Service (MATS). The MATS would be under US Air Force control but would combine resources of the Air Transport Command and the Naval Air Transport Service. Although intended to function mainly as a transport arm, MATS would be the parent command of a small number of special services, one of which was

The Alaskan Wing Search and Rescue Squadron of ATC, which activated in December 1943, saw the largest use of Noorduyn UC-64 Norsemans, with eight assigned. The letters "CL" preceding this Norseman's serial no. (43-35444) were postwar code for the metal-and-fabric-covered UC-64. The first 299 UC-64As delivered to the USAAF left the production line in Olive Drab with light-gray undersides. Follow-on production of 449 Norsemans was factory-painted silver. *Courtesy of David Menard collection*

the Air Rescue Service, which came under MATS when it was activated on June 1, 1948.

The assignment breathed new life into air rescue, whose leaders set their sights on optimizing the service with more-skilled personnel and the best equipment available. With regard to aircraft, that could only mean finally settling on a type built specifically for air rescue. Fortune smiled on the Air Rescue Service, since that would happen both with fixed and rotary wing.

The air force revised its aircraft designation system in 1948, which had the B-17H redesignated as SB-17G, the Catalina becoming the SA-10A, and the C-47 renamed the SC-47, with the "S" denoting search and rescue as the primary mission. The second letters in the prefix stood for aircraft type, be it cargo, amphibian, bomber, etc. Early that year, Colonel Kight's yearlong plan for extending rescue service into overseas areas was implemented. Small units with few aircraft were established. They were the 512th base Unit at Dhahran, Saudi Arabia, the 2154th Rescue Unit at Wheelus Field, Tripoli, and the 2152nd Rescue Unit, which dispersed its few SB-17Gs and SA-10As among flights at Newfoundland, Labrador, Bermuda, and the Azores. The Azores, Portugal, held geographical value as an Atlantic air connection between Europe and North and South America. The main operating base, on Terceira Island, was British-named Labens Field, which was renamed Lajes Field in 1953.

Illustrating the adaptability of an Air Rescue unit to its area of operations was the 1060th Rescue Unit at Dhahran, which became Flight D of the 7th Air Rescue Squadron in September 1949. Unit members became keenly aware of

customs and the way of life in their host countries. This especially held true in Saudi Arabia, where King Saud maintained strict oversight of all foreign nationals on his soil, allowing only 225 US military personnel at Dhahran, forty-one of whom were assigned to Flight D. Equally daunting was adapting to the region's climate, which meant enduring blistering desert heat and frigid nights as well as fierce desert sandstorms, and traversing high, soft sand dunes of the Rub al Khali Desert. Aircraft assigned to Flight D included a pair of SB-17Gs and a float-equipped H-5H helicopter.

An important element of the unit was a land rescue team manned by volunteers and consisting of two 6×6 Diamond T trucks and a 4×4 Dodge ambulance, all adapted for desert travel, rescue, and recovery. One truck was painted red and carried 800 gallons of gasoline, 50 gallons of oil, spare parts, tools, and maintenance equipment. The other was painted white and carried 500 gallons of drinking water, rations, a generator, and radio sets. Since the land rescue team was tasked with gathering information for an air force survival manual, desert survival training was conducted throughout Saudi Arabia. Often, these long trips entailed searches for aircraft wrecks and then applying yellow paint for identification. In an account of his fifteen-month tour in 1950 and 1951 with Flight D as an aircraft crew chief and flight mechanic, Ted A. Morris wrote:

A French Navy F4U, an RAF Anson, and a US B-29 were among the old wrecks located, identified and painted. We also collected anything that crawled, slithered, walked, ran or otherwise moved in the desert. Spiders, snakes, lizards, foxes, and gazelles were among some of the more identifiable desert life we collected. There was no natural life, no moisture, no shade, and no protection from the fierce wind-driven sand. Our best recommendation to the survival pamphlet authors was for aircrews to never become stranded in the "Empty Quarter."

During the return from our survival information gathering trip into the Rub al Khali, we were refueled and resupplied by air in a large gravel-plain area called Abu-Bahr on the northern edge of the desert. Selecting a large, fairly level area, we used the large trucks to mark off a landing zone several miles long by driving back and forth to indicate the actual landing strip. An SB-17G with two 300-gallon bomb bay tanks, one filled with truck gas and the other with drinking water, landed and provided replenishment to our very dehydrated desert traveling party. On other resupply flights, mail, food, and spare parts, including spare tires, were dropped by parachute.

To enable the aircrew to recover the parachutes and outgoing mail when a landing was not possible, a rudimentary rig consisting of a grappling hook on the end of a nylon line was lowered from the SB-17G. On the ground, a nylon line and container were strung between the two large trucks. The SB-17G flew between the trucks, quite low to the ground, and snatched the pick-up line. The aircrew then hauled the container hand over hand into the aircraft.

Due to its proximity to the Persian Gulf, Flight D traded its two SB-17Gs for Grumman SA-16A Albatrosses. Morris describes the changeover:

These were the first SA-16As assigned outside the Continental United States. Four pilots, two crew chiefs / flight mechanics (including myself), and two radio operators were quickly sent to MacDill AFB for two weeks transition training and then to the Grumman factory in New York to pick up the 21st and 22nd SA-16As delivered to the air force. These were serial numbers 49-074 and 49-075. Behaving as two crew chiefs assigned to a godforsaken backwater, TSgt. Nilo P. Pollo and I scrounged every available spare part not tied down at the Grumman plant in order to get our aircraft to Dhahran and keep them flying once we arrived. At that time a major problem existed with the exhaust system of the R-1820-76A Wight Cyclone engines. Nine cylinders emptied into six exhaust stacks, and the clamps holding this system together had a bad habit of cracking and breaking apart. This then allowed the unsupported exhaust stacks to crack and break at the cylinder, creating a severe fire hazard. Needless to say, we made off with every spare exhaust clamp we could lay our hands on.

Now that we had an aircraft which could land on water, much training was needed. Our water practice takeoffs and landings took place in the Persian Gulf, one of the saltiest bodies of water on earth. Corrosion was a serious problem. The normal water supply at Dhahran was brackish and had to be distilled for drinking. The aircraft wash-down procedure involved using the fire truck water supply to wash the salt off, after which the distilled water supply from the 500-gallon white desert truck was used to wash off the corrosive brackish water.

Since Dhahran Airfield (the king forbade calling it a base) was the only one in the region that could support B-29s, the Air Weather Service set up a detachment with three WB-29s. Flight D then added to their schedule weekly intercepts of WB-29s with at least one engine out. To see a Flight D SA-16A providing close escort was a welcome sight to those weather fliers.

When the Military Air Transport Service (MATS) absorbed the Air Rescue Service, nineteen Catalinas were on hand. Within a few months that number would top out at twenty-four SA-10As, but the amphibians were tired, and the time had come to replace them with amphibians designed for rescue. With its long, multiservice history, the proven Catalina, albeit an optimized model, seemed the obvious choice. But defense planners desired something even more rugged, and American-manufactured. Grumman Aircraft Corporation officials felt that they could fill the bill. In a letter sent to the deputy commander of ATC, Lt. Col. Littleton J. Pardue, Air Rescue headquarters requested that procurement of PBY5As be stopped and the Grumman be procured instead. The letter stated, in part, "After studying and comparing the Grumman with the PBY5A, it has been determined that the Grumman is the more desirable aircraft."

The 71st Air Rescue Squadron in Alaska prior to November 14, 1952, had been Flight A, 10th Air Rescue Squadron. The color scheme for Alaska-based aircraft was aluminized lacquer and Insignia Red. Here, 71st ARS, 10th ARG personnel, and H-5A serial no. 43-46632 pose for the camera at Elmendorf AFB, Alaska, in 1952. *Courtesy of USAF*

Jet-assisted takeoff (JATO) was an early German innovation first applied to US military aircraft in 1941. The system proved especially useful in takeoffs from rough seas, which made it a standard fixture on the Albatross. This SA-10A (serial no. 44-33956) of the 4th Rescue Squadron departs McChord AFB with two JATO units producing 1,000 pounds of thrust each for fourteen seconds. The Catalina was withdrawn from use in late 1952 and stored at Brookley AFB, where it was scrapped. *Courtesy of Jim Sullivan collection*

During World War II, Grumman's engineering team drew from its decade of experience designing amphibious aircraft to meet the navy's requirement for an amphibian to replace aging Catalinas. In 1944 the navy's Bureau of Aeronautics accepted Grumman's proposal for its Model G-64, which was a continuation of its earlier twin-engine G-21 "Goose" design, albeit on a larger scale. One month after the US Air Force was established, Grumman's prototype lifted from Bethpage, Long Island, New York, on its maiden flight. The timing could not have been better. Air force officials immediately took interest, and after the second prototype flew in 1948, a marriage that would last more than two decades was consecrated. During his interview with the author, retired Col. Richard Kight recalled:

Experimental SA-16s were built with money provided by the coast guard. The coast guard had no money to start production. It just happened that the air force had procurement money that was budgeted for another aircraft that was not as advanced as the SA-16. We were able to switch the money over to Grumman and got production started.

The air force not only took over a large order canceled by the navy, but ordered additional aircraft. Initially labeled the "Pelican" and later "Albatross," the sturdy amphibian was designated SA-16A by the air force, and the UF-1 by the navy. Not to be left out, the coast guard placed an order for Albatrosses under the designation UF-1G.

As the Air Rescue Service grew, it seemed in a perpetual state of organizational flux. In February 1948, squadron and detachment designations gave way to the consolidation of all personnel under the 8th and 9th Rescue Units (RUs). The 8th had flights at Hamilton and March Fields, California, and McChord Field, Washington, while the 9th was based at Lowry Field, Colorado, with flights at Biggs Field, Texas, and Selfridge Field, Michigan. Headquarters ARS moved to Gravelly Point, Virginia, with its flight section assigned to Pope Field, Fort Bragg, North Carolina. The assignment of air rescue to MATS resulted in formation of the 1050th Rescue Unit in Newfoundland, with flights in Labrador, the Azores and Bermuda; the 1061st RU in Tripoli; and redesignation of the detachment at Dhahran to the 1060th RU. Only two months would pass before these units received new designations: the

8th became the 2150th, the 9th became the 2151st, the 1050th became the 2152nd, the 1060th became the 2153rd, and the 1061st became the 2154th. The 5th Rescue Squadron maintained its training role at MacDill, while providing rescue coverage with flights at Westover and at Pope.

Beginning in September 1949 the Air Rescue Service had stretched its protective arms sufficiently to create numbered squadrons that would provide global rescue service. These assignments did not affect the operational control held by commanders in overseas areas. They were as follows:

1st Rescue Squadron
Headquarters and Flight A, MacDill AFB, Florida
Flight B, Albrook AFB, Canal Zone
Flight C, Ramey AFB, Puerto Rico
Flight D, Waller AFB, Trinidad, British West
    Indies / Kindley AFB, Bermuda

2nd Rescue Squadron
Headquarters and Flight A, Kadena Field, Okinawa
Flight B, Kadena Field, Okinawa
Flight C, Clark AB, Philippine Islands
Flight D, North AB, Guam, Mariana Islands

3rd Rescue Squadron
Headquarters and Flight A, Yokota AB, Japan
Flight B, Yokota AB, Japan
Flight C, Misawa AB, Japan
Flight D, Ashiya AB, Japan

4th Rescue Squadron
Headquarters and Flight A, Hamilton AFB, California
Flight B, March AFB, California
Flight C, McChord AFB, Washington
Flight D, Hickam AFB, Hawaiian Islands

5th Rescue Squadron
Headquarters and Flight A, Lowry AFB, Colorado
Flight B, Biggs AFB, Texas
Flight C, Maxwell AFB, Alabama
Flight D, Selfridge AFB, Michigan

6th Rescue Squadron
Headquarters and Flight A, Westover AFB,
    Massachusetts
Flight B, Ernest Harmon AFB, Newfoundland
Flight C, Goose AB, Labrador
Flight D, Bluie West 1, Greenland

7th Rescue Squadron
Headquarters and Flight A, Wiesbaden AB, Germany
Flight B, Lajes Field, Azores
Flight C, Wheelus Field, Tripoli, Libya
Flight D, Dhahran Field, Saudi Arabia

These changes had the 5th RS relinquishing its training role to the 2156th Air Rescue Unit, Tactical Training Unit (TTU), on January 21, 1950. Besides instruction in all aspects of each rescue aircraft type, the TTU provided specialized training for most elements of rescue, including land rescue, emergency medicine, survival (Arctic, desert, and jungle), special vehicle operation, land navigation, native culture, mountain climbing, advanced swimming, communications, and aerial-delivery techniques. When the TTU relocated from MacDill AFB to West Palm Beach AFB (formerly Morrison AAF) in July 1952, it was redesignated the 1707th Training Squadron (Amphibious) of the 1707th Air Base Wing of MATS. The squadron trained SA-16A crews at the joint civil-military base until 1959, when it was moved to Brookley AFB, Alabama, and redesignated the 1797th Flying Training Squadron (Amphibious).

Missing from this list is the 8th Rescue Squadron, which was reactivated in October 1950 but assigned to Strategic Air Command (SAC) for its exclusive support. Since the SAC mission went hand in hand with the nuclear war mindset, the 8th RS flew ski-equipped SC-47s in the event SAC bombers were sent to the Soviet Union over the polar region; SAC was also prepared to address deteriorating conditions in the Far East, which brought SAC and Air Rescue leaders together to work out air evacuation plans should an atomic offensive occur. With MacDill AFB selected as the jumping-off point, SAC then ordered URC-4 radios for long-range evacuation communications; modified C-119s, along with a C-47 derivative, were evaluated as evacuation aircraft. The C-47 modification was the result of airworthiness requirements imposed for commercial use of existing DC-3 airframes. While unsuccessful from a commercial standpoint, despite increased

In the postwar period, airborne lifeboats were included in the air force redesignation of watercraft, receiving hull numbers 1 through 650. The A-1 boat carried by this SB-17G (serial no. 44-83711) wore the emblem of the 5th Rescue Squadron. *Courtesy of USAF*

After World War II, about thirty B-29s were converted to SB-29s for air-sea rescue duty, supporting air units that flew long distances overwater. Defensive armament was retained with the exception of the forward lower gun turret, which was replaced with search radar. The first SB-29 "Super Dumbos" were assigned to the ARS in mid-March 1947 and served throughout the Korean War and into the mid-1950s. Besides the A-3 airborne lifeboat, this SB-29 (serial no. 44-87644) carried extra crew and survival kits. *Courtesy of Lionel N. Paul*

speed and payload, the refined "Super DC-3" grabbed the interest of the air force, which labeled it the YC-129, and later the YC-47F. A single example was test-flown in June 1949 but was passed over in favor of Convair's C-131. The Super DC-3 found a home in the navy as the R4D-8, later designated C-117. Concurrently, SAC commander Gen. Curtis E. LeMay worked with the director of intelligence, US Air Forces Europe, and the CIA to formulate escape and evasion plans with MATS leaders when it appeared that Russia might move against the air force during the Berlin Airlift. Although the Strategic Air Command had fast developed a reputation for being autonomous, its leaders eventually were persuaded to place training of their air rescue support in more-capable hands, and the 8th RS was transferred to the ARS, which then provided rescue support for SAC. In conjunction with the move, in 1951 the USAF Survival School and the 3904th Composite Wing, which trained SAC aircrews in survival, moved from Camp Carson, Colorado, to Stead AFB, Nevada, to capitalize on the Sierra Nevada's ideal setting for survival training. Stead

would become home for the 61st and 62nd Air Rescue Squadrons, which were among four squadrons assigned to the 8th RS when it was elevated to group status; the other two were the 63rd and 64th ARS at Norton AFB, California. Jerry Jones remembers:

> Before going to pilot training, I was assigned to the 61st ARS at Stead, Reno, Nevada, as a navigator. Our mission was to bring the SAC crews home after their probable one-way mission to Russia. One of our squadrons was always in England. We initially deployed to RAF East Kirkby and in 1956 changed to RAF Greenham Common. We flew SC-47s equipped with JATO. I don't know what legal altitude requirements were back then, but we were authorized flight down to 100 feet during daylight and 500 feet at night.

The 9th Rescue Squadron had not been reactivated since its closure during the final days of World War II, but it was reactivated in 1952. The 10th remained under control of the

Alaskan Air Command until July 1950, when it was transferred to the Air Rescue Service.

The air rescue organization in Alaska served as a shining example of total SAR coverage and function as an integral part of military and civil aviation. Since Alaskans were accustomed to seeing aircraft and land rescue teams throughout the territory, it was no surprise that the 10th ARS was widely known as "the Guardian of the North," and "the Sourdough Retriever," the latter referring to experienced prospectors called "sourdoughs." Initially consisting of two flights, and later three, the 10th by 1952 had grown to group status, with four Air Rescue squadrons—the 71st through 74th—along with detachments at Lake Hood, Cold Bay, Shemya, Galena, and Naknek.

As Air Rescue's global net became fully operational, it was discovered that two-thirds of its alerts were false, pointing to the need to educate both civilian and military pilots, who generally had become accustomed to laxness in reporting termination of flights, late flight arrivals, and changes in flight plans. As the situation improved, false alerts gave way to a workload of using onboard navigation and communication gear to intercept and escort aircraft in distress.

Manpower shortages, lack of funds, and antiquated aircraft and equipment continually plagued Air Rescue during the late 1940s. Such drawbacks could not dampen the spirit of rescue, which burned brightly in those who made their living answering the call. A call to Kight from one of his squadron commanders brought to light an issue yet to be explicitly defined and logged as gospel. The commander asked if he could send an airplane to rescue a civilian. When Kight asked, "What the hell do you have to ask me that for?," his man said that air force policy restricted rescue to the military. After saying, "Go ahead anyway," Kight scoured the manuals but found nothing that forbade military aircraft from helping civilians. It had been done previously, but it had to be made official. He wrote regulations stating that anyone, whether wearing a US uniform, any other uniform, or no uniform at all, would get help from Air Rescue. In addition, he authorized local commanders to decide if help was needed and to launch the mission. Kight knew that helping people in distress was bigger than Air Rescue and bigger than the air force itself. His concept was bought all the way up to the Pentagon; it was bought cautiously and with reservation, but it was bought, and that was all that Kight had asked.

Instilled with a profound sense of purpose, rescue men knew that there could be no limits on their humanitarian service. Above all else, it fell upon them to be the friends in high places to anyone who needed help. There could be no better tool of diplomacy. Although the dawning of the Cold War was a call to arms, it motivated America to establish a global peacetime presence. Humanitarian airlift operations demonstrated to the world the versatility of airpower. Humanitarian airlift was nothing new—as early as 1919, US Army aircraft dropped food to stranded flood victims along

During December 1948 and January 1949, eighteen snowstorms in twenty-seven days hit the Rocky Mountain and upper Great Plains states, dropping temperatures to –40°F and threatening thousands of livestock with starvation. As part of the relief effort called Operation Hayride (interchangeably with Operations Haylift and Snowbound), the 2151st Rescue Unit at Lowry AFB, Colorado, flew SC-47, SC-82, L-5, and H-5 aircraft to drop and deliver lifesaving supplies. This M-29 Weasel of the 2151st, which was flown to Scottsbluff, Nebraska, by SC-82, delivered feed to starving sheep in February 1949. *Courtesy of USAF*

the Rio Grande—and Kight and his successors remained dedicated to the concept.

Although the air force operated on a constricted budget, it was imperative that budget appropriations for the SAC and TAC remain solvent, should world peace be threatened. However, the dire need to address the problem of outdated and too few aircraft in air rescue left DoD officials no choice but to make budget allowances. The Air Rescue Service could not be expected to expand global coverage with its inventory of World War II–vintage SB-17Gs, SB-29s, OA-10 Catalinas, SC-47s, and L-5s, and a small fleet of helicopters. The rescue B-29, a rudimentary form of which flew in the final weeks of the war, was the newest of the bunch, having been refined into the SB-29 and introduced to air rescue in March 1947.

During this period, the question arose of what to do with the air rescue boats. Despite General Vandenberg's limit on the length of air rescue boats, many of the 63-footers were spared and put to use in numerous crash rescue boat flights formed by the air force after World War II. Three years after setting out as a separate branch, the air force changed the "P" designation of air rescue boats briefly to "R-1" and then "R-2," followed by the boat's three-digit number.

A carryover from the war that would become a key element of air rescue was the Douglas C-54 "Skymaster," which served as the ATC's chief long-range transport since 1943. Based on the famed DC-4 commercial airliner, the first military model—the C-54A—featured a strengthened floor, a large cargo door, and increased fuel capacity, and its four Pratt & Whitney engines were uprated to 1,450 hp. At its inception, the MATS inherited 234 C-54s from the ATC; in 1950, four C-54Ds powered by R-2000-11 engines went to the Air Rescue Service.

None received special modifications for search and rescue with the exception of one flown by Flight D of the 10th Rescue Squadron, which mounted search radar. The four served until 1954, when air rescue acted on large-scale plans for the C-54, but more on that later.

Thankfully, Grumman's Albatross filled the urgent requirement to equip rescue units with amphibious aircraft. When the SA-16A was introduced to the air force in 1949, first to go was the Catalina. An initial order for thirty-two Albatrosses was followed by eleven delivered during 1950, with production for the air force peaking at 225 aircraft during 1951. By the end of 1953, the air force had taken delivery of 293 SA-16As, which gradually replaced SB-17s, SB-29s, and SC-47s. True to its namesake, the Albatross was built for prolonged operation over the world's saltwater oceans. Initial 1948 and 1949 production batches of SA-16As did not feature "wet" floats. On

November 16, 1950, a trio of SA-16As, modified with wet floats holding 210 gallons of fuel each, plus underwing tanks, completed an endurance flight of 2,400 miles from Travis AFB, California, to Hickam AFB, Hawaii. Wet floats then became standard on succeeding models. With a full fuel load, the rugged, twin-engine, high-wing Albatross had a range of 2,680 miles. To expand their versatility, unique triphibian gear was installed on 145 air force SA-16As, enabling them to operate on snow and ice, as well as on water and on land. This made it necessary that pilots undergoing training in the SA-16A qualify on all four surfaces. The Albatross proved tailor made for rescue. It was a superb combination of performance, ruggedness, and versatility, thanks to its structural integrity, powerful engines, and excellent hull design. Although designed to operate in 4-foot seas, it has managed in 8-foot swells, with and without jet-assisted takeoff (JATO) units. Four JATO

Displayed in 1952 with an SA-16A of Flight D of newly activated 9th Rescue Squadron at Wiesbaden AFB, Germany, is equipment packed into two life rafts. Warrant Officer W. S. Smith demonstrates a corner reflector developed by the USAAF in 1944. Opened like an umbrella and set up in a raft, the reflector was a frame loosely covered with metal fabric to transmit radar echo that could be picked up 20 miles distant. Its drawback was its fragility. Flight D replaced Flight A, 7th RS, which relocated to Wheelus AB, Libya. *Courtesy of USAF*

units—officially termed RATO, for rocket-assisted takeoff—could be affixed to the Albatross, each of which produced 1,000 pounds of thrust.

The first operational use of JATO with the SA-16A occurred during July 1952, when an Albatross from Ernest Harmon AFB, Newfoundland, became stranded on the Greenland ice cap during a scientific mission. On July 4, four JATO bottles were parachuted to the crew. With Robert E. Freshwater at the controls, the Albatross broke free of its snowy bonds.

Since the Albatross filled the requirement for a go-anywhere rescue aircraft, the search was on for other types to make ARS fully and optimally functional. Tempering the SA-16A's unmatched versatility was its inability to haul large cargo loads, often necessary to support global rescue operations. Fortunately, during the war Fairchild Aircraft had begun development of a large cargo hauler to satisfy an army requirement for a C-47 replacement. First flown in 1944, production of Fairchild's C-82 "Packet" was too late for wartime duty; however, MATS leaders were quick to eye its potential. Air Rescue leaders also saw the Packet as their solution to the problem of long-range transport of heavy equipment, such as helicopters, radio trailers, and land rescue vehicles.

Operational experience proved that the Packet was underpowered—single-engine performance was dismal—its cargo area was not up to its intended structural strength, and it was difficult to maintain. These shortcomings, along with limited downward visibility for the pilots due to an oversized flight deck, kept C-82 production low, with only 223 examples built. Regardless, Air Rescue headquarters saw value in the Packet, so in 1947 they requested from the commanding general of the Tactical Air Command (TAC) that they train the initial batch of ARS pilots and aerial engineers. The general obliged and made arrangements for TAC's 316th Troop Carrier Group at Pope Field to begin training. The MATS acquired a large number of C-82As, at least thirty-seven of which were converted to SC-82A rescue variants for its Air Rescue Service.

Triphibian versions of the SA-16A that could operate on water, land, snow, and ice typically were assigned to the 6th and 10th Air Rescue Groups, which operated in Arctic climates. *Courtesy of J. B. Chessington*

The Packet's long flying duration and easy loading through rear, removable clamshell doors made it ideal for rescue support, not to mention a "Paratainer" belly hatch, which allowed rescue equipment to be dropped with accuracy at low levels; helicopters could be carried long distances beyond their range and be unloaded quickly to fly searches in rugged terrain.

From 1947 to 1953, Air Rescue SC-82A Packets served more than two dozen rescue units across the US and Europe, and in Panama, Newfoundland, and Libya. The 5th RS at MacDill AFB, Florida, boasted the largest number of SC-82As, having thirteen assigned. Also at MacDill was the 2156th TTU, assigned two SC-82As for pararescue training. Ten Packets were assigned to the 4th RS at Hamilton Field, California. SC-82As of the 2151st RU at Lowry AFB, Colorado, were vital participants in relief efforts Operations Hayride (later Haylift) and Snowbound, when blizzards imperiled ranchers and livestock of eight western states during the brutal winter of 1948 and 1949. Food, blankets, and medicine were dropped to isolated residents and to trains that had become stranded. The Packet's high-tail/rear-loading configuration set the standard for air force cargo haulers. Refinement of the C-82 resulted in Fairchild's successful C-119 "Flying Boxcar," the unofficial name originally given the Packet.

When the Air Rescue Service came into being in May 1946, its light-plane inventory included more than thirty Stinson L-5 Sentinels. Two years later, when the ARS was absorbed into MATS, that number had been reduced to twenty-three. The L-5s flown by Flight D of the 4th Rescue Squadron at Hickam AFB, Hawaii, were adapted to the region by being equipped with an underwing, droppable one-man lifeboat, while mounted on opposite wing struts were a tidal-wave warning siren and loudspeaker. Six L-5s flown by MATS as trainers were retired by 1953, while L-5s of the ARS served beyond the Korean War, into the mid-1950s. Although a large number of Piper L-4s were passed to the air force at its inception, only one is known to have been flown by air rescue, believed to be serial no. 43-1037 at West Palm Beach Airport, and later ARS Headquarters. Various models both of L-4s and L-5s had served dutifully since the beginning of World War II, flying primarily liaison, observation, search, and medical-evacuation missions. To augment its stable of "L" planes, air rescue leaders found irresistible the multiple features of the Convair-produced L-13, which was designed in 1945 as the Model 105 by Stinson, then a division of Consolidated-Vultee.

The L-13 was purposely overbuilt; its roomy, amply windowed cabin allowed various configurations that accommodated six passengers, or a pilot, medical attendant, and two stretchers. Its huge, high-mounted wings not only enabled it to be towed as a glider but gave the aircraft short-takeoff-and-landing (STOL) characteristics, enabling takeoffs and landings within 230 feet. Of the three hundred examples built by 1947, twenty-eight left the production line as L-13Bs tailored for Arctic use with a powerful cabin heater and fittings for skis or floats. One of the names for the L-5 was "Flying Jeep," a term that was also applied to the L-13, but as it related to transportability. Stinson designers used the jeep as the measurement to which the L-13 could be compacted for loading into cargo aircraft or ground towing. The L-13's wings could be folded back, its tail surfaces hinged upward, and its landing gear rotated 180 degrees, reducing its track to that of a jeep. By 1949, thirty-eight L-13s were part of the ARS fleet, only to be retired from rescue duty the following year.

Alaska's treacherous combination of terrain and climate humbled aviators and made for a busy rescue tableau. Civil aviation contributed to the majority of SAR missions, since more than 20 percent of Alaskans flew aircraft, with the expected number of mishaps attributed to unskilled pilots and rapidly changing weather conditions. Thus, more than half of Air Rescue's missions were body recovery, and often in inhospitable terrain. Besides rescue, missions of the 10th RS included radar and communications site support, humanitarian missions to villages, combat exercises, bomb range support, forest firefighting, and supporting the recovery of high-altitude rocket capsules launched from Poker Flat

Research Range in interior Alaska. Accordingly, the Alaska-based 10th Rescue Squadron possessed its own brand of specialized aircraft. Nearly all aircraft flown by the 10th RS either could operate directly from water and tundra surfaces or were adaptable for skis or floats. From the Grumman "Ironworks" came the OA-12A "Duck" amphibian, the original version of which first flew in 1933. To negotiate Alaska's lakes and rivers, the air force in 1948 acquired eight surplus US Navy J2F-6 Ducks. Redesignated OA-12A, five went to the 10th Rescue Squadron. Powered by the dependable 1,050 hp Wright R-1820-54 engine, the two-place biplane was a stable performer in rugged Alaska.

The search for a fast, rugged light airplane for Arctic search and rescue led officials to Cessna's model 195, powered by a 300 hp engine. Popular in civil aviation since 1947 as the "Businessliner," the military version—designated LC-126A—differed in having enlarged cargo compartments, a door added for loading two stretchers, a pilot escape hatch, a main-door jettison system, and parachute-adaptable seats. Adding to the appeal of the all-metal aircraft were fittings for Edo floats or Federal skis, and a swing-out engine carriage for easy

After World War II, the air force acquired eight Grumman J2F-6 "Duck" amphibians from the navy, five of which were winterized as OA-12As for the 10th Rescue Squadron in Alaska. The Duck was powered by a 1,050 hp Wright R-1280-54 engine, allowing a top speed of 188 mph; range was 780 miles. *Courtesy of USAF*

maintenance of the 300 hp Jacobs R755-A2 radial engine. The LC-126A could carry 1,250 pounds of cargo, and pilots noted that it performed well on instruments. The air force purchased fifteen LC-126s, six of which went to the 10th Air Rescue Squadron in Alaska in March 1949. Float versions were flown by the squadron's Flight B at Lake Hood until late 1952, when both wheel and float LC-126s were transferred to the army, and their mission was assumed by helicopters.

Although seemingly a perfect fit for search-and-rescue work in Alaska, few Noorduyn UC-64A "Norsemans" found their way into the air force inventory. Introduced during the 1930s, the Canadian workhorse was a pure "bush" airplane, rugged, dependable, and able to take on bulky loads and operate on rough terrain, whether on wheels, skis, or floats, and its cabin was well insulated. The Norseman cut its teeth wearing USAAF Olive Drab during World War II, having served mainly with the Eighth and Ninth Air Forces in Europe, the Tenth Air Force in the CBI theater, and the Alaska Wing. Of 903 Norsemans built during a span of two decades by Noorduyn Aviation Ltd. and later Canadian Car & Foundry, 764 went to the USAAF, all but sixteen of which were Mk. VI models powered by the stalwart 600 hp Pratt & Whitney R-1340. When the Military Air Transport Service was formed in 1948, it inherited only eight UC-64As, two of which are known to have flown with Alaska's 10th Air Rescue Squadron.

Also in the light-plane category and favored in rough terrain and Arctic climes was de Havilland Aircraft of Canada's L-20 "Beaver." Having gained high marks in the field of utility aircraft, the air force acquired nearly two hundred L-20s during the 1950s, some of which entered Air Rescue service. Known for its versatility, reliability, and durability, Beavers proved a favorable slow, high-wing platform for search and rescue, and for supplying land rescue teams. The L-20A could carry seven passengers or 1,000 pounds of cargo.

Completing Air Rescue's fixed-wing inventory between the wars were light twins from the reputable Beech Aircraft Corporation of Wichita, Kansas, undeniably the birthplace of the golden age of aviation. Outgrowths of Beech's prolific Model 18, AT-7A "Navigator," and AT-11 "Kansan" trainer aircraft, along with the popular C-45 "Expeditor," were regular fixtures of the 10th ARS in Alaska during postwar years. Although low wing and generally ill suited for search and rescue, AT-7As were viewed by rescue men as dependable and reliable for search, along with transport and utility duty. Six are known to have been float-equipped and nine were winterized for cold climates.

Two fixed-wing aircraft considered for Arctic rescue duty are worthy of mention, given their uniqueness. With the demand for large combat aircraft stilled at war's end, Boeing Airplane Company eyed diversification by allowing its Stearman Division at Wichita to engage the US Army search for a light plane to replace its wartime "L" planes. Boeing/Stearman, as it was called, in 1947 introduced a small 125 hp aircraft to fulfill the army requirement and gain a foothold in the civilian small-airplane market. In view of the airplane's decidedly military characteristics, the L-15 "Scout" was a better fit for military buyers but receded into the shadow of Cessna's L-19 Bird Dog. Weighing only 1,500 pounds, the all-metal, two-place Scout featured a roomy gondola-like cabin with ample windows for all-around visibility. A large rear door permitted supply drops by an observer in a 360-degree swivel seat. The Scout's oversized wings with combination flap-ailerons, called "flaperons," gave it STOL ability with a slow speed of 36 mph and enabled it to be towed as a glider. Like Convair's much-larger L-13, wing surfaces could be folded back for transportability, a byword in air rescue. Watching closely the L-15's testing by army ground forces, air rescue leaders liked what they saw but reverted to development of the helicopter for its search-and-rescue mission. Army ground forces also passed on the concept in favor of more-powerful light planes and the emerging helicopter. Only twelve L-15s were built, all of which were handed over to the US Forest Service and the Fish & Wildlife Service in Alaska.

Equally unique was Northrop Aircraft Company's contender as an air rescue workhorse, the C-125 "Raider." The design was based on its predecessor, Northrop's N-23 "Pioneer," intended as a replacement for the Ford Trimotor. Although the fatal crash of the prototype spelled the end of the civilian venture, air force interest in the N-23 held firm, resulting in a 1948 contract for twenty-three YC-125s: thirteen as assault transports and ten C-125Bs for Arctic search and rescue; the latter version could accommodate twenty stretchers. After the YC-125A made its first flight on August 1, 1949, aircraft began extensive testing at Edwards, Eglin, and Wright-Patterson Air Force Bases. With a configuration similar to the classic Trimotor, the Raider was powered by three Wright R-1820-99 engines for a total 3,600 hp to carry its 21-ton maximum weight. The Raider's range was 1,900 miles.

The C-125 was a classic example of what happens when demands placed upon a sound design become so excessive that they seal its doom. Air rescue planners strongly influenced the Raider's design and submitted their requirements, which included extra fuel, additional crew, large heaters, and rescue equipment, while the army required structural reinforcement to carry artillery, plus paratroops. Unfortunately, no increase was made in horsepower to compensate the additional weight of these requirements, resulting in an underpowered airplane. Despite these findings and unfavorable test pilot reports following the crash of serial no. 48-628 at Eglin, air rescue officials insisted on further tests of the Arctic rescue version. They were given the go-ahead, so YC-125B serial no. 48-622 in 1950 was tested with skis as part of the air force's "Sliding On Ice And Snow" (SOIAS) project. Results were favorable, prompting further cold-weather tests with a YC-125B at Bemidji, Minnesota, in 1951. The Raider was deemed to be a good short-field performer; however, its instability with full payload on skis sounded its death knell. The Raiders were relegated to Sheppard AFB as ground maintenance trainers until 1955.

Serial numbers allocated by the air force for the ten YC-125Bs were 48-618 through 48-627. Accurate air rescue markings for the period seen on *Arctic raiders* were strictly a Northrop marketing ploy to illustrate the close association with the Air Rescue Service; at no time during the entire project were the aircraft officially assigned to the service.

Markings for air rescue aircraft were a goal of the Air Sea Rescue Agency during the postwar period, to develop a standardized, distinctive, high-visibility scheme for aircraft. The result was painted aluminum overall with orange-yellow (also called chrome yellow) wingtips, floats, partial wing areas, and fuselage band, all bordered with black, and the word "RESCUE." The scheme included hull markings for amphibians, which quickly wore off, and the practice was discontinued. Eventually, all coast guard, navy, and air force rescue aircraft wore the basic scheme into the 1960s, although numerous variations were used, depending on aircraft configuration, unit policy, and regions in which aircraft operated. Aircraft that operated in Arctic regions, for example, typically wore large Insignia Red panels, with International Orange also used for high visibility. Helicopters often were painted overall yellow with large RESCUE lettering.

Possibly due to the glider's success during World War II, air rescue officials had an affinity for the powerless craft when building their postwar aircraft inventory. This is apparent not only in the glider capability of the L-15, L-13, and C-125, but in Waco CG-15 gliders used for air rescue; Alaska's 10th ARS operated a glider, serial no. 45-5399, from 1950 to 1952. Towed by the squadron's SC-47s, the glider, even fully loaded, with large skis could land on thinner ice than most aircraft. The glider's Achilles' heel, however, was the inability of its structure to withstand weather extremes.

Often, Mother Nature determined not only the course of a rescue mission, but its outcome. Nowhere was the contest between rescuer and weather more relentless than on polar ice caps. For example, the seven men aboard a C-47 that crash-landed on the Greenland ice cap on December 7, 1948, escaped serious injury, and they had survival gear sufficient to sustain them for a time; having a medical officer among them offered even-greater assurance. Despite immediate radio contact with Bluie West 1, nightfall prevented the 2152nd Rescue Unit at Goose Bay Labrador, from finding them. When an SB-17 spotted the survivors the next day and dropped supplies, all seemed routine. But the temperature nosedived and winds whipped into cyclonic proportion. First, an SB-17 with a crew of two landed on the deceptively safe-appearing snow surface and nosed over. Next, a glider with two aboard was released and slid to a safe landing, but strong winds foiled three pickup tries and tore the glider apart. Another glider with a pilot was brought in but was damaged on the pickup attempt. Now the number of men stranded on the ice cap numbered twelve. A C-47 with JATO racks was summoned, but nasty weather kept it grounded, first at Goose Bay and then at Bluie West 1. Meanwhile, the aircraft carrier *Saipan*, with helicopters aboard, headed for the area. Finally, three weeks after the initial crash landing, a C-47 with seasoned Arctic rescue pilot Lt. Col. Emil Beaudry at the controls landed and made a JATO takeoff with all survivors aboard.

Veteran rescue man Herb Hardin recalls some of his experience with Arctic rescue:

> After graduation from Keesler AFB in May 1951 as an airborne radar mechanic, I was assigned to the 5th Air Rescue Squadron at Westover AFB, Massachusetts. That squadron flew the SA-16A Albatross. I was only there for a month before I was reassigned to the 6th Air Rescue Squadron at Harmon AFB, Newfoundland. The 6th had two flights: A and B. I was assigned to Flight A, and as luck would have it, in August 1951, Flight A was transferred to Bluie West 1, a reactivated World War II base at Narsarssauk, Greenland. Our flight had four SB-17s and one C-47.
>
> Our squadron presence in Greenland was primarily to provide for the safe passage of the many fighter planes that were going from and to Europe via Goose Bay, Bluie West 1, Iceland, and Prestwick. When flights were coming through, our planes would orbit, which was called "Duckbutt," either halfway between Goose Bay or Iceland, to provide rescue coverage if a plane went down. We also participated in several search missions for aircraft that were lost. One I remember quite clearly was a search for the SA-16A that was assigned to the 6th Air Rescue Squadron, Flight C, at Keflavik, Iceland. The aircraft had passed through BW1 only a few days prior to it being lost, and I had a long conversation with the crew chief. I didn't go on that search mission, but what I remember was the crew chief's body was the only one they found when they came across the wreckage. Best I can remember, this was an older-model SA-16A without deicer boots, and icing was the cause of the crash.

Deicer boots along the leading edges of wing and tail surfaces would become standard on Albatrosses.

The four flights that composed the 6th ARS would shift, with Flight A based in Greenland, Flight B in Newfoundland, Flight C in Iceland, and Flight D in Labrador. In 1950, an SC-47B, s/n 45-1013, believed to be from Flight D when it was based at Bluie West 1, Greenland, like the aircraft it was sent to rescue, fell to the mercy of Arctic weather on Iceland's largest glacier. In a rescue scenario that captivated Icelanders, the incident began when a DC-4 (C-54 s/n 44-9014) named "Geysir" of Loftleidir Airlines crashed on Jokull glacier on September 14. The crash site was found four days later, and the following day the SC-47B landed near the wreck and took its six crewmen aboard. Geysir's cargo of fourteen caged dogs and the body of an American woman in a coffin were left for later recovery. The SC-47B's skis, which had warmed from the friction of landing, had melted the snow, which froze and held the aircraft captive. JATO bottles were used to break the glacier's icy grip and attempt takeoff, but two attempts only damaged the airplane.

Meanwhile, an ad hoc rescue team comprising twenty-four members of an Alpine climbing team and skiing tourists had reached the site. It was decided that the four SC-47 crewmen and six survivors of the DC-4 would hike out with the team. The SC-47 was left on the glacier and abandoned. The following spring, Loftleidir, after purchasing the SC-47B from the US Air Force, sent a team to free the aircraft from the ice, tow it from the glacier, make repairs, and fly it to England, where it was converted to a civilian airliner. In Loftleidir livery, the C-47 wore registry TF-RVP and the name "Jokull," after the glacier from which it was rescued.

THE HELICOPTER GROWS UP

Many air rescue aircraft were war weary and deemed unsuitable for the mission. To its credit, not only was the emerging Sikorsky R-5 helicopter a relative newcomer, it had not undergone the protracted strain of combat. Sikorsky's R-4 and R-6 helicopters had proved the value of rotary-wing aviation during latter months of the war. These conditions set the stage for Igor Sikorsky to prove beyond all doubt the helicopter's place in aviation. He and his engineers knew that their Model S-51, or R-5, had to be the showstopper, the machine that convinced both civil and military aviation communities that rotary wing was the wave of the future. Most convinced were the leaders of air rescue, and they would be the driving force behind the R-5's success. When initial tests of the S-51 easily demonstrated its superiority over the R-4 and R-6, it was called the "Cadillac of helicopters," and it was continually updated, ensuring wide civil and military use.

First flown in August 1943, with deliveries beginning in February 1945, more than three hundred S-51s were built before production ended in 1951. The streamlined, all-metal R-5 featured tandem seating for a pilot and crew member. Power for its three-blade wood-and-fabric main rotor was driven by a 450 hp Wasp Junior engine. In the final months of the war, an Army Air Force order for 100 R-5As was reduced to thirty-four machines, twenty-one of which (serial nos. 43-46606 and -46640 through -46659) were converted to R-5Ds. Modifications included increasing power with a 600 hp Pratt & Whitney engine, seating for a second passenger, adding a nosewheel, provisions for an auxiliary fuel tank, and a hydraulic rescue hoist with cable length of 75 or 110 feet and able to lift 300 pounds.

Next came the YR-5E, which identified five machines converted to dual control. In 1947 the air force procured eleven commercial S-51s, which were designated R-5Fs when fit with four cabin seats, increased gross weight, and an all-metal 49-foot-diameter main rotor, which offset the penalty imposed by float gear. Metal blades became standard on succeeding models and were retrofit on earlier variants. To augment its helicopter assets, in 1948 the Air Rescue Service ordered thirty-nine rescue versions that were similar to the F model and were designated H-5G, the "H" prefix used in compliance with a June 1948 directive changing the "R," for

rotorcraft, to "H," for helicopter. Sixteen H-5H models purchased for air rescue in 1949 featured a combination wheel-pontoon undercarriage, increased gross weight, and fuselage protrusions to accommodate three patients crosswise in the cabin; a medical attendant had access to only the two patients positioned forward. All previous models carried two litters externally, using various types of mounts. Sikorsky Archives reported that in late 1949, the first two H-5Hs went to the 2nd Air Rescue Squadron on Guam, one with pontoons and the other with a hoist for land rescues.

Air Rescue was pleased with its H-5s, which were dispersed among rescue units worldwide, often making the difference when fixed-wing aircraft were unable to get into an area to effect rescue. The S-51 quickly gained popularity on a global scale, guaranteeing Sikorsky's place in the helicopter industry. US Air Force orders would total 131 H-5s in six models. Since tradition died hard in the military, the helicopter did not enjoy sweeping acceptance. Yet, they were barter in the army–air force squabble over aircraft and tactical authority that would simmer for years to come. Even after the air force was established as an independent service in 1947, it took two additional years of army–air force negotiation to arrive at basic agreement on the question of what each could have. Some resolve permitted the army to have helicopters not exceeding 4,000 pounds. Further agreements over another two years governed army helicopters solely in terms of function. Having become more optimistic about the helicopter's potential, the air force during the early 1950s formed a helicopter transport force; however, it was short lived in lieu of a pilot shortage and the army's advances in troop-carrying helicopters. The business of helicopter airlift, air force leaders realized, was best left to the army and marines. Besides, the air force was more interested in developing more Cold War requirements and redirected their focus on helicopters best suited for utility and rescue work. John Caldwell, who began flying P-51 and P-47 fighters in World War II and ended up flying H-5s and H-19s in the Korean War, probably said it best: "The air force should have had its butt kicked seventeen different ways for not recognizing early enough the value of rotary wing. The smartest thing they did with that was turning it over to the army, because they probably would have screwed that up too."

A top contender in the helicopter industry was Bell Helicopter, which developed one of the most versatile, if not popular, designs of all time, the Bell Model 47, known in military circles as the R-13, and later the H-13. Because the Model 47 was not designed at the behest of the military, the budding Department of Defense (DoD) showed little interest. The army and air rescue service, however, showed great interest, ordering eighteen YR-13s. The first machine was delivered to the army on New Year's Eve 1946, and the next two (serial nos. 46-228 and -229), built as winterized YR-13As, left the Bell plant in a C-82 on January 6 for cold-weather tests in Alaska; serial no. 46-230 would follow. Examples were also

Air force interest in Bell Helicopter's Model 47 resulted in a four-month test period in 1948 of this crop duster version of the 47D (military designation H-13B). This demonstrator (NC167B) featured a Bell-designed litter kit and split canopy, the upper half of which was replaceable with an abbreviated windshield. Vented engine panels were removed for portions of the trials. *Courtesy of US Army Aviation Museum*

The enlarged rear cockpit of the H-5D provided room for this parajumper of the 3rd ARS to exit the aircraft in 1951. A wind spoiler was added to the doorway's forward edge. The "R" designator (rotorcraft) was changed to "H" (helicopter) in 1948. *Courtesy of USAF*

Seen near its home base Hamilton Field, California, in April 1947, this Sikorsky R-5D (serial no. 43-46640) was painted overall orange yellow. This model featured an enlarged rear cockpit, four-position landing gear, and loud hailers on the rear fuselage underside. *Courtesy of William T. Larkins*

Attached to this H-6A (serial no. 43-45398) is a locally fabricated folded litter support. In the folded position, the device doubled as a supply container. Pride of ownership is evident in the name "RONNIE" on the rotor pylon, and stars on the wheel covers. This was one of two H-6As operated by the 2nd Rescue Squadron at Kadena AB, which supported Okinawa's tactical reconnaissance wing, and an F-51 squadron at Naha AB, Okinawa. *Courtesy of A. W. George*

tested in the hot climes of southern states. Beginning in October 1948, an H-13B underwent four months of testing by the air force. No large orders were forthcoming, but the air force would add the H-13 to its training syllabus in 1948, remaining in the curriculum until 1958. Thereafter, Sioux helicopters that remained in the inventory, while not officially assigned to Air Rescue units, could be found serving as the rescue element of tactical units. H-13Gs, for example, shared the flight line with jet interceptors of the 15th Fighter Group at Niagara Falls AFB during the late 1950s. In the same period, a pair of H-13s were assigned to the flight line of California's Vandenburg AFB.

Garnering more interest than the Model 47 was its lesser-known predecessor, the Model 42, which had its military equivalent in the XR-12. The air force ordered two XR-12s for trials as a rescue aircraft. A production order was canceled; however, a larger variant, the YR-12B, would get the attention of air force leaders. A prototype and ten machines were ordered to begin service trials during late 1946. Developmental

problems, unfortunately, led to cancellation of the program, causing the air force to shift its attention back to Sikorsky's proven H-5. They were pleased to discover that Sikorsky had plans for bigger and better helicopters.

Sikorsky, in less than a year, designed, built, and flew its model S-55 as a company-funded project. This was a radical design departure from Sikorsky's R-4, R-5, and R-6 by placing the engine below and forward of the cockpit, resulting in a large cabin below the main rotor. This design feature, along with the use of offset hinges in the main rotor head, allowed a significantly broadened center of gravity.

The design drew immediate interest from air force leaders, who ordered the first five machines, which were given the military designation YH-19. First flown on November 10, 1949, the H-19 boasted a 600 hp Pratt & Whitney engine to carry ten passengers and lift 1,800 pounds externally. Sikorsky designers had maintenance personnel in mind, not only placing the engine at ground level behind clamshell doors, but designing all major components to be quickly replaced.

The air force ordered fifty-one H-19As and wasted little time in doling them out to air rescue units, where they joined forty H-5s. The SH-19 would eventually replace the H-5, but not before both types amassed remarkable save records during the war in Korea.

With the requirement for a dependable, Arctic-capable, fixed-wing aircraft met by the Albatross, the 1949 search for a helicopter with like attributes ended at the Piasecki Helicopter Corporation. The search for a long-range, cold-weather performer began in 1946, since the Arctic was critical to the rapidly expanding Cold War. Downed crews of intercontinental B-29 and B-36 bombers flying polar routes to the Soviet Union would have to rely on a rescue helicopter capable of operating and being maintained in extreme subzero temperatures. Especially desirous was a helicopter that could accomplish other missions, such as support of the construction and maintenance of a chain of early-warning radar stations in Alaska and Canada. Frank N. Piasecki was committed to the development of tandem-rotor technology as an alternative to the single-rotor concept, which required a tail rotor to counteract the effects of torque caused by a large main rotor. Not only did the tail rotor tap valuable power needed for lift, but the single rotor imposed center-of-gravity restrictions. Piasecki first was awarded a contract for his massive YH-16 "Transporter," which the air force rejected as a SAR platform and turned over to the army. Piasecki then submitted another design, in both single- and twin-engine versions, which were modifications of its HRP-2 already in production for the US Marine Corps.

Piasecki's single-engine version was selected by the air force, having edged out Sikorsky's emerging H-34. Although not designed for Arctic use, the H-34 was adaptable to air force cold-weather requirements and would, in fact, later serve the Air Rescue Service. Initially named "Arctic Rescuer," Piasecki's design PD-22 was given the military designation YH-21 and renamed "Work-Horse." The YH-21 was first flown on April 11, 1951, with an order for eighteen YH-21s delivered between February and August 1953. Per air force specifications, the H-21 could be float-equipped and carry twelve litters, and it mounted a rescue hoist. Powering its tandem rotors was a 1,150 hp Wright Cyclone R-1820 engine. The air force then ordered 32 H-21As, which proved to be solid performers in the subzero temperatures of the Far North. Eventually, the air force took delivery of 163 H-21Bs, featuring increased power with the Wright Cyclone 1,425 hp R-1820-103 engine with pilot-activated supercharger.

As the Air Force Helicopter School grew to keep pace with the growing numbers and types of helicopters, often it was relocated; so many times, in fact, that it was named "Gypsy School." In 1949 it was moved from San Marcos to James Connally AFB, Texas, and back to San Marcos in 1951. For the next few years two courses were offered: training with the H-5, H-13, H-19, and H-21 for air force pilots, and training with the R-6, H-13, and H-23 for Army Ground Force liaison pilots. The large number of army personnel caused aircraft and instructor shortages, which were alleviated when the army established its own helicopter school in 1956. The air force school then relocated to Randolph AFB, Texas, pulling up stakes again in 1958 for the move to Stead AFB, Texas, to take advantage of the region's mountainous terrain for high-altitude training. School staff found the Bell H-13 underpowered for this advanced training, and it was phased out. The school remained at Stead for eight years before relocating to Sheppard AFB, also in Texas.

SA-16A (serial no. 49-075) and 49-074, when assigned to Flight D, 7th ARS Dhahran, Saudi Arabia, in 1950, were the first Albatrosses assigned outside the continental US. They joined two SB-17Gs, a float-equipped H-5H, and a three-vehicle land rescue team. Orange-yellow markings on painted aluminum included "RESCUE" on the hull, which was soon eliminated due to wear. Midway through SA-16A production, wing-mounted APS-31 search radar was relocated to a nose radome. Two 295-gallon Mk. 8 drop tanks extended the Albatross's range to 2,600 miles. *Courtesy of Lt. Col. Ted A. Morris, USAF (Ret.)*

Cessna's LC-126A, the military derivative of the Model 195, as an excellent performer in Arctic rescue was a favorite with the 10th ARS. Adaptable for wheel, float, or ski landing gear, the LC-126A had a top speed of 175 mph and a range of 850 miles. Flight B flew float versions, such as serial no. 49-1949, seen here at Lake Hood, Alaska. *Courtesy of H. B. Allen*

This SC-82A (serial no. 44-22982) loads 5 tons of hay for air drop to stranded livestock in Nevada and Utah in January 1949. After loading, the "Packet" flew to Ely, Nevada, to pick up stockmen, who directed the crew to their cattle. Hay then was dropped through bomb bay–like doors in the center of the fuselage. *Courtesy of USAF*

RESCUE GETS BETTER

Since replacement of the SB-17 and SB-29 by the SC-54 Rescuemaster and SA-16A Albatross was gradual, the obsolescent bombers turned rescuers underwent improvement. The SB-17G tested improved airborne lifeboat designs, while SB-29 Super Dumbos, carrying additional crew and fuel plus a wide variety of survival gear, were pressed into service during the Korean conflict. After the war, eighteen B-17Gs were transferred from the Army Air Force to the US Coast Guard, which converted them into PB-1G rescue platforms patterned after the Dumbo; they remained in service until 1959, while US Air Force SB-17Gs

served until 1953. As the SB-29 supplanted the SB-17G, the search was on for an improved airborne lifeboat. Edo Corporation, named after its founder, Earl Dodge Osborn, in 1947 developed the all-aluminum A-3 airborne lifeboat, which eventually succeeded the wooden Higgins A-1. While retaining many of the features built into the A-1, the A-3 featured large stabilizing fins for descent. Since the boat fully equipped weighed 2,736 pounds, it was dropped with the largest parachute standardized by the air force. With a capacity for fifteen people, the boat could do 8 knots on calm water, with power derived from a four-cylinder, Red Wing Meteor 20 gasoline engine.

A number of things happened when the A-3 splashed down: a sea anchor dropped, the stabilizing fins and parachute jettisoned, and a keel guard that protected the rudder and prop during splashdown released. Especially interesting is evidence of technology of the day; through radio control from the rescue aircraft, the boat's engine vents opened and a blower activated to clear the engine compartment of fumes. Then the engine was cranked and choked, the clutch was engaged, the throttle was advanced, and the boat was steered toward the survivors. Besides grab rails built into the hull, a recessed hull ladder could be lowered into the water. Once aboard, survivors could assume manual control of the boat. Two-way radios eventually were added to the A-3's extensive inventory of survival gear. More than a hundred A-3s were built, which were numbered successively beginning with 501.

Although the A-3 was deemed the optimum lifeboat, its mother aircraft required special modifications, and mechanical failure could cause drifting or swamping. To eliminate these shortcomings, the Air Material Command's Air-Sea Rescue Unit in late 1951 came up with a droppable lifeboat encased in an aluminum cylinder. Unit personnel then took the concept to Douglas Aircraft Corporation, which had a wealth of experience in droppable stores. The uniqueness of the device lay in the versatility derived from its dimensions; it was 20 feet in length and 21 inches in diameter, matching those of a torpedo so that it could be launched from a PT boat or submarine. Packed inside the torpedo-like casing was a 22-by-8-foot raft, an inboard engine, remote control radio, fuel for a 300-mile range, a two-way radio, a canopy, and survival equipment that included a distillation kit and dehydrated food.

The lifeboat could be dropped from any aircraft fit with sturdy bomb racks. Two minutes after release from an altitude of about 75 feet, carbon dioxide cartridges inflated the package. Its engine could then be started and the raft steered toward survivors by remote control from the launching aircraft or vessel. After tests, little was heard of the novel device, likely having passed into obscurity with the advent of the helicopter.

Undoubtedly, the most remarkable record of persons rescued with an A-3 airborne lifeboat occurred during the Kansas-Missouri floods in July 1951. Tons of supplies were dropped by aircraft, including the SA-16As of the 5th ARS and SB-29s of the 4th ARS. Vital among the items dropped was an SB-29's A-3, which was used to rescue 439 persons in one day.

By 1954, the Air Rescue Service had completed changeover of SB-29s and H-5 helicopters to SA-16As and H-19 helicopters. Typical squadron strength was four SA-16As, two H-19s, and one or two C-47s. Each air rescue squadron had at least one of its primary aircraft and a crew on alert status around the clock; a second aircraft and crew were on standby and moved to alert status if the alert crew was "scrambled." Able to home in on any signal on standard frequencies thanks to its array of communication equipment, the SA-16A lived up to its reputation as a dedicated SAR platform. With a range well exceeding

An A-1 airborne lifeboat undergoes testing with an SB-17G. Cutouts were made in the ex-bomber's bomb bay doors to mount the boat, while a rubber skirt between the boat and fuselage enhanced aerodynamics of the mated pair. Higgins Industries began producing the 27-foot A-1 in 1944. *Courtesy of USAF*

Most unusual among air rescue's fleet of unique aircraft was a pair of Curtiss SC-46D "Commando" transports flown in the Far East. This Commando (serial no. 44-78542) was assigned to the 3rd Rescue Squadron at Misawa, Japan. When it first flew in 1940, the C-46 was the largest twin-engine transport in the world. Thanks to massive loading doors, jeeps could be driven into its cavernous fuselage. *Courtesy of J. Chessington*

This SC-46D, serial no. 44-78420, was assigned to the 2nd Rescue Squadron at Kadena Field, Okinawa. *Courtesy of A. W. George*

Queen of the "Mayday"

In answer to the airman's emergency distress signal, "Mayday, Mayday", the Albatross has grown from a speck to a queen to many a man marooned in a dinghy or on an icecap. Flown by skilled crews of the Air Rescue Service of the U. S. Air Force, the U. S. Navy and Coast Guard, the Grumman Albatross can land and take off from snow and ice as well as land and sea. Though she doesn't fit into the airman's survival kit, she's part of it.

GRUMMAN AIRCRAFT ENGINEERING CORPORATION
BETHPAGE · LONG ISLAND · NEW YORK

Designers and builders also of Cougar jet fighters, S2F sub-killers, metal boats, and Aerobilt truck bodies

The YL-15, genetically, was a Stearman, having been conceived at Boeing's Wichita plant by its subsidiary Stearman. Positioning the cabin beneath wings and tail boom allowed all-around visibility for pilot and observer, with the latter position able to swivel rearward. Beside this vital search feature, the Stearman's STOL characteristics and adaptability for floats or skis earned it a close look for Arctic rescue work. This L-15A "Scout" (serial no. 46-521) was among only twelve built for testing by the Army Ground Force. *Courtesy of US Army*

2,000 miles, the Albatross could cover large areas of land and water. Two search patterns were used, with the "creeping line," with 2-mile separation of search legs, flown over relatively smooth terrain and water. Altitudes were 500 feet overwater and 800 feet overland, and 2,000 feet over both at night. Mountainous terrain called for a "contour" search, which was a descending, circling pattern. With the Albatross not having "blister" windows, as did other search aircraft, its crewmen had difficulty scanning below. Felix McLarney, whose long career as an NCO with the 304th Air Rescue Squadron included thirteen years the unit flew the Albatross, remarked:

We often wished we had bulged windows, and felt the coast guard had the better idea when it came to scanning below the aircraft. We had to rely upon the pilots and radio operator to pick up objects in front of us or we might go directly over them and not be able to look down. Of course the expanding search patterns were designed to eventually expose all of the

surface to the searchers, but unfortunately we knew that some saw us but we didn't see them. The navigator's wave-swell-measuring scope was truly the only device that could look straight down, and it wasn't designed for searching.

At sea, the SA-16A crew marked the survivor's position with smoke and evaluated the sea state in order to land in the least violent manner. Albatross pilots quickly developed a healthy respect for the sea and learned to read its many features. On the open sea, visual references were nonexistent, mountainous swells created mammoth troughs and crests, and "confused seas" interspersed calm areas and crisscross wave patterns. On the water, the aircraft approached survivors to bring them in the left-side rear doorway. The starboard engine (opposite the survivor) could be used to maneuver the aircraft. A sea anchor could be used for positioning, or the landing gear could be lowered to induce drag and enhance stability. Survivors could then be brought aboard using a sea rescue platform below

One patient was loaded crosswise into this H-5H (serial no. 49-2009) through downward-hinged "blisters" on both sides of the helicopter. One patient fit in the rear, while two fit in the forward cabin. Crew consisted of pilot and medical attendant. *Courtesy of J. J. Tarsitano*

Only ten H-5Hs were built, some of which were float-equipped. Since the patient loaded through the blister had no cabin access due to a 200-amp generator mounted above, the station was rarely used. *Courtesy of USAF*

Aircraft of Flights A and D of the 4th Air Rescue Squadron at Hamilton AFB, California. The SC-82A is serial no. 44-23033, while the SB-17G is serial no. 44-83781. Farther down the line is an SA-16A and C-45. *Courtesy of David Ostrowski collection*

the doorway, a lifeline could be fired to the survivor, or a pararescueman, tethered to the aircraft, could swim to them.

Droppable gear aboard the Albatross consisted of the MA-1 kit with two twenty-man rafts and three survival containers, all connected by floating rope. The package was dropped so it could be wind-blown to survivors. The SA-16A could also drop a six-man life raft, URC-4 radio, D-1 survival kits, and medical equipment.

THEY CALL HIM PJ

Prudent aviators knew that some terrain forbade the best efforts to save lives using aircraft, vessels, vehicles, and ground teams. Such seemingly impossible rescues in such regions turned the spotlight on the element of air rescue that was an absolute necessity—pararescue. A variety of similar sobriquets would be used to identify this elite bunch, but the term "parajumper" would stand the test of time and be shortened to "PJ." The flight log entry "PJ" had already been in use to indicate parachutists on board. Although it is generally noted that pararescue traces its beginnings to World War II, it dates further back. Credit for giving rise to the birth of pararescue goes to the US Forest Service (USFS). The USFS smoke jumper concept, which coincided with the development of US Army airborne units, was born in 1939 and led to experiments the following year in the Pacific Northwest. On July 12, 1940, USFS smoke jumpers Earl Cooley and Rufus Robinson demonstrated that parachutists could land on target using a newly invented steerable parachute. That same year, USAAF Medical Corps physician Capt. Leo P. Martin, chief flight surgeon at Walla Walla Army Air Base, was trained by the USFS at Seeley Lake, Montana, as the first "para-doctor." An initial cadre of AAF parajumpers was formed and attended the USFS smoke jumper school to evaluate the steerable

"Derry Slotted Chute." In 1943, about half of the twenty-five military personnel trained by the smoke jumper school were Second Air Force flight surgeons and personnel of the 2nd and 3rd Arctic SAR squadrons.

Pararescue activities during World War II were uncoordinated and without organizational structure, and techniques often varied according to geography and lessons learned. Standardized training, equipment, and procedures were nonexistent. There was only the presumption that there were survivors and that they might be unable to use items dropped to them, which could be verified only by parachuting rescuers to the site. The only other constant on which old hands in the PJ community agreed was its alliance with the US Forest Service Smoke Jumpers Center. In keeping with its mission, the US Coast Guard also relied on the USFS for jump-training rescue specialists. This came on the heels of a passenger plane crash in Alaska in January 1943. After realizing that a rescue party parachuted to the site would have better served the mission, US Coast Guard chief boatswain A. H. Hook trained a group called the Ketchikan Paratroopers Squad. The Canadians followed suit, training a team, and both teams became an element of air-sea rescue in the Northwest Territory.

After Col. Kight took command of the Air Rescue Service in 1946, he recognized the value of a special group of rescue men who could jump into sites, especially those deemed inaccessible by other means. Pararescue's charter had yet to be sealed, leaving it vulnerable to planners who wielded the budget ax. In May 1947, when the need for pararescue was being debated, pararescue doctor Capt. Pope B. Holliday jumped from a Catalina into a B-17 crash site in forbidding Nicaraguan jungle and saved the life of the pilot. Holliday's actions, along with his earlier testimony to ATC officials supporting pararescue, convinced decision makers that

A fine study of a Stinson L-5 (serial no. 42-98572) of Flight A, 8th Rescue Unit, at Hamilton Field, California, in June 1948. In the background are P-61 Black Widows. *Courtesy of William T. Larkins*

The L-13 was the Army Air Force's first all-metal liaison aircraft. Its large wings not only gave it STOL characteristics but allowed the L-13 to be towed glider-like by a C-47. The L-13 cruised at 92 mph and could land at 44 mph. The USAF buzz code for both L-13s and L-20s was "LG." *Courtesy of Boardman C. Reed*

Delivery of equipment, including aircraft, to an operating site was important to air rescue. One of the L-13's selling points was its ability to be compacted for loading into cargo aircraft, or to be towed by ground vehicle. This was one of two XL-13 prototypes powered by a 245 hp Franklin engine.

pararescue was here to stay. On a broader scale, that mission, and others, slowly placed Air Rescue on solid footing. In November 1947, five enlisted men, two doctors, and a headquarters officer attended a two-week course at the Forest Service's "Fire Jumpers" school at Missoula, Montana. This was the first step of Col. Kight's implementation of pararescue teams. These eight parajumpers formed the nucleus of instructor staff for a pararescue survival school conducted by the 5th Rescue Squadron at MacDill AFB. The school soon had instructors from many areas of expertise from all branches of service, under the leadership of Lt. Perry C. Emmons, a colorful character formerly of the OSS. Pararescue teams would comprise a doctor, two medics, and two survival experts.

Although PJs were, in many ways, a cut above most airmen, a tragic incident would drive home the lesson that dedication alone was not always enough to accomplish their mission. In what became known as "the Clobbered Turkey Incident," an air force doctor and two parachutists jumped to an aircraft crash site nearly 100 miles north of Nome, Alaska, on December 27, 1947. Four days earlier, the doomed aircraft, an F-13 (s/n 45-21775) named "Forlorn Turkey," a photoreconnaissance version of the B-29, crashed with a crew of eight. The three rescue jumpers, who were unaware of horrendous surface wind and far-below-zero temperatures, were found some distance from the site, having been dragged by their chutes and frozen to death. Ground rescue teams that were sent two days later also found the frozen bodies of the plane's pilot and navigator, who had attempted to walk out; six of the F-13's crew were rescued. During the fallout of the incident, it became instantly clear that the trio of rescuers was poorly trained and inadequately equipped. Not only did the incident bring about immediate change in those areas, it also spurred the centralization of air force rescue operations of all commands under Air Rescue Service.

A more successful mission in December 1947 demonstrated the value of the C-82/R-5 helicopter team when Flight D, 5th Rescue Squadron, flew from Westover Field to Goose Bay, Newfoundland, to rescue six survivors of a C-54 that had crashed.

A shortage of doctors in 1949 had paradoctors replaced by Medical Service Corps officers, who underwent the same training as enlisted PJs, along with a nineteen-week supervisor's course at the School of Aviation Medicine at Gunter AFB, Alabama. Graduates then taught seasoned PJs advanced medical care. One of the officers was Capt. John C. Shumate, who became commandant of the MacDill school. With all rescue units aligned under the Air Rescue Service, a training syllabus was assembled, which included Army Airborne School at Ft. Benning, Georgia, and Air Force Pararescue and Survival School at West Palm Beach, Florida. To qualify as a rescue specialist, candidates underwent jungle training in Florida, desert training in California, mountain and arctic training in Idaho, and saltwater operations in the Gulf of Mexico.

This 85-foot Type II Air Rescue Boat was originally Army hull number P335, one of five built by Julius Peterson of Nyack, New York. It was delivered in 1944 and served in the Pacific theater. The 85-footer (Model 379) was designer Diar Long's answer to the US Army Quartermaster Corps request for an ARB faster than the 104-footer, but larger than the 63-footer. Postwar color scheme was white hull, yellow deck, and orange house. A total of 140 Type IIs were built by thirteen different boatbuilders. *Courtesy of USAF*

Still wearing war paint, this SC-47D (serial no. 45-1012) of Detachment 6, Rescue Unit A, was based at Biggs Field, Texas, in 1948. *Courtesy of William T. Larkins*

Northrop's YC-125 "Raider" was the military version of the commercial N-23 "Pioneer." Air Rescue visionaries held high hopes for the C-125 in the Arctic rescue role; however, tests found the Raider unstable on skis. The aircraft could carry 21 tons and cruised at 171 mph, with a range of 1,900 miles. This YC-125B (serial 48-620) unofficially wore the air rescue scheme. *Courtesy of Gerald Balzer / Northrop*

This Canadian Vickers-built SA-10A (serial no. 44-33924) began life as PBV-1A BuNo 67888. It is seen here in June 1948, fit with early underwing metric wave radar, which was an array of dipole antennae. The "OB" Army Air Force buzz number signified Observation (O) and OA-10A Catalina (B). *Courtesy of William T. Larkins*

Finished in natural metal, this pair of Piasecki YH-21s (serial nos. 50-1239 and 50-1238) were among eighteen YH-21s ordered by the air force. Originally designed as an Arctic rescuer with winterization features allowing operations at –65°F, it was also adaptable to wheels, skis, or floats. *Courtesy of USAF*

THE PROP AND TRIANGLE

When World War II ended, many of the duties carried out by the Civil Air Patrol could be resumed by the Army Air Force. This abrupt change in status significantly narrowed CAP's scope of activities, placing its very existence in question. Evidence of the military's quandary over what to do with CAP lay in its assignment under a half-dozen commands during a two-year period from 1943 to 1945. The CAP's future seemed even more uncertain beginning in April 1946, when drastic budget cuts in the AAF halted funds to CAP. Gen. Arnold called a conference of CAP's wing commanders to examine postwar CAP, which led to a plan to incorporate. Follow-through had President Truman on July 1, 1946, signing into public law the CAP as a nonprofit organization without financial assistance from the AAF. Under federal charter, CAP was obligated to a multifaceted program of promoting both civilian and military aviation and conducting various flying projects. The organization would also take on projects specially requested by the AAF, but the arrangement defied clarity of the relationship between the CAP and the AAF. Finally, postwar CAP would find its place months after the air force was established as a separate arm in October 1947. On May 26,

1948, the Senate passed a bill establishing the CAP as a permanent civilian auxiliary of the US Air Force.

War-born CAP had become a tremendous resource of skill and dedicated manpower in search of a peacetime mission. Government donations and loans of material including aircraft and vehicles were sowing seed from which the government reaped great returns. The passing of L-4, L-5, and C-45 aircraft to CAP from the AAF continued during the postwar era. Surplus equipment was distributed to each state, which were called "wings" and grouped geographically into eight "regions." At the national level, CAP was organized under an air force commander and headquarters staff, along with a liaison officer at each wing headquarters.

While the primary purpose of postwar CAP was to maintain a trained, organized reservoir of potential airmen and a civilian flying corps should war abroad tax the military, the air force established search and rescue as CAP's primary mission. The light airplanes, wearing the three-bladed prop within a triangle, and their pilots and observers became a component of the Air Rescue Service. When activated for a SAR mission under ARS authority, CAP volunteers set off on the mission not only in aircraft, but by whatever means their

During the postwar period, some AAF planners saw the value of new helicopter designs for rescue. When Bell Helicopter developed a military version of its Model 42 with a car-like cabin in 1946, the USAF ordered two examples designated XR-12. Pictured here is the first airframe (serial no. 46-214), while -215 was tested with flotation gear, a rescue hatch, hoist, litters, and life rafts. A production order was canceled; however, a larger variant would get the attention of USAAF leaders. *Courtesy of Bell Helicopter*

Having sold some USAAF officials on its XR-12, Bell Helicopter developed the larger and more powerful YR-12B. Deliveries of a prototype and ten aircraft for service trials began in late 1946. Developmental problems led to cancellation of the program during the late 1940s, with the air force shifting its attention back to Sikorsky's proven H-5 for air rescue. This YR-12B (serial no. 46-222) was written off following fuel starvation on August 22, 1951. *Courtesy of Bell Helicopter*

Designed by Air Material Command and built by Douglas Aircraft, the aluminum "Torpedo Lifeboat" was slightly more than 20 feet long and 21 inches in diameter. Self-inflated by carbon dioxide on impact, the aluminum cylinder contained a 22-by-8-foot life raft, inboard engine, remote-control radio, fuel for 300 miles, two-way radio, and survival equipment. The SA-16A carried two underwing orange-painted cylinders during testing. *Courtesy of USAF*

In December 1951, the Torpedo Lifeboat undergoes testing at Long Beach, California, near Douglas Aircraft Corp. With six men aboard and the raft still being inflated, it is already under power by its four-cylinder engine, with the cylinder acting as stiffener and keel. *Courtesy of USAF*

Dog teams were used for search and rescue prior to expanded use of helicopters. Parajumper and malamute "Trooper Joe" of the 10th Rescue Squadron prepare to jump from an SC-47 at Ladd Field, Alaska. Attached to the fuselage near the doorway is a parachute-rigged survival kit. *Courtesy of USAAF*

In April 1949, an injured plane crash survivor is eased down a mountainside in the Black Forest of Colorado by students of the USAF Pararescue and Land Survival School, based at MacDill AFB, Florida. A six-week course began in Florida's Everglades, followed by two weeks in the Rocky Mountains and the desert of West Texas. The survivor was taken to an M29 Weasel track vehicle for transfer to a ski-equipped L-5 aircraft. *Courtesy of USAF*

An A-1 airborne lifeboat rests on its ground-handling carriage during the early 1950s. Dual propellers are protected by cages, and grab rails for survivors are affixed topside and to the hull. *Courtesy of USAF*

Fully stocked with survival equipment, the A-1 airborne lifeboat featured removable stabilizers necessary for its parachute descent. *Courtesy of USAF*

region dictated; that could mean swamp boats in Florida, horse-mounted teams in the West, skis and dogsleds in Alaska, and a wide range of vehicles.

Air Rescue Service commander Gen. DuBose stated in 1952:

In the event ARS aircraft and aircrews are required to deploy from the ZI for any reason, the Civil Air Patrol will be called upon to perform a higher percentage of the air rescue mission in the United States. Air Force Regulation 45-49 assigns the war mission of the CAP[,] which entails, in part, participation in search and rescue service as an auxiliary of ARS. This headquarters envisions a heavy requirement upon the Civil Air Patrol during any national emergency.

At that time, CAP volunteers were conducting nearly 80 percent of the total SAR hours under ARS. Many missions

By 1948, when MATS assumed control of the Air Rescue Service, fewer than two dozen L-5s were in the inventory. Although postwar markings of ARS aircraft varied, most were painted overall aluminum with yellow-orange high-visibility markings. The lettering on this trio of L-5Bs leaves no doubt as to their function. *Courtesy of A. W. George*

During the postwar period, a few float-equipped Beech AT-7As, including serial no. 41-21161, served the 10th Rescue Squadron in Alaska. *Courtesy of David Menard collection*

Never too young to learn. When parajumpers of the 3rd Rescue Squadron in Japan jumped from an SA-16A in April 1951, "Dozo" went along. Two parajumpers, SSgts. Oswald Fleming and Kenneth Blackwell, prepare Dozo for the jump to test a miniature parachute specially rigged for her. *Courtesy of USAF*

were conducted for other national, state, and local agencies for countless varieties of tasks, often of humanitarian nature during natural and human-made disasters.

By the end of 1952, CAP boasted a fleet of more than 7,000 light aircraft. In that year alone, 486 were military acquisitions; 335 Aeronca L-16s were loaned by the air force, thirty aircraft were returnees from the European theater of operations, nine Beech C-45Gs went to liaison offices, while the remainder came from Army National Guard units replacing five-year-old aircraft. Although US forces had become embroiled in war in Korea, the growth of CAP and its expanding air operations kept open the pipeline for surplus military equipment.

Shown to good effect in 1952 are the high-visibility markings of this SB-17G (serial no. 44-83705) of Flight A, 6th Rescue Squadron, at BW1, Greenland. *Courtesy of Herb Hardin*

Five seemingly short years after the end of World War II, in June 1950 the Air Rescue Service would be tested when Korea flared into a hotspot in the Cold War. Combat rescue, which demanded more equipment and personnel and presented new tactical challenges, would change the face of air rescue. It would also take the alliance between air rescue and special operations far beyond that employed during World War II. Assistance for South Korea called for in "United Nations Resolution 25 June 1950" initially would come from forces serving occupation duty in Japan, which included elements of the Air Rescue Service. Although rescues behind enemy lines had been accomplished during World War II, in Korea they occurred regularly.

At war's outbreak, rescue coordination centers were quickly established, and the two closest rescue squadrons were made available to the Far East Air Forces (FEAF); the Philippines- and Okinawa-based 2nd ARS served the Thirteenth and Twentieth Air Forces, while the Japan-based 3rd ARS served under Fifth Air Force. Flights A and B of the 2nd ARS were based at Kadena Field, Okinawa, while Flight C was at Clark Air Base, Philippines, and Flight D at Guam, equipped with a mix of SA-10As, SB-17Gs, and SB-29s. Flights would be repositioned to take full advantage of each aircraft type's speed and abilities. All four 3rd ARS flights—at Johnson (A), Yokota (B), Misawa (C), and Ashiya (D) Air Bases—flew SB-17Gs; Flights B, C, and D also flew H-5 helicopters, only nine of which were H-5F models, the most powerful of the breed. Flights B and D were equipped with L-5s. Squadron records also indicate SC-47s and a detachment of Flight D at Seoul, South Korea. An earlier detachment at Itazuke Air Base, Japan, was equipped with three SB-17Gs, a PBY-5A Catalina, and two L-5s for rescues of airmen and Japanese fishermen, and for surveillance of shipping in the Sea of Japan.

The 3rd ARS spent many flight hours calibrating mountaintop radar-warning systems. Due to its proximity to the war zone, the squadron was quickly drawn into the conflict and bore the brunt of air rescue operations. This meant tapping the 2nd ARS for manpower until troops arrived from the US. Although more distant at Okinawa, the 2nd ARS was active as well. Aircraft types were spread thin among rescue squadrons, and when new types finally arrived in theater, maintenance men had to learn their new systems in order to raise aircraft flyability rates. Until their arrival, weary but dependable SB-17Gs did the job.

During the first few weeks of the conflict, reconnaissance units had yet to arrive, so the job fell to Air Rescue's SB-17Gs. It was an SB-17, in fact, that flew the first air rescue sortie of the conflict. Capt. James A. Scheib of Flight A, 3rd RS, was at the controls of the Dumbo to fly a US Army general from Japan to the vicinity of Seoul so that he could reconnoiter the ground situation. Far East Air Forces (FEAF) relied on the Flying Dutchmen to fly long-duration target recon and weather recon missions over hostile territory in preparation for planned strikes against North Korea. Besides these missions, the SB-17Gs flew Duckbutt sorties, escorted aircraft in distress, and flew searches for missing aircraft. Searches along the North Korean coast, combined with recon duty, soon had units reinstalling armament on B-17s. The SB-17G's crew then consisted of pilot, copilot, navigator, radar operator, flight engineer / top turret gunner, radio operator, two waist scanners/gunners, and tail scanner/gunner. Three months into the war, FEAF commandeered three of the rescue forts for classified missions, foretelling the role that air rescue would play in clandestine operations.

July 1950 proved a busy month for the 3rd RS. On the seventh, the squadron's pair of L-5s and an SC-47 were sent to conduct rescues in enemy territory. The planes proved inadequate for much of the region's terrain, shining the spotlight on the helicopter as the ideal method of evacuating the wounded. Wounded at the front lines were transported by vehicle to Taegu's airstrip for evacuation to hospitals in Japan, but not all survived the long, rough overland trip. Helicopters were the answer to getting wounded off the battlefield and relaying them from aid stations to collecting points, and finally to major airstrips. With the squadron's few H-5s in constant demand, Col. Kight found it necessary to draw the distinction between medical evacuation and rescue using helicopters, recommending that his H-5s be used for rescue and that separate units be formed to perform medical evacuation. Some relief came on July 22, with the formation of Detachment F at Pusan. In September, the sixty-six men and few H-5s composing the unit set up shop at Taegu. Within days the unit had flown badly wounded Eighth Army soldiers to field hospitals. FEAF commander Lt. Gen. George E. Stratemeyer and 5th AF commander Maj. Gen. Earle E. Partridge, both of whom were staunch opponents of airpower restrictions handed down from policymakers in Washington, and being genuinely concerned for the safety of their troops, pushed for more H-5s to be sent to Korea. Within two weeks, six of the 3rd Rescue Squadron's nine H-5s were committed to Korea, and fourteen additional H-5s were pulled from other units and shipped to the war zone. The operational plan had H-5s on strip alert, with requests for missions screened through

A number of SB-17Gs were refit with armament for the Korean War, although search radar that replaced the original chin turret was retained. This SB-17G of Flight C, 3rd Rescue Squadron, carried an A-1 airborne lifeboat. *Courtesy of David Menard collection*

After the loss of 28 B-29s to bomber-hunting MiG-15 "Fagots," B-29 raids were limited to night-only missions. The undersides of serial no. 44-87768 of Rescue Squadron B, *seen here*, were painted black to escort similarly painted bombers. When B-29s based in Japan began flying night missions in late 1952, an SB-29 of the 3rd RS escorted the bomber formation and then orbited offshore awaiting their return. Although fully armed, 768's lack of search radar and an airborne lifeboat indicates the escort role only, although droppable survival equipment was aboard. *Courtesy of USAF*

Eighth Army surgeon's office. Missions also arose from pilots of T-6 "Mosquito" air controller aircraft, who notified their base when fliers were downed. Always close to the action, H-5s of Detachment F were protected by Rescue Combat Air Patrol (RESCAP), usually F-51Ds of the 18th Fighter Bomber Group. Assistance also came from the Marine Corps when Observation Squadron 6 (VMO-6) arrived in August with Sikorsky HO-3S (H-5) helicopters and Stinson OY-1 (L-5) light planes.

When Air Rescue H-5s flew into the battlefield to rescue wounded and downed aircrew, they carried only a pilot, accompanied by a medic who could jump out to tend the wounded and load one or two onto the chopper. This lifesaving scenario became the lasting tableau of future wars. To more clearly identify its mission among the flow of units into the war zone, rescue squadrons in August 1950 were redesignated air rescue squadrons.

US Army officials, particularly Eighth Army surgeon Col. Chauncey Dovell, who had closely watched 3rd Air Rescue Squadron's activities in Korea, followed the squadron's lead in adopting helicopters for medical evacuation. Dovell's efforts were rewarded in November 1950, when the army's 2nd Helicopter Detachment arrived in Korea with four Bell H-13s. After a thorough training period to become familiar with the aircraft and terrain, the detachment became operational on January 1, 1951, and was attached to the 8055th Mobile Army

An H-5 of the 3rd Air Rescue Squadron approaches the newly installed helicopter deck of the hospital ship USS *Constellation* (AH-15) in December 1951. The chopper was carrying wounded US and South Korean marines on the last leg of an operation in which thirty-seven were evacuated from a seaside airstrip. *Courtesy of US Navy*

The airborne medic and pilot of a 3rd RS H-5G prepare a patient for flight in a side litter that accommodates a windowed full enclosure. The pilot wears a stylish six-shooter. *Courtesy of USAF*

Air Rescue crewmen use a raft to rescue a flier downed in Korean waters. *Courtesy of USAF*

More than thirty Boeing B-29 Superfortress bombers were converted to SB-29s for air rescue. These "Super Dumbos" retained their defensive armament with the exception of the forward ventral turret, which was removed to make room for an AN/APQ-13 radome. Equipped with the aluminum A-3 airborne lifeboat and droppable survival gear, the SB-29's primary mission was support for bombers flying long distances overwater. This SB-29B (serial no. 44-84078) of the 3rd Rescue Squadron carries the A-3, which was built by the Edo Corporation. Known for its production of aircraft floats, Edo, in 1947, built A-3s to replace the SB-17's Higgins A-1 lifeboat. Built specifically for the SB-29, the 30-foot A-3 could hold fifteen persons and used a single 100-foot parachute. A four-cylinder Meteor engine built by Red Wing Motor Co. allowed a top speed of 8 knots. *Courtesy of USAF*

With their post–World War II overall yellow painted over with Olive Drab for war in Korea, only the yellow serial number background of these H-5s was retained. Serial no. 48-560 was an H-5G, while no. 47-480 in the background was an H-5F. *Courtesy of USAF*

Surgical Hospital (MASH) at Ascom City. By the end of the month, the unit had evacuated more than five hundred casualties from battlefields. Also in January, the 3rd and 4th Detachments arrived with H-13s for assignment to MASH units. The 1st Helicopter Detachment arrived in February; however, it became nonoperational on May 14, when the remaining three were redesignated army units, which became the 49th, 50th, and 52nd Medical Detachment Helicopter Ambulance in 1952. Each unit flew four H-13 "Sioux" helicopters, which, periodically, were augmented with Hiller H-23 "Raven" helicopters. Like the H-5, H-13s carried two externally mounted litters.

The air force possessed two YH-19 prototypes. Important to air force leaders were the H-19's power over the H-5 and its ability to carry eight evacuees and a medical attendant. Army leaders closely watched air force trials with the pair, and the August 1951 arrival in Korea of Marine Medium Helicopter Squadron HMR-161, equipped with its version of the H-19, the HRS-1. Gen. Matthew Ridgeway, who had succeeded Gen. MacArthur as United Nations commander in Korea in April

In July 1951, a 3rd ARS H-5G (serial no. 48-555) heads for a hospital with a wounded Korean marine in encapsulated litter after he was transferred from the Albatross at left (serial no. 49-084). The H-5 was shot down in October. Sikorsky H-5s accounted for the largest number of rescues during the war, 730 of which were behind enemy lines. Grumman's SA-16A rescued 322, 122 of which were behind enemy lines. *Courtesy of USAF*

Fairchild's C-82 "Packet," which became the SC-82 in the Air Rescue Service, originally was labeled the "Flying Boxcar," the name later given Fairchild's C-119 transport. *Courtesy of USAF*

1951, enthusiastic about his observations, requested helicopter-equipped transport battalions in November 1951. During the long wait for H-19s, the army–air force debate over responsibility flared anew, with medical evacuation becoming army responsibility, and the air force returning to the business of air

rescue. The argument became a moot point since the army did not receive its H-19s until late in the war, performing double duty carrying cargo and wounded soldiers.

The first helicopter pilot to rescue a downed pilot behind enemy lines in Korea was Detachment F's Lt. Paul W. Van Boven, who on September 4 rescued F-80 pilot Capt. Robert E. Wayne after he was shot down while attacking targets in the north. Wayne's comrades of the 35th Fighter Bomber Squadron flew cover while one climbed to altitude to radio for the chopper. The longest-distance H-5 rescue was flown on October 10, 1950, by Lt. David C. McDaniels, when he flew 125 miles deep inside North Korea to rescue a British Sea Fury pilot. Severely wounded and trapped in the wreckage, the pilot held off the enemy with his revolver while his flight mates kept the enemy at bay. An hour later, McDaniels and an onboard doctor landed and worked to free the pilot, while keeping the enemy's heads down with automatic weapons. They freed Lt. S. Leonard of 807 Squadron, the doctor administered a blood transfusion on the chopper, and he made a full recovery. That month a few L-5s were added to the detachment for pickups in areas suitable for landing and takeoff, and by the end of 1950 the detachment's L-5s and H-5s recorded the lion's share of missions: 618 medical evacuations and eighty-seven rescues behind enemy lines by H-5, and fifty-six medical evacuations and seventeen rescues behind enemy lines by L-5. The mission deemed the most hazardous

Nearly forty SC-82s served the Air Rescue Service, including this SC-82A (serial no. 44-22978) seen at Hamilton Field in March 1949. *Courtesy of William T. Larkins*

1Lt. William A. Bright, SB-29 commander, *at left*, briefs his crew of Flight B, 3rd ARS, at Komaki AB, Japan, in February 1952. The unit had relocated from Yokota AB to Komaki near Nagoya in September 1951. Bright, a veteran of World War II, was awarded the Distinguished Flying Cross in Korea for a mission that saved the lives of two downed US Navy aircrewmen. *Courtesy of William A. Bright / Jeffrey Bright collection*

by the overworked men of the detachment occurred on February 15, 1951, when they were tasked with supplying badly needed medical supplies to embattled and surrounded 2nd Division soldiers. Six H-5s flew until nightfall, getting supplies in and bringing out thirty wounded. Two helicopters broke down but four repeated the process at daylight, by afternoon flying through a blizzard, and by nightfall accounting for twenty-two additional wounded.

As the air war over Korea intensified, the demand for rescuing downed airmen increased, as did casualty evacuation. Besides its two-man crew—pilot and medical attendant—H-5s could carry only two casualties in externally mounted stretchers. But the men who flew and maintained the worn H-5s knew that their choppers compressed an hour of rough land travel to a flight of a few minutes. And they knew that their work doubled the save rate of those wounded during World War II. As carryovers from World War II, the fabric-covered L-5s not only were obsolete and weary but were unsuitable for Korea's rugged terrain. But air rescue's L-5 pilots persevered,

often casting an envious eye toward Cessna L-19 "Bird Dogs" arriving to replace army "L" planes. The 213 hp, all-metal Bird Dog, complete with radio and instrument packages, flaps, heater, and shoulder harness, and, above all, combat-tested in Korea, would end up in the air force inventory more than a decade later. Much of the flying over Korea was done under Visual Flight Rules, following roads for a number of reasons. Magnetic compasses proved unreliable among mountains, in which armed guerrillas would not hesitate to shoot at aircraft. In addition, main supply routes (MSRs) were traveled and offered the few places where forced landings were possible. Eventually, it became common knowledge among pilots that rescue aircraft would begin their search along supply routes. The practice of following roads led to the first loss of an H-5 to enemy action. On October 1, 1950, the chopper was flying at low level along a road when it detonated an antitank mine, blowing the aircraft into a hillside. The first operational loss of an H-5 occurred on July 25, 1950, when the pilot extended his search for a downed navy flier—whom they picked

The time-honored, venerable Douglas C-47 enjoyed a strong presence in the Air Rescue Service. This ski-equipped SC-47B "Gooney" (serial no. 43-48765) of Flight A, 6th Rescue Squadron, shows to good effect its high-visibility orange-yellow at Greenland's Bluie West airfield in 1952. Earlier, number 765 featured Insignia Red panels, which were standard Arctic markings. The short-lived Northeast Air Command also flew ski-equipped, up-engined C-47s from Greenland's Narsarssauk. *Courtesy of Herb Hardin*

up—and the helicopter ran out of fuel. The aircraft landed safely and the three were rescued, but attempts to drop fuel were hindered by enemy fire. Three were rescued and the chopper was destroyed by airstrikes.

Besides difficulty in obtaining replacement parts and the effects of harsh weather on the H-5s, pilots quickly learned to adapt to combat flying in unarmed and unarmored helicopters that flew at 60 knots. Flight patterns had to be constantly altered, and overloading required that missions be flown with minimum fuel loads and careful attention given the use of ballast for takeoff; staying within reasonable center-of-gravity limits was accomplished by placement of a 60-pound weight—the more people taken aboard, the farther rearward the ballast. The first H-5 crew lost in combat was killed when their helicopter was hit by enemy fire on September 13, 1951. Although the pilot made it back to friendly lines, at 300 feet a rotor blade went out of track and severed the tail boom.

Successful aircraft are generally the result of the right design coming along at the right time. For duty in Korea, this seemed especially true of Grumman's SA-16A Albatross and Sikorsky's

H-19 helicopter. The Albatross made its mark early in the conflict when on August 5, 1950, one of the first SA-16As to arrive in the war zone landed in heavy seas to rescue a Corsair pilot who had ditched in enemy waters on his first combat mission, launched from the carrier *Philippine Sea*. Capt. Charles E. Schroeder was at the controls of the Albatross, which had three F-51 escorts. With the need for helicopters in air force colors no longer in question, two prototype YH-19s were sent with a test team to Korea to join Detachment F. The group arrived on March 23, 1951, and the next day worked with the detachment's H-5s to evacuate wounded paratroopers from a drop zone just south of the thirty-eighth parallel. The paradrop, which was part of Operation Ripper, was the second-largest airborne operation of the war, having placed nearly 5,500 paratroopers on the ground, along with 220 tons of equipment. Before long, the Chinese rallied and the choppers were flying through small-arms and mortar fire, with two H-5s hit but not put out of commission. By nightfall of the twenty-fifth, the H-5s and YH-19s had flown seventy-seven sorties to evacuate 148 paratroopers. Operations continued into the next day, with battle sorties totaling 147.

The crew of an SA-16A stands preflight inspection; crew consists of pilot, copilot, navigator, radio operator, flight engineer, and two pararescuemen. The door for the main entrance hatch was a two-section "Dutch" door, the bottom half of which was kept closed to increase freeboard in rough seas. A smaller hatch on the opposite side of the fuselage is open. Visible at far lower left is the shock strut and skid attached to the keel, indicating that this is a triphibian. *Courtesy of Robert F. Dorr*

This SA-16A wore the markings typical for Korea-based Albatrosses. Red trim on the drop tank of serial no. 49-096 likely was a personal or squadron marking. A boarding ladder is in place by the aft Dutch door, along with a padded support for the often-tail-heavy Albatross. The dark shape above the aft keel was a flush antenna. *Author's collection*

Throughout the war, helicopters sometimes flew the wounded from the battlefield to areas where an SC-47 could land and fly the wounded to hospital settings. The venerable Douglas "Gooney Bird" continued to prove its versatility, flying not only medical evacuation but search missions, supply runs, and pararescue support.

In June 1951, the 3rd Air Rescue Squadron's Detachment F was redesignated Detachment 1 and divided into four flights,

serving the 8055th MASH, the army's 25th Division near the battlefront, alert duty at Seoul, and transport for truce negotiators at Munsan-ni. Seldom equipped with more than ten helicopters, the detachment could assign only one or two H-5s, sometimes with an L-5, to the many sites near the ever-changing front lines. Later that year, H-5s took up station on the islands of Paengyong-do and Cho-do, which were designated bailout zones for aircrews. Although Cho-do was dangerously close to the North Korean coast and north of the thirty-eighth parallel, rescue H-5s and SA-16As on alert were vital since downed airmen stood little chance of survival in the Yellow Sea in winter. Oddly, island-based units received no opposition from enemy aircraft, although it was known that enemy pilots seldom ventured out over open sea since they had no air rescue capability. Helicopter pilot John Caldwell recalls:

> South Korean nationals flew with our choppers to Cho-do and Paengyong-do, where they assisted us in many ways, including camp maintenance and aircraft battery installation. Batteries were removed and kept near stoves in cold weather. When alerts occurred, there was a coordinated rush to dress alert crew in survival suits, and everyone worked to start the alert bird as the crew dressed. Preparation included the chopper's engine being warmed up.

Beginning in late December 1951, a pair of Detachment 1 H-5 helicopters, along with army and marine helicopters, conducted trials to determine the practicality of flying the wounded directly to a hospital ship lying offshore the Korean coastline. For the trials, the hospital ship USS *Consolation* (AH-15) was fitted with a 60-by-60-foot helicopter landing pad on its afterdeck. The three-week test period, during which more than two hundred wounded were flown to *Consolation*, proved conclusively the success of such missions, a practice that not only continued but became commonplace in Southeast Asian waters more than a decade later.

The SB-29 Super Dumbo was the first *new* aircraft assigned to the 3rd Air Rescue Squadron, arriving in Korea on July 29, 1950. The first Albatrosses to arrive were four SA-16As, along with thirty-four personnel, assigned temporary duty from Lowry Field, Colorado, as the newly formed Detachment E of the 5th Rescue Squadron. The contingent arrived in Japan on July 28 and within three weeks had rescued six downed fliers. Detachment E was relieved by the 3rd ARS when it received its own SA-16As four months later. Albatrosses stood alert at various bases, and if seas permitted, they were the preferred aircraft to make the rescue. As more SA-16As arrived, the SB-17G's days were numbered, although the "Old Reliables" still performed, despite a dwindling supply of parts. On December 6, 1950, an SB-17G made the first boat drop of the war after a B-26 crew bailed out at night over the Korea Strait. A search at daybreak, although in a snowstorm, by air rescue boats and aircraft failed to turn up the missing airmen, until one was spotted in a raft two days later. High seas ruled out landing the SA-16A after crewmen spotted the survivor, so an SB-17G was summoned. Its airborne lifeboat landed 50 feet from the survivor but disappeared in snow and poor visibility. Two days later an SB-17G crew spotted the lifeboat beached, and an SC-47 was able to land to rescue the lone survivor. The same SB-17G pilot, Lt. Carl P. Dimmitt of Flight D, 3rd ARS, on April 7, 1951, performed the second and final successful wartime rescue with an A-1 airborne lifeboat. Dimmitt's crew was flying a Duckbutt orbit for B-29 strikes when one of the bombers exploded in midair. Spotting a survivor in a raft, Dimmitt released his A-1 lifeboat, and shortly thereafter an SA-16A landed to pick up the survivor. Only one other operational A-1 boat drop had been made during the war, but the survivor had perished.

By the end of 1950, the 3rd ARS had fourteen H-5 helicopters, eight Albatrosses, six SB-17Gs, five SB-29s, three SC-47s, and three L-5s. Early in 1951, Flight A had replaced its SB-17Gs with Albatrosses, Flight D's two remaining "Old Reliables" were gone by August, Flight B followed suit, and Flight C flew its last SB-17G mission in October. Grumman's Albatross had taken center stage in the rescue business, one of which, with Lt. John Najarian at the controls, exhibited the mettle both of air rescue man and machine. After Capt. Kenneth Stewart had bailed out of his flak-damaged F-51 at night over the Taedong River on June 11, 1951, Najarian landed his SA-16A in the shallow, debris-filled river to snatch Stewart. As F-51s raked enemy guns along the riverbanks, others used their landing lights to illuminate low-hanging high-tension wires, enabling Najarian to take off.

After the 3rd ARS had received its full complement of twelve SA-16As by March 1951, aircraft and crews were rotated between Korea and Japan bases every two weeks. This not only minimized crew fatigue, it allowed more-extensive aircraft maintenance at Japan bases. Aircraft introduced into a combat theater typically present new problems for maintenance crews, and the Albatross was no exception. Problems with SA-16A propellers, especially with their reversible feature, were compounded by a lack of specialized tools. Engine failures, five of which occurred during March 1951 alone, forced the decision to reduce maximum gross weight to single-engine capability until the problem was solved. The very nature of rescue work added to the woes of hardworking maintenance crews. Operations in rough seas often resulted in damage that highlighted the SA-16A's ability to convert from airplane to boat. For example, on June 28, 1951, 3rd ARS operations officer Lt. Col. Theodore P. Tatum took aboard a physician and assistant and flew the Dumbo (s/n 49-082) 400 miles to the cargo ship USS *Whiteside* to treat a passenger with acute appendicitis. Faced with a decision that weighed the life of one man against those of his crew, Tatum full-stalled his Albatross onto heaving seas, bouncing off three swells. A wing dug into the water, severely damaging a flap, ruling out takeoff. After a hazardous raft transfer of crew and passengers to the ship, *Whiteside* took the aircraft in tow. The weather worsened,

so Tatum, the true captain of his ship, stayed aboard in case the bilge pump was needed. After thirty hours of battering by mountainous waves, he traded places with two of his crew. A tug relieved *Whiteside*, and two days after landing, the entire crew boarded the Albatross within the shelter of Tokyo Bay. To the crew's astonishment, the engines roared to life, so Tatum water-taxied to the Yokosuka seadrome, lowered the gear, and went ashore.

Within the SA-16A's first year in theater, Dumbo crews had accomplished thirty water rescues, twenty-two of which occurred during the month of October 1951, the peak period of the war for water rescue by SA-16A. That number, which represented one-fifth of all the downed aircrew rescued by Albatrosses during the war, was attributed to maximum-effort B-29 missions over North Korea, intended to bring the enemy to an armistice. A number of changes occurred during the month of November, not the least of which affected the operational chain of command by placing Korean-based Albatrosses under control of helicopter-equipped Detachment 1, 3rd ARS, at Seoul City. A squadron directive followed, outlining that SA-16A mission priority was water rescues, then orbits, and search and rescue as directed by Fifth Air Force. Medical evacuations were excluded from the directive, although they were flown when necessary. Also that month, the 2nd Air Rescue Group based two SA-16As at Pohang, Korea, to augment the 3rd's coverage of waters surrounding the Korean Peninsula. Veteran Albatross pilot Aaron Ellis explains that not all Albatross missions were high drama but made for interesting telling, nonetheless:

The little island off the northwest coast of Korea and in enemy territory was where our fighter boys would go and bail out, and try to get on the leeward side, where we could land in open sea and pick them up. Air cover would go there to protect the rescue. My classmate who was stationed at Johnson Field had taken off full of fuel in the mains and drop tanks. They had to stay on station all day, and when fighters got shot up, they'd head there. Bob and his crew were somewhere near there when they lost an engine, fully loaded. They "feathered" and dropped the drop tanks but only one fell away, making them use nearly all aileron and cross control, but they were still losing altitude. Bob asked his flight mechanic to use the carbine from the rear hatch to drain the tank, but he was afraid of fuel fire. So Bob got up out of his seat and ran back, opened the hatch, and used the carbine to shoot out the drain plug, draining all the fuel and making it home rather than ditching in enemy waters, and the airplane and crew were saved. I can't remember the medal he received, but the citation mentioned one of the laudable items was shooting his own aircraft.

Three SA-16A losses due to operational causes are recorded as having occurred during the conflict. The first loss occurred on January 20, 1951, when the ocean claimed the amphibian during a practice water landing. The second loss happened on January 13, 1953, when an Albatross crew left its Duckbutt orbit to land in icy seas in search of a fighter pilot. So much ice had accumulated on the aircraft that both takeoff and water taxi in rough seas were ruled out. Finally taken in tow by vessel, the pair made it to an island, where the damaged, ice-encrusted Albatross sank just minutes after the last crewman was helped aboard the tow boat. Exactly one month later, a Dumbo crashed into a mountain on a medical evacuation mission; the cause was never determined.

DICKEY'S BOATS

Just four months prior to the outbreak of war in Korea, the FEAF had eliminated air force crash boat operations west of Hawaii, with the exception of Manila's port. No boats were in Korea, and those at Guam were turned over to the navy, with boat personnel dispersed among other fields. No sooner had all taken place when war broke out in Korea, and FEAF leaders wanted immediate crash boat coverage in the Sea of Japan. Beginning at the top, orders were given and the "buck passing" stopped at Lt. Phillip Dickey, last commander of the crash boat unit at Fukuoka. Dickey's hunt for men with boating skills ended three months later with more than eighty men. When Dickey went to Yokohama to gather boats, he found the army reluctant to part with 63- and 85-foot ARBs, since they were earmarked for spook missions. Dickey managed to talk them out of a 104-footer, four 85-footers, six 63-footers, and four shallow-draft vessels. Digging up spare parts, especially engines, along with technical material, proved difficult.

Dickey's boats became a component of the 8th Fighter Wing until July 1950, when it relocated from Itazuke to Suwon Air Base, Korea (K-13), as the 6160th Air Base Wing; the ARBs were called Detachment 1. The four 85-footers operated initially from Pusan (K-9), Aino Shima, Miho, and Fukuoka Air Bases. The single 104-footer was based at Tsushima Island, where, in 1951, it caught fire during refueling and was destroyed. Despite numerous requirements by FEAF commanders, boats and crews were spread thin throughout the war. Under call sign "Soda Water," mainly 63- and 85-foot boats saw combat duty, and they were constantly moved as tactical needs dictated. Boat duty was harsh. Despite their open-helm stations, many were without heating systems, and they were unarmored. Crews, which often were skippered by NCOs, lived onboard for periods of two to three months, returning to safe harbor for supplies, fuel, and maintenance, with major repairs made in Japan. Duty for the 85s often consisted of one-to-two-month stints north of Cho-do behind enemy lines, which had crews inserting or retrieving agents or delivering supplies into North Korea, China, or Manchuria. The 85s were the obvious choice for missions north, since they were armed with a Quad-50 forward, .50 cal. machine guns in midship turrets; the 20 mm cannon aft was later replaced in favor of the longer-ranged .50 cal.

In early 1952, the army turned over two 85-footers at the behest of new unit commander Capt. James Beene. Later that year, on June 16, Detachment 1 was redesignated the 22nd Crash Rescue Boat Squadron. As they had in World War II, crash boat crews wore navy clothing, which included authorized chambray shirts and blue dungarees; the latter could be cinched at the bottoms to assist with flotation. During the war, only the 63s were painted the high-visibility scheme, while the 85-footers wore gray. After the armistice, most boats were painted the bright colors. While most crash boats operated with the 22nd CRBS during the war, other boat units served various commands; however, all were under air base groups.

The coordination of rescue operations with other combat units was accomplished through an air rescue officer of FEAF staff. Rescue coordination centers soon sprang up at Johnson, Itazuke, and Misawa Air Bases, with a naval liaison officer assigned to each. The 3rd ARS operated a radio network around the clock to direct and coordinate all rescue activities in Korea and Japan. If necessary, rescue units at Iwo Jima, Guam, Okinawa, and Hawaii could be called upon to assist. As in World War II, rescue coverage was included in mission planning. Another carryover from that war was having SB-17Gs taking off well ahead of bomber formations to intercept the faster B-29s at the rendezvous point. Some measure of relief came on September 1, 1950, when Flight B, 3rd ARS, began flying four SB-29s from Misawa AB, Japan; 3rd ARS SB-17s, SC-47s, and SC-46s flew shorter-range missions, often orbiting off Korean or Japanese coasts. In November, they operated from Yokota AB, and in September 1951, Flight B relocated to Komaki AB. There, Super Dumbo crews took advantage of nearby Lake Biwa to conduct practice lifeboat drops using a locally fabricated sight that surpassed the Norden bombsight used previously. It wasn't until May 1952 that four Okinawa-based "Airedale" Super Dumbos of Flight D, 2nd ARS, began flying orbits over the Korean coastline until the bombers headed inland, and were offshore again until the last B-29 reached the coast. Among the hard lessons learned were those concerning calculated allowances for fuel consumption affected by full ammo loads and boat drag; when SB-29s of the Okinawa-based 2nd ARS began flying bomber escort missions, some didn't make it back due to fuel starvation, making it necessary to reduce, or even delete, ammo loads. The SB-29s also covered bomber takeoffs, escorting each one on takeoff, landing only after all were safely outbound. After acquiring its first few SB-29s, the squadron's Flight B began flying bomber escort missions in early September, along with search missions. In November, the flight was tasked with SAR escort for classified RB-45 missions flown by the 91st Strategic Reconnaissance Wing. Flight B's first loss of an SB-29 occurred on January 31, 1951, when the aircraft (s/n 44-84124) crashed on takeoff from Yokota AB, killing three crew members. In June 1952, Flight B provided rescue coverage for Operation Hightide, in which B-29s modified as KB-29M tankers refueled F-84 aircraft en route to Korea.

Demonstrating the coordination among the variety of rescue assets was a mission on the night of October 31, 1952. After reporting problems with two engines, a B-29 returning from Korea to Kadena was intercepted by an Airedale SB-29. When a third engine quit, the bomber ditched in open sea. Airedale's crew lost sight of the bomber but dropped its lifeboat in an area illuminated by a flare. The flare burned out, causing the wreckage and boat to disappear in the blackness, but an H-19 helicopter that had been summoned was led to a light spotted by an SC-47 crew that had also responded. The chopper crew lowered its sling to pick up the survivor but backed off as an air rescue boat, which could make a safer pickup, was approaching. The H-19 lingered using its spotlight to illuminate the area, while the crash boat rescued two additional survivors.

By spring 1952, 3rd ARS had eight H-19s, two of which were pontoon-equipped for water rescue. They could perform more safely than Albatrosses, which sometimes were unable to land on water due to ice or choppy seas. The H-19, along

On April 6, 1951, SA-16A (serial no. 48-602) of Flight D, 5th ARS, crashed at Mt. Clemens, Michigan, near Selfridge AFB. The Albatross was returning from a SAR mission in Tennessee when it lost an engine on approach to Selfridge. Four were injured. The right propeller is feathered. *Courtesy of USAF*

Beginning with SA-16A (serial no. 49-082), three rescue aircraft share the flight line with a B-29 in Korea. The float-equipped H-19A is serial no. 51-3847. *Courtesy of USAF*

with improvement of the H-5—the H-5H—which was also pontoon-equipped, brought to an end the use of L-5s for rescue in the combat zone. The US Navy brought the HO3S-1 to the war zone aboard carriers, using them mainly for water pickups close to ships. The navy also flew two amphibians—Martin PBM Mariner and P-5 Marlin—however, they were used for antisubmarine patrol, minesweeping, and escort.

TRANSATLANTIC FLIGHT

Besides Korea, H-19s began to appear on the inventories of air rescue squadrons across the globe. Two that were destined for the long trip from the Sikorsky plant to the 9th Air Rescue Squadron at Wiesbaden AFB, West Germany, would begin their career with a record flight. Air Force captain Vincent McGovern, after flying ninety-six missions in the H-5 in Korea, was assigned to Air Rescue Headquarters. Impressed with the H-19, McGovern formulated a plan to deliver the pair of H-19As by making the first transatlantic crossing by helicopter. On July 15, 1952, the two H-19As, christened "Hop-A-Long" (s/n 51-3893) and "Whirl-O-Way" (s/n 51-3890), with three 100-gallon fuel tanks added to their cabins and stripped of all unnecessary equipment, took off from Westover AFB, Massachusetts, to begin the 4,000-mile journey. The trip took twenty days and accounted for fifty-two hours of flying time. The pair was shadowed by an SC-54 named "Playmate" carrying spare parts, mechanics, observers, and a Sikorsky technical representative. Two days after signing on with the 9th ARS, the two H-19s saved the crew of an American bomber that had crashed in the Rhine.

The number of personnel assigned to 3rd ARS increased from nearly 540 during August 1950 to a wartime high of more than a thousand by February 1952. During August 1952, Air Rescue got a new boss, Brig. Gen. Thomas Jefferson Du Bose, who, like Kight, stood the helm with enthusiasm and drive. Although the nature of air rescue fostered a high accident rate, Du Bose was relentless in his insistence on safety. On November 14, 1952, a complete reorganization of rescue units had most of the squadrons, which were numbered 1 through 12, upgraded to air rescue groups (ARGs), resulting in eleven groups and forty-one squadrons; many of these squadrons had been detachments or flights. Groups and squadrons abroad came under theater commanders. The 3rd Air Rescue Squadron's Flight A, then, became the 36th ARS; Flight B, the 37th ARS; Flight C, the 38th ARS; and Flight D, the 39th ARS. Under the new 2nd ARG, Flight A became the 31st ARS; Flight B, the 32nd ARS; Flight C, the 33rd ARS; and Flight D, the 34th ARS.

SPOOK MISSIONS

Because of the skill and dedication, and the high risk associated with air rescue and what is today termed special operations, seldom have the two been far apart. They would close the distance during the Korean War after Pentagon planners came up with a scheme to combine several overt and covert missions to counter the Communist threat. The result was activation on February 23, 1951, of the Air Resupply and Communications Service (ARCS) under the Military Air Transport Service. It was all a ruse, of course, with the ARCS mission vaguely described as psychological warfare and aerial resupply, which translated to the infiltration and extraction of clandestine operators in the enemy's backyard.

Planners envisioned seven ARCS wings, each having five squadrons for assignment in the US and abroad. Three wings would actually be formed; the 580th, 581st, and 582nd, with the 581st sent to Korea. While documentation of the unit's operations remains obscure, it is known that it began on a small scale with nineteen personnel and four helicopters. Twelve airmen, who were fresh from the helicopter maintenance training school at Sheppard AFB, arrived during summer 1952. Finding no semblance of the 581st, they were put to work with air rescue at Seoul City Air Base, better known as K-16 among base designations assigned by United Nations Command. When six helicopter pilots arrived at K-16 on October 5 and asked where the 581st was, they too were met with shrugs and "There's no such outfit in Korea."

Finally, someone remembered where the dozen airmen had gone, and then assumed that there was a connection between these six pilots and four crated helicopters awaiting pickup at Kisararzu, Japan. Expecting castoff helicopters from air rescue, the pilots were elated to find they had been given factory-fresh H-19s. After quickly retrieving their aircraft from Japan, the pilots, the dozen wayward airmen, and an NCO line chief who had been an H-13 ground school instructor colocated with air rescue at K-16 under operational control of B Flight, 6167th Air Base Group (ABG).

Receiving their orders from intelligence organizations with a string of deceptive names, the small unit was tasked with infiltrating and extracting intelligence-gathering agents and saboteurs in North Korea. Agents often had been parachuted behind enemy lines by B-26, C-46, C-47, and B-17 aircraft of B Flight; those aircraft types also were equipped with the All American Engineering winch system for pickup of agents and downed fliers. Shortly after the outbreak of the war, select personnel of Flight A, 3rd ARS, in Japan were trained in flying a pair of B-17s at low level at night, blacked out and without communications. Beginning in September, on clear nights with a full moon, the B-17s flew from Johnson AB, Japan, to Miho AB, where agents loaded with radio and survival gear boarded. After being flown to mountainous regions near the Korea-Chinese border, the agents slipped from the B-17's modified bomb bay, parachuting from 500 feet onto sandbars formed by river bends. More than one veteran relates that agents, at times, were young South Korean teenagers who would go unnoticed as they observed enemy activities. Their motivation for night parachute jumps came from parents who received handsome payments from the government.

The mettle of crews flying the H-19s was matched only by their skill as they flew 50 feet above the waves at night,

Settling into its open-sea landing to pick up plane crash survivors in June 1952, this SA-16A (serial no. 49-095) of the 2nd Rescue Squadron offers a good view of its topside features. *Courtesy of USAF*

without the benefit of radar or radio altimeters. Relying on visual references and basic altimeter settings, they flew blacked out, under radio silence, and usually single ship. Even before spook missions began in December 1952, the rescue commander requested that rescue markings of the four H-19s be painted over. Since the enemy knew that rescue did not fly at night and its aircraft wore rescue markings, air rescue staff avoided placing added risk on its crews. Appearances aside, air commandos and rescue men worked hand in hand when it came to rescue.

When SA-16As arrived at K-16 in spring 1953, they too balanced rescue missions and harrowing jaunts north to pick up agents. On deep-penetration missions, they flew 100 feet above the waves to avoid radar detection, escorting the H-19s and providing navigation and then orbiting offshore for the chopper's return trip. Like the H-19s, the Albatrosses, along with B-17s of the 581st ARCW, were painted overall black in keeping with their nighttime operations. Aaron Ellis remembers:

In SA-16 Black Birds, we had all-day missions along the China coast since our RB-50s from Japan were being chased out by jets, and navy surveillance P2Vs were being shot down; China was then getting jets as production of MiG-15s increased for war needs. We had to be there if B-50s could make it to the coast, where we could pick them up. Of course, it had to be a clear day and they wouldn't even let us take a gun. The only protection we had was flying at 200 feet with hatches open for scanners to spot, and hopefully outmaneuver them, and that they, with short-time jet experience, would misjudge and scrape the water and we could become an ace! We passed over sampans, most of which had radios. But we were radio silence from the 100-mile radar boundary for over twelve hours. We went up and down the coastline, matching the routes of B-50s. We did take special people to islands, and they'd go ashore in rubber rafts or meet someone in a boat, and with special codes we'd leave or stay out in the open sea just floating with engines shut down and watching from atop the aircraft for proper signals, or to go home and come back another day. We never knew what the mission was.

On March 1, 1953, when the 2157th Air Rescue Squadron was activated at K-16 from Detachment 1 of the 3rd ARS, it absorbed the four H-19As of the 581st ACRW; its aircraft inventory was then a record high—ten H-5s and eight H-19s. John W. Caldwell, who was assigned to the 2157th ARS as a helicopter pilot, recalls an H-19 mission he calls "the Miracle":

It was 29 May 1953 at Cho-do Island, and the sea was still fiercely cold as we headed north in our H-19A, call sign "Pedro," to respond to a mayday call. After we became airborne we were put in touch with an SA-16, call sign "Dumbo," already in the vicinity of a downed F-84 pilot. The Dumbo was unable to make a water landing because of the numerous sandbars in the area. His options were further complicated by ground fire from the beach less than a mile from the downed pilot, almost in the mouth of the Chong River. It was my first H-19 mission from Cho-do, my earlier missions having been flown to MASH hospitals along the Main Line of Resistance (MLR) in the H-5. I was being supervised, observed, and graded by Major Jim Blackburn, the coolest man I ever saw under fire.

The Dumbo guided us into the general area of the downed pilot and departed for points south. He had already stretched his fuel by waiting as long as he had. It took some minutes for us to locate the pilot, and from Dumbo we had already learned that he was being fired on from shore. When we finally spotted him, we rushed in with the hoist sling extended, and with absolute minimum hover time we plucked him neatly from his one-man raft and headed out to sea with him still dangling 10 to 12 feet below the chopper as we moved away from the unfriendly beach as fast as possible, while hoisting him into the helicopter. Routine? Not quite.

Our downed pilot had followed his overwater bailout procedures to the letter. He had inflated his dinghy and crawled into it just as his parachute had lowered him to the surface, and he sat in that dinghy until plucked out by our sling-hoist operation. Believe it or not, his dinghy was on dry land, and I could not have thrown a rock from his dinghy to the water. We immediately headed south for Cho-do, by now low on fuel.

H-19s were rarely able to take off from Cho-do with a full fuel load. Rescue equipment, two pilots, and a medic limited us to about two hours' fuel on all but cold, windy days. This particular day was cold but not windy. Accordingly, we immediately headed south, parallel to the coastline and about 3 miles out in a direct line to Cho-do. No sooner had the medic reported that the pilot seemed uninjured than the change in his voice became noticeable. I'll never forget his words: "Sir, there is a bent-wing airplane headed our way, and it's not an F-86." As I turned back to the right, I was able to confirm his report. It was not an F-86. Our situation was not good—an unarmed 80-knot chopper was certainly at

the mercy of a MiG-15, and then the miracle happened. Our uninvited guest dove, pulled up, rolled his fighter, and headed north. We proceeded south to our island destination—still parallel to the mainland of a hostile North Korea. Then Jim Blackburn started laughing. It had been a trying day for me—a search while drawing gunfire, a hover and pickup of a downed pilot, and a thoroughly frightening interception by an enemy fighter aircraft. Had Jim become hysterical? Not bloody likely. He was laughing at me as I flew the chopper while leaning all the way to the right side of the cockpit, as far away from North Korea as I could get.

We landed on the beach at Cho-do and turned our very lucky charge over to a C-47 crew which had been dispatched, complete with flight surgeon. I spent the next nine weeks at Cho-do and scrambled from there twenty-six times, which included two more successful "you call, we haul" missions, but the memories of that pilot sitting in his dinghy on dry land and the MiG escort are the ones that come back most often.

In a postscript, Caldwell noted that his hope of meeting the downed F-84 pilot became reality, thanks to aviation author Robert F. Dorr's *Air Force Times* article based on the incident. The pilot, now Dr. John Gaskins of North Carolina, along with Caldwell and Dorr, attended the 2002 reunion of the US Air Force Helicopter Pilots Association.

Among the few operational boat drops during the war by SB-17s and SB-29s, the last drop occurred just hours before the armistice on July 29, 1953. An RB-50 on an intelligence-gathering mission over the Sea of Japan was shot down by a Soviet MiG-15. One survivor reached the lifeboat and was picked up the next day by a US Navy destroyer. A two-day search by SB-29s and RB-29s failed to turn up more survivors, unsurprisingly, since about fifteen Soviet patrol boats were seen leaving the area. The lone survivor had heard fellow crew members shouting in the water, leaving the status of twenty-four crew members unresolved, with the speculation that they are additions to the long list of Korean War MIA.

Pararescuemen, better organized and trained than they had been during the post–World War II period, were the preferred medical crewmen aboard air rescue aircraft. While medical service personnel were forbidden to get off the aircraft, pararescuemen not only left the aircraft to aid downed fliers but often made their way to a site on foot, spending one or two days on the ground. In 1952, shortly after Gen. DuBose replaced Col. Kight as commander of Air Rescue, he directed that Medical Service Corps officers be phased out of pararescue, to be replaced by senior noncommissioned officers assigned as team commanders. DuBose's directive stated, "Based on our past experience, the hazards inherent with parachute activities far outweigh the gain obtained where Medical Corps Officers have participated in parachute jumps at the site of a disaster." An aircraft down in terrain that was inaccessible by any other means meant that PJs were strapping on parachutes. Pararescue teams also were inserted into drop zones as an advance element preceding massive paratroop assaults. In October 1952, Gen. DuBose reduced the number of pararescuemen in a team from seven to five to fill other slots in Air Rescue and in the interest of economy. The cut went hand in hand with his directive that the number of teams be reduced from forty-five to twenty-nine.

While slight variances are recorded in the number of persons saved by the 3rd Air Rescue Squadron during the thirty-seven months of the war, most—including USAF accreditation—agree that ARS crews flew 9,680 to safety, all but 461 of them by helicopter; 996 were rescued from behind enemy lines. Of these, helicopters are credited with 846, with H-5s accounting for 730 and the remainder by H-19s. Igor Sikorsky could not have been more proud. Grumman's SA-16A is credited with 322 saves, 122 of which were behind enemy lines. Although airborne lifeboat-equipped SB-17s and SB-29s saw less action during the war, their service is testimony to the skill and dedication of their crews and illustrates the creative use of assets. Their mere existence paid dividends in morale, since aircrew knew that if they had to go down, a lifeboat could be dropped to them. These accomplishments grounded the air rescue concept as a vital component of combat forces, but they could not make guarantees for the future.

By 1951, SB-29 Super Dumbos were operational with the A-3 lifeboat, which form-fit to the underside of the bomber-turned-rescue aircraft, seen here, which was assigned to Flight C of the 5th Rescue Squadron. *Courtesy of Kelly McLarney*

A very fine line existed between operations of Air Rescue and the secret Air Resupply and Communications Service, which was formed for the Korea War in 1951. Air commandos and rescue men served side by side in rescue mode; however, "spook" aircraft later were required not to wear rescue markings. This H-19 (S/N 51-13883) belonged to the 3rd ARS but was marked for the Air Resupply mission. *Courtesy of Kelly McLarney collection*

THE 1950S

When the shooting stopped in Korea, Air Rescue was able to divert more of its attention to peacetime missions, in the US and throughout the Free World. This did not, however, come without a price; during the few years following the armistice, the ranks of Air Rescue personnel, which had grown to a force of nearly nine thousand airmen, were reduced to one-fourth that number. The demands of the Cold War were not lost on anyone, and the nuclear war mindset that prevailed erased the wartime mission from the national search-and-rescue plan, leaving the US unprepared for combat SAR. The Korean conflict, much like World War II, had taught valuable lessons and brought about changes likely not to have occurred under less strenuous conditions. But only "Air Force Manual 20-54," dated October 15, 1952, served as official guidance for USAF Air Rescue. Although the manual addressed rescue in combat operations, by the mid-fifties the service would be fighting for its very existence, resulting in the deactivation of rescue units supporting combat operations. Until then, the Air Rescue Service had been allowed to keep the thirteen groups and nearly fifty squadrons established during, and shortly thereafter, the Korean War. Expansion of Air Rescue, though limited, enabled the service to amass impressive statistics throughout the world. Gen. DuBose, on the tenth anniversary of ARS in May 1956, stated:

To me it has always been a source of wonder and pride that the most potent and destructive military force ever known should create a special service dedicated to saving life. Its concept is typically American. All over the world Air Rescue affords daily proof that as Americans we hold human life to be the most precious commodity on earth. To the people of foreign lands who see Rescue in action it serves as a constant rebuttal to those who propagandize against us.

An example of Air Rescue's global influence is seen in Col. Robert Rizon, who took command of the 12th Air Rescue Group, established in March 1952. Contributing to the expansion of air rescue in Central Europe was tension between the US and the Soviet Union over Berlin. After training and equipping the four squadrons that composed Rizon's group, in November they deployed to Europe, where the headquarters and the 81st, 82nd, and 83rd Air Rescue Squadrons set up shop at Bordeaux Airfield, France, as did the 84th ARS at Furstenfeldbruck Air Base, Germany. Rizon then assumed the role of diplomat, establishing relationships with European government leaders. He and his personnel worked with rescue agencies of Italy, France, Spain, Norway, and Denmark. Rizon noted:

One of the highlights was our association with the Spanish. The Spanish have always had a small rescue arm but only recently started to develop it. They sent several of their crews to the United States, and they trained at West Palm Beach at our school. The Spanish air force obtained, through the Military Assistance Program, the same type of equipment that we use—SA-16s and SH-19s. Early in 1954 we offered, through the joint United States Military Advisers Group in Madrid, to help in the transition from the type they had been using to the new equipment.

They accepted this offer, and we went to Madrid and then on to the island of Majorca and worked with the people in command of the Spanish air rescue service. We gave them all of our operating procedures and we also gave them advanced open-sea training in the SA-16, using our instructor pilots. As a result, the present Spanish air rescue service is modeled on our own.

Although the group's main mission was support of the Twelfth Air Force, civilian emergencies received the group's full attention. When in February 1953 the dikes burst in Holland,

Rizon gathered nearly fifty helicopters and more than thirty fixed-wing aircraft to aid the Dutch. Dubbed Operation Humanity, it was then the largest peacetime rescue operation in history. Then there were the avalanches in Austria and floods in Bavaria and at Italy's Po River valley. The list goes on.

Also providing air rescue coverage in Europe was the 7th ARS, which had been reactivated on September 1, 1949. Squadron headquarters and Flight A were based at Wiesbaden, Germany; Flight B, at Lajes Field, Azores; Flight C, at Wheelus Air Base, Libya; and Flight D, at Dhahran Air Base, Saudi

"We'll come back for it in spring" might have been on the minds of 10th RS crewmen of SA-16A serial no. 51-059 when it became stranded on Alaska's Taku glacier in December 1953. By the time crewmen had dug out fuel drums that had broken free of their parachute harnesses during the drop, a snowstorm had half-buried the Albatross. After fifteen days of captivity by Mother Nature, the Albatross was flown out. *Courtesy of USAF*

Built as a C-53 paratroop variant during World War II, serial no. 42-15894 served the 10th ARS and later the 54th ARS. Seen here in Alaska with an SA-16A, the "Skytrooper" was winterized, was long range thanks to extra fuel tanks, and featured a navigator's astrodome and enlarged portside paratroop doors. Named "JATO BRONC," it ended up in the US Navy as BuNo 06994. *Courtesy of Jack Barry / James Gremmell*

Arabia. In 1952, the 7th was replaced by the reactivated 9th ARS, based at Bushy Park, England, with Flight A at Prestwick, Scotland; Flight B at RAF Manston; Flight C at RAF Burtenwood; and Flight D at Wiesbaden. Headquarters 7th ARS relocated to Wheelus AB.

The specially modified C-53 42-15894 "JATO BRONC" wore nose art in the post–Korean War era. *Courtesy of Jack Barry / James Gremmell*

Reorganization became a byword in the Air Rescue Service during the 1950s. Throughout the decade, the service underwent numerous changes that reflected prevailing mindsets and budget considerations. To reflect its expanding role, beginning in 1952 the Air Rescue Service upgraded its squadrons to group status, while subordinate flights became numbered squadrons. Designations too were changed to reflect unit function. As land rescue teams and air rescue boats faded from the picture, the designation "rescue squadron," which had been assigned on January 28, 1948, became "air rescue squadron" on August 10, 1950. By early 1954, when Air Rescue Headquarters moved to Orlando AFB, Florida, the service had reached peak strength with thirteen groups and more than eight thousand personnel.

Air Rescue boats that did not serve in Korea usually were culled from army and navy storage for use in crash rescue boat flights (CRBFs) beginning in March 1950. Just when most of the boats had passed into history, production, in fact, resumed to equip boat flights. Navy Mk. III boats built during 1952 and 1953 that were pressed into air force service were designated R-37-, followed by the boat number. The Mk. III was an upgrade of the Mk. II, with an all-electric galley, pressurized freshwater system, surface search radar, and improved communications and

When control of Military Air Transport Service operations in Iceland was passed to the US Navy in July 1961, two USAF H-19Bs—serial nos. 52-7004 and 52-7538—were transferred to the navy to continue rescue service to the region. They were redesignated BuNos 150193 and 150194, respectively. The pair was redesignated UH-19Fs in 1962. The air force rescue scheme was retained, with service titles changed and tail code "FN" of navy FASRON 107 added to the rescue band. Fleet Air Service Squadron 107 was stationed at NAS Keflavik, Iceland, until June 30, 1960, when it was deactivated. *Courtesy of US Navy*

An SA-16A makes a difficult rescue in churning seas of Okinawa's Buckner Bay in 1953. The crew has deployed a raft with pararescueman to transfer a sick seaman from a launch of a Korean ship. The Albatross was unable to take off in high seas and taxied to shore. The SA-16A was one of six assigned to the 2nd Air Rescue Group at Kadena AB, Okinawa. *Courtesy of USAF*

Against the rugged Iceland background in 1954 is SA-16A (serial no. 51-057) of the 53rd ARS at Keflavik AB. The triphibian's drop tanks are red, and wheel covers wore a flashy design. *Courtesy of Leonard H. Clark*

navigation equipment. Mk. IV boats built during 1953 and 1954 were designated by the Air Force as R-37A-, followed by the boat number. Major improvements in the Mk. IV featured an aluminum drop transom and propeller guards to protect people in the water. Typically assigned to busy airfields near bodies of water, CRBFs were small versions of World War II emergency rescue boat squadrons, from which some crash rescue boat flights evolved. The crash boat detachment of the 1st Emergency Rescue Squadron at Bermuda, for example, descended from the World War II 791st Quartermaster Boat Company. The largest number of crash boats was assigned to the 15th CRBF, based at Canal Point near Florida's West Palm Beach AFB. Since SA-16As of the amphibian training facility at the base often used nearby Lake Okeechobee, crash boats of the 15th provided rescue coverage. Beginning in late 1954, contracted salvage divers worked with crash boats to recover from the ocean bed debris from thousands of rocket launches from Cape Canaveral at the height of the Cold War. When rocket launches had been expanded to the Bahama Banks at the end of the decade, divers and crash boats were joined by a low-flying B-17 whose crew spotted rocket debris in the shallow, clear water. Besides CRBFs stationed along the continental US coastline, units could be found supporting air bases at Bermuda, Puerto Rico, Libya, Panama, Hawaii, Okinawa, and Japan, among others. Most common of the boat types were the 85-foot Model 379 and the 63-foot Miami, although smaller types were used. All crash rescue boat flights were inactivated by July 1956; however, a small number remained in service. Most of them were gone by mid-1957 as helicopters became increasingly effective in rescue work. The remainder survived into the 1960s for special purposes such as drone, missile, and dummy torpedo retrieval; anti-mine training; and towing targets for helicopter gunship training. All boats were mustered out by the early 1970s; crash rescue boat flights were not officially disbanded until September 1984.

In anticipation of downsizing that typically follows war, while standardizing and upgrading its equipment, leaders of Air Rescue focused on reducing the types of aircraft in its inventory. Ideally, they agreed, there would be two basic aircraft: a long-range fixed-wing plane and a powerful helicopter with greater range and payload. Two fixed-wing types already were in the MATS inventory and were battle proven; the select helicopter was just coming on board.

Easily surviving the cut was the venerable Douglas C-54. When the decision was made in 1953 to replace the SB-17 and SB-29 with a rescue version of the C-54, the modifications proposed by Air Rescue were so extensive that it was almost considered a new airplane. The amount of changes necessary to adapt the Skymaster to rescue work, along with slow replacement of the type in MATS, delayed its arrival to October 1955, one year later than originally planned. Rescue men found the wait worthwhile in view of the SC-54D's capabilities, including greater range and endurance than the Albatross. Its greater speed, plus the safety margin afforded by four engines, added to its appeal for long missions, which often involved rendezvous with aircraft in trouble. The SC-54D used less runway than its predecessors, its engine-out performance was better, and parts were easier to obtain.

First to get the Rescuemaster was the 36th ARS at Johnson AB, Japan. The squadron flew the first mission by an SC-54 in the Far East on December 21, 1955, when it searched for a USMC F3D Skyknight from NAS Atsugi. Within one year, the 36th, in addition to its trio of SC-54s, had four SA-16As and a pair of SH-19s.

More than sixty SC-54s would serve Air Rescue, the majority of which underwent modification to SC-54D "Rescuemaster" by Convair Fort Worth. Range increase was achieved with two 450-gallon fuel tanks installed in the fuselage, for a total of 3,720 gallons, which allowed flights lasting more than eighteen hours. Power was improved with Pratt & Whitney R-2000-11 Twin Wasp engines. Extensive remodeling of the interior included upgraded electronic and communications equipment, along with a galley and bunks for long-duration missions. Rescuemasters were winterized, which included floor heaters. Special seats were added at waist scanner positions where large blister windows from B-36s were installed. A unique antiskid braking system and a pneumatic floor-mounted flare launcher included in the conversion were firsts in air force aircraft. A specially built rear fuselage door could be opened in flight for paradropping PJs and MA-1 air rescue kits (ARKs). The SC-54D carried two ARKs, which comprised five bundles each; four forty-person inflatable lifeboats, which were inflated by static lines, were connected by 840 feet of floating line, and three survival kits were equally spaced along the line. The ARK was dropped upwind of survivors so that it would drift toward them, enabling them to grab the line to get into the boats and then pull in the survival kits. The ARKs enabled a single SC-54 to get 160 people out of the water, compared to the fourteen-person capacity of the SB-29's aluminum A-3 lifeboat.

Besides the SC-54Ds, a small number of SC-54Es and SC-54Gs were flown by Air Rescue. The E model featured revised fuel tanks and more-powerful engines, and its interior was easily converted from cargo to passenger. The G model was basically an E model but with upgraded engines. Since C-54s were built in a wide variety of models flown globally by military and commercial concerns, the availability of parts kept downtime to a minimum. Some SC-54s were serviced at Brussels by SABENA, the Belgian national airline, which flew the C-54's commercial equivalent, the DC-4.

Finished in natural metal with red trim, an SC-47A (serial no. 42-101000) of the Strategic Air Command at Baltimore-Friendship Airport, Maryland, in October 1958. The 8th Air Rescue Group, which was activated at Stead AFB in 1954 with the 63rd and 64th squadrons, eventually assumed the search-and-rescue role for SAC aircrew in polar and Pacific regions. The black-painted area on the aft fuselage is a mask for the APU exhaust. *Courtesy of Wayne Schultze*

An SB-29A "Super Dumbo" flies over Japanese waters in 1955 with a Grumman F9F-5P photo recon "Panther" of Det F, VC-61, aboard USS *Boxer* during a WestPac cruise. *Courtesy of US Navy*

Wearing a "tree suit," Pararescueman Harold Birtel demonstrates the jump position from an SA-16A of the 84th ARS during the 1950s. To his left is the inward-swinging rack for mounting two JATO units. Birtel was among the first group of PJs assigned to Southeast Asia in 1964. *Courtesy of USAF*

Besides Albatrosses and H-19s, the 48th ARS operated no fewer than a half-dozen SC-54s from 1956 to 1965. Based at Eglin AFB, Florida, the squadron, along with the Air Proving Ground Center, with five C-54s, served as good cover for the secret 1045th Operational Evaluation & Training Group, whose Detachment 2 flew ten C-54s to Tibet and against Cuba beginning in 1960.

Seldom, if ever, mentioned in historical annals is the SA-16A's involvement in America's protracted testing of atomic power. "Pacific Proving Grounds" was the name given the many sites in the Marshall Islands, along with other sites in the Pacific, where the US tested nuclear weapons from 1946 to 1962. The Air Rescue presence at the first atomic tests in 1946 was Task Unit 159, formed with a pair of SB-17s based at Eniwetok Island. Successive tests saw a large number of SA-16As assigned to various projects, beginning with Project Greenhouse in 1951. Albatrosses assigned to the project formed Air Task Rescue Unit 3.4.7, based at Kwajalein. Seven SA-16As were assigned for nuclear weapons experiments conducted under Operation Castle in 1954. And in 1956, an astounding number of Albatrosses, a total of seventeen, were on hand during atomic testing labeled Operation Redwing at Bikini Atoll. During 1955, 1956, and 1958, Hawaii-based 76th ARS maintained aircraft at Johnson Island for atomic bomb tests. From October 1957 to August 1958, the five SA-16As of the 64th ARS participated in Operation Hardtack, the multiple atomic tests that encompassed both Bikini and Eniwetok Atolls, as well as Johnson Island. Albatross crews flew more than two thousand hours, which included ten SAR missions. The 64th, which flew SA-16As and SC-47Ds since its activation at Norton AFB in April 1954, was transferred to Bergstrom AFB, Texas, in August 1959. By year's end the squadron's aircraft were being absorbed by the 41st ARS pending deactivation of the 64th in June 1960.

Equally impressive were the SA-16A's remarkable achievements in less destructive environs, such as 3rd Rescue Squadron's SA-16A s/n 49-082's rendezvous with USS *Whiteside* in 1951. On July 29, 1955, an Albatross of the 58th ARS, after rescuing nineteen survivors of a C-47 that had ditched in the Mediterranean, was unable to take off and thus taxied 90

True to its namesake, the Albatross was at home on the water. Here, SA-16A (serial no. 51-7177) of the 304th ARS beaches at Lake Washington, NAS Sand Point, in the 1950s. Veteran 304th Air Rescue pilot David Wendt said, "Beaching was fun. Land on the water, lower the landing gear taxiing in the water, approach the ramp at a fairly high speed, and hope you don't slide sideways and slip off a slimy, slippery ramp." *Courtesy of Ray Dowell / Felix McLarney collection*

Pararescuemen conduct a simulated rescue in Japan in May 1963. The rescue platform below the Albatross's Dutch door would not see use in Southeast Asian combat since its attachment and removal was too time consuming. Below the empennage is the weighted LORAN trailing antenna, which was wound on a drum in the aft compartment. *Courtesy of USAF*

miles to land. The following year, an Albatross was skillfully landed among 15-foot waves to rescue a B-26 bomber crewman. Since the unforgiving seas ruled out a takeoff attempt, the pilot turned sea captain and taxied his aircraft 98 miles back to Okinawa, an unofficial record. Topping the list for number of days on the water was HU-16B s/n 51-5279 of the 48th ARS at Eglin AFB, Florida. After recovering a nose cone from a missile launched at Cape Canaveral in February 1964, sea conditions rapidly worsened, which ruled out takeoff. For two days, the aircraft taxied in rough seas toward land, consuming nearly all its fuel. With a fuel truck lashed to its foredeck, the Coast Guard cutter *Hollyhock* arrived on scene two days later and took the Albatross in tow. Although a long fuel line was floated to the aircraft to top off its fuel tanks, huge waves kept the aircraft waterborne for another night. On the fifth day, with no break in the weather, the decision was made to attempt takeoff. The first run failed when an engine inadvertently feathered. On the second attempt it happened again. While the prop power panel was dried, the weather worsened. Tension mounted. Finally, with *Hollyhock* acting as a wind break at full speed, the pilot applied power, fired the JATO (jet-assisted takeoff) bottles, bounced the airplane three times, and broke free of its watery bounds. After a refueling operation not found in the manuals, and five days on rough open seas, that HU-16B went on to fly combat rescue missions over the South China Sea.

The Albatross repeatedly proved its worth, often in the worst that Mother Nature could deliver. In December 1953, a hapless crew of the 10th RS spent fifteen days on Alaska's

Taku glacier, when their triphibian SA-16A (serial no. 51-059) got bogged down in wet snow during the first of thirty to forty planned touch-and-go landings. After most of the aircraft's fuel was used taxiing in search of dry snow, plans were made for C-54s to drop drums of fuel. Meanwhile, on the glacier, a geological research team being supported by the Albatross made daily ski trips with supplies to the aircraft. Two parachute drops of fuel drums failed when the drums broke loose and became buried in 8 feet of snow, one drop a half mile from the aircraft.

On the twelfth day, the aircraft heater failed, so the pilot taxied down the glacier to the research site. Then the weather set in, and when it cleared, the crew discovered that they were over a 100-foot-deep crevasse. Finally, on the fifteenth day, an ARS SC-54 successfully dropped a fuel drum. The crew dug the aircraft out, hand-filled the wing tanks, and flew out, which required a takeoff run on more than a mile of snow.

The record length of time for an Albatross to remain stranded in snow began on January 7, 1954, when serial no. 51-5290 of the 51st ARS became stuck on the Greenland ice cap near Narsarrsauk during a snow-training flight. Weather held the aircraft captive for forty-seven days while two ski-equipped SC-47s made a total of thirty-one landings nearby to shuttle personnel and supplies. The SA-16A finally was dug out, fit with four JATO bottles, and flown out.

Throughout the decade, commercial fliers were warned to exercise caution in view of increased Communist air activity in the region of the South China Sea off China and Vietnam. When those warnings went unheeded, Albatross crews of the 31st Air Rescue Squadron at Clark Air Base, Philippines, worked in dangerous waters. On July 23, 1954, two Communist Chinese fighters shot down a Cathay Pacific Airways DC-4 off Hainan Island in the South China Sea. When the mayday sent by the crew of the stricken airliner was received by the

Besides an uprated engine, improved transmission, and autopilot, the H-21B featured hardpoints for mounting two 165-gallon external fuel tanks. Use of a single tank was common practice, as seen on this SH-21B (serial no. 53-4354) of the 54th ARS at Mud Lake, Goose AB, Labrador, in 1959. *Courtesy of Carl Damonte*

This SA-16A (serial no. 51-7168) of the 4th ARS at Hamilton Field proudly wore the squadron's Outstanding Unit Award for the unit's rescue of more than five hundred persons during the 1955 Northern California floods. Squadron aircrew flew both Albatrosses and SH-19s during the floods. *Courtesy of William T. Larkins*

31st ARS at Clark, two SA-16As (s/n 51-009 and 51-018) were scrambled. No. 009, flown by Captain Jack Thompson Woodyard (call sign "Dumbo 4-5"), landed in rough seas to rescue the nine survivors afloat in a dinghy. Accounts told by the survivors testified to the danger in the region and the treachery of the Communist regime.

To say that the Grumman SA-16A Albatross had proven indispensable was an understatement. Since the amphibian's versatility and dependability far outweighed its shortcomings, it was decided to put it through a modification phase to optimize its performance, versus designing a new aircraft around its fine points. Its keel already had been modified for better handling on the water, and mounts for JATO units, and an overhead flare pistol mount had been added.

Air Rescue officials and Grumman engineers collaborated to refine the SA-16A's basic design. Their conclusions called for increasing the wing area, enlarging the vertical and horizontal tail surfaces, and adding high-pressure deicer boots on cambered wing leading edges; each wing float doubled as a 206-gallon fuel tank. In its new configuration, the "Old Reliable" showed marked improvement in all phases of performance and handling. The amphibian's single-engine performance advanced from

The 55th ARS at Thule AB, Greenland, flew this colorfully marked SH-19A (serial no. 51-3856). Since metal "hot dog" floats added 385 more pounds than wheeled landing gear, they were replaced by nitrogen-filled floats. *Courtesy of USAF*

inferior to favorable, including the ability to climb on one engine. The first production SA-16B flew on January 25, 1957, with 241 SA-16As eventually upgraded.

Concurrent with modification of the Albatross was upgrading the SC-47 fleet, which comprised nearly eighty aircraft. As the oldest aircraft in the air force, the "Gooney Bird" was long obsolete, yet it was important to Air Rescue as a support and SAR platform until the fleet was up to strength with modernized aircraft. Limited modifications of SC-47s included improved electronics, a redesigned fuel system, and provisions for mounting JATO units to get the 30,000-pound aircraft off the ground. An MA-1 air rescue kit was routinely carried. The first improved Rescue Gooney was delivered in April 1956. Detachment 1 of the 60th ARS at Ashiya AB, Japan, was formed later that year to operate ten JATO-equipped SC-47s for short-field work. Before the squadron was deactivated just nine months later, it had flown SC-47s from Itami AB

(renamed Osaka Airport in 1959), along with SH-19s from Ashiya and Formosa. The SC-47s passed from the scene quickly as more Albatrosses and Rescuemasters appeared. Thirty remaining SC-47s were retired from air rescue during late 1958, with the very last Rescue Gooney pulled from frontline service in 1959. Other derivatives of the venerable C-47 would serve the air force for another decade, even adding another war to its long history.

The helicopter that Air Rescue officials envisioned as their primary rotary-wing platform was Piasecki's H-21 "Work Horse." Although the army was satisfied with the tandem-rotor H-21 as a troop and cargo transport, Air Rescue personnel had misgivings about its ability to perform the rescue mission. To help it adapt, proposed changes included an uprated Wright R-1820-107 engine, reinforcement of the hoist to lift 400 pounds, adding a radio compass, and a command radio that was more reliable in northern latitudes. Key modifications were

A survivor of a Northeast Airlines Convair 240 that crashed at Nantucket, Massachusetts, on August 15, 1958, is unloaded at Boston by an Air Rescue SC-54G. Serial no. 45-637 was the last SC-54G built. *Courtesy of USAF*

During the 1950s, an army L-20 "Beaver" at Ladd AFB, Alaska, periodically was requested by the 74th Air Rescue Squadron to air-drop equipment into areas not accessible by the squadron's Albatrosses. The Beaver often joined air force H-5 helicopters and Albatrosses in support of a rescue team that brought down climbers on Mt. McKinley. Here, a parajumper attaches food supplies to the Beaver's bomb shackle. *Courtesy of James LaCasse*

winterization, and mounting provisions for two external fuel tanks, extending its range to 650 miles. Deliveries of the SH-21B began in 1956 to the 6th and 10th Air Rescue Groups, which had squadrons in frigid climates. The Work Horse proved to be a good performer in temperatures well below zero, and it was well liked by those who flew and maintained it.

Not more than twenty SH-21A and B models were committed to Arctic rescue by 1957, its peak year of use. Safeguarding the SH-19's title as Air Rescue's main helicopter, nearly all of the SH-21Bs would be phased out of the ARS by 1961 due to their limited range and slow cruise speed. The Chickasaw's capabilities had been demonstrated in July 1952, when H-19As "Whirl-O-Way" and "Hop-A-Long" crossed the Atlantic to become the first helicopters to do so. The flight was intended to evaluate the practicality of ferrying helicopters over the North Atlantic, devise techniques to extend the helicopter's range, and study pilot fatigue.

Air Rescue squadrons of the early 1950s were equipped with a mix of Stinson L-5s, Sikorsky H-5s, medium-range Catalinas, SC-47s or SC-82s, and long-range SB-17s or SB-29s. By 1955, only a handful of SB-17s remained in service, along with about fifteen SB-29s. The 37th ARS (formerly Flight B, 3rd Rescue Squadron), when it relocated to Yokota AB, Japan, in mid-1954, flew the SB-29 to fill the long-range, overwater function for the Far East; the 37th ARS was deactivated on May 8, 1955. Later in the decade, the typical squadron flew SA-16s, SC-54s, and SH-19s.

The exception was Alaska's 10th ARS of the Alaska Air Command, which was reassigned to the Air Rescue Service in July 1950. The squadron's wide variety of wheel-, ski-, and float-equipped aircraft included a CG-15 glider. In November 1952, the squadron was redesignated the 10th Air Rescue Group, and its flights became the 71st and 72nd Air Rescue Squadrons at Elmendorf, the 73rd ARS at NS Adak, and the

74th ARS at Ladd AFB. Air force withdrawal from the Aleutian Islands caused inactivation of the 72nd and 73rd ARS in September 1953. A rescue coordination center was maintained around the clock at Elmendorf AFB. The 10th ARG made full use of its wide range of resources, which included land rescue teams with ground vehicles, dog teams, pararescuemen, helicopters, and amphibious and conventional aircraft. The group deployed entirely in Alaska, flying more missions than any other except the 3rd ARG in Korea. Most missions were for weather-related accidents and involved major search-and-rescue operations. Despite that responsibility and widespread support to civilians and the growing air defense forces of the Alaska Air Command, the decision was made to eliminate the 10th ARG completely in January 1958. Stripping Alaska of all air force search-and-rescue capabilities by deactivating the 71st ARS in March 1960 was the final blow, which drew fierce opposition from AAC officials and citizens alike.

Although the rescue coordination center remained, and four SH-21s were turned over to the AAC (albeit without flight and maintenance crews), the Civil Air Patrol took up the slack, along with other private and government agencies.

Termination of air force Air Rescue operations in Alaska signaled the beginning of an austerity program that in June 1957 had targeted ARS for a reduction to seven groups and sixteen squadrons. No longer could ARS perform its multifaceted mission; it was restricted to direct support of USAF air activity along established lines of communication, and it could no longer support combat operations, should they become necessary. Air Rescue policy had to be rephrased. Some leaders at USAF Headquarters levels inferred that ARS curtailment was the result of overemphasis on the humanitarian aspect of the Air Rescue mission, to the extent that it appeared as the primary mission. The performance of Air Rescue during peacetime, they contended, in actuality, was to train for combat. USAF Headquarters made clear its position with a letter to MATS Headquarters in 1958, affirming withdrawal of its wartime mission from the National Search and Rescue Plan. The letter, dated September 26, stated this in part:

> The Air Rescue Service will be organized, manned, equipped, trained, and deployed to support peacetime air operations. No special units or specially designed aircraft will be provided for the sole purpose of wartime search and rescue. Wartime rescue operations will be dictated by the capabilities of equipment used for peacetime SAR.

Reductions took the form of reorganization, which saw the 53rd ARS established at NS Keflavik, Iceland. Another change on the organizational chart of US Air Force, Europe (USAFE), was consolidation of the UK-based 66th and 68th ARS into the 67th ARS.

In the Pacific, in June 1958 the 2nd ARG was inactivated at Wheeler AFB, Hawaii, which it had called home since November 1955. Air Rescue leaders were reminded of the importance of supporting the Strategic Air Command in its long-range mission. To erase the blurred line between the primary mission (SAC coverage) and secondary mission (ARS capability in a combat theater) of the 8th Air Rescue Group, it was ordered to support SAC exclusively.

Further provisions of the reorganization had the Coast Guard designated as the Maritime Region Coordinator, meaning that USAF Air Rescue units venturing into maritime regions could expect to be approached by the Coast Guard, seeking agreement to use ARS facilities. That, in turn, had Air Rescue Headquarters asserting its position that "in all search and rescue incidents concerning distressed or lost US Air Force aircraft, equipment, or people, Air Rescue Service will be designated as the controlling agency at any time we so request." Air Rescue Headquarters avowed reciprocation with other services, maintaining its position as Inland Regional Coordinator and as the primary air rescue agency for the air force. In effect, the lines had been drawn, and everyone knew where they stood.

After the improved SH-19B helicopter had entered service during the mid-1950s, their number peaked, with more than one hundred serving Air Rescue worldwide. Improvements over the SH-19A included a more powerful Wright R-1300 engine, horizontal stabilizers to replace inverted types, a 600-pound-capacity rescue hoist, and downsloping the tail boom 3 degrees to prevent main rotor blade strikes during hard landings.

Noteworthy among the H-19's thirteen years of service in Air Rescue are humanitarian missions flown by the 59th ARS at Dhahran AB during flooding in Iraq's Tigris River valley in April 1954; SH-19A crewmen airlifted 15 tons of food to four thousand flood victims. In September 1958, a single SH-19B manned by rescue men of the 57th ARS saved forty-eight people aboard the Portuguese ship *Arnel*, which had run aground in the Azores. It took nearly five hours to rescue survivors by hoist and fly them to a nearby hilltop. During October 1959, an H-19 of the 33rd ARS hoisted twenty-nine crewmen from the grounded Japanese freighter *Zenko Maru*.

During the 1950s an air rescue capability was added to the Air Force Reserve, with activation by the Continental Air Command of five air rescue squadrons equipped with the SA-16A/HU-16B Albatross. Joining the Reserve force in 1956 were the 301st ARS at Miami International Airport; the 302nd at Luke AFB, Arizona; and the 303rd at Long Beach Airport, California. The 304th ARS came on board at Portland International Airport in 1957, and in 1958 the 305th at Michigan's Selfridge AFB.

During the decade, pararescuemen continued to apply their stock in trade as precision parachutists, medical technicians, and survival experts to save life. On April 16, 1954, Sergeants Elliot Holder and Robert Christiansen jumped to the crash site of a navy patrol bomber on Greenland's ice cap. High winds nearly dragged Holder to his death over a

True to its name "Arctic Rescuer," Piasecki YH-21 prototypes (serial nos. 50-1236 and -1240) arrived at Thule AB, Greenland, America's northernmost base, for evaluation in September 1953. Number 1240 crashed on November 17. No. 1236 is seen here testing first-generation float gear, which was found to be unwieldy and, therefore, was replaced with fuselage float gear.

1,900-foot precipice. Landing more than a mile from the crash, tremendous effort was required to reach the site. At one point the pair spent three hours traveling a quarter mile on steep, icy slopes. In the wreckage they found that all nine crewmen had perished. A howling Arctic storm with 100 mph winds pinned the rescue men down for eleven days. On the twelfth day, the winds subsided to allow a helicopter to pick them up.

A more successful mission occurred on February 13, 1953, when Sergeants Charles Abbott and John Bowers jumped at night to the flaming crash of a B-36 near Goose Air Base. It was 20 degrees below zero when they exited their SC-47. After crawling 300 yards through deep snow, they reached the survivors and treated the injured, and at dawn fourteen survivors and the pararescuemen were rescued by helicopter. By jumping, pararescuemen saved hours, even days, that it would take for ground parties to reach a disaster site. Countless rescues depended solely on the skills and fortitude of pararescuemen to reach a disaster scene to effect rescue and recovery.

WHAT GOES DOWN MUST COME UP

In this strange twist of logic, the air rescue community was approached to get a feel for its becoming involved again with pickup systems to retrieve equipment and humans from the air and from the ground. Although the practice of making snatches with specialized equipment and techniques had receded into the shadows with the advent of the helicopter after World War II, technology had opened the door to new possibilities in aerial recovery. Initiatives within various branches of the US military during the Cold War focused on snatching balloons conducting high-altitude surveillance of the Soviet Union. Under a multitude of code names, such activities had All American Engineering (AAE) providing retrieval equipment installed in USAF C-119 aircraft. The winch used was AAE's Model 80C, the same unit used for glider pickup during World War II. Further to that was exploiting Air Rescue Service expertise in aerial retrieval.

Although the extensive history of surface-to-air and air-to-air recovery was not widely publicized until modern times, personal accounts by those directly involved sidestep military secrecy to shed light on the major players involved. As interest in pickup systems gained momentum, all branches of the US military, along with various government agencies, participated in trials of the technique, using a wide variety of aircraft. The success of such trials left no doubt as to their value in air rescue.

The idea of using aircraft to snatch objects and humans, and even animals, from the ground and in midair is nothing new. The unorthodox practice dates back to the late 1920s, when dentist and inventor Dr. Lytle S. Adams devised a mail pickup system for the US Postal Service. Short of both funds and clout to pursue his ambitions, Adams teamed with Richard C. du Pont, which led to formation of the company All American Aviation (AAA). Refinement of Adams's system

led to regular mail pickups using Stinson SR-10 aircraft and later Noorduyn Norsemans, concurrent with secret research and development using a variety of aircraft during World War II. Having researched Nazi Germany's use of gliders in the invasion of Crete, du Pont theorized that his company's system could enhance glider operations. Dependent on a fleet of Stinson SR-10Cs, engineers at AAA quickly went to work testing the pickup of a glider and a man in a harness. In demonstrations of both techniques conducted at Fort Monmouth, New Jersey, on July 8, 1941, and at Wright Field in September, the standard AAS-4 airmail winch installed in an AAA's SR-10C successfully snatched a small "Midwest" glider and a weighted dummy. Afterward, a company report touted air pickup of heavier gliders, downed pilots, espionage agents, and numerous objects. The report was not far off the mark by mentioning the possibility of refueling aircraft in flight by

Significant aerodynamic improvements that resulted in the SA-16B included a 16-foot, 8-inch wing extension, which had a drooped leading edge with high-pressure deiced boots, replacing the A-model's leading-edge wing slot. The droop improved air flow over the wing, which kept ailerons effective up to a stall. Tail surfaces were enlarged, and most antennae were made flush. *Courtesy of USAF*

A Sikorsky SH-19B (serial no. 53-4455) faces into the wind, indicated by a floating smoke marker, to rescue a survivor off Honolulu Airport during the late 1950s. The helicopter was assigned to nearby Hickam AFB. *Courtesy of USAF*

The 1950s witnessed continuous development of the helicopter, with serial number prefix dates reflecting contract dates, and not year of manufacture. Tail boom and stabilizer configurations of H-19s changed continually from 1949 to 1955, with overhaul and field updates further confounding aircraft identification. This SH-19B, for example, has the droop tail boom introduced in 1955, although its serial number is 52-7521. *Courtesy of Raymond E. Vogler*

The SC-54G of the 9th Air Rescue Group, based at RAF Bushy Park, England, refuels at RAF Burtonwood. During its US service from 1942 to 1958, this Rescuemaster covered the Transatlantic Transport Route. Atop the fuselage of serial No. 45-556 are compass loop, nav dome / escape hatch, and glide path antenna. The small window above the "S" is the radio operator's station; opposite was the navigator's position. This aircraft went on to serve NASA and Aero Union as a fire bomber. *Author's collection*

After sustaining damage while alongside a merchant ship during the late 1950s, SA-16A (serial no. 51-7202) of the 58th ARS was taken in tow by the British frigate HMS *Wakefield* for an 18-mile trip to Malta. The Albatross crew had boarded the merchant ship to treat a critically ill sailor. Four tow lines and the aircraft's sea anchor were used for the tow in rough seas. *Courtesy of USAF*

Rescuers become the rescued. An SH-19B and USAF air rescue boat work in concert to rescue the crew atop a foundering Albatross in the Mediterranean near Wheelus Air Base in 1956. Green sea dye marked the hapless aircraft's final resting place. *Courtesy of USAF*

Few de Havilland L-20 Beavers are known to have been assigned to the Air Rescue Service. Although used mainly in a utilitarian role, L-20s could accommodate two litters with removal of the right-rear cabin seat. This L-20A (serial no. 52-6102) was attached to Detachment 15, Central Air Rescue Center, at Goodfellow AFB, Texas, during the late 1950s and early 1960s. *Courtesy of Norm Taylor*

using tanker gliders. Tests, first at du Pont Airport in Wilmington, Delaware, and later at Clinton County Airport in Wilmington, Ohio, used C-47s and eventually B-23, B-25, B-26, and B-17 aircraft. Besides gliders, improved winch systems were snatching P-47 and P-51 aircraft, minus their propellers to allow the pickup fitting to be attached to the propeller shaft. In 1943, AAA devised the Model 15 winch to bring snatch loads to within human tolerance, permitting the first human pickup to take place on September 5. The landmark event occurred at Wright Field, where pilot Norman Rentoul at the controls of an AAA Stinson SR-10C successfully snatched paratrooper volunteer Lt. Alexis Doster from the ground. Ensuing human pickups were accomplished by Norman S. Benedict, who during his US Army Air Corps / Air Force career was involved with aviation safety engineering. Benedict picks up the story:

The SA-16A (serial no. 51-7172) of the 28th ARS undergoes maintenance at Ramey AFB, Puerto Rico, during the early 1950s. The bow-mooring cable wrapped around the radome and was secured atop the fuselage, where it was accessible from the bow hatch, which has been removed. Pilots' overhead hatches are open. The SA-16A (serial no. 49-089) is in the background. *Courtesy of USAF*

USAF veteran Harry Conway of All American Engineering is snatched from AAE's airfield in Georgetown, Delaware, in November 1957. In one of three tests of the rescue technique, Conway is being reeled in through the cargo doorway of an ARS HU-16B (serial no. 51-7169) flying at 138 mph. AAE pioneered the technique prior to Lockheed Aircraft assuming the program. The AAE facility included the airfield, shops, jet car tracks, and arresting gear equipment. *Courtesy of USAF*

On May 3, 1966, off Pt. Mugu, California, the first HC-130H (serial no. 64-14859) made the first live surface-to-air recovery (STAR) pickup by a USAF crew. After the single-man pickup, the same day the first USAF two-man pickup occurred when ARRS commander Col. Allison C. Brooks and A3C Ronald Doll were snatched by the specially modified Hercules. *Courtesy of US Navy*

I entered this business as a 2nd lieutenant, design and development officer, at Wright Field on 1 January 1944, assigned to the Tow Target and Aerial Pickup Unit, Equipment Laboratory. I believe the first airplane snatched was a propellerless Cub in 1941. Aircraft known to be snatched include the Waco CG-4A glider and propless P-47s and P-51s. I believe the heaviest aircraft was a prototype Laister CG-15 glider that weighed 15,000 pounds, requiring a specially equipped B-17. My own trials with the lumbering Noorduyn Norseman C-64A were farcical. The Pentagon firmly insisted on the C-64A, which was a lumbering, unmanageable airplane. Nevertheless, on 23 September 1944 I successfully flew the second, third, and fourth human pickups at Wright Field.

While a 2nd lieutenant with a good pre-WWII background, I kept insisting the C-64A was headed for trouble. In the meantime our old C-47 with AAA winch arrived and I started making innumerable CG-4 pickups on wear-out tests. I insisted the flight path and "getaway" could be better made with the C-47. Subsequently, the "Hump" people asked for help, and I traveled there with a winch operator and 1,000 pounds of equipment. I had no trouble picking an able pilot, gave him eight passes knocking down the rope strung between two poles and two cargo passes with a 220-pound load. I then got in the harness to prove some points, becoming the first C-47 pickup subject.

During the Korean conflict I returned to the Inspector General Directorate of Flight Safety Research at Norton AFB, California. Despite critical duties there, the 3rd Air Rescue people in Japan demanded training, so I again embarked as an instructor pilot. The human pickup poles were 20 feet high compared to the glider heights of 12 feet to accommodate the large 1¼" nylon rope. All runs were conducted strictly to the 135 mph requirement. The pickup hook affixed to the lowered arm is about 40 feet from the pilot's seat, so it fell upon pilots to extrapolate these factors. Initially, "knockdowns" were required by flying through the station at the required height and airspeed—no drastic pull-ups. After about ten knockdowns, a 220-pound cargo container was added to also train new winch operators. The excellent pilot was given eight knockdowns and two cargo pickups before I climbed in the harness. In both wars I heard of no accidents, injures, or fatalities.

During training a brown C-47 landed, occupied by an "indigenous crew," that is usually an American pilot and copilot, and Asian crewmen. The C-47 had no insignia and not a single number anyplace. Its major approached me by name, advising that when the 3rd Air Rescue group was trained, I was to detach to his organization. I explained my stateside responsibilities and that he'd have to obtain the inspector general's permission for my extended stay. That died underway, since 3rd Air Rescue had enough pressing problems getting H-19 voluntary pilots for missions north of the parallel.

The "brown C-47" observed by Benedict likely belonged to the CIA-affiliated Joint Advisory Commission, Korea (JACK), which modified the AAE system to snatch agents from North Korea and mainland China.

While the pickup system was not widely used by conventional Allied forces during World War II, it saw frequent use for covert operations. A postwar switch to Beechcraft D-18s modified for mail pickup allowed passenger service. The company's widespread services resulted in a separation, with All American Aviation becoming All American Airways and flying DC-3 passenger service—which became Allegheny Airlines in 1952—and All American Engineering (AAE) for military contract work. The latter set the stage for an extensive program involving the US military using an interesting variety of aircraft modified with pickup equipment based on Dr. Adams's original design.

After surface-to-air recovery evolved into midair pickup of reconnaissance cameras and film capsules, US Air Force C-119 Flying Boxcars used during the 1950s were later replaced by helicopters and modified Lockheed JC-130s, which brought USAF Air Rescue closer to direct involvement. Meanwhile, All American Engineering had been placed under contract to design a new recovery system in the C-130. As early as September 1958, the USAF Air Rescue Service affirmed its plan to form units to recover camera equipment, space capsules, and personnel, both in midair and from the ground. Since the C-130 was its baby, Lockheed during the early 1960s agreed to develop the first mission capability, which was snatching people from the ground. Not only the concept but also live testing of air-to-ground pickup using a four-engine aircraft was hardly groundbreaking. At Eglin AFB in 1951, a TB-29 (s/n 44-70113), while trailing a hook line, skimmed the ground to snatch a live pig, and then a volunteer. Although the pig was enraged and the man was injured going through the hatch cut into the B-29's tail, tests proved the technique technically feasible for extracting persons from behind enemy lines. However, the project was dropped in view of the risk of a four-engine aircraft flying close to the ground, and to pursue higher-priority projects. Planners wisely drew from the experience and from those with experience in the aerial-recovery business to give the C-130 pickup capability. Lockheed then turned to All American Engineering and the Fulton Company, pitting them against each other in competitive bid.

The Fulton System was the brainchild of inventor Robert Edison Fulton Jr., who decided to refine All American Engineering's pickup system by placing the pilot's aim point straight ahead, versus AAA's system, which had the hookup behind the airplane, unseen by the pilot, where a hook snatched a load line strung between two poles. Basically, the Fulton-equipped aircraft drops by parachute a packet containing a harness attached to the braided nylon lift line. At the end of the line is a large balloon plugged into a helium bottle. The person to be rescued opens a valve to inflate the balloon, and

Secured to a steel drydock cradle, a damaged 63-foot ARB Mk. II is brought ashore at Naha, Okinawa, in 1954. The air rescue boat is designated R-2-692 and wears the name "HOT TACO" on its pilothouse. Doing the lifting is a Dravo Corp. barge derrick (BD 6235) of the 101st Marine Maintenance and Harborcraft Co. *Courtesy of US Army Transportation Museum*

Wheelhouses of USAF crash boats of the 1950s were painted either orange or orange yellow. Boat crews called the high-visibility scheme "Clown Colors." This view of the Mk. II R-2-692 of Naha Detachment, 22nd CRBS, at Okinawa in 1954 shows the "star and bars" insignia on the forward deck, and markings on the pilothouse awning. *Courtesy of US Army Transportation Museum*

another valve seals the balloon when it becomes fully inflated. The aircraft, with two extended nose prongs that form a 28-foot span, engages the lift line, which is guided into the crotch of the yoke. There, a mechanism locks it into place. With contact made, the balloon tears loose and the line trails back along the fuselage until a crewman in back snares the line with a long hook. He brings it inside, where it is transferred to a winch. Initial lift for the person in the harness is vertical, with gradual acceleration. The line gradually straightens with the line of flight, and the person is reeled aboard.

Joseph Pogue, whose credentials include Air National Guard pilot, aeronautical engineer, and AAE project engineer, explains:

The Fulton system required several steps that AAE would never use in their manned systems. One was knotting of the lifeline and another was cutting the lifeline. With the Fulton system, they flew directly into the lift line so that it was gathered by extended arms into the center, where a motor triggered to knot the lift rope so that it was attached to the aircraft nose. The pilot would then go into a steep climb to make the line fall along the bottom of the fuselage so the crew in back could swing a Shepard's [shepherd's] crook into the slipstream to snare the lift line and pull it into the aircraft, where it was transferred to a winch. This is where it got tricky, because the lifeline had to be cut once it was attached to the winch in order to reel in the line.

Fulton demonstrated his system using a B-17 and won the contract. We, at AAE, were perplexed by the choice; because of Fulton's lesser experience, that fact that his system knotted and cut the lifeline required extensive modification to the recovery aircraft, and a variety of other shortcomings. The only rationale we could come to was that by using the Fulton system, Lockheed would be able to sell a completely new line of C-130, which is exactly what they did. Several years after the new C-130 with the Fulton system went into service, AAE was contracted to design a system that could be quickly installed into the back of the Fulton recovery planes. Yes, the AAE system was eventually added to the Fulton system. Go figure.

Named "Skyhook" by Fulton, the system was funded by the US Navy's Office of Naval Research (ONR) beginning in 1950. The CIA took immediate interest, appropriated the project, and turned it over to the navy in 1954. Coined the "Skyhook Aeroretriever" in navy circles, the system garnered a great deal of attention by various US Navy labs, culminating on August 12, 1958, with the first human pickup, which took place at Quantico, Virginia. The Naval Air Development Unit (NADU), which had conducted the majority of tests, used its Lockheed P2V-5 Neptune aircraft to snatch Marine sergeant Levi W. Woods. The event was kept under wraps by the Department of Defense until October 1959. In contrast, a well-publicized rescue demonstration took place at NAS Patuxent River, Maryland, on June 14, 1961, during which a NADU P2V-7 snatched a Navy UDT member from a raft and, for the benefit of photographers, snatched another frogman from the beach. By the time of the event, the navy boasted more than five hundred pickups, seven of which were humans, nineteen animals, two hundred instrumented dummies, loads weighing up to 500 pounds, sixty-five night pickups, in all types of terrain. Nine different aircraft, both single- and multiengine, had been fit with the Fulton system. For the crewmen of the recovery aircraft, Woods's pickup was a welcome change from trial pickups of sheep and pigs. Some sheep did not survive, and one of the pigs spun uncontrollably in the air; once inside the aircraft, the enraged porker attacked the crew.

As a major player in the Skyhook project since its inception, the CIA kept its hands on the project even when it was in navy hands. "The Company" is known to have tested a Skyhook P2V-7, in air force guise as an RB-69A, during the late 1950s. The first operational use of the system had the CIA using a Skyhook-equipped B-17 to investigate an abandoned Soviet spy station on an Arctic island. Air Force captain James Smith and an ONR scientist, Lt. j.g. Leonard LeShack, parachuted from the B-17 onto the ice island and were picked up by the Skyhook Fortress six days later.

Seldom was a clear line drawn between air rescue and special operations, or, for that matter, between air rescue and any government program in which air rescue's skilled personnel, techniques, and aircraft could be employed. Even before transition of the Fulton system from navy to air force, some Air Rescue aircraft served dual roles testing pickup systems and flying search and rescue. In 1957, for example, an Air Rescue HU-16B Albatross was used in pickup tests at the AAE facility. Although the versatile Albatross was a good fit for Air Rescue, it proved unsuitable for pickup systems. The ideal pickup platform would be found in Lockheed's C-130. The business of snatching people from the ground by using USAF Air Rescue's HC-130H model, mounting both the Fulton and All American Engineering systems in the same aircraft, would come into its own during the 1960s.

Besides limited use in the training syllabus, some USAF Bell H-13 helicopters were put to use as base rescue aircraft. This H-13G (serial no. 53-3791) provided rescue coverage for F-86D Sabre pilots of the 15th Fighter Group of the Air Defense Command at Niagara Falls (New York) Municipal Airport. The H-13 crashed near the base on September 26, 1955, killing both pilots. *Courtesy of USAF*

Organizational charts of Air Rescue units throughout history illustrate periods of flux, which added to the complexity of the ARS mission. The charts document not only numerous changes in unit structure, designations, and locations, but activations and deactivations, often in on-again/off-again fashion. Severe reductions were imposed early in the decade, when, from March through December 1960, fourteen Air Rescue squadrons were inactivated, leaving three squadrons by year's end, along with 1,450 personnel. Of note is the Base Rescue Section at Hamilton Field, organized after the Hamilton-based 41st Air Rescue Squadron was deactivated. Led by Capt. Henry P. Fogg, base personnel, including flight crew, pararescuemen, and medics, took it upon themselves to provide around-the-clock rescue service with an SH-19B helicopter, a swamp glider, and a 40-foot air rescue boat named "Lady Hamilton." The boats covered San Pablo Bay off the end of Hamilton's runway. Besides conducting water recovery training, the unit worked with the Civil Air Patrol, coast guard, and civil authorities when called upon.

Concurrent with the cutbacks, USAF planners investigated new missions for the ARS, such as a local base rescue (LBR) program involving helicopters. Another area under consideration—transferring inland SAR responsibility to ARS—became reality on February 1, 1961. Rescue coordination centers (RCCs) at Robins AFB, Georgia; NAS Dallas; and Hamilton AFB, California, were renamed the Eastern, Central, and Western Air Rescue Centers (ARCs), respectively. The Central ARC shortly thereafter was relocated to Richards-Gebaur AFB, Missouri. It fell upon these centers to coordinate all search-and-rescue organizations available in the US. The severe cutbacks imposed in 1960 were short lived, thanks to newly elected president John F. Kennedy, who overwhelmingly supported the military; on June 18, 1961, most of the squadrons deactivated the previous year went back in business. Overseas, the 67th ARS at Prestwick, Scotland, stationed two detachments in Germany, two in France, and one in Spain. Southern Europe was served by the 58th ARS in Tripoli, with

detachments in Italy and Turkey. In the North Atlantic, the Labrador-based 54th ARS fielded detachments in Greenland and Newfoundland. Covering the vast Pacific region was the 33rd ARS at Okinawa, with a detachment in the Philippines. The 36th ARS in Japan had three detachments in country and one in Korea. The 79th ARS in Guam provided coverage for the Far East. The Eastern Seaboard was the responsibility of the 55th ARS at Bermuda, while the 48th ARS was positioned in Florida. Global response to aid other countries often paid dividends in foreign relations. For example, Air Rescue's assistance to the people of Spain during 1962 floods resulted in automatic renewal of base rights agreements, which otherwise required prolonged negotiations.

As part of a service-wide aircraft redesignation system in 1962, the "S" prefix for rescue aircraft was changed to "H." The Douglas SC-54, for example, became the HC-54. Forty HC-54s were in the air rescue inventory when the new designation system went into effect. By 1965, thirty Rescuemasters were on the inventory, with twenty-four in service dispersed among twelve air rescue squadrons.

At the beginning of the decade, Air Rescue Headquarters was at Orlando AFB, Florida. Major overseas air rescue centers were the Atlantic ARC at Ramstein AB, in Germany, and the Pacific ARC at Hickam AFB, Hawaii. Subordinate to the Pacific ARC was the rescue coordination center of the 51st Fighter Interceptor Wing's Air Defense Control Center (ADCC) at Okinawa. The ADCC's primary mission was defense of the Ryukyuan Islands, with rescue as a secondary mission. Regional rescue coordination centers were located in Panama and Alaska, with smaller centers in Japan, the Philippines, and Vietnam. Early in the 1960s, the center in Vietnam soon was in dire need of rescue service and would attain proportions never imagined at the beginning of the decade. Before addressing the Vietnam situation, Air Rescue leaders planned strategy after ARS was tasked in 1961 with the search for and recovery of space hardware and all manned space missions. Adding to Air Rescue's workload in 1961 was the Berlin Crisis,

Although insufficient range and low cruising speed limited the SH-21B's effectiveness, it saw use with the 58th ARS in Libya to stand downrange alert during manned space missions. Here, serial no. 52-8666 trains with a Mercury capsule in the Med in April 1963. Practices were held day and night prior to staging on Mauritius Island, Indian Ocean, which was a secondary splashdown site for Mercury. Compared to the H-21A, the B model had a larger rear doorway, autopilot, and mounts for jettisonable fuel tanks. By 1961, Air Rescue retired all but four SH-21Bs, which performed the local base rescue mission in the US. *Courtesy of James LaCasse*

Moroccan flood survivors are taken aboard an SH-19B (serial no. 52-7498) of the 58th ARS when heavy rains caused rivers to overflow their banks in January 1963. *Courtesy of USAF*

which had ARS units committing aircraft and crews to cover the deployment of units staged for possible intervention in Europe. More than a hundred citizen airmen of the Reserve air rescue squadrons voluntarily assumed active duty to deploy Albatross amphibians to provide rescue coverage for Air National Guard jet fighters sent to Europe. Four Albatross aircraft and crews went to Goose Bay, Labrador, and Prestwick, Scotland; two stood alert at Eglin AFB, Florida. In fall 1962, Air Rescue crews and aircraft again deployed to bases in Florida to participate in the Cuban Missile Crisis, this time with HC-54 Rescuemasters and HH-43B helicopters joining HU-16Bs; ARS units operated throughout the Caribbean during this tense period. Although the five Albatross-equipped Reserve Air Rescue squadrons did not maintain an alert posture, they flew almost every type of Air Rescue mission. Roger Ferguson, who proudly served as part of an Albatross crew, provides this insight:

It wasn't until I started to read my logbook that I came to the realization of what a benign aircraft the HU-16 Albatross was. Not like the B-52 I had flown on active duty—multiple engine failure, blown tires, electrical failure, explosive decompression, a duck through the copilot's window. No Sir! The log proclaims no flight problems in the two years that I had flown as the "Nav" for the "Weekend Warriors" of the 305th Aerospace Rescue and Recovery Squadron.

The '16 got us where we intended with no emergencies. It took forever at 150 knots airspeed (sometimes a lot slower with a mean headwind) but we arrived, did our job, and went home. Every so often we lost the weight attached to the trailing wire antenna for the LORAN. But we wound the cable in slowly, without it strangling the tail structure.

The equipment was ancient. The radar was old and sometimes temperamental. The LORAN was a spiky display which left you wondering which blip to select for your navigation plot. But the plane was sturdy and reliable. The '16 wasn't sleek and it wasn't symbolic of man's conquest of the air. But it left the ground easily and returned you there safely.

As a reservist, the '16 wasn't a day-to-day relationship. We flew mostly on weekends. However, these men, who had other jobs, came together quickly when an authentic rescue mission suddenly developed. We searched for a lost white Cessna that had crashed in an area covered with snow, and [for] military aircraft down in the Atlantic. We did our search patterns over many miles of the earth's surface trying to find a pilot who changed his destination without altering or closing his flight plan. While he slept in some rented room, we strained our eyes in vain, seeking that glimmer of light which told us we had gotten there and located the survivor's desperate signal.

I will never forget my first water landing. It was on the warm waters of Pensacola Bay. The nav's visual reference outside the aircraft consisted of a small window mounted under the wing. I thought we had sunk! Once we touched down, the outside world was blotted out by a solid wall of green water. After the landing had been completed, my heartbeat returned to normal as the water receded and daylight returned.

In June 1965, the '16 proved its mettle when our crew tried to find the crash site of a military transport near the Bahamas. Operating out of Homestead AFB, we had been searching most of the day at low level. Turning for home, we were confronted with a wall of thunderstorms which had drifted off the Florida land mass. The aircraft could not climb

What might have been . . . this was Boeing-Vertol's 11th Model 107II, which won a fly-off against Sikorsky's S-61R. An air force order for twelve machines to replace H-21s for Arctic rescue was canceled in late 1962 due to contractual issues, and the switch was made to S-61Rs. The Model 107—which fell into the USAF designation system as the XH-49A—was painted white with both USAF markings and civil registration N6679D. *Courtesy of Boeing-Vertol*

The unmistakable similarities of Kaman's marine HOK-1 and the air force H-43 leave no doubt as to the latter's lineage. Spawned from the US Navy and Marine Corps HTK-1, HOK-1, and HUK-1, the air force H-43 began life in 1958 as the third-produced HOK-1, complete with USAF markings and a rescue hoist over the left doorway. Kaman billed its HOK-1, including BuNo 125530 seen here, as a "Flying Fire Engine." *Courtesy of US Navy*

The USAF Helicopter School relocated from Randolph AFB, Texas, to Stead AFB, Nevada, in July 1958, with the H-43A as part of the syllabus. The arrival of the first H-43B Huskie in April 1960 marked the school's conversion to all-turbine helicopters. This H-43A (serial no. 58-1834) works with a derelict B-29 fire trainer at Stead. *Courtesy of USAF*

An HH-43B flight engineer directs his aircraft to a positioner pole to place the 900-pound fire suppression kit on its specially built heater trailer at MacDill AFB in 1963. This was the original "soft-hose" FSK nicknamed "Sputnik." "Bear-Paw" skis were standard landing-gear components. *Courtesy of USAF*

above the towering anvils, so we chose the middle route—between the cells, using radar to detect the weakest area of return. Navigation was forgotten as I kept my face pressed into the radar glare shield. Left and right and right some more, we snaked our way through the buffeting storms. We would float up on an updraft and get slammed down on the downdrafts. But the airplane (no. 17169) took the storms in stride. The engines never faltered and the wings stayed on—what more could one ask?

One of the most spectacular flights was a night self-illumination mission. Parachute flares were dumped out the door in a timed sequence, then the aircraft quickly descended to land on the water while the descending flares provided the light necessary to see the surface. Over Lake Huron, one of the flares burned through its parachute and fell like a bomb into the lake. Since the flare had its own oxidizer, it continued to burn even when it hit bottom. The burning flare lent a surrealist effect as the light was diffused under the water. A nearby lake freighter glided over the light like a ghost ship. Wish I had a video camera that time.

Most of our flight time was spent at lower altitudes. It became an event if we ever had to buckle on the oxygen mask. I believe the highest I had been in the '16 was 13,000' MSL. It must have been rare since I recorded it in the log.

Circling takeoffs on water were always thrilling. There we would be, going around in circles trying to build up speed while trying not to bury the wing in the water or hit boaters attracted by the maneuver. Some pilots, no matter how often they tried, could not get the aircraft up on the "step" sufficient to break the water friction and achieve takeoff. For others, it was a "piece of cake."

Some bold aeronautical engineer designed mounting lugs for JATO bottles to achieve takeoff speed quicker. These things were really rockets that were difficult to mount on the aircraft exterior when you are bobbing around on the water! But once those things were in place and working properly, they produced a lot of thrust in a hurry—and you were up, up and away!

We said goodbye to the HU-16 in February 1966, when it was replaced by the HC-97, a converted air force tanker. It was a good two years for me. I always felt safe in that airplane. But then again, we were RESCUE!

LOCAL BASE RESCUE

When the local base rescue (LBR) concept—that of using base helicopters for aircraft accidents—was examined during the mid-1950s, a 1956 study determined that since 51 percent of accidents (49 percent on landing and 2 percent taxiing) occurred on base, they were best handled by emergency land vehicles. This led examiners to the conclusion that the LBR concept would make air rescue assets available in areas of lesser need than for flight emergencies and crashes beyond the immediate response of base crash units. The results of a two-year government study stated in 1958 that 96 percent of

crashes occurred within a 61-mile radius of air bases. Both studies pointed to the need for a fast and reliable method of rescuing aircrew in areas inaccessible to ground fire apparatus. Planners felt that the solution could be found in a small, high-performance helicopter that could perform hoist rescue, carry firefighters, and transport the injured.

During the 1950s, air force officials had kept a close eye on marine corps experiments with helicopters in the firefighting role. The concept was not new to the marines, who early in the decade attached a "Helitank" to an H-19's hoist cable. Comprising two 50-gallon water drums, a pump, and 300 feet of hose, the unique package self-released when it touched the ground. Kaman Aircraft Corporation in 1957 capitalized on the marine experiments by billing its HOK-1 as a "Flying Fire Engine." The Marine Corps had taken its cue from the US Navy, which took delivery of the HOK-1 prototype in 1950. Early Kaman models got the attention of air force officials, who conducted trials with the third-built HOK-1. Carrying the fire suppression kit on its cargo hook, sporting a rescue hoist over the left doorway, and wearing US Air Force markings, the HOK-1 sold itself to the "Blue-suiters." The air force sent out proposals for bids to fulfill its LBR helicopter requirement. Kaman's winning design quickly led to a contract for eighteen piston-powered H-43As, which were based on the Marine HOK-1. The first two H-43As went to the 3640th Pilot Training Wing at Laredo AFB, Texas, during January 1959.

Each of the three air rescue centers (ARCs) controlled a reactivated squadron comprising H-43 LBR detachments for air base coverage across the US. Under the Eastern ARC, the 44th ARS in March 1959 began LBR coverage with eleven detachments at seventeen air bases; all were assigned H-43Bs except Detachments 53 and 54, which had H-43As. By the end of the 1960s, the squadron had twenty-two detachments, including those in Canada, the Canal Zone, and Greenland. The Central ARC controlled the 43rd ARS, with fifteen LBR detachments (five with H-43As) covering sixteen bases beginning in January 1959. By 1970, that number rose to eighteen detachments. Under the Western ARC, the 42nd ARS in October 1960 began with nine LBR detachments covering seventeen bases; only Detachment 16 flew the H-43A. By 1970, thirteen detachments of the 42nd were covering twenty-one bases.

During the army's search for a new turbine-powered helicopter, Lycoming developed the T53 power plant; however, the army's XH-40—which evolved into the famed UH-1 "Huey"—was not ready for flight test. Under air force contract, on the army's behalf, the Kaman HOK-1 was selected for the turbine installation. Charlie Kaman could not have been happier, since the air force follow-on order both for piston-powered H-43As and turbine-powered H-43Bs was changed to an all-turbine line.

During initial tests with fuel fires, a phenomenon had come to light that told the air force they got more than they bargained for. Kaman's counterrotating, intermeshing rotors,

In July 1964, the Federal Aviation Administration tested the HH-43B "Huskie's" rotor downwash ability to blow a path through flames of crashed commercial airliners. The test was conducted using a Boeing C-97 at the FAA's facility near Atlantic City, New Jersey. *Courtesy of USAF*

they discovered, exhibited the ability to generate huge volumes of low-velocity air with a forward thrust, which opened a "cool" corridor through the flames. Further testing showed that firefighters could walk through this pilot-directed corridor unharmed to fight fire from within and reach the aircraft to rescue trapped occupants. Since rescue was paramount, it became more important to form a path and control the fire, rather than attempt complete extinguishment.

During February 1958, the air force placed an order for twenty H-43Bs, powered by the 825 hp Lycoming T53-L-1A gas turbine engine. Replacing the H-43A's piston engine with the turbine allowed complete redesign of the cargo compartment to accommodate four litters and a medic, or firefighting or rescue crew. Deliveries of H-43Bs powered by upgraded 860 hp T53-L-1B engines began in June 1959. Initially, H-43A and B models were assigned under various commands, in contrast to their intended rescue mission. Some filled the LBR role by using fire suppression kits (FSKs). The original FSK used with air force H-43s comprised a 78-gallon water tank topped by a 5-gallon foam tank. When pressurized, 690 gallons of aerated foam mixture could be discharged through a 150-foot "soft" hose and nozzle. When not slung beneath

the aircraft, the 950-pound FSK, nicknamed "Sputnick," stood ready atop a trailer featuring a heater burner beneath the water tank.

A typical crash scenario had the tower alerting the LBR detachment that an aircraft in trouble was inbound. The pilot lined up with a positioner pole, which placed him over the FSK, which was quickly attached to the H-43's cargo hook. The helicopter followed the aircraft during its landing run, and in the event of crash or fire the FSK was quickly lowered to the ground. Onboard firefighters were offloaded, pressurized the FSK system, and advanced the hose to clear a path through the flames. Simultaneously, the pilot hovered about 10 to 20 feet off the ground with the rotor system at the edge of the fire, creating a path and helping to roll the foam pathway. Upon reaching the aircraft, firefighters were busy locating crash exits, disarming ejection seats, cutting power supplies, and removing victims. Through constant practice, firefighters and crew honed the coordination and skills necessary to save lives.

In December 1960, the air force chief of staff directed that all independent LBR units be placed under the Air Rescue Service. The changeover was complete by October 1961, and by year's end, sixty-nine LBR H-43s were operational at all major

Stranded and pitching on heavy seas 140 miles east of Grand Abaco Island, Bahamas, in March 1964, the HU-16B (serial no. 51-5279) is held fast by the coast guard tender *Hollyhock* while the ship's crew floats a fuel line to the aircraft. Unable to take off in rough seas, for two days the Albatross had taxied toward land, consuming nearly all of its fuel. Aircraft and crew spent five days on the water before bad weather subsided, permitting JATO-assisted takeoff. *Courtesy of US Coast Guard*

air force installations. A typical LBR unit consisted of two aircraft, one of which stood twenty-four-hour alert. The LBR force included seventeen H-43As, fifty-eight SH-19Bs, and four SH-21Bs. The rescue H-19s and H-21s were not equipped for fire suppression and were phased out as more H-43Bs were delivered. By December 1961, seventy LBR elements were based worldwide, with 148 helicopters assigned. Under the revised designation system implemented in 1962, the H-43B became the HH-43B, which crews named the "Huskie." US Air Force orders for H-43Bs would total 175 aircraft.

The Huskie's crew initially comprised pilot, firefighter, and medical technician. That was soon increased to include copilot, flight engineer, and an additional firefighter. Kaman supplied the first fire-extinguishing unit for its helicopters; however, the H-43's FSK was designed by the Wright Air Development Division at Wright-Patterson AFB, Ohio, and built by Surface Combustion Corporation of Columbus, Ohio. An improved skid-mounted FSK appeared in the mid-1960s. Rigid, reel-mounted hose replaced fabric-covered, rubber-lined hose, and stabilizing vanes were added to prevent oscillation in flight. Huskies that were stationed near large bodies of water were equipped with emergency flotation gear, which consisted of inflatable bags contained in fairings at each side of the fuselage and between the tail booms; it was found that the bags alongside the fuselage, when inflated by their gas actuators, pressed against cabin doors, impeding their opening.

Detachment 1 of the 54th ARS at Thule Air Base, Greenland, conducted the first tests of the flotation system in late 1963.

In September 1963, the commander of Detachment 3, a rescue control element in Vietnam, submitted a requirement study that included recommendation for a combat-modified HH-43B. Faced with the realization that Huskies would be operating in the unfriendly skies of Southeast Asia, air force planners and Kaman engineers went to work to improve the HH-43B's combat survivability. A more powerful Lycoming 1,100 shp (shaft horsepower) T53-L-11A engine replaced the original T53-L-1. Fuel tanks were made self-sealing, and a 150-gallon tank was installed in the cabin to increase range to 140 miles. Nearly 800 pounds of titanium armor was added to doorways, cabin, cockpit floor, oil cooler, engine, and lower windshield; the windshield itself was reinforced. The rescue hoist cable was lengthened from 100 to 217 feet; attached to the cable was the new Kaman-developed forest penetrator, which replaced the time-honored kapok horse collar. The first six of the new models designated HH-43F emerged from the Kaman factory in October 1964; another six were delivered one year later. Only these twelve machines featured the armor installation for duty in Southeast Asia. During 1970 and 1971, 155 of the 208 "B" models produced were brought up to HH-43F standard with the uprated engine.

When the USAF Helicopter School relocated to Stead AFB, it became the 3638th Flying Training Squadron (Helicopter). Student pilots arrived fixed-wing-rated but underwent training in the H-21B and H-19B. This H-19B (serial no. 51-3928) wears the squadron livery for H-19s. Before the squadron made its next move to Sheppard AFB, in 1965, its H-19Bs had flown numerous SAR missions and had participated in a variety of assignments, including SAR for rocket and nose cone recovery during Operation Dominic atomic tests in the South Pacific. *Courtesy of USAF*

SPLASHDOWN

Just weeks after its creation in October 1958, the National Aeronautics and Space Administration (NASA) began training astronauts in preparation for space flights. Beginning in 1961, NASA embarked on a protracted program during which it conducted thirty-two US manned spacecraft missions, ending in 2004 with space shuttle flights. Prior to rocketing Alan Shepard into space on May 5, 1961, NASA had worked closely with the Department of Defense to establish a global recovery network to ensure safe recovery of astronauts, regardless of the circumstances of their return to Earth. Since all manned space flights would terminate in Mother Earth's oceans, US Navy ships and their aircraft took center stage as the primary means of recovery. Included on the long list of support forces committed to the space program was the USAF Air Rescue Service. A tall order went out from NASA to friends in high places. From Air Rescue, NASA required helicopters to pick up astronauts and their capsules if the launch was aborted on the pad or immediately after liftoff. NASA's second requirement was fixed-wing aircraft in the launch abort region from Bermuda to the African coast. And last, fixed-wing aircraft designated primary recovery teams at bases around the globe to respond to radar-predicted contingency splashdowns of space vehicles.

Helicopters aboard US Navy ships did the close-in work at splashdowns if missions went according to plan. Aboard the helicopters were navy frogmen of UDT teams that had trained extensively for their recovery roles. In the event that splashdowns occurred far distant from planned target areas, and air force aircraft were first to arrive on scene, PJs who had been trained and were equipped for astronaut recovery were aboard the aircraft to parachute into the ocean. The pararescuemen were part of the crew of large ARS aircraft:

the SC-54 and HC-97, and later the HC-130. Even elite navy frogmen noted that their air force counterparts jumped from their aircraft at altitudes of about 1,000 feet with full SCUBA gear and other equipment, a feat the frogmen described as significantly more difficult and dangerous than their 15-to-20-foot jump from a hovering helicopter.

It was PJs who took center stage on May 24, 1962, when the "Aurora 7" spacecraft with astronaut Scott Carpenter splashed down 250 miles from recovery ships. Pararescuemen A1C John Heitsch and SSGT Ray McClure of the 41st ARS jumped from an SC-54 to pay a surprise visit to Carpenter as he floated in his raft in the Atlantic, east of Puerto Rico. Heitsch reached the raft first, surfacing on Carpenter's blind side, reached up, and tapped him on the shoulder. The startled spaceman heard simply, "Hi," and asked Heitsch, "How did you get here?" When McClure joined them, they inflated rafts, secured the flotation collar, and waited for the navy; USS *Intrepid* made the pickup. On March 17, 1966, when Gemini 8 made an emergency splashdown in the East China Sea, an HC-54 (call sign "Naha Rescue") of the 79th ARRS (Aerospace

This HH-3C (serial no. 63-9683) was the first in Air Rescue. Here, in September 1965, using its low-response cargo sling, it conducts lift tests of a dummy Gemini 8 module while assigned to Detachment 15, Eastern Air Rescue Center, at Florida's Patrick AFB. The 8,000-pound-capacity sling reduced load shift feedback by keeping the load close to the center of gravity, thereby improving control. *Courtesy of USAF*

One of the priorities in designing the Model S-61R (H-3) was its ability to float. A boat hull was laid first like a ship's keel, with large sponsons added. The S-61R (H-3) was then designed around the engines. Initial deliveries briefly wore this pea-green scheme. Serial no. 63-9681 was photographed at Eglin AFB, Florida, in 1965. *Courtesy of John Lindgren*

Showing details of the CH-3C's underside, serial no. 64-14224 of Det 15, EARRC, at Patrick AFB practices astronaut recovery with an early hoist prior to Gemini launch. Detachment 15 was responsible for astronaut recovery over the entire Cape Canaveral launchpad. *Courtesy of James LaCasse*

One of Detachment 15's four CH-3Cs sits on the Banana River west of Cape Kennedy after an engine driveshaft failure. CMSgt. Robert Hamilton, who had cut his teeth on B-17 maintenance in World War II, asked pilot Carl Damonte if he could power it to shore on one engine. The helicopter was stripped to reduce weight, then Damonte taxied to shore for an engine change and the flight back to Patrick. Converted to CH-3E with the more powerful GE-T58-5 engine, no. 63-9688 spent its entire USAF career in the state of Florida. *Courtesy of USAF*

Rescue and Recovery Squadron) arrived in time for pilot Capt. Lee Schneider to see the splashdown. Capt. Creighton W. Frost of the 33rd ARRS was at the controls of an HU-16B 100 miles from splashdown and arrived as the HC-54 was lining up to deploy its PJs, flotation collar, and MA-1 kit. Frost was told he was the final authority and could land for the pickup. After the commander of the 33rd ARRS radioed, "Go!," Frost went down to 100 feet for his sea evaluation: "Sea condition favorable, swells 10 feet, wind calm, swells running 500 feet apart. Making final run." And then the HC-54 radioed: "Search Three, this is Naha Rescue, radio relay from Pacific Net Control, cancel pickup by HU-16." Frost was ordered not to land because, it was later explained, the commander of Project Gemini feared the Albatross might break up on the water. While it's possible the commander was unaware of the HU-16B's fondness for water, or Frost's skill, the more believable reason is the navy's aversion to the air force stealing the show. The trio of PJs attached the flotation collar to the capsule and opened the hatches for astronauts Neil Armstrong and David Scott as they awaited the arrival of USS *Leonard F. Mason*, still three hours away. The HC-54 remained overhead, while another HU-16B piloted by Capt. David A. Sisson arrived to orbit at higher altitude to relay radio transmissions.

Although improvements in the space program resulted in near bull's-eye splashdowns until the end of Mercury missions, NASA retained involvement of the Air Rescue Service for upcoming Gemini and Apollo programs. Although support of space programs along with traditional requirements defined the course for the ARRS, by the late 1960s, expanding NASA endeavors and subsequent ARRS support were depleting Air Rescue capabilities. Preparation for support of the space program included an intense regimen of NASA-ARS training missions. One such mission in 1964 underscored the danger in the air rescue business.

Among a series of training missions off Bermuda was an exercise on June 29, in which PJs aboard two aircraft were to jump into the ocean and practice securing a Gemini capsule. The two aircraft—HC-97G serial no. 52-2773 of the 55th ARS at Kindley AB, Bermuda, and HC-54D serial no. 42-72590 of the 57th ARS at Lajes AB, Azores—collided and crashed, killing all seventeen aboard both aircraft. Just seconds before the collision, five PJs had jumped from the HC-54 and two

Actor Yul Brynner with the 36th Air Rescue Squadron at Tachikawa AB, Japan, in 1964, during filming of *Flight from Ashiya*. Brynner portrayed a pararescueman in the film. *Courtesy of Bill Lyell*

The rescue version of the C-54 was easily identified by its pointed nose, which housed APS-42 search radar, and by large blister windows at waist scanner positions. The national insignia of HC-54D (serial no. 42-72696) covers a specially built, inward-opening door for paradrops. A cargo drop guide was stowed nearby to aid in ejection of MA-1 air rescue kits. The Rescuemaster is seen at Prestwick, Scotland, in March 1965 while assigned to the 67th ARS, which flew four HC-54Ds and two SA-16A amphibians. *Courtesy of Jean Magendie*

from the HC-97. The remaining PJ, A2C Larry W. Carleton, went down with the HC-97.

So committed to the space program were some air rescue squadrons that in July 1965 they were redesignated air recovery squadrons. Units known to have undergone the change are the 33rd, 36th, 48th, 54th, 57th, and 67th ARS. On January 1, 1966, concurrent with the redesignation of the Military Air Transport Service (MATS) as the Military Airlift Command (MAC), the Air Rescue Service became the Aerospace Rescue and Recovery Service (ARRS) to reflect its expanded role of worldwide rescue and recovery support for NASA's manned space flights. All squadrons then became aerospace rescue and recovery squadrons.

Indicative of the broad scope of ARS involvement is the fact that between thirty and fifty aircraft might be standing alert or airborne during launch and splashdown. More than thirty HC-130Hs, which covered the launch abort area from Bermuda to the African coast, would be deployed worldwide for up to fifteen days. Meanwhile, CH-3Cs of Det 15, EARRC,

Taken from the tanker KC-130F (GV-1) BuNo 148891 of Marine Aerial Refueler Transport Squadron 252 (VMGR-252) on December 15, 1965, this photo records the first H-3 air-refueling connection. Using JH-3C serial no. 62-12580, this was a feasibility trial, with no fuel transferred. The center-mounted refueling boom was relocated to the right side, since it provided only marginal stability and interfered with access to the avionics compartment. The shift also improved the pilot's ability to line up with the tanker's drogue. *Courtesy of USAF*

With the 17-foot dummy refueling boom moved to the right, the JH-3C/E undergoes tests with the JHC-130P (serial no. 65-0988), the first-built "P"-model rescue Hercules in mid-1966. The HH-3E (serial no. 65-12777), the first-built "E" model, was also used in the tests conducted by the Aeronautical Systems Division at Wright-Patterson AFB. Test director and HH-3E Project test pilot was Capt. William Eastman, along with Maj. Robert Nabors. Air Rescue project pilots were captains Carlton Damonte (HH-3E) and William Tripp (HC-130P). Two hose reel pods were from a USMC KC-130F, each containing 85 feet of hose. *Courtesy of USAF*

at Patrick AFB, covered the launch site area. As long as spacecraft could splash down on target near navy recovery ships, ARS aircraft maintained a standoff, yet alert, posture, with PJs in wetsuits and NASA-supplied capsule flotation collars ready. Les Robbins reveals a little-known fact:

I was part of contingency recovery crews for each Gemini mission when I was a radio operator in the 58th ARS/ARRS from 1964 to 1967. On the HC-97Gs, we carried six Army Special Forces guys with us on several missions in addition to our PJs. They ensured that nobody but US contingency teams got to the capsule and its astronauts if they came down at an unplanned location. Those guys were super serious

about it (but they were lousy poker players). They were badass fun guys.

Although Geminis 3, 4, and 5 missed their splashdown targets, navy recovery forces saved the day. But things didn't always go as planned, and it was Air Rescue, well, to the rescue.

Besides manned space flights, the ARS was regularly involved with unmanned space flight recovery operations. Recovering equipment from space was nothing new for Air Rescue. During the Cold War, in particular, the air force launched numerous spy satellites to take pictures or monitor various transmissions. Since early satellites were unable to transmit information to ground stations, they descended

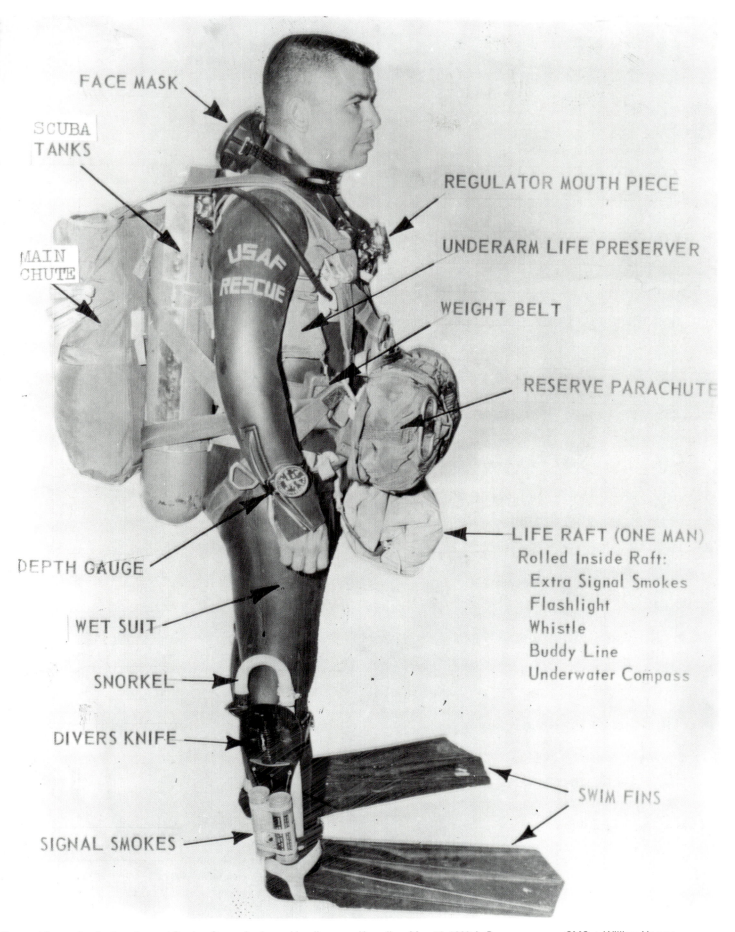

FACE MASK

SCUBA TANKS

MAIN CHUTE

REGULATOR MOUTH PIECE

UNDERARM LIFE PRESERVER

WEIGHT BELT

RESERVE PARACHUTE

DEPTH GAUGE

WET SUIT

SNORKEL

DIVERS KNIFE

SIGNAL SMOKES

LIFE RAFT (ONE MAN)
Rolled Inside Raft:
    Extra Signal Smokes
    Flashlight
    Whistle
    Buddy Line
    Underwater Compass

SWIM FINS

Dressed for work prior to astronaut Gordon Cooper's planned landing near Hawaii on May 14, 1963, is Pararescueman CMSgt. William Vargas. Revered among his peers, Vargas culminated his USAF pararescue career as commandant of the USAF Pararescue School at Eglin AFB. After retirement he remained a dedicated leader of emergency operations. *Courtesy of USAF*

The first HC-130H (serial no. 64-14852) awaits its first test flight at Lockheed's Marietta, Georgia, plant on December 8, 1964. Nicknamed "Humanitarian Dragonfly" during testing, the rescue Hercules was equipped with the Fulton Recovery System, the balloon recovery forks of which, when spread, spanned 24 feet, 8 inches from tip to tip. The window at left was an observer's position. *Courtesy of USAF*

from low orbits to release small craft containing film canisters. Slowed by drogue parachutes, the containers descended over the Pacific or the Atlantic, where Air Rescue aircraft either snatched the package in midair or recovered them by helicopter after splashing down. Declassification of documents early in the twenty-first century confirms that Air Rescue squadrons, particularly the 55th and 57th ARRS, were tasked with spy satellite recovery under the MARS (Mid-Air Retrieval System) program; Detachment 1 of Florida-based 48th ARS became involved in 1960. Air Rescue aircraft and crews assigned to or working in conjunction with units under the cover title "test" squadrons or groups performed dual roles—MARS and SAR.

Lockheed HC-130s and Sikorsky H-3 helicopters were key participants in aerial recovery of space hardware. For several years, All American Engineering had been developing an improved winch for ARRS HC-130s. The model 80G winch was incorporated into a hydraulically powered davit mounted to the HC-130H's aft ramp. Capable of recovering 2,500-pound packages, twelve systems were built for distribution to five ARRS bases throughout the world. The 48th ARRS at Eglin—which through experience had earned the redesignation "air recovery squadron"—was first to obtain the air-to-air equipment. The 6550th Operations Group at Florida's Patrick AFB received their equipment in 1966, which was used to recover data capsules and Ryan Remotely Piloted Vehicles (RPVs) on the Eastern Test Range; this was a 5,000-mile range beginning at Cape Canaveral Air Force Station, extending over the Atlantic Ocean. After training at Eglin, the West Coast 41st ARS received the equipment for their HC-130s in early 1967. Operating from Howard AFB, in the Canal Zone, the 41st accomplished the first "live" recoveries on April 2, 1967. In 1969, fifteen HC-130N models were ordered, which differed

from the H model in having advanced direction-finding equipment for retrieving space capsules. They were without the Fulton STAR system but were equipped for air refueling. In keeping with their combat SAR function, armor protection was added at crew stations.

Model 80G winches later removed from HC-130Hs were modified to model 80H configuration for installation in CH-3Cs, bringing the MARS helicopter fleet to fourteen. By 1970, RPVs had grown to 4,000 pounds, which pushed the CH-3C's lifting ability. US Air Force officials then decided to modify CH-53s for the mission. This was not a landmark innovation since the HH-53 already was being evaluated for support of manned space flight.

The aforementioned 57th ARS seemed to specialize in support of covert operations. Flying SC-54s, aircrews of Detachment 2 of the 57th supported U-2 flights from Greece and Turkey. So expansive was use of the U-2 that in January 1958, the 60th ARS was reactivated and based at Ramey AB, Puerto Rico, to support U-2 atmospheric research projects conducted for various government organizations. In March 1959, the squadron was redesignated the 64th ARS (with a detachment at Ezeiza, Argentina) and relocated to Bergstrom AFB, Texas, to continue support of U-2 programs. The U-2 served many masters during two hundred atmospheric research flights between 1956 and 1960, a portion of which were covert CIA flights. US Air Force U-2 operations came to an end in 1968.

IMPROVING THE FLEET

During the 1950s, manufacturers were making huge advances in aircraft design, which leaders of various air force commands deemed adaptable to their missions. The Air Rescue Service was no exception, having long planned modernization of its aircraft fleet. A major factor in the development of high-performance helicopters was the turbine engine. The light General Electric T58 engine, which offered a very high power-to-weight ratio, in particular, held promise of adapting well to helicopters due to its rapid acceleration and ability to maintain constant rotor rpm. The switch from reciprocating to turbine-powered helicopters for the air force began with the US Navy. Navy officials proposed updating its Sikorsky HSS-1 "Seabat" antisubmarine warfare (ASW) helicopter with turbine engines, but in January 1957, Sikorsky had a better idea: a larger helicopter powered by twin T58s, with a boat hull for overwater operation. Designated HSS-2 and named "Sea King," the first example first flew on March 11, 1959. Sikorsky then proposed a version of its Model S-61 with a rear cargo ramp to satisfy the US Marine Corps search for a new amphibious assault helicopter. Sikorsky's design lost to Boeing-Vertol's commercial 107II, which became the marine CH-46 Sea Knight. The appeal of Sikorsky's Sea King, however, was not lost on air force planners.

An air force requirement called for twenty-eight tandem-rotor, turbine-powered, twenty-eight-passenger helicopters

The CH-3C crew that accomplished the first recovery of the camera cassette of Saturn III pose with the device immediately after landing at Patrick AFB on February 26, 1966. *From left*, John Vandergraaf, PJ A1C Hanon Combs, aircraft commander Capt. Carl Damonte, copilot Capt. Ramon LeFevre, PJ SSgt. David E. Milston, and flight engineer TSgt. Johnny Tindal. Crew and aircraft staged from Marsh Harbor Airport on Abaco Island, Bahama Islands. Air Rescue used the CH-3C for the first time on June 18, 1965, when a crew recovered camera cassettes from a Titan IIIC launched one hour, fifteen minutes earlier. *Courtesy of USAF*

to replace H-21s that serviced radar-warning sites, called the "Texas Towers," along the North Atlantic coast. Other roles for the new chopper included recovering drones in the Gulf of Mexico, supporting missile sites in the US, and Arctic search and rescue. The air force closely monitored the army's 1960 evaluation of the BV-107II, which was passed over in favor of the larger CH-47 Chinook. An air force–sponsored fly-off in 1961 between the Boeing-Vertol 107II and a navy Sea King favored Boeing-Vertol. The air force then placed an order for twelve BV-107IIs, which the air force labeled XH-49A in its designation system. In the interim, a review by DoD and Air Force Systems Command concluded that a single-rotor helicopter was a better selection for the speed and range

necessary for the rescue mission, which was becoming more prominent. The decision to change was sealed when it became obvious that Boeing-Vertol could not meet the delivery date. The project manager, Lt. Col. Willis R. "Joe" Kusy, was then directed to halt procurement of the Boeing-Vertol, cancel the order for twelve machines, and request from Sikorsky a stretched S-61 with rear cargo ramp. Sikorsky agreed, and, in the meantime, to prepare the air force for its new helicopter, six Sea Kings went to the air force, which labeled them CH-3Bs. Three were loaned from the navy, and three came from Sikorsky's production line in 1962. The first example of Sikorsky's new Model S-61R (USAF serial no. 62-12577), with stretched fuselage, tricycle-retractable landing gear, larger tailplane, and hydraulically operated rear ramp, and powered by twin 1,300 shp T58-GE-1 turbine engines, was delivered to the air force on January 30, 1964. Designated CH-3C by the air force and nicknamed "Big Charlie," the type became the first twin turbine to be certified by the Federal Aviation Administration (FAA). The first Big Charlie to join the Air Rescue Service performed the first rescue with an H-3 on July 8, 1964, while the type was undergoing testing. Carl Damonte, colonel, USAF (ret.), was the copilot that day when the CH-3C made a water landing at night to rescue two passengers from a stranded boat. Damonte provides these details:

The mission occurred while we were conducting the Category III Test of the CH-3C helicopter. Aircraft S/N 63-9683 was the first H-3 assigned to the Air Rescue Service. We started as Detachment Provisional 1st, HQ ARS at Tyndall. We started there because facilities were not yet available at Patrick AFB, where we subsequently moved in September 1964. At Patrick we became Det 15, EARRC, and supported the Gemini program. Also, Tyndall had a couple of CH-3Cs for drone recovery and qualified instructor pilots (IPs). We used their IPs to check us out in the CH-3C. I was the first one checked out as instructor pilot for the Air Rescue Service. On this mission, I made the water landing. One interesting note about the landing was, once we landed, we discovered that all the lights were below the waterline and were submerged. It got dark! The searchlight was subsequently placed above the water line in the nose of the helicopter on later models. The CH-3C evolved into the HH-3E "Jolly Green Giant." I flew them in Southeast Asia in 1967 and 1968.

As CH-3Cs arrived, both CH-3Bs and CH-3Cs performed numerous roles, including test phases, drone recovery, missile site support, assignment to the helicopter school, and support of space programs.

In 1964, most of the CH-3s went to Eglin AFB for assignment to the Tactical Air Command (TAC). During that period, the air force endeavored to exploit the tactical abilities of its CH-3C. Foremost on the minds of TAC officials was competition between air force and army for the short-range intratheater delivery mission, moving supplies from large cargo aircraft to remote units. The army proposed its very capable de Havilland Caribou transport, while the air force promoted its CH-3C, which nearly matched the Caribou's cargo capacity. Former air force helicopter pilot John "Jay" Merz provides insight to his experience with the early Sikorskys:

I was assigned to the Tactical Air Warfare Center (TAWC) at Eglin AFB for a year, starting in late spring 1964. I had attended the CH-3C/S-61R factory School in the winter of 1963–64 because SAC was expecting some of the early-production H-3s to support the new Minuteman Wing at Malstrom AFB. I was a 1Lt and aircraft commander because

The Albatross never looked so good. Adding to this SA-16B's good looks are women associated with the "Rain Makers," which was a social group of businessmen that highlighted events in the Portland area beginning in 1958. The Albatross was serial no. 51-5293 of the 304th ARS. *Courtesy of Felix McLarney collection*

I had attended the H-3 Factory School. At this point in my career I had flown a thousand hours in the H-19 at Malstrom.

All the Eglin H-3s came from Sikorsky with a shiny silver paint job. We took them all immediately over to the depot at Mobile, Alabama, for their green war paint. The depot green paint was dissolved by the ever-present leaking fluids on the H-3s. All of us were getting this paint on our boots, gloves, and flight suits during routine preflights. The crews had a deep dislike for the green slime. This led to numerous derogatory names for the H-3s that eventually was the source of the ARRS "Jolly Green" call sign. The Eglin unit wanted the H-3 to drag loads off the C-130 drop area. The old-style sling on the H-3 could not safely drag large loads, because the sling required a lot of forward cyclic. This would drive the H-3 into the ground if the load suddenly separated. A new "swing sling" in later models solved the problem.

To prove the air force's ability to support army forces, the Tactical Air Warfare Center (TAWC) from June through September 1964 conducted a three-phase exercise called Indian River, which had participating CH-3Cs painted with the temporary green paint that Merz describes. Army–air force rivalry over approaches to air mobility culminated in November with the US Strike Command's exercise Goldfire I, held at West Plains, Missouri. The showy war game had the TAWC, which had been activated one year earlier, committing twelve CH-3Cs and six new UH-1F helicopters, along with cargo and fighter aircraft, against a fictitious enemy force. Few major changes came of the exercise; the army got the go-ahead to develop its air assault division, which became the famed

When the helicopter school moved from Randolph AFB to Stead AFB in 1958, the H-13 was found underpowered for advanced training, and it was phased out of the program. Some H-13s were retained, including this dual-control H-13E (serial no. 51-13809) at Edwards AFB. Its color scheme was overall Olive Drab with white lettering, yellow skid caps, and red tail rotor guard. *Courtesy of Norm Taylor*

1st Cavalry Division, and the air force would beef up air support to the army but place greater emphasis on air rescue.

Among the many uses of new CH-3Cs was their role in international relations, particularly with a Sikorsky modification package that lightened the aircraft. Former USAF helicopter pilot and test pilot William D. "Don" Eastman explains:

In 1964, the US State Department and Treasury Department were pursuing payments from NATO members for the deployment of the large number of US armed forces in Europe. It was called the "Gold Flow Reversal." The US wanted NATO and particularly Germany to buy US weapons. One of the USAF items to sell NATO members was the CH-3C with fixed landing gear. The project was called "Project Bueckeburg" because the primary base of operation was German army airfield Bueckeburg from August to October 1964. Three CH-3Cs were shipped to Germany along with three air force pilots, four mechanics, and Sikorsky maintenance personnel. We installed the fixed gear and then began a ninety-day demonstration of the helicopter. Sling loads of over thirty

types of German army equipment were demonstrated, including high-altitude mountain landings, low-altitude attack missions, internal loads of missiles and army vehicles, and IFR cruise missions. German pilots and maintenance personnel evaluated the helicopter. The most significant load was a USAF T-33 aircraft. Another, which I flew once and declared a hazardous load, was a 110-foot amphibious boat with outboard engine and all equipment installed. At 40 knots it wanted to fly and carry the helicopter along with it. A real accident waiting to happen. I wouldn't let German or USAF pilots fly it. At the end of the project, we demonstrated two standard CH-3Cs in France, Italy, Egypt, Saudi Arabia, the Med, and Greece.

Closer to US shores, the air force made maximum use of its CH-3Cs. While observing testing in 1961 of the H-43 Huskie for midair recovery of target drones, US Army major Myron Wilson envisioned army CH-37 "Mojave" helicopters recovering drones in midair over New Mexico mountains, thereby avoiding landing damage. When tests with the CH-37 proved successful, Wilson coined the system "Mid-Air Retrieval

System" (MARS), the air force got involved, and a contract went to All American Engineering to install MARS gear in the new CH-3Cs. A prime example of the air force commitment to the MARS program, while retaining SAR capability, was the 6594th Test Group, which had been activated at Hickam AFB, Hawaii, in 1958. Documents declassified in 1995 reveal the unit's primary purpose of recovering film canisters ejected from Corona Project spy satellites. Initially flying specially configured JC-119 Boxcars and H-21 helicopters, the 6594th began midair retrieval in 1960. If the JC-119 could not make the midair snatch, H-21s retrieved the canisters from the ocean. Eventually JC-130Bs replaced the Boxcars, while six CH-3C helicopters replaced the H-21s. Three World War II Liberty ships were extensively modified as Longview-class missile range instrumentation ships with helipad and hangars to support helicopter operations. Because all operations took place over the West Pacific, pararescuemen were part of the aircrew. In late 1974, HH-53Cs returning from the war replaced the CH-3Cs. Code-named "Crested Rooster," the Super Jollies were extensively modified with internal auxiliary fuel tanks, inertial navigation systems (INS), and capsule recovery apparatus. When not busy with their primary mission, the unit assumed the SAR role in conjunction with the US Coast Guard and other agencies. As a secret MARS/SAR unit, the 6594th Test Group achieved a commendable record of open-water rescue. On January 7, 1985, one of the unit's Super Jollies set a world record for the longest overwater helicopter rescue without landing. The 1,380-mile round trip was flown to hoist a seriously ill crew member from a distant cruise ship. A submerged Soviet sub detected in the recovery area prompted engineers to quickly devise a method to develop and relay canister film in orbit, eliminating the possibility of film canisters falling into the wrong hands, thus drawing to a close the HH-53's recovery mission.

Carl Damonte, who flew CH-3Cs of Detachment 15 of the EARRC, describes an ocean recovery during NASA–air force testing of the Saturn-series rockets, which later took man to the moon:

These rockets employed boosters to increase thrust. At approximately 100,000 feet the boosters burned out and separated from the first stage. Since proper separation was critical for a successful launch, two camera cassettes that recorded the separation were installed in the first stage. After photographing booster separation, the cassettes were ejected and fell to Earth. To aid in their recovery, the cassettes were equipped with a UHF transmitter that gave a signal allowing tracking-equipped aircraft (our CH-3C, HC-130, and HC-97) to continuously take bearings during descent and after impacting the ocean. They were also equipped with dye marker and a flotation device that deployed on impact.

Prior to launch from Cape Kennedy, engineers predicted the impact area downrange over the Atlantic. This area was known as the "footprint" and was normally 30 miles long

and 20 miles wide and about 250 miles from the cape. An HC-130 or HC-97 was positioned at each corner of the footprint. Two CH-3Cs from Detachment 15 deployed out of the Grand Bahama Island and held clear of the footprint until impact. The CH-3Cs were fit with an internal 1,000-gallon fuel tank that gave an eight-hour endurance.

As the cassette fell to the ocean, the fixed-wing aircraft at each corner of the footprint took continuous bearings that allowed a fairly accurate position of the impact point. Once that occurred, the CH-3C was vectored toward the impact point by an electronic-intelligence (ELINT) EC-121 that monitored the entire operation. When close, the CH-3C picked up the homing signal on its ARA-25 tracking equipment and homed to the floating cassette, with the dye marker aiding sighting.

With the CH-3C at a hover, two pararescuemen jumped and swam to the cassette. The CH-3C's sea anchor was used as the recovery device and was retrieved with the rescue hoist. The PJs were then hoisted aboard and the cassette was flown to Patrick AFB.

Throughout manned space flight training, the CH-3C proved an excellent vehicle for astronaut rescue after abort during the critical launch phase. All four Detachment 15 CH-3Cs flew each training mission, with each flying a specific orbit prior to simulated launches. Each helicopter crew consisted of two pilots, two PJs, crew chief, flight surgeon, and photographer. One CH-3C had the launch site recovery commander on board to oversee operations.

A total of seventy-four CH-3Cs were produced before factory installation of the General Electric T58-GE-5 engine, rated at 1,500 shp. The uprated engine resulted in the new designation CH-3E in early 1966. The CH-3Cs were eventually converted, with air force H-3 production totaling 133 aircraft. With the dire need for rescue helicopters in the widening war in Southeast Asia, CH-3s would shift from their tactical cargo role to combat rescue, which meant a number of modifications for survivability, and a new designation and nickname. Meanwhile, another turbine-powered helicopter was coming on board.

THE HUEY

Since 1955, Air Force officials had watched closely the development of Bell Helicopter's turbine-powered Model H-40 for the army; in the army–air force designation system this became HU-1 (for helicopter, utility, model 1), or "Huey." In keeping with the army's practice of naming its aircraft after Native American tribes or woodland animals, the HU-1 was named "Iroquois." Seldom was the name heard, while "Huey" became universal.

In 1962, USAF officials approached Bell Helicopter about developing a special version of the UH-1 using the 1,325 shp GE T58-GE-3 engine. The air force possessed an ample stockpile of the turbine power plant since it had been intended for the H-3 helicopter. In June 1963 the air force named Bell the winner of the competition for a turbine-powered replacement of the H-19 for missile site support. The air force felt that its Huey could also be used for staff transport, cargo delivery, security, and rescue. Bell engineers proposed their Model 204 short cabin, which was a continuation of the UH-1B series, labeled the H-48 in the USAF designation system; H-48 was soon changed to UH-1F. The 48-foot rotor of the long-cabin Model 205 was used, which required the 205's longer tail boom for rotor clearance. To fit the T58 engine in place of the Huey's standard Lycoming T53, a gearbox changed the direction of drive, which had exhaust routed to the right side. At mission gross weight of 9,000 pounds, the UH-1F had a top speed of 120 mph and a range of 350 miles.

The UH-1F made its first flight on February 20, 1964, with the first two examples delivered to the 4486th Test Squadron at Eglin AFB in late September. The arrival of the UH-1F was the final step in converting to an all-turbine air force helicopter fleet. By 1967, a total of 119 UH-1Fs had been delivered, along with twenty-six TH-1F trainer variants, which joined the HH-43 and CH-3 at the helicopter school. Although the majority of UH-1Fs went to the Tactical Air Command, where they also performed rescue duty, UH-1Fs gradually replaced H-19s in air rescue squadrons. Wearing the orange-yellow and black markings of Air Rescue, the UH-1F earned high marks, which meant future orders from the air force for larger and more-powerful Hueys.

THE "STRATO-RESCUER"

The modernization plan for the Air Rescue Service focused on the ultimate combination of a high-powered, long-range helicopter and a long-range, fixed-wing aircraft. The Sikorsky H-3 satisfied the rotary-wing requirement, with the decision made to fill the fixed-wing requirement with a rescue version of Lockheed's C-130 Hercules. Although the C-130A became operational in the air force in late 1956, an order for forty-three rescue HC-130H models could not be filled by the retirement

The second Bell UH-1F (serial no. 63-13142), along with no. 63-13141, after delivery went to Eglin AFB for testing. All left the factory painted Glossy Dark Blue (FS 15042), with white cabin roofs, earning them the name "White Tops." *Courtesy of USAF*

Wearing the colorful air rescue scheme, the HH-43B (serial no. 58-1848) is inspected by Capt. Fialko and SSgt. Bucknall at Clark AB, Philippine Islands, in 1964. Huskies stationed near large bodies of water were equipped with emergency flotation gear. Flotation bags were contained in fairings below cabin doors. Forward of the fairings were gas actuators that inflated the bags. *Courtesy of USAF*

date of the Douglas HC-54. Since the Rescuemaster was showing its age, and support of the space program was priority, an interim aircraft was needed to fill the gap pending arrival of the rescue Hercules. Studies showed that Boeing's KC-97 tanker was the ideal candidate, since its expeditious replacement by the jet-powered KC-135 extended the KC-97's service life. The type was reliable, large, long range, and available.

The Aircraft Service Division of Fairchild Hiller Corporation was the logical choice for the conversions, since it had modified and repaired US military aircraft, including KC-97s, since its founding as Fairchild Stratos Corp. in 1961. In the beginning of 1964, twenty-eight Strato-Tankers went to the firm's St. Augustine, Florida, facilities for conversion to the HC-97G Strato-Rescuer. The aerial-refueling boom was replaced by clamshell cargo doors taken from retired C-97 cargo variants. The large doors could be opened in flight for deploying pararescuemen and rescue equipment. External underwing fuel tanks were removed; however, more tanks augmenting those retained in the fuselage gave the Strato-Rescuer impressive twenty-three-hour endurance and a range of 5,000 miles. Since many search missions were flown at lower altitudes, air-conditioning was added to the flight deck. To satisfy the Pratt & Whitney 4360 engines' voracious appetite for oil at low level, a 50-gallon oil tank was added. Updated radio and electronic search equipment with corresponding radio operator's position completed the conversion. A typical HC-97G crew comprised two pilots, navigator, two flight engineers, radio operator, and two PJs. The large aircraft could accommodate rescue coordination staff to operate an airborne command post. Between May and November 1964, deliveries were completed, with the HC-97Gs assigned to the 55th ARS

at Kindley AB, Bermuda; the 58th ARS at Wheelus AB, Libya; and the 76th ARS at Hickam AFB, Hawaii.

Eight KC-97Gs, four of which were from the 500th Air Refueling Wing at Selfridge AFB, were rotated through the three rescue squadrons to train crews until the three units were operational with the Strato-Rescuer. In 1965, two of the trainer aircraft were converted to C-97G command support platforms, complete with air rescue livery, which caused observers to believe that HC-97Gs numbered more than twenty-eight. One C-97G was assigned to the 55th ARS, and the other to the 76th ARS. The 55th and 58th Squadrons each operated eight Strato-Rescuers, while the 76th had eleven assigned, due to the expanse of the Pacific, for which it was responsible. All three air rescue squadrons were heavily involved in providing support for NASA's Gemini space program. NASA had pressed the air force for increased support when experience with the Mercury space program showed that spacecraft could easily miss their targeted splashdown by more than 90 miles.

When conversion plans were made in 1963, little thought was given to the simmering situation in Southeast Asia. By the time that deliveries of HC-97Gs began, Vietnam loomed as a major aspect of rescue in the Pacific. From mid-January 1965 onward, a pair of HC-97Gs of the 76th ARS was assigned temporary duty at Clark AB in the Philippines to free HU-16B Albatross aircraft of the 31st ARS for combat SAR missions. Soon, HC-97Gs of the 76th were also deployed to Okinawa and Japan to augment the 33rd ARS and 36th ARS, respectively. Eventually, Strato-Rescuers were commonly seen at air bases in Vietnam and Thailand.

Beginning in 1956, the Air Staff had decided to include six air rescue squadrons in the Air Force Reserve, which in 1948 had dismantled detachments and reorganized to establish squadron-size units. By 1958, five of the six squadrons, the 301st through 305th Air Rescue Squadrons, were operational with SA-16A/B Albatross aircraft. When in 1963 the Air Staff

Albatross no. 51-7177 of the 304th ARS strains to "get up on the step" for its takeoff run. *Courtesy of Ray Dowell / Felix McLarney collection*

On March 17, 1966, Gemini 8 astronauts Neil Armstrong and David Scott await the recovery ship USS *Leonard F. Mason* with PJs A1C Eldridge M. Neal, SSgt. Larry D. Huyett, and A2C Glenn M. Moore. Their raft at right was boldly marked "USAF RESCUE" after the media wrongly credited the 1962 Aurora 7 recovery to navy frogmen. *Courtesy of USAF*

The absence of air rescue assets at Thule AB, Greenland, was addressed in 1960 with assignment of two SC-54Ds to the 4683rd Air Base Wing of the Air Defense Command. "ARCTIC RAVEN" (serial no. 42-72524), seen here, initially was named "THULE KNOT" after a native Greenland bird. The other SC-54D (serial no. 42-72747) was named "THULE PRINCESS." An adjustable tail support was standard equipment aboard SC-54s to prevent the tail from lowering during loading. The installation of AN/APS-42 weather radar gave the SC-54 a bulged nose. *Courtesy of Frank MacSorley*

The Mk. 13 signal flare had a daytime end that emitted orange smoke, while the nighttime end produced a bright flare. Both uses of the Mk. 13 are used here in Florida's Biscayne Bay to signal an Albatross of the 301st ARRS. *Courtesy of USAF*

An SC-54D (serial no. 42-72527) of the 54th ARS takes on fuel in its "wet wings" at Goose Bay, Labrador. The Rescuemaster typically operated with a crew comprising pilot, copilot, navigator, radio operator, and two PJs. As a long-range rescue platform, the SC-54 featured MA-1 rescue kits, scanner positions, search radar, crew comfort provisions for long-duration missions, and a flare launcher. The launcher, in the rear cabin floor, could eject parachute flares, float lights, and sea marker dye cartridges. *Courtesy of Steven Southiere*

considered changing Reserve air rescue to an all-helicopter force, the 303rd and 305th were omitted from the plan in order to maintain global SAR capability. The Air Staff and Air Rescue Headquarters were apprehensive about reserve squadrons not only maintaining the multiengine HC-97G, but taking on larger numbers of aircraft and assuming global responsibility. As HC-130Hs began to arrive at the three active squadrons, eighteen of their HC-97Gs were slated to be divided between the 303rd and 305th Reserve Air Rescue Squadrons; the remainder went into storage. Beginning in 1966, both the 303rd ARRS and the 305th ARRS maintained peak efficiency while flying a wide variety of missions around the globe. Dispelling the initial apprehension of air force officials, reservists expertly flew and maintained their Strato-Rescuers, often on extremely busy schedules, until 1972, when they too were replaced by the HC-130H.

The organizational chart of the Air Rescue Service in 1965 showed twelve air rescue squadrons, five reserve air rescue squadrons, and sixty-one local base rescue units. The squadrons are as follows:

31st ARS Clark AB, Philippines
33rd ARS Naha AB, Okinawa
36th ARS Tachikawa AB, Japan
41st ARS Hamilton AFB, California
48th ARS Eglin AFB, Florida
54th ARS Goose AB, Labrador
55th ARS Kindley AB, Bermuda
57th ARS Lajes Field, Azores
58th ARS Wheelus AB, Libya
67th ARS Prestwick AB, Scotland
76th ARS Hickam AFB, Hawaii
79th ARS Andersen AFB, Guam
301st ARS Homestead AFB, Florida
302nd ARS Luke AFB, Arizona
303rd ARS March AFB, California
304th ARS Portland International Airport, Oregon
305th ARS Selfridge AFB, Michigan

Missions performed by both active and reserve air rescue squadrons when equipped with HC-97Gs included search and rescue, support of the space program, training, augmenting other rescue units, airlift, escort for aircraft ferried to war in Southeast Asia (and their return), airborne command post, support of U-2 flights, and alert during immediate buildup of US forces following North Korean seizure of USS *Pueblo* in January 1968. During the late 1960s, a two-plane element of the 305th ARRS stood alert at NS Keflavik, Iceland, as the rescue element for F-102 interceptors that responded to increased activity by Russian long-range bombers.

QUEEN OF THE FIXED-WINGS

Air Rescue's modernization program of the early 1960s focused on arrival of Lockheed's rescue version of the C-130 "Hercules," designated HC-130H. The Air Rescue commander, Col. Allison C. Brooks, stated in 1967, "This aircraft will be the primary fixed-wing rescue aircraft for some time to come." How correct he was, for the C-130 holds that title nearly six decades later; the prototype C-130 first flew in 1954. The HC-130H was the combat rescue version of the C-130E and C-130H, powered by four Allison T56-A-15 turboprop engines, rated at 4,590 shp each. The multirole rescue Hercules was configured for airborne mission control and long-range, overwater search. External fuel tanks and two additional 1,800-gallon tanks in the fuselage permitted a range of just over 5,000 miles. Equipped with the Fulton Recovery System combined with All American Engineering equipment, the HC-130H could retrieve personnel in midair from land or water, as well as satellite equipment. A large radome on the upper fuselage housed a Cook satellite

reentry-tracking system, which was requested and funded by NASA. The ARD-17 aerial tracker's ultrasensitive high frequency and S-band direction finder proved ideal for locating downed fliers through the use of their locator beacons. Standard on each HC-130H were three MA-1 sea survival kits, overhead delivery system, dual radios with direction-finding ability, and automatic flare launch system. The "H" had a top speed of 380 mph and a ceiling of 32,800 feet.

The first flight of the Rescue Hercules occurred in December 1964, followed by testing of initial JC-130s at Dyess AFB, Texas, and Edwards AFB, California. On July 26, 1965, Col. Brooks accepted the first HC-130H (s/n 64-14860) for the 48th ARS at Eglin AFB. The following month, an accelerated HC-130H training program began with the 48th. By year's end, sixteen HC-130Hs had been delivered and were operational with air rescue units.

Planning and fabrication of the Fulton Surface-to-Air Recovery System had begun at Lockheed-Marietta in 1962. Seldom publicized are concepts considered for newly developed systems. Although often deemed outlandish, some have merit and are added to test programs. The potential of pickup

The HC-97G's nose radome, which was a carryover from the KC-97G, housed antennae for the glide slope indicator and the AN/APS-42 search radar. The radome atop the fuselage housed the AN/APX-29A IFF interrogator antenna. Serial no. 52-2754 was assigned to the 305th ARRS at Selfridge AFB, Michigan. *Courtesy of USAF*

A CH-3E (serial no. 64-14225) and crew of Det 15, EARRC, used in the 1969 filming of *Marooned*, pose at Cape Kennedy. Flight engineer SSgt. James Burns, *fourth from left*, noted, "We had to keep this one bird in commission the whole time, which was not a big chore because the H-3 was a very reliable helicopter." Actor David Janssen, one of the stars in the film, is third from right, and director John Sturges is at far right. Commander of Det 15, Lt. Col. Frederick C. Faust Jr., is third from left. *Courtesy of James Burns collection*

systems was tested to such a degree. For example, years after the STARS had become a fixture in the world of special operations, during the late 1980s, USAF Special Operations Command revisited the system, with plans to beef up the equipment for its "Talon I" C-130s. They then hoped to be able to snatch four- or six-man special-operations teams. The weight of one such pickup would dangerously approach the lift line's 1,500-pound load limit. Scheduled into a test program, code-named Project 46, were fifty-six trial pickups using dummies. The plan abruptly ended during a heavyweight test with C-130 serial no. 64-0551 when the lift line broke on the fifty-third test pickup.

Also noteworthy is the first midair snatch of a parachute jumper, validating the prospect of rescuing airmen during parachute descent over enemy territory. It happened on August 29, 1966, when Charles M. Alexander, test parachutist for Pioneer Parachute Company, jumped from a Cessna 180 at 10,000 feet over All American Engineering's airfield. Flavoring the rarity of the event was the snatch aircraft, a rare Chase YC-122 (s/n 49-2886/N5904V), forerunner of the C-123 aircraft. Alexander had dropped only 1,000 feet when the YC-122 crew snagged his chute and reeled him aboard. Then there was the combination parachute-balloon called a "Ballute," which kept an airman not only aloft but able to ascend, while awaiting the snatch aircraft.

JOLLY GREEN GIANT

To ensure optimum combat rescue capability, the HC-130H's teammate, the CH-3C/E, required modifications to maximize its efficiency and survivability. To extend the CH-3's range for anticipated use in combat rescue, in August 1964 the air force issued a requirement for air-refueling capability. This became reality after extensive testing, along with additional changes made by Sikorsky. Prior to the installation of air-to-air-refueling equipment, six CH-3Cs in production were fit with increased internal fuel capacity, and plumbing inside the sponsons for 200-gallon jettisonable fuel tanks used on the F-100. Fuel tanks in the cabin floor were made self-sealing, and 1,000 pounds of titanium armor protected crew and vital components. The six—serial numbers 64-14227 and -14229 through -14233—were shipped directly from production to Thailand. Follow-on production included Doppler navigation equipment, automatic flight control, all-weather instrumentation, and multiple radios. The original H-3's electric hoist, located in the forward cabin, used a series of pulleys to assist in loading cargo up the aft ramp. It was slow and had only 100 feet of cable, which was unacceptable for combat rescue. A temporary tripod hoist outside the cabin doorway was replaced by a high-speed, hydraulic hoist with

240 feet of 600-pound-capacity cable with forest penetrator. Attached to the hoist cable, the penetrator was heavy and pointed, to penetrate jungle canopy. Three arms folded against the device could be lowered as seats for survivors, or to lower PJs. The switch to 1,500 shp T58-GE-5 engines allowed a top speed of 163 mph. Two crew-served 7.62 mm M60 machine guns added a measure of protection. A tritone camouflage scheme adopted for aircraft in Southeast Asia completed the new model, which was designated HH-3E but was more popularly known as the "Jolly Green Giant." The air force took delivery of the first HH-3E on November 5, 1965. The same month, two HH-3Es joined a pair of CH-3Cs that had been shipped to Udorn Royal Thai Air Force Base (RTAFB), Thailand, four months earlier. Standard crew for the Jolly Green Giant was pilot, copilot, flight engineer, and PJ. Only fourteen HH-3Es came from Sikorsky production, with the remainder derived from the conversion of CH-3Es, forty-five of which were built. Filling out the total of 133 S-61R models built for the US Air Force were seventy-four CH-3Cs.

Seven PJs of the 41st ARRS, along with manikins wearing a tree suit and a wetsuit, pose at Hamilton AFB, California, in January 1969. *Standing left to right:* William Tracey, Dennis J. Kraft, Gary W. Senter, Herbert H. Romisch, and Howard T. Favour. Kneeling is David M. Wichman, and sitting is Duane D. Hackney. On May 26, 1966, the USAF Chief of Staff approved the maroon beret for pararescuemen. *Author's collection*

The HC-54D with serial no. 42-72564 at Elmendorf AFB, Alaska, in March 1964. At least one Alaska-based HC-54 was assigned to the CIA to provide navigational aid for U-2 flights over the Soviet Union. Especially important in HC-54s that operated in cold regions were heating units to prevent waist observation blister windows from fogging and icing. *Courtesy of Norm Taylor*

The development and refinement of air-to-air refueling began on December 15, 1965, when a CH-3C flown by veteran air force helicopter test pilot William "Don" Eastman connected with a marine corps KC-130F aerial tanker in the sky over Dayton, Ohio. Eastman skillfully guided a 16-foot-long dummy probe attached to the helicopter's nose into the tanker's drogue at the end of a long fuel hose. From then until 1967, about six hundred air-refueling tests, including ninety night refuelings, were accomplished. Veteran helicopter pilot Capt. Carl Damonte describes his involvement in the tests:

Initially there was controversy as to how air-refueling H-3s from C-130 tanker aircraft should be accomplished. One school of thought was for the hose and drogue to be installed on the helicopter and the probe on the C-130. This had some merit in that it would allow the C-130, with the greater speed envelope, to do all the maneuvering for the contact, and the helicopter would just fly straight and level and get pumped full of gas. However, installation of the hose (140 feet in length), the drum,

and all associated hydraulics on the helicopter was impractical because of the increased weight factor. Besides, a proven C-130 tanker was already operational with the Marines, and Lockheed was tooled up to produce C-130 tankers for the air force. So the probe went on the H-3.

Early in 1966, feasibility tests were conducted at Marine Corps Air Station Cherry Point, North Carolina. A modified CH-3C with dummy probe was able to make contacts on the marine tanker. This proved the concept, although no procedures as such were established. The probe on these tests was installed in the center of the CH-3C nose. It was subsequently moved to the right side of the fuselage to provide the pilot better visibility when aligning the probe for contact with the drogue. All initial tests were conducted using the dummy probe.

The official air force test program got underway at Wright-Patterson AFB on 14 July 1966. I had been selected as the H-3 pilot for Project Fast Gas for the ARRS. On 18 July, I flew on my first air-refueling test mission. The left hose

Members of the 58th ARRS at Wheelus AB, Libya, gather to recount the squadron's most historic operation, and the largest noncombat rescue mission: the Tunisian flood of 1969. During October and November, the 58th flew its three HH-3Es to rescue people and deliver supplies. On one mission alone, an HH-3E evacuated sixty-eight people. The 58th's three HH-3Es were serial nos. 67-14715, 716, and 717. *Courtesy of USAF*

and drogue was the normal refueling position. Because of wake turbulence, prop wash, etc., the right refueling was very turbulent and required more power. Normally, all join-ups were made to the HC-130's left side. If right-side refueling was required, a crossover maneuver had to be accomplished. The first time we attempted a crossover resulted in an exciting experience. We assumed that all that was required was to slip back behind the HC-130 and slide across to the right side. However, as we did this we entered severe turbulence. Aircraft control was almost impossible, and we recovered about 500 feet below the HC-130. We only tried this once. We altered the procedure so that as we slid back we climbed 50 feet above the HC-130's vertical stabilizer and then moved across in "clean" air.

The initial test program lasted until 23 August 1966. The second phase was flown from 14 December 1966 through 13 January 1967. I went back to Wright-Patterson in December 1966 and on these missions actually transferred fuel and learned to operate the air-refueling panel in the H-3. In

January 1967, I left for Vietnam and there started the in-country air-refueling training program. On 8 May 1967 I flew the first combat SAR mission in a Jolly Green where air refueling was utilized. We didn't get the downed HH-43 guys of "Pedro 9-6" because we took extensive battle damage during the pickup attempt, including wounded on board; one of our PJs lost a leg.

When I look back, I think the Air Refueling Test Program was probably the best thing I accomplished during twenty-eight years in the air force. I wrote the helicopter procedures for the Aerospace Rescue and Recovery Service, which were published and subsequently in an air force technical order. As far as I know, they still air-refuel helicopters the same way today.

There was no better concurrence of Damonte's view of air refueling than a record-breaking transatlantic journey accomplished by two HH-3Es in 1967. The factory-fresh HH-3Es (serial nos. 66-13280 and -13281) of the 48th ARRS at Eglin AFB departed NAS Brooklyn on May 31, for the Paris

Air Show. The helicopter piloted by Maj. Donald Maurras clocked twenty-nine hours, thirteen minutes to London's Heathrow Airport, while Maj. Herbert Zehnder reached Paris nonstop in just under thirty-one hours, covering 4,157 miles. Each HH-3E was air-refueled nine times by HC-130Ps staged along the route. Four days later, both aircraft were shipped to Vietnam for assignment to the 37th ARRS at Da Nang.

After Maj. Harry P. Dunn, who was part of the original test team, had proved his theory throughout testing that the H-3 could safely refuel by flying on the slipstream of the powerful Hercules, USAF Air Staff approved an initial order for eleven HC-130Hs converted for the aerial-refueling role. Modifications made at Lockheed's Marietta, Georgia, plant included additional interior fuel tanks, along with drogue

kits mounted to pods under each outer wing. Lockheed delivered the first modified Hercules, redesignated the HC-130P, on November 18, 1966. As more HC-130Ps arrived, rescue crews reported to the 48th ARRS at Eglin AFB to begin the second phase of tests and training in aerial refueling. The multimission HC-130P "Combat King," equipped with the Fulton Recovery System, in-flight refueling, and the latest avionics and teamed with the HH-3E, exceeded air force expectations as the ultimate search-and-rescue and airborne mission control platform. Twenty HC-130Ps would roll off the production line, while twenty-one were modified from HC-130Hs . . . and none too soon as the need for "friends in high places" in Southeast Asia rose dramatically.

Equipped with emergency flotation gear, HH-43B (serial no. 60-0255) was one of four Huskies assigned to the 58th ARRS at Wheelus AB during the 1960s. Others were nos. 62-4517, -4532, and -4558. Three HU-16Bs were also assigned: serial nos. 51-5290, -5305, and -5306. *Courtesy of Jack M. Friell*

At the beginning of the 1960s, there was no escaping the fact that conflict generalized as the "Vietnam War" actually involved the Southeast Asian countries of Vietnam, Laos, Cambodia, and Thailand. For America, the region had been a quagmire beset with political struggle since World War II. US aid to Laos begun in 1955 paved the way for military advisors placed in Laos and South Vietnam by the end of the decade. To avoid an overt military commitment to the region, in early 1961, President Kennedy authorized the delivery of sixteen Sikorsky CH-34 helicopters to the CIA's air arm, Air America. However, US military intervention in President Kennedy's rapidly worsening crisis was unavoidable, generating the first code name of the war—"Bell Tone." This identified four F-100 tactical fighter squadrons that rotated through Takhli Royal Thai Air Force Base (RTAFB) beginning in February 1961. Their purpose was protection of reconnaissance flights begun in April, which were code-named "Field Goal." Takhli was the first Thai air base upgraded by the US to prevent the civil war in Laos from spreading into Thailand. With the commitment of combat aircraft came the realization that an air rescue capability was needed; history was then repeated.

Post–Korean War austerity led to a large reduction in the ranks of air rescue personnel. Worse, the nuclear war mindset that prevailed erased the wartime mission from the National Search and Rescue Plan. Instead, combat SAR descended merely to an extension of the peacetime air force mission. Since the 1947 separation of services, disputes between army and air force over function and missions, and subsequent aircraft procurement, were ongoing. Finally, in 1954, the air force, having become focused on development of a strategic bomber force and jet interceptors, relented and army aviation came into its own. The volatile situation in Southeast Asia led to deployment of six army aviation units, one of which was the 57th Medical Detachment at Ft. Meade, Maryland. Equipped with the new HU-1A Huey, in March 1962 the 57th "Original Dustoff" established a foothold in the business of combat rescue and medical evacuation. Air force H-43Bs

were not far behind, although the first Huskies in theater were a pair passed to the Thai government in June 1962 for search and rescue, accompanied by USAF pilots as advisors. Among a number of varying sources is a report indicating that the first air rescue helicopters in Southeast Asia were two H-19s of Detachment 14 of the Eastern Air Rescue Center. The helicopters and four pilots left Langley AFB, Virginia, in September 1961 for Takhli RTAFB, for a six-month assignment supporting F-100 flights.

A sharp increase in enemy activity prompted President Kennedy, in October 1961, to send assets of the 4400th Combat Crew Training Wing to Bien Hoa AB, South Vietnam. Code-named "Farm Gate," the 150-man unit, with a mix of T-28s, C-47s, and B-26s, was to train the Vietnamese air force (VNAF) in counterinsurgency operations. Secretary of Defense Robert McNamara's authorization two months later allowing the air force to engage in combat operations in Vietnam changed the course of the war; American casualties were inevitable. No longer could there be concern that forming a combat search and rescue (CSAR) structure in Southeast Asia would draw attention to increased air activities intended to appear as training. The lessons of unpreparedness learned after World War II and Korea had been ignored, with economic and political pressure instead of experience governing the status of air rescue. But the conceptual differences that simmered between the army and air force over which service would assume responsibility for CSAR caused delays in deploying rescue forces. Army leaders contended that with few aircraft modifications and a training program, they could manage CSAR. The directive by the Joint Chiefs of Staff doused the embers of rivalry by assigning the CSAR mission to the air force, a decision that was largely responsible for expansion of the air force helicopter inventory.

At the beginning of April 1962, Detachment 3, Pacific Air Rescue Center, was activated at Tan Son Nhut AB, South Vietnam, its sole function being to coordinate and control SAR operations. It was "learn as you go" for the meager staff of Detachment 3 as

AND ANGELS

War and, subsequently, helicopters were nothing new in Southeast Asia. Valerie Andre pioneered helicopter rescue in the region when France fought in Indochina during the 1950s. Qualified as an army surgeon, parachutist, and helicopter pilot, Andre's dedication to helicopter rescue saw her rescue 165 persons during nearly 500 missions. Capt. Andre poses with her litter-equipped Hiller UH-12A (Model 360) in 1952. The Hiller saw limited use by the French in Indochina, with two having flown medical evacuation missions from 1949 until the 1954 truce. During 1949 and 1950, the USAF procured two Model 360s for evaluation.

During the early 1960s, prior to the commitment of USAF rescue units, helicopters of CIA-operated airline Air America were the only rescue helicopters in Southeast Asia. Air America flew Sikorsky H-34 "Choctaws" and Bell Model 204 Hueys, such as this 204 seen at Bong Son Special Forces camp. *Courtesy of Ed Lemp*

they mustered whatever resources were available to attempt rescue of downed airmen. These included Air America, along with Vietnamese and US air and ground forces.

Air force leadership now had to atone for the depletion of its rescue forces and lack of a plan for rescue in a combat environment. Without the personnel, aircraft, and structure to meet the mounting demand for rescue in Southeast Asia, existing crews and their aircraft would be required to do the job, devising tactics and gaining experience with the resources available. But more was needed; much more.

Thankfully, in the few years preceding conflict in Southeast Asia, improvements had been made in the Air Rescue Service to meet global SAR commitments. The performance of Grumman's Albatross amphibian had been improved, and the SC-54 had replaced World War II–era bombers modified for search and rescue. On the downside, helicopters were underpowered, slow, and short ranged. Even the most modern helicopter in the inventory, Kaman's H-43B, was designed for local base rescue (LBR) and firefighting in a peacetime setting. Pararescue was ahead of the game, having been selected in 1958 as the ideal means of ocean recovery of space hardware

and support of manned space flights. That had prompted PJ Earl Casto of the 76th ARS at Hickam AFB to submit a study on the feasibility of parachuting with SCUBA gear. Approval by ARS Headquarters led to attendance at US Naval Underwater Swimmer Schools at Pearl Harbor and Key West. Enhancing its reputation as a special breed that epitomized the term "jack-of-all-trades," pararescue then began its own intensified training in extended, deepwater operations. Graduation from US Navy and Army Special Forces SCUBA schools meant another notch added to the pararescueman's belt.

Due to political infighting and army domination of helicopter operations in Vietnam, the case for establishing an air force combat rescue force still had not been made. Convinced that the war would only worsen, the Detachment 3 commander, Maj. Alan W. Saunders, in September 1963 submitted a report to the 2nd Air Division recommending that an air force rescue force be assigned to Vietnam. Already, nine USAF aircraft had been shot down, with nineteen airmen dead or missing; army losses were higher, with twenty-six aircraft shot down and twenty crewmen lost. Saunders pointed out that search and rescue by allied aircraft was haphazard and that crews lacked formal rescue training and equipment. His study trudged up the chain of command, meeting the expected opposition from the army. The Air Rescue Service commander, Gen. Adriel N. Williams, grabbed the reins and requested six Sikorsky CH-3 helicopters then in development. With the first few CH-3s committed to the space program, foresighted leaders had already taken steps to beef up the combat survivability of Kaman's HH-43B Huskie. Since the HH-43F would not be ready until October 1964, six HH-43Bs were earmarked for airlift to the combat zone in March. Their arrival was delayed, however, due to continued wrangling over responsibility between Commander in Chief Pacific and army-dominated Military Assistance Command Vietnam (MACV). Sticking points were the need to maintain the appearance of minimal US involvement, and ongoing army–air force squabbling over the use of helicopters. Finally, Joint Chiefs of Staff assigned the Southeast Asia air rescue mission to the air force.

Confirming Maj. Saunders's belief that things could only get worse, war erupted in northern Laos, revealing that the enemy had erected a lethal air defense network. With USAF air rescue assets yet to arrive, Air America filled the gap, and the Thai government granted permission for air force aircraft to launch from Thai bases to support air rescue in Laos. Air America UH-34D helicopters had begun rescuing downed military aircrew

in early 1961. "The Company's" first SAR for a US military pilot came on June 6, 1964, when USN lieutenant Charles F. Klusmann was shot down in Laos in his RF-8A Crusader. Klusmann was captured and used as bait for rescue forces, but he later escaped. Later that month, by mutual agreement with USAF officials, Air America SAR operations in Laos became part of air force rescue procedures, with both services working under a single coordinating and controlling agency.

The first rescue components were to have set up shop at Da Nang, Bien Hoa, and Soc Trang, South Vietnam; however, they were diverted to Nakhon Phanom RTAFB (NKP) near the Laotian border to provide cover for "Yankee Team" reconnaissance flights. Capture of an American airman in Laos would create an international incident, which had to be avoided at all costs. On June 19, 1964, two HH-43B Huskie helicopters and thirty-six personnel arrived at NKP on temporary duty from Naha AB, Okinawa, to form Detachment 3 (Provisional) of the Pacific Air Rescue Center. Concurrently, two US Marine H-34s were positioned at the Marine fire base Khe Sanh for rescues in eastern Laos. In addition, the 33rd ARS at Naha was directed to send a pair of HU-16B Albatrosses, along with crews and ground crew, to Korat RTAFB to fill the role of airborne rescue control for Thailand and Laos. Additionally, the 31st ARS provided one HU-16B with crew.

To utilize the HC-54's more sophisticated communications systems, in June 1965, Pacific Air Forces transferred three Rescuemasters from Japan to Udorn RTAFB, replacing HU-16B Albatrosses that served as "Crown" air controllers. Here, HC-54D (serial no. 42-72658) of Guam-based 79th ARS is escorted by an A-1E (serial no. 52-133888) of the 1st Air Commando Squadron. Air Rescue retired the HC-54 in late 1965, when the first HC-130Hs arrived. *Courtesy of Don Clemens*

By this time, Air America's helicopter assets had dwindled from sixteen H-34s to four, due to combat losses and mechanical issues.

The Gulf of Tonkin incident in August placed increased demands on air rescue, which had LBR detachments in the US quickly dispatched to Korat, Thailand, and Da Nang, and Bien Hoa, South Vietnam. Responsibility for LBR at Takhli RTAFB was assigned to Korea-based Detachment 4 of the 36th ARS. Thus began a system of continual global movement of LBR detachments to keep pace with tactical requirements. Temporary (provisional) assignments became permanent, with Detachment 4 at Bien Hoa and Detachment 5 at Da Nang receiving three each of the first examples of the HH-43F Huskie.

The numbers of aircraft lost in combat over Laos grew, yet rescue remained an ad hoc affair. Crewmen of US Marine and Air America H-34s did their best pending the arrival of major USAF air rescue assets. In the meantime, Thailand-based A-1E Skyraiders of the 1st Air Commando Squadron provided limited support of Air America rescue in Laos and Vietnam. US combat aircraft finally received authorization to participate in combat search and rescue, providing the covering firepower so desperately needed to effect rescue. Hindering such efforts were the HH-43B's limited range of 140 miles, and the negligibility of Royal Laotian Air Force rescue capabilities. It was painfully apparent that air rescue had to be well organized if it was to succeed. Timeliness too was essential for air rescue to be successful. When an airman went down, the race was on between the enemy and rescue forces to snatch the survivor, and the enemy had a good lead. The faster, longer-range HH-3E helicopter was expected to shorten the time to reach the survivor.

The first large-scale SAR effort of the war occurred on November 18–19, 1964, when an F-100D "Ball 0-3" was shot down in northern Laos. The effort, under Air America control, involved USAF HU-16Bs, F-105s, F-100s, and HH-43s, US Navy Skyraiders; and Air America H-34s, T-28s, and a C-123, totaling forty-four aircraft. The next day, an Air America H-34 copilot lowered from his H-34 found that the Hun pilot had died.

By June 1965, Detachment 3, PARC, at Tan Son Nhut AB was controlling seven helicopter detachments and two

The first search-and-rescue task forces in Southeast Asian combat were composed of HC-54 or HU-16B "Crown" controller platforms, two HH-43 Huskie helicopters, and US Navy Skyraiders. Here, a USAF air commando looks over a US Navy A-1H after a pair of Skyraiders with full rocket loads landed at Nakhon Phanom RTAFB in early 1965. The two "Spads" were BuNos 137496 and 135226 of VA-95 aboard USS *Ranger*. The latter was shot down over Laos on April 11. *Courtesy of Neil McCutchan*

fixed-wing detachments. The temporary-duty shell game could no longer match the war's quickening tempo, prompting the Air Rescue Service and its parent Military Air Transport Service to reorganize search-and-rescue forces in Southeast Asia. On July 1, 1965, the 38th ARS was reactivated at Tan Son Nhut AB, replacing Det 3, PARC, and assuming control of all helicopter units. Fixed-wing assets retained temporary-duty status until the 37th ARRS became operational in summer 1966. By the end of 1965, the 38th ARS had fourteen HH-43 detachments throughout Thailand and South Vietnam. They were as follows:

Det 1: Phan Rang AB, SVN, initially at Nakhon
    Phanom RTAFB
Det 2: Takhli RTAFB
Det 3: Ubon RTAFB
Det 4: Korat RTAFB
Det 5: Udorn RTAFB
Det 6: Bien Hoa AB, SVN
Det 7: Da Nang AB, SVN
Det 8: Cam Ranh Bay AB, SVN
Det 9: Nakhon Phanom RTAFB, later Pleiku AB, SVN
Det 10: Binh Thuy AB, SVN
Det 11: Tuy Hoa AB, SVN
Det 12: U-Tapao RTAFB
Det 13: Phu Cat AB, SVN
Det 14: Tan Son Nhut AB, SVN, also Da Nang and
    Bien Hoa AB

While the LBR Huskie detachments at Korat and Takhli were available for SAR, the NKP-based unit was dedicated to CSAR for Yankee Team flights. The downing of an F-100D of the 613th TFS in Laos on November 18, 1964, triggered the largest SAR effort so far conducted in the war. The pair of Huskies, using call signs "Pansy 8-8" and "Pansy 8-9," joined a pair of navy A-1 Skyraiders over Laos. By day's end, the search involved thirty aircraft, all controlled by an HU-16B airborne mission controller, call sign "Tacky 4-4." The F-100 with its deceased pilot was found by an HU-16B crew the next day.

Despite their limited range, HH-43s penetrated deep into Laos and North Vietnam to rescue downed fliers. The first combat rescues in North Vietnam occurred on March 2, 1965, when HH-43 crews rescued pilots of two F-105s downed during the first day of Rolling Thunder strikes. The daring missions, which sometimes brought Huskies within 40 miles of heavily defended Hanoi, were accomplished a number of ways. Huskies devoid of US markings were positioned in Laos to gain a distance advantage. To extend operating range, fuel was stored at forward sites called "Lima Sites"; a 55-gallon fuel drum usually was lashed in the cabin and tapped into the aircraft's plumbing. When empty, the drum was simply pushed out of the aircraft. This method enabled rescues of airmen downed in North Vietnam. It was learn as you go, which led to planned procedure, with one Huskie descending for the

Space limitations and a busy cabin limited HH-43 crewmen to handheld weapons. Since the Huskie's rear clamshell doors were not used in the theater, some crewmen took extra measures for rescues in enemy territory by manning heavier weapons. Here, Pararescueman Daniel E. Galde mans a Browning Automatic Rifle (BAR) rigged for firing from the rear cabin opening of an HH-43B of Det 3 (Prov) at NKP in 1964. *Courtesy of James Burns collection*

rescue while the other maintained orbit, its crew working in concert with fixed-wing escorts to suppress ground fire. Kaman Aircraft Corporation offered to mount armament systems on its HH-43s, but Air Rescue officials passed on the idea, with the explanation that they didn't want to turn their rescue aircraft into gunships. Besides, there was little room for machine gun installations, and the flight engineer and PJ would be too busy with rescue of survivors. The Huskie's offensive capability was limited to personal weapons. Since the Huskie's large rear clamshell doors were not used in Southeast Asia, heavier weapons, such as BARs and M60s, sometimes were suspended with straps in the large cabin opening.

Combat operations took their toll on Huskies, limiting their availability. During the first attack on an American air base, which began on October 31, 1964, at Bien Hoa AB, three HH-43s were damaged and one destroyed. Earlier that year, two had been damaged in accidents in Thailand, and one sustained battle damage. On June 3, 1965, an HH-43F was shot down and destroyed; fortunately, the crew was rescued. The next Huskie crew shot down was not so fortunate. On September 20, two NKP-based HH-43Bs, call signs "Dutchy 4-1" and "Dutchy 2-2," launched from a Lima site when notified by an SC-54 controller that an F-105D, call sign "Essex 0-4," was shot down over North Vietnam. With a pair of Skyraiders covering, Capt. Thomas Curtis slowed the Huskie to a hover over the downed pilot; the enemy sprung its trap, shooting down the helicopter and capturing the crew, along with the survivor. The second Huskie was driven off by heavy ground fire. The HH-43B copilot, 1Lt. Duane Martin, later was killed in an escape attempt. The Air Rescue flight engineer, A1C William Robinson, and PJ A3C Arthur Black became the first USAF enlisted men to become POWs.

After serving as a training aircraft to prepare crews of the 55th and 76th ARS for the arrival of HC-97Gs, this KC-97G (serial no. 53-0217) underwent conversion to a C-97G in early 1964. In January, it was assigned to the 76th ARS as a support aircraft. Wearing rescue markings, the C-97G is seen here at Da Nang AB in early 1965. Aircraft of the 76th ARS commonly were deployed to Pacific bases to augment rescue units. The KC-97G serial no. 53-0216 was the only other conversion to C-97G trainer/support aircraft, thereafter assigned to the 55th ARS. *Courtesy of David W. Menard*

The enemy displayed an intense, almost uncanny determination to block all rescue attempts, or at the very least to make them costly in lives and aircraft. US forces countered with equal intensity to pull downed airmen from enemy clutches. A favored tactic had the enemy exploiting that determination by using downed airmen as bait. Knowing that survivors awaited inbound rescue aircraft, they sprang the trap when the pickup helicopter was most vulnerable, in a hover. The enemy also used the "bear hug" technique, in which they closed with the survivor to rule out close air support. Often, however, the enemy did not factor in the skill of helicopter gunship crews and Skyraider pilots that could place ordnance "danger close" to survivors.

In June 1965, the 31st ARS at Clark AB, Philippines, began rotating three Albatrosses through Da Nang AB to provide rescue coverage and mission control in the Gulf of Tonkin. To meet increased demands of the Air Rescue Service by a buildup of forces and mounting airstrikes, two additional HU-16Bs were assigned to Da Nang on a rotational basis. When the two Thailand-based HU-16Bs joined the Albatross element at Da Nang, on January 6, 1966, they formed the 37th Air Rescue Squadron. Intensifying combat over Laos and North Vietnam made it increasingly difficult for the Albatross, with limited communications capability and being

cramped, unpressurized, and unheated, to continue in the airborne mission control role for the SAR task force. Although only moderately more effective in the controller role, the HC-54 was selected to fly the airborne mission control, call sign "Crown," inland. The Rescuemaster's high-altitude capability, its additional room, which improved crew efficiency, and its ability to stay airborne for eighteen hours offered the best interim capability pending the arrival of the Lockheed HC-130H. Russell Vick, who served as an HC-54D navigator, explains the Rescuemaster's role:

As far as the "Original Crowns," the HC-54D was deployed to Southeast Asia at the same time as the HU-16. Four HC-54Ds were temporary duty (TDY) from the 79th ARS at Andersen AB, Guam, and the 36th ARS at Tachikawa AB, Japan, to Detachment 5, 38th ARS, at Udorn until the first HC-130s arrived. Composite crews were from home squadrons and from the 48th ARS at Eglin, 57th ARS at Lajes, and 58th ARS at Wheelus. The HC-54 served as the airborne Rescue Command and Control aircraft for combat rescue missions in Laos and North Vietnam, while the HU-16s served in the same capacity offshore North Vietnam, with the added capability of landing in the sea.

The HC-54 Crown crews consisted of aircraft commander, copilot, navigator, two flight engineers, and a radio operator; we did not carry PJs. Our mission was to orbit in northern Laos from first light until dark. Early-morning departure was at 0400, and the afternoon replacement took off at 1300. Remaining aircraft and crews stood alert. The early departure flew unarmed and unescorted north until within sight of the Red River valley in North Vietnam and relayed weather conditions to Seventh/Thirteenth Air Force. There was a lot of coordination with Air America and with Lima sites, where Jolly Greens were predeployed and often remained overnight.

The only specialized equipment on the HC-54 was a NASA "SARA" receiver tuned to "Guard" channel. It was used many times to locate downed aircrew or aircraft locator beacons and survival radios. Using our radar, we also led Jolly Greens through and around frequent thunderstorms during monsoon season.

To my knowledge, the only Crown aircraft hit by anti-aircraft fire, other than small arms, was an Andersen-based HC-54 hit in early spring 1966 while doing an electronic search too close to Mu Gia Pass, North Vietnam. Damage to the aircraft was minimal, and no crewman was injured when the 37 mm round hit the rear of the aircraft.

At the start of HC-130 operations, Crown HC-54s had amassed over six thousand hours of combat flying time and three thousand hours of combat support time. Those crews gathered from all over the Air Rescue Service established from nothing the tactics and procedures which accounted for success in combat aircrew recovery for the remaining years of the war.

As the HC-54 was phased out of the Air Rescue Service, filling the gap pending the arrival of additional HC-130s were HC-97Gs, some of which, flown by the 76th ARS, were stationed at Okinawa and the Philippines to cover for HU-16Bs flying combat missions.

Air Rescue in Southeast Asia was coming together as an organized force—specifically called a search-and-rescue task force—although much refinement was needed. Fixed-wing support, now labeled "RESCAP" (for Rescue Combat Air Patrol), relied on air force and navy fighter-bombers, along with VNAF Skyraiders and "Water Pump" T-28s; Water Pump was a program to train Laotian pilots in the aircraft, with combat missions usually flown by US pilots. Army Hueys and H-21s, along with Air America and marine H-34s, plus navy UH-2 "Seasprites," aided USAF HH-43s. Although none were pure rescue aircraft, they did the job pending arrival of the HH-3. The Douglas A-1 Skyraider emerged as the obvious answer to the need for a dedicated RESCAP aircraft. Although a throwback to the Korean War, the rugged piston-powered Skyraider was able to carry its own weight in ordnance and fly low and slow to provide close air support. The first USAF A-1s arrived at Bien Hoa at the end of May 1964, to replace the Farm Gate contingent, but were not specifically tasked

with the RESCAP mission until August 1965. Shortly after the bombing campaign against North Vietnam began in early 1965, commanders at air bases in Thailand, from which strike aircraft operated, requested Skyraiders to fly SAR cover. The requests were denied until months later, when the A-1-equipped 602nd Fighter Squadron at Bien Hoa was directed to fly SAR cover for F-105 strikes against surface-to-air (SAM) missile sites around Hanoi. The four Skyraiders were ordered back to Bien Hoa, and in August the 602nd began rotating four A-1s to Udorn RTAFB for two-week periods to cover airstrikes into high-threat zones. The success of those missions led not only to the transfer of the 602nd to Udorn, but to the Skyraider's role as a vital element of the SAR task force.

Finally, in early July 1965, the first faster, longer-range helicopter for combat operations in the spreading war in Southeast Asia arrived—Sikorsky's CH-3C "Big Charlie." Borrowed from the Tactical Air Command at Eglin AFB, two CH-3Cs (s/n 63-9676 and -9685) were assigned to Provisional Detachment 1 at Nakhon Phanom RTAFB. The pair had been camouflaged with pea-green, water-soluble paint, which earned them the name "Jolly Green Giant." Jerry W. Jennings, then a captain and helicopter pilot with the 38th ARS, answers the question "Where and when was the name 'Jolly Green Giant' first used?":

Well, it all began in July 1964 at Eglin AFB, Florida. When the 4488th Test Squadron of the 4485th Test Wing began preparing for Indian River, it was determined that the CH-3s should be painted a camouflage color—flat OD Green. The CH-3s were flown to Pensacola Naval Air Station for painting. When the first painted CH-3 returned to Eglin, a group of us were on the ramp to welcome it home. As the chopper approached, one of the flight mechs said, "Look, it's the Jolly Green Giant."

Nothing more was said about the Jolly Green Giant until July 1965, when two CH-3s, two flight crews, and maintenance support personnel from the 4488th were sent TDY to NKP to begin rescue operations in North Vietnam and Laos. When asked what call sign the CH-3 rescue choppers would use, all pilots agreed that "Jolly Green" and the last two digits of the tail number would be their call sign each and every day. The fighters used different call signs for each day and sortie. We figured that because the enemy knew a rescue chopper would try to rescue every pilot or crew shot down, there was no reason to change the call sign. They would know it was a rescue chopper anyway when they saw it on radar.

On 4 October 1965, the 38th ARS arrived at Udorn. When the 38th commander, Major Baylor Haynes, was told about the Jolly Green call sign, he agreed that it should remain the same.

I was in the 38th ARS, having arrived from Eglin with most of the other squadron members. On 13 October, I was the AC (aircraft commander) on the first pickup accomplished by the 38th ARS. The other crew members were Captain James "Digger" O'Dell, CP (copilot); MSgt William G. Daniels (PJ);

In alert mode, Huskies, when scrambled, hovered and crept to a positioner pole to align the cargo hook with the FSK's sling. This pair of "F" models (serial nos. 63-9714 and -9716) of Det 6, 38th ARRS, stands alert at Da Nang AB in February 1966. Armor added to the HH-43F included panels that replaced lower portions of windshields. *Courtesy of James Mardock*

"Pedro 9-7" of the 40th ARRS on April 12, 1966, on the battlefield of Operation Abilene the day after PJ William Pitsenbarger was killed. Pitsenbarger's fellow PJ Harry O'Bierne is at far left. *Courtesy of Mark Schibler, Lt. Col., USAF (Ret.) collection*

While this HH-43B hovers at the positioner pole, the fire suppression kit is hooked to the cargo sling. The local base rescue crew consisted of pilot, copilot, aeromedical technician, and two airborne rescue men / firefighters. *Courtesy of USAF*

and SSgt Harold R. Schrader, FM (flight mechanic). We picked up Major James Edward Prestle Randall III, an F-105 jock of the 562nd TFS, 25 miles northeast of Dien Bien Phu.

Randall was fortunate to be rescued, since he was pursued by villagers with rifles. Adding to his good fortune was the Jolly Green Giant's pre-positioning at the forward Lima Site 36, enabling the dash into North Vietnam to reach Randall first.

Still short of filling the requirement for the ultimate combat rescue helicopter, the CH-3C quickly underwent modifications to increase the CH-3C's combat survivability. Subsequently, during November and December, six CH-3Cs (s/n 14227 and -14229 to -14233) left the production line for direct airlift to NKP, Thailand. These were officially designated HH-3Cs in January 1966, the only examples so labeled. Eventually, they were redesignated HH-3Es, but only two would survive the war and return to the US, where they were fit with refueling booms. Of the original two CH-3Cs, no. 63-9676 was transferred to Udorn RTAFB in December and assigned to the 20th Helicopter Squadron on January 10. No. 63-9685 was a combat loss, the details surrounding its shootdown serving as testimony to the remarkable lengths to which US forces were willing to go to attempt rescue.

The shoot-down of "Oak 0-1," Lt. Col. George McLeary flying an F-105, on November 5, 1965, set in motion four days of combat search and rescue that ended not only with little success, but with the loss of McCleary, two helicopters, two Skyraiders, battle damage to four aircraft, and five airmen taken prisoner. In addition, the crew of CH-3C s/n 63-9685 of Detachment 5, 38th ARRS, had the unenviable distinction of being the first Jolly Green loss of the war. Successive shootdowns during the SAR caused expansion of the effort that involved navy aircraft, one of which was a Skyraider flown by Gary Gottschalk; he picks up the story:

Aboard USS *Oriskany* on 6 November, orders came to my attack squadron, VA-152, to man a two-plane section for a search mission. Four USAF rescue helicopter crew members were down about 40 miles southwest of Hanoi. The skipper chose Commander Gordon Smith, our squadron executive officer, to lead the flight, and I volunteered to fly wing with him.

Our two Spads were strapped to the catapults and launched at 1730 hours into a lowering sun, followed by a two-hour flight heading northwest. En route and *feet dry*, we started receiving a weak emergency signal from a pilot's survival radio. Responding to the signal with onboard homing equipment, we diverted toward the signal, since it could be a credible one. It could also be a false one, since some of our emergency radios had fallen into enemy hands. Our flight of two was soon circling an area of rough terrain where the signal was coming from. Shortly after, we were bracketed by intense AAA and automatic-weapons fire, some of which put holes in both aircraft, but with no major or disabling damage. It was a "flak trap," and we got out of the area.

Continuing on to the area of the downed helo crew, we arrived after sundown, but with visual conditions and a rising half moon. We started to search with the hope of establishing communication with any of the downed airmen. As we circled an area approximately 3 miles in radius, we encountered AAA and automatic weapons, which we avoided. We searched for perhaps an hour with some help from moonlight as we flew low over the precipitous mountainous terrain, with dense jungle canopy in the valleys between. Then we received a weak signal from nearby, terrain having blocked the line-of-sight signal earlier. We homed on the signal and were able to establish radio contact with one of the airmen. Gordon then had me climb to about 2,000 feet above the area and plot the position as closely as possible, while he tried to pinpoint the survivor's location from low altitude.

We made many low passes close to the airman's position as Gordon communicated with him. We hadn't yet pinpointed a location that would enable the rescue helo to make the pickup. On one of the low passes, Gordon clipped some of the jungle canopy, which we later found on his aircraft. Fuel was now becoming a concern. Then an idea occurred to Commander Smith that probably saved the airman's life. Gordon asked him if he had a flashlight in his survival equipment. He didn't. Smith asked, "Do you have a cigarette lighter?" He did. Gordon told him to flash the lighter whenever he heard the airplane fly directly overhead. Gordon located the position precisely after a few more passes by spotting the small flame in the darkness through the jungle canopy. On a subsequent pass he flashed his navigation lights momentarily from over the position, and I was able to accurately plot it on my charts. We got what we came for, but now fuel was more of a concern since we were about two hours from *Oriskany*, and with about two hours fuel remaining.

We remained on station for about another fifteen minutes, waiting for another flight to relieve us. A flight of four USAF F-4s arrived and we departed. Now it was a game of "do we have enough fuel to make it to *Oriskany*, and if not, where to land?"

Gottschalk and Smith pointed their Spads toward the carrier, giving them the option to ditch alongside the on-station rescue destroyer positioned halfway to the flattop. Smith, meanwhile, radioed a request that the carrier steam in their direction to lessen flight time. *Oriskany*'s captain obliged. When the tailwheel of Gottschalk's Skyraider touched the deck, the engine quit. Smith too made a successful trap aboard. Thirty-five years later at a reunion, the Spad drivers discovered that Capt. Bartholomew Connolly took *Oriskany* into dangerously shallow water to bring the pair aboard.

At first light the next morning, SSgt. Berkeley Naugle, the flight engineer of Jolly Green 8-5, was hoisted aboard a navy Sea King helicopter of HS-2, call sign "Nimble 6-2," launched from USS *Independence*. Naugle's three fellow crewmen had been captured almost immediately after bailing out of their burning CH-3C. Gordon Smith had stayed far beyond his mission time to find the Jolly Green crew. And he went out again the next day to help search for the remaining three. That day he also escorted bullet-riddled Nimble 6-2 to a safe mountaintop clearing, where its crew was rescued.

Months earlier, on July 27, the ill-fated CH-3C no. 9685 had performed the first combat rescue by a Jolly Green in Southeast Asia. Capt. George Martin and crew, call sign "Shed 8-5," penetrated deep into North Vietnam to rescue F-105 pilot Capt. Frank Tullo, one of six shot down during a major strike against SAM sites; only Tullo was rescued, the others having been killed or taken prisoner. Joe Ballinger, who was assigned to the original NKP detachment and would eventually log more than 4,300 hours in nearly every H-3 variant, recalls:

I could go on forever about the H-3 as a forgiving, versatile helicopter. It is the "Gooney Bird" of helicopters. I had two CH-3Cs in my detachment at NKP in 1965. When the shock wore off that we were flying combat missions over North Vietnam with H-43Bs, Tom Curtis and I wrote a fast report on what kind of helicopter was needed for the job; kind of a dream sheet, thinking about a two-engine Lockheed Cheyenne, all-weather instrumented with extended range drop tanks, armor, and guns-a-go-go. Two weeks later, the two TAC CH-3Cs arrived on our ramp. Too big (hell of a target), not enough power, not fast (the H-43 could outrun it at high altitude), Mickey Mouse cargo hoist, no guns, no armor, internal fiberglass fuel tank, but it did have two engines! You can imagine the shock of the TAC crews when we told them what our mission was. But they jumped right in and joined us. Those guys had balls!

George Martin made the first North Vietnam "Jolly Green" combat rescue on 27 July 1965. George's engines were so power-deteriorated, they screamed and bawled, but he went anyway. He picked up Captain Frank Tullo less than 50 miles from Hanoi. The hoist quit in the down position, so he landed in a rice paddy, while the crew pulled in Frank. They took some hits but no one was hurt.

They got safely back to Lima Site 36, where the bad engine had to be changed. We sent an engine up by Air America, and by the time I got word from higher headquarters that an engine couldn't be changed in the field without a special hoist kit, George was on his way back to NKP. A rope over one of the rotor blades with twenty Laotians pulling might not be in the tech manual, but Site 36 was not a place to stay overnight.

With air losses increasing over North Vietnam, and with the range extension offered by the increased fuel capacity of the HH-3Cs deemed only marginal for air rescue in the combat theater, modification of the CH-3 for air-to-air refueling on the basis of ongoing testing became paramount. Meanwhile, on January 8, 1966, the Air Rescue Service was redesignated the Aerospace Rescue and Recovery Service (ARRS) to reflect

Air Rescue's role in the space program. On the same day, the ARRS activated the 3rd Aerospace Rescue and Recovery Group (ARRG), headquartered at Tan Son Nhut AB. The 3rd ARRG was responsible for the 38th ARRS, with thirty-two HH-43B/Fs assigned to fourteen detachments: ten in Vietnam and four in Thailand. About that time, HH-43 crews adopted the name and call sign "Pedro," revived from the Korean War when H-19 crews of the 2157th Air Rescue Squadron used the call sign. The 3rd ARRG charged newly activated 37th ARS at Da Nang with responsibility for rescue in North Vietnam, Laos, and the Gulf of Tonkin.

In August 1965, the helicopter school at Stead AFB conducted an escalated training program for crews selected for the first HH-3Es. Under the code name "Limelight 36," crews and support personnel trained as a unit to learn the rescue helicopter. Until the end of September, crews trained under the tutelage of Korean War rescue veteran Maj. Baylor R. Haynes. On November 3, two HH-3Es arrived by C-133 transport at Bien Hoa AB. Maj. Haynes and fellow aircrew flight-tested the pair before flying them to their duty assignment with Detachment 5, 38th ARS, at Udorn RTAFB. By the end of 1965, Detachment 5 counted six HH-3Es, one CH-3C, and three HH-43Bs. Two HC-54Ds remained on the unit inventory, the last Rescuemasters in theater. Russel Vick, who served as a rescue crew navigator, noted: "I was TDY to Det 5, 38th ARS, in 1965 and '66 with the 'Crown' HC-54Ds and had the honor and pleasure of knowing and working with the original Jollies. These guys were the first to fly and establish the tactics and combat rescue record of the HH-3. They were the original 'Right Stuff.'" Rescue forces throughout Southeast Asia at year's end also comprised five HU-16Bs, along with four HH-43 Pedros, of Detachment 7, 38th ARS, at Da Nang AB. An additional nineteen HH-43s were stationed at Takhli, Korat, and Nakhon Phanom Royal Thai Air Force Bases, and at Tan Son Nhut, Bien Hoa, Pleiku, and Binh Thuy Air Bases, South Vietnam.

Concurrent with familiarization courses conducted in the HH-3E at Stead AFB in August 1965, similar training with the next upgrade in rescue aircraft was occurring in Florida at Eglin AFB. Prior to deployment of the first HC-130Hs to the war zone, accelerated transition and rescue training was conducted with Eglin's 48th Air Rescue Squadron. In December, two HC-130Hs, on temporary duty from the 36th ARS in Japan, arrived at Udorn RTAFB to replace the HC-54s. When three additional HC-130Hs arrived in March 1966, the five rescue Hercules formed Detachment 1, 37th ARRS. In April, the HC-54s departed the combat theater.

Featuring the latest electronic equipment, air-droppable rescue gear, and huge fuel capacity, plus fit with the Fulton Recovery System, the HC-130H was the ultimate multifunctional rescue and airborne controller platform. The Cook AN/ARD-17 tracker was considered the heart of the H model's vast array of electronics, since its extremely long range could detect signals of emergency beepers attached to airmen who

After this HH-3E (serial no. 65-12786) of the 37th ARS was hit by ground fire on October 16, 1968, it sank off Con Co Island, North Vietnam. The crew of "Jolly 2-4" scrambles to the upper fuselage for rescue by a hovering Jolly Green helicopter. *Courtesy of Gary Bryant*

flew the dangerous skies. The highly versatile Hercules with ample crew could direct an entire search-and-rescue mission throughout the expanse of the war zone.

BLUE-WATER SAR

No historical treatment of air rescue during the war in Southeast Asia is complete without looking into the US Navy's search-and-rescue experience. The US Navy had maintained a presence in the West Pacific since World War II, with Task Force 77 (TF 77) as the operational command. When hostilities flared, all of the navy's attack carriers (with the exception of USS *Kennedy*) along with five antisubmarine warfare support carriers served at least one Vietnam cruise, beginning in August 1964. Multiple carriers were positioned in the northern portion of the Gulf of Tonkin on "Yankee Station," where TF 77 became known as the "Tonkin Gulf Yacht Club." Before sufficient land bases were established, a single carrier to support ground operations in South Vietnam was positioned off the southern coast at "Dixie Station" from May 1965 to August 1966. Early in the war, until USAF aircraft became

widely available, navy A-1 Skyraiders supported Air America helicopters on rescue missions. Navy A-1s were key players in the first major rescue effort of the war when, on November 18, 1964, an HU-16B airborne controller requested navy A-1s to join a pair of HH-43B Huskies over Laos in the search for an F-100 pilot.

Although the CSAR mission was the primary responsibility of the air force, the northernmost regions of North Vietnam and the Tonkin Gulf lay beyond the reach of land-based helicopters, even those flying from Lima sites in Laos. Combat SAR then too became a navy responsibility; however, the navy, like the air force, was unprepared, untrained, and ill equipped for combat search and rescue. By April 1965, combat attrition had plane guard UH-2A/B "Seasprite" helicopters aboard destroyers of TF 77 performing search and rescue on a contingency basis. Antisubmarine SH-3 Sea Kings aboard four carriers followed suit after being stripped of primary mission gear deemed unnecessary in the absence of enemy submarines. Seasprite and Sea King crews generally held to waters ("feet wet") off Vietnam's coast. Although a UH-2B crew of Helicopter

US Air Force and Navy aircraft often worked as a team during rescue operations in the Gulf of Tonkin and off North Vietnam. Navy A-1 Skyraiders aboard carriers on Yankee Station regularly escorted HU-16Bs. The pilot of this A-1H of VA-145, aboard USS *Intrepid* in 1967, opens the dive brakes for HU-16B flight engineer Tom Hansen's camera. Underwing of this "Spad," call sign "Electron," are rocket launchers and a forty-five-minute smoke marker.

TEMPORARILY SUSPENDED?
NEED A
PICK-ME-UP?
Contact:
CROWN
Sandy JOLLY
Pedro GREEN

243.0 Mcs

JOLLY GREEN

CONFUSED? FOLLOW THESE STEPS

1. Use your head.
2. Stay with chute/aircraft.
3. Conserve flares and radio.
4. Advise others of your position and condition
5. Do exactly as instructed by SAR aircraft
6. Stay calm-others have been rescued under worse conditions than yours.

We bring 'em back alive

AFSC · EGLIN AFB, FL

Combat Support Squadron 1 (HC-1), Det A, made the first sea-based helicopter rescue in North Vietnam on September 20, 1965, longer-range Sea Kings of helicopter antisubmarine (HS) squadrons, beginning with HS-4 aboard *Yorktown*, began dangerous treks inland to effect rescues. The "Golden Falcons" of HS-2 became the hard-luck squadron, suffering heavy losses, which tempered fifteen saves during its first three combat cruises.

Improvements of the SH-3A "Protector's" SAR capability had begun in March 1965, focusing on refueling Sea Kings from fleet destroyers. Destroyers, having been fit with 7,000-gallon jet fuel tanks for the unsuccessful QH-50 antisubmarine drone helicopter, would become the fuel source for SH-3s conducting long-range inland rescues. The "hover in-flight refueling" (HIFR), "High-Drink," technique pioneered by HS-2 proved successful and later was adopted by air force HH-3s. Aboard USS *Hornet* in 1965, five SH-3As of HS-2 were stripped of sonar equipment, were armed with machine guns, and had their high-visibility markings painted over to blend with their dark-gray livery. Steel fuel tanks beneath the cabin floor (which shipboard regulations forbade being kept full) were removed in lieu of two centerline drop tanks from A-4 Skyhawks, kept in wooden cradles. Their combined capacity of 1,000 pounds of JP-5 jet fuel extended the Sea King's range by 200 miles. Similar modifications to SH-3s of HS-6 "Raunchy Indians" were taking place aboard the carrier *Kearsarge* in 1966.

The navy was losing two helicopters for every three aircrew rescued, and one crewman killed or captured for every two aircrew rescued, highlighting the overwhelming need for a dedicated combat SAR unit. On September 1, 1967, HC-1 was divided into four different squadrons, one of which was

US Coast Guard lieutenant Jack Ritticher (*right*) with LCmdr. Lonnie Mixon with an HH-52A prior to deployment to Vietnam for the USAF pilot exchange program, during which the pair flew Jolly Green helicopters. *Courtesy of US Coast Guard*

This photo was taken by an HH-43B pilot as it supported rescuers wading into the ocean to assist the crew of an F-4C (serial no. 64-0769) of the 558th TFS, 12th TFW. The Phantom ended up in the surf while trying to abort takeoff from Can Ranh Bay AB on March 27, 1967. Both crewmen survived. *Courtesy of Dick Van Allen*

Helicopter Combat Support Squadron 7 (HC-7). Although the squadron was the sole unit tasked with CSAR, it absorbed various detachments, including the "Clementine" UH-2A/B Seasprites aboard ships.

Efforts were under way to increase the combat effectiveness of the Seasprite helicopter, including modifications for High-Drink refueling from ships. In early 1966, a single UH-2 of HC-1, Det 5, was stripped of nonessential gear, fitted with armor, and painted two-tone green camouflage. The detachment, aboard USS *Coontz*, proved so successful that it spawned five detachments that eventually were absorbed by HC-7. Eventually, both Sea Kings and Seasprites were repowered with "Gold Stripe" GE T58 engines, which were rated for higher operating speeds and temperatures to provide emergency power. To adapt to the intensifying tactical environment, Kaman Aircraft Corp. drew from its experience testing a Seasprite as an army gunship to develop an armed rescue Seasprite. Featuring twin engines for safety and added power, the combat-dedicated Seasprite emerged as the HH-2C. Ample armor, a four-bladed tail rotor, crew-served machine guns, additional radios, and nose-mounted 7.62 mm minigun turret brought the HH-2C's gross weight up to nearly 13,000 pounds, requiring dual-wheel main landing gear. Compromises, which commonly result from improvements, included doubled fuel

consumption requiring drop tanks that proved unreliable. Worse was the increased likelihood of engine stall while hovering, caused by salt water ingested into engine intakes. It was also found that jolts from deck landings caused the minigun to fire a few rounds, spelling a quick end to the turret installation. Just days after the first of six HH-2Cs became operational, all single-engine Seasprites were removed from SAR duty. To give heroic, spirited helicopter crews the best chance of success, Sikorsky and the navy began work on the ultimate CSAR Sea King.

US Army UH-1 Huey helicopters came in for their share of rescues, mainly in southern delta regions, where air force assets were limited. The sheer number of Hueys of all services soon committed to Vietnam proved vital in expanding the overall SAR network.

FEET WET

As additional HC-130Hs arrived in theater, at least two flew eight-hour shifts monitoring aerial activity. Albatross amphibians then were committed mainly to flying tracks off the coast of North Vietnam. During these long-duration missions, the HU-16Bs typically were accompanied by a pair of navy Skyraiders, which provided cover should the Albatross make a water landing to rescue downed airmen. In that event, the droning monotony of the mission abruptly changed to high drama.

For example, on March 14, 1966, an F-4C Phantom—call sign "Pluto 2"—was badly damaged by antiaircraft fire during a strike in North Vietnam. Knowing the chance of rescue was greater if he reached the gulf, Maj. James Peerson nursed his crippled jet to the coast, where he and Capt. Lynwood Bryant ejected. Flying the sixth hour of their on-station orbit, Capt. David Westenbarger and his Albatross crew heard the "mayday" call and turned for the area. Spotting the pair in the water 2 miles from shore, Westenbarger jettisoned drop tanks and full-stalled the Albatross onto the sea. As scores of enemy boats converged on the aircraft, PJ James Pleiman jumped into the sea to pull Peerson toward the aircraft. Suddenly, the shoreline erupted with enemy fire, while crewmen exchanged rifle fire with an approaching boat. Two shells bracketed the aircraft and a third found its mark on the Albatross, which exploded and burned. Radio operator A1C Robert Hilton was killed and flight mech SSgt. Clyde Jackson was blown out of the aircraft. The PJ was hit and the navigator, Capt. Donald Price, was burned by igniting JATO bottles while trying to leave the airplane. Once in the sea, among burning fuel, he pulled the F-4 pilot clear of the blazing, sinking Albatross.

Within minutes, a pair of VA-115 "Arab" Skyraiders flown by Lieutenant Commanders Jerry Tabrum and Manny Benero arrived and made rocket runs on the shore batteries. With 5-inch rockets expended, they turned to cannon fire to silence mortar fire. Benero, now on-scene commander, called for rescue helicopters for the eight men now in the water. The PJ went down with the aircraft, to which he had been tethered. Tabrum noted:

The NVA attempted to capture the survivors by sending three small boats to the scene. I made one rocket run firing two nineteen-shot pods of 2.75-inch FFARs in salvo on the boats, and they disappeared. We continued remaining in sight of

Another parachute will be added to the save scoreboard of this Jolly Green. The return of rescued airmen was a much-celebrated affair, with returnees usually greeted by base officials. This fortunate pilot arrives at Nakhon Phanom ("Naked Fanny") RTAFB in spring 1968. *Courtesy of Ron Angelly*

This Skyhook balloon was inflated at Nha Trang AB in March 1970. In the background is a special-operations C-130E "Blackbird," one of only a few operated by the 15th Special Operations Squadron in support of the army's Studies and Operations Group (SOG). *Courtesy of Neal R. Schneider / Dave Hansen, Wonderchief Archives*

the burning amphibian, eventually vectoring in two "Fetch" SH-3 helos from *Yorktown*, who, despite taking enemy fire, rescued five crewmen before being forced out of the area. By this time a very low overcast had come in from seaward, forcing us to remain at a very low altitude in order to remain in visual contact with the amphibian. The final crewman was rescued by an H-34 helo vectored in from the guided-missile cruiser USS *England*, terminating a two and a half hour ordeal.

Hilton and Plieman became the first air rescue crewmen killed in action during the war. Obviously, the rescue business was one of highs and lows, wins and losses. Tom Hansen, then an A1C flight mechanic nearing seven years of service, recalls a rescue off the coast of North Vietnam that had a brighter outcome:

In the course of a year of service with the 37th ARRS, and flying 121 missions, this was the only actual rescue in which I participated. I was assigned to the 37th ARRS, stationed at Da Nang from 17 August 1966 to 16 August 1967, as a flight mechanic on Grumman Albatross HU-16B aircraft. By 1966, the '16 was the only amphibious aircraft (excluding the equally famous HH-3 helicopter) in the US Air Force.

Our higher headquarters was the 3rd Air Rescue Group at Saigon. Even though I belonged to a flying unit in the combat zone, we were still part of MAC, and not TAC, or Seventh Air Force like all the other USAF squadrons in the combat zone.

The date is 10 September 1966—this will be my twelfth mission since arriving in country. It is the morning mission, call sign "Crown Alpha." Takeoff time for the Alpha mission was 0500, which would put us on station at 0630. But, possibly delayed by a predawn rocket attack on the base, records show

The moment of pickup when a naval officer is snatched by a Skyhook C-130 during a "Gabriel demonstration" at the PACAF Jungle Survival School at Clark AB, Philippines. *Courtesy of Robert J. Donaldson*

us arriving on station at 1315 hours, normally the time of the afternoon Bravo mission.

Our aircraft for the day is HU-16B 51-7182, not one of our own, which were camouflaged Sea Blue with white underneath. It belongs to the 33rd ARRS, based at Naha AB, Okinawa—one of our sister squadrons with whom we exchanged crews and aircraft. The plane is painted dull aluminum overall with standard and current USAF markings. Only the gloss chrome yellow wingtip and fuselage bands are deleted. These were standard Air Rescue markings worldwide, but in this case overpainted to tone down conspicuous markings. There are bad guys out there who like to shoot at airplanes, and they don't care if they happen to be rescue birds. Our pilot is Major Henry Irwin, an HU-16 record holder. Copilot is Major Don Purdy, navigator unknown, radio operator James Rogan, and PJ SSgt Dan Schmidt.

The preflight, engine start, taxi, and takeoff are routine, no surprises. Takeoff gross weight is 36,000 pounds max.

Fuel load is full mains, full drop tanks, floats empty. Equipment load is standard MA-1 kit, twenty SA-8 parachute flares, smoke floats, and four 15KS-1000 JATO cylinders. And, of course, personal survival gear, parachutes, and weapons.

We take off to the north from Da Nang's 10,000-foot runway, in between the variety of aircraft that flew over there. We head for our central orbit station, 1.5 hours flight time, as the lumbering HU-16 at max gross flies. Our station lies between Vinh and Than Hoa, North Vietnam, and between Chinese Hainan Island and North Vietnam, about 30 to 35 miles off the coast.

As we arrive on station, we check in with our controlling agency, a navy destroyer leader ship, call sign "Royal Lancer." Lancer tells us that our fighter escort of two Skyraiders is off somewhere doing an electronic and visual search for another carrier aircraft, call sign "Robbie," also a Skyraider, but the multirole version. This is an EA-1F, an electronic snooper and countermeasures aircraft. Robbie has talked to Lancer a while ago concerning electrical problems and has not been heard from since. Royal Lancer gives us coordinates of Robbie's last known position, along with the info that they had broken off from their mission and were going back to recover aboard their carrier.

The two A-1s that are assigned to us for RESCAP are off somewhere snooping around, looking for some sign of their comrade. They are from VA-25, call sign "Canasta," off USS *Coral Sea*. We are now in contact with them and heading for their area. They tell us they are picking up an occasional faint beeper signal, but they have not been able to home on it. We tell Canasta lead that now we too are starting to pick up a beeper signal but can't get a steer on it. We are in the area now and initiate an electronic search, using our Sarah receiver. This is a beacon homer that we've been told is on loan from NASA. We start picking up a stronger signal. So do the Canasta birds, which are closer and get there first. The two A-1 drivers spot survivors in rubber rafts. Canasta lead holds down his transmit button for ten seconds so we can get a bearing on him, and shortly we are over the guys too.

As we approach in a shallow descent, our PJ suits up to go into the water. Canasta lead calls Lancer, informing him that we have located four survivors in rafts, apparently in good shape. He gives Lancer their position relative to the ship, which had a TACAN beacon for working with aircraft. Canasta also tells Lancer that they better send their helo, "Lancer's Angel," a Kaman Seasprite. Lead doesn't think we can land in those swells safely to make the rescue. Lancer asks our pilot what he thinks. Irwin is an old head in '16s, and his reply is "No sweat."

While radio traffic goes back and forth, we overfly the survivors in a shallow, descending turn. There are four soaked fliers bobbing in one-man rafts. They have a Mk-13 smoke flare deployed, and sea dye-marker in the water around them. This is a visual-sighting aid that turns the water into a bright-aqua-blue-green patch near the rafts. As we make our pass over them, I arm and toss out the open Dutch door in back, a forty-five-minute smoke float. This gives our pilot a read on the surface wind velocity and direction and also gives him a reference point to aim for on final approach, as once we are down low just above the waves, we won't see the rafts.

The weather and sea state is relatively sunny, high haze layer, moderate wind, about 4- or 5-foot swells. We can handle it. I don't recall if we had to get permission from 3rd ARG, call sign "King," to make this pickup—on later pickups we did. The radio operator would call them on HF because of the range (almost 400 miles). Intense rivalry existed between the helos and we HU-16s to get the pickups.

After passing over our guys in the water on our downwind leg, and dropping a smoke float for the pilot, we jettison our drop tanks. They depart with their characteristic audible bang, as they are held to the underwing bomb shackle by four explosive squibs. I make a quick eyeball check on both sides to make sure both tanks are gone, and call the pilot on interphone to tell him so. We swing around in a tight left turn, lining up into the wind for final approach, heading for the thin column of blue-gray smoke that is our aiming point. We are about 9 miles offshore of North Vietnam, well within SAM range. The SA-2 Guideline has a slant range of 27 miles, but we are down real low; we are safe . . . I think.

We are all strapped in tight now. This is going to be a rough ride. The power is on just enough to keep us a tad above stall speed, full flaps, the nose is up, wave tops are flashing past. The pilot picks his moment, left hand on the wheel, right hand on the throttles on the overhead—he yanks the throttles back. We stall onto a wave crest with a mighty thump and a big splash; props go into reverse. Engines bellowing, water flying all over the place, we rapidly decelerate. From my vantage point in the back end, all I can see is water. We could be upside down, for all I know. Now the engines are idling, props coming out of reverse, and I can see out the window again. We are bobbing and heaving on the swells. I spring out of my seat and make a fast bilge check (six underfloor watertight compartments) and report to the pilot, "Bilge check OK." The master has done it again. The survivors are very close, passing close aboard our left wingtip as we get into position to pull them aboard. The pilot jockeys the throttles between idle and reverse, maneuvering us the last few yards to the rafts, which are, like us, bobbing and heaving all over the place. I am now at the open back door on interphone calling out the raft positions to the pilot, who is now backing us toward them. When we have them about 10 yards from our Dutch door, the PJ leaps into the water, and in a few strokes he is up to them. We have a line on the PJ, so as soon as he grabs a raft line, the nav and I haul them in. They are now at the door, and we start grabbing bodies and hauling them inside; nothing fancy, grab 'em and haul 'em in, headfirst, or whatever. They don't have any injuries.

In short order we have four soaked, unhurt, grateful fliers and our fearless PJ aboard. I inform the pilot we have

everyone aboard, door is closed, let's go! Throttles to the firewall, now we find out what this old Grumman is made of. We slowly begin to accelerate, slamming and pounding into the waves. There is no time for finding seats and strapping in—this is a combat rescue. We are a pile of wet bodies in the back end, trying to find something to hang on to as we are thumping and banging into the waves, trying to get up on the step.

We finally get up on the step—airspeed comes up better now, but it is still a mighty rough ride. Finally we break free, we are airborne. On the water about six or eight minutes, takeoff run is about fifty seconds.

There were no boats, no bad guys, no shooting. We climb and head back to Da Nang (TACAN channel 37, call sign "Panama") at METO power all the way. The pilot and RO make all the appropriate radio calls (Royal Lancer, who in turn calls the carrier *Roosevelt* to let them know their guys are safe), RCC at Saigon, call sign "King," 37th ops at Da Nang, etc. Everyone knows we have the four-man navy crew aboard. Everyone finds a seat, and we find out what happened. The EA-1F crew from VAW-13 had launched from *Roosevelt* on an electronic snooper mission. Their commo and electronics started going down, and later they had a complete electrical failure. They lost a generator and then had an engine fire. Not only did they lose all navaids and radios to tell someone they were going down, they had to make a quick choice: bail out or ride it down and ditch. The pilot makes the call—they stay together and rider 'er down. The pilot did a good job because they all got out with no injuries.

When we called squadron ops and told them we made the pickup and were inbound, they scrambled the alert crew ("Crown Charlie") to take over the rest of our mission. We're done flying for the day. This gets logged as a combat mission. Ordinarily, our missions are combat support. Back at Da Nang we taxi to our very congested parking area. Everyone from our ops is out to greet and congratulate us. This is what Rescue is all about—finding and bringing people back! The navy guys get a ride to the hospital to get checked over and debriefed, dry clothes, and a shot of "cough medicine." Their ship would send a COD, a C-1A transport (also a Grumman aircraft), to bring them back to the "bird barge."

As soon as our bird was parked, I climb up on the wing to dip the fuel tanks as part of the postflight. The big maintenance item is an immediate and thorough freshwater washdown for corrosion control after an open-sea landing.

I felt like I was part of an elite group. Sure, we had old airplanes, but we had a first-class mission, and there was not one other aircraft in the entire inventory that could do what we could do. The Jolly Greens were amphibious, but their water landings and takeoffs were from a hover. I think going in the water for them was a last resort.

When I found out I had gotten assigned to Air Rescue, and HU-16s no less, I felt very fortunate. I had admired the Albatross since I was a kid. Never did I dream that someday

I would be on a rescue crew on an HU-16. The bird I flew on that day of the rescue is still around.

In detailing the art of making an open-sea landing in an Albatross, Hansen explains:

As we are just prior to touchdown—slam-down would be more appropriate—we are just barely above the crests of the swells. The power is just enough to keep the bird from stalling in. Flaps are full down, the nose is up. That isn't just for landing attitude, it is also to keep from hitting a swell with the nose and caving in the nose gear doors. This almost certainly results in a sinking. We are probably doing about 80 knots, and the wave tops are flashing past, seemingly at eyeball level looking out the window in back. When the pilot picks his spot, the intent is to set it down on a crest, not in a trough. The timing must be exquisite. There is no gentle squishing down into the water. When you hit, you know you have arrived. Prop reverse was always used to shorten the landing run-out considerably, and lessen the pounding and banging.

A WELL-OILED MACHINE

By the end of 1966, the war in Southeast Asia was in full swing. Bombing campaigns against North Vietnam and Laos, interdiction of the Ho Chi Minh Trail, and tactical support missions placed high demands on air rescue. Eventually, new equipment and aircraft, along with refined tactics and techniques, allowed the spirited and dedicated men of the ARRS to meet those demands to give downed airmen the best chance of survival; a well-oiled machine indeed. At the beginning of 1967, the ARRS counted more than fifty aircraft in theater: HU-16Bs at Da Nang to cover the Gulf of Tonkin; twenty-nine HH-43s, HH-3Es, and HC-130s. In mid-January, the six HC-130s at Udorn RTAFB—formerly Detachment 1 of the 37th ARRS—became the 39th Aerospace Rescue and Recovery Squadron. Detachment 2 was then formed at Udorn to meet the demands of rescue in Laos and North Vietnam. By February, aircraft of the rescue force were identified by standard call signs: the HH-43B/Fs Huskies became "Pedro," HH-3Es were the "Jolly Greens," HU-16B Albatrosses—and their replacement in the

In mid-1968, an unmarked HH-3E is refueled at Lima Site 98 in Laos. Rescue helicopters stood alert at forward sites to shorten the time and distance to airmen downed during strikes into North Vietnam. *Courtesy of Ray Sancton*

Proclaiming their dedication to rescue, personnel of the 37th Aerospace Rescue and Recovery Squadron at Da Nang AB posted these signs of encouragement on a revetment wall. Displayed left of the Jolly Green character is the Air Force Outstanding Unit Award ribbon. *Courtesy of Rodney Aukshun*

airborne mission controller role, HC-130s—were labeled "Crown" and later "King." CSAR-dedicated A-1 Skyraiders were "Sandys" throughout the war.

Ramp space at Udorn became such a premium that in May 1967, the HC-130-equipped 39th ARRS relocated to Tuy Hoa AB, South Vietnam. Living conditions were poor, and wind-whipped sand challenged maintenance crews. Enemy activity was never far from Tuy Hoa, as evidenced by a sapper attack on July 29, 1968, that left two HC-130Ps destroyed and seven aircraft damaged. Despite periodic shortages of HC-130s, the 39th flew daily orbits over the Gulf of Tonkin and central Laos. Although aerial refueling had been approved in January, the squadron's first aerial refueling between an HC-130P and an HH-3E occurred on June 21; by September the technique had become routine, spelling the end of the HU-16B's combat service. Despite aerial refueling, forward-operating locations and Lima sites in northern Laos saw frequent use to shorten the distance to downed airmen.

Despite political limitations, widening and vastly improved enemy defenses, and the constant effort to catch up to technology, Air Rescue personnel made do on fortitude and ingenuity. Their pride ran deep; their dedication and camaraderie were without question. As experience was gained and lessons were learned, basic procedures governing search and rescue were written with built-in flexibility that allowed decision-making on scene. These guidelines professed, "In a search and rescue effort, certain calculated risks must be taken, risks that must be measured against the odds of losing additional men and aircraft. Only those risks having a strong possibility of salvaging an otherwise hopeless situation with a reasonable degree of safety should be considered." The A-1 Skyraider proved to be a vital element of the SAR team, its dual function being to locate survivors and provide suppressive fire for recovery helicopters. Its speed was compatible with that of the Jolly Green, enabling it to escort the helicopter and provide continuous close cover during the survivor pickup and egress. Its loiter time of five hours enabled it to remain in the SAR area for long-enough periods to reduce the number of relief aircraft. Normally, a SAR team comprised four Sandys, two Jolly Greens, and a Crown control aircraft. Sandys worked in two flights of two aircraft each: Sandy 1 and 2 being the low element, and 3 and 4 the high element. A Sandy usually assumed the role of on-scene commander, or the job might go to a forward air controller (FAC), whose small aircraft was equipped to manage communication and mark targets; initially, FACs were Cessna O-1 Bird Dogs, followed by O-2s, and eventually North American OV-10A Broncos. Other resources came into play, often because they were available and in proximity. These might include fighter aircraft, fixed-wing and helicopter gunships, flare ships, refueling aircraft, and ground forces, from any service. The air mission commander, who was aboard the HC-130P King, juggled numerous and diversified resources in addition to providing weather, navigational, and intelligence information.

Held in high esteem on the air rescue team was the pararescue element, the highly trained PJ who can operate in almost any environment. About one-third of downed crewmen needed the PJ's help. The survivor, often wounded or trapped, was unable to assist in his own rescue, requiring that the PJ go down the helicopter's hoist to find survivors, provide medical aid, possibly fight off the enemy, and get victims onto the hoist of the hovering helicopter. The two PJs aboard Jolly Green helicopters usually tossed a coin to determine which one went down the hoist. Pararescuemen were also part of the crew of HH-43 helicopters committed to aircrew recovery. The PJ's ride down the hoist was not always to rescue downed airmen, but soldiers wounded in ground combat. Most army medevac Hueys had yet to be equipped with hoists, so Air Rescue flew missions called "Troops in Contact," or TICs. Pedro crews of Detachment 6, 38th ARRS, based at Bien Hoa Air Base, got their share of TICs.

WHAT MAKES YOU DO IT?

Milton Caniff, American human-interest cartoonist of *Steve Canyon* fame, asks the question in a passage he wrote that pays homage to the men of Air Rescue. Answers vary and are elusive but, on the whole, seldom are explained by a humble rescue man. It's deeper than that. In the words of legendary PJ Duane Hackney, "I don't really go for the idea of killing. I would rather save a life."

On March 7, 1966, PJ A1C William H. Pitsenbarger of Detachment 6, 38th ARRS, was lowered from a hovering helicopter onto a burning minefield to rescue a wounded Vietnamese soldier. "Pits" was seasoned, having survived more than 250 combat missions. One month later, on April 11, Pitsenbarger was aboard HH-43 "Pedro 7-3" when it and "Pedro 9-7" hurriedly lifted off from Bien Hoa's pad. They had been scrambled to rescue wounded soldiers of the 1st Infantry Division under attack while engaged in a sweep named Operation Abilene.

When the pilot, Capt. Harold Salem, arrived over dense jungle where Charlie Company had been cut off and was fighting for its life, he had to descend below the treetops for the 200-foot hoist cable to reach the ground. Pitsenbarger, after being lowered, signaled flight mechanic Sgt. Gerald Hammond to lower the litter. Continually exposed to heavy fire, Pitsenbarger treated the wounded and prepared them for the litter ride up the hoist. Shortly after the second Pedro left with a load of wounded, Salem and his copilot, Maj. Maurice Kessler, returned to extract more wounded. Salem describes what followed:

> We had just worked into position in that narrow opening. It was almost impossible to see anything below because of the smoke. Hammond was lowering the litter basket, still 10 feet above Pits's head, when all hell broke loose.
>
> The VC really poured it on us, apparently aiming everything they had right at us to knock us out of the treetops. We took hits all over the aircraft, including our oil lines, and we immediately began losing rpm at a rapid rate. We either had to go down or get out of there fast before we lost all power.
>
> Hammond could see Pitsenbarger below, looking up at us. And when Hammond beckoned him to grab the basket and come out with us, Pits just gave him a wave-off. So we hauled out of there—or tried to. The basket got hung up in the trees, and we had to cut the cable loose to get out.

Seeing the helicopter taking multiple hits, and Hammond waving at him, Pitsenbarger made the instant decision to stay with the wounded. Army sergeant Fred Navarro, one of three survivors of his ten-man rifle squad, later told how Pitsenbarger continued to treat the wounded as the large enemy force mauled Charlie Company. When ammo ran low, he ran from man to man collecting clips, which he distributed to those

This US Marine Corps F-4 Phantom crew, Lt. William C. Ryan Jr. (*left*) and Lt. Gary L. Bain, were shot down twice during 1969. Both were rescued on the first shoot-down; however, only Bain survived to be rescued the second time. *Courtesy of Gary L. Bain collection*

who could still shoot. Pitsenbarger then added to the defensive firepower. As the enemy prepared for an all-out assault at dark, their female soldiers slipped in to steal weapons, carry off their dead, and slit the throats of US wounded. In desperation, the infantrymen called in danger-close artillery throughout the night.

The next day, Detachment 6 crews at Bien Hoa were told the zone was too hot to continue medevacs. 1Lt. Mark Schibler, the pilot of "Pedro 9-7," remembers:

Everyone in the unit had been up most of the night worrying about Pitsenbarger, and my crew was the first up the next morning. We got the call from the RCC in Saigon that the army thought the area was safe enough for us to get into, so we launched. When we arrived, the army had already dropped off some combat engineers, who were felling large trees to make an LZ [landing zone] large enough for Chinooks to land in. Since the small clearing was already large enough for us to get into, we landed and took on three wounded, which was all we had room for lying on the floor in the back of the HH-43. Our PJ, Harry O'Bierne, wanted to stay on the ground and search for Pitsenbarger, so we took the first three to the local MASH facility and returned as soon as we could. When we landed, Harry met us and said, "If anything happens to me, I just want you to know that Pits didn't make it." That remark just totally drained me, and I could hardly fly the rest of the evacuations. We were concerned since Pits hadn't met us when we landed, but confirmation was just heartbreaking. I didn't understand totally what Harry was telling us, because he didn't elaborate that the army was still experiencing sniper fire and they still didn't have a secure perimeter. We made two more trips before the engineers had the clearing enlarged enough for the Chinooks, so we returned to base.

Photographs taken of rescuers and the rescued were common during the war. On December 3, 1968, the two crewmen of an OV-1A Mohawk of the 245th Aviation Company "Redeye" ejected near Kham Duc, South Vietnam, after being hit by ground fire. With covering fire from 6th SOS Skyraiders, they were rescued by an HH-3E Jolly Green crew of the 37th ARRS. Front row is the HH-3E crew: Capt, Jon Hannan, Maj. Robert D. Shular, PJ Eugene Nardi, and FE Charles Severns. Back row is Maj. Donald Dineen, "Spad 1-1"; Sgt. Robert Christianson, "Redeye 22B"; Capt. Norman Svarrer, "Redeye 22A"; Capt. Seely, Redeye wingman; and Maj. Carl Richards, "Spad 1-2." *Courtesy of USAF*

A few months later, the air force chief of staff, Gen. John P. McConnell, presented the Air Force Cross to Pitsenbarger's parents—the first awarded to an enlisted man. Schibler notes, "Years later, PJ Harry O'Bierne was one of the individuals who worked tirelessly to get Pitsenbarger's Air Force Cross upgraded to the Medal of Honor." Not until thirty-four years later did that occur.

Six weeks prior to the battle of Abilene, Gen. McConnell had authorized a distinctive uniform change for pararescuemen: maroon beret with pararescue emblem, and trousers bloused in combat boots.

The pararescueman's star shined brightly, but those who wore the maroon beret, confident in their skills and imbued with selflessness, found their extraordinary deeds unremarkable. But even they hailed some among their elite ranks as legends.

On February 6, 1967, an FAC, Capt. Lucius Heiskell, bailed out of his O-1F Bird Dog after it was hit by enemy fire over North Vietnam. Crewmen of two Jolly Green Giant helicopters of the 37th ARRS ("Jolly Green 0-5" and "3-6") that scrambled from NKP arrived to hear Heiskell radio that he was evading the enemy. Pararescueman A2C Duane Hackney rode the jungle penetrator down to rescue Heiskell but found only enemy footprints during two hours of searching. Worsening weather forced an end to the mission until hours later, when the pilot again was heard on the radio. The HH-3Es launched to attempt another rescue. Hackney recalled:

We knew we had to get him out before dark, because after the sun dropped, our chances for getting him would drop from about 90 percent to 30 percent. A Sandy told us not to go over this one ridge because of heavy AAA and small-arms fire. But we had to—that's where the pilot was!

Once we got over the area, they lowered me on a hoist again, and this time I found the pilot. He was pretty messed up. I got him onto the hoist, but on the way back up the helicopter started drawing more fire, so the Sandy dropped in and knocked them out. Then the enemy's antiaircraft gun picked us up on radar. The first hit jarred us pretty bad, and there was a lot of fire and smoke. I knew we had to get out of the chopper.

I kept my emergency parachute hanging on the forward bulkhead near the left scanner's window. I grabbed it and helped the survivor put it on. I left the survivor by the crew entrance door and headed aft to find another parachute. I found one hanging by the ramp and began to put it on. That's when the second burst of flak hit us. There was an explosion and I was thrown backwards—hard. I felt a sharp pain in my left arm. I tried to get my balance and was surprised to see my helicopter flying away from me. I had been blown out the aft ramp of the HH-3. I did not have the parachute completely on yet and was only a couple of hundred feet above the treetops.

Hackney instinctively pulled the ripcord and held tight to the parachute harness. The chute did not fully open, but it slowed his fall into the trees. From there he plummeted downward onto a ledge in a crevasse about 80 feet above the jungle floor. Hackney was semiconscious, [was] wounded by shrapnel, and suffered third-degree burns, but he was alive:

When I came to on the ledge, I could look up and see the Vietnamese jumping from one side of the ravine to the other, looking for me. If they had looked down, they would have spotted me. About an hour later I heard an A-1 Skyraider over me and popped a flare.

Capt. Oliver O'Mara, "Jolly Green 3-6," piloting the high bird, descended to lower his PJ, Sgt. Luther Davis. Davis risked his life to get Hackney, now in shock and badly injured, out of the jungle. Hackney was later told that he was the sole survivor of the mission; HH-3E pilot Maj. Patrick Wood and his crew, including copilot Capt. Richard Kibbey, flight engineer SSgt. Donald Hall, and the survivor Hackney had rescued, died when the burning, uncontrollable helicopter crashed. O'Mara made several low passes over the scene, but the Jolly Green had crashed violently and there were no signs of survivors.

Nineteen-year-old Hackney had made good on the air force commitment to make every effort to recover downed aircrew. His survival was miraculous, some say instinctive as a result of intensive training and combat experience. Hackney already had been awarded numerous lifesaving awards, including four Distinguished Flying Crosses. This mission earned him the Air Force Cross, making him the first living recipient of the award. Eventually, Duane Hackney became the most highly decorated enlisted man in US Air Force history. He and PJ Luther Davis went on to serve additional combat tours. Hackney would survive, only to succumb to a fatal heart attack at age forty-six; Davis survived a helicopter crash in Vietnam but climbed into the burning wreckage to save a fellow crewman trapped in the flames. The man survived, but Davis succumbed to his severe burn injuries on the flight to a hospital in Japan.

Pararescuemen performed almost unbelievable feats so often that they considered their actions ordinary: "I was just doing my job," said Duane Hackney. In the embrace of fatalism, pararescuemen knew that *doing their job* brought them to the brink of disaster. At first light on Christmas Day 1968, PJ A1C Charles King was aboard an HH-3 of Detachment 1, 40th ARRS, inbound to snatch an F-105 pilot shot down the previous night in Laos. King was lowered on the hoist to free the pilot's body, suspended in a tree. After King fastened the body to the penetrator and radioed, "Pull us up," the enemy sprang the trap. King was hit and the helicopter came under intense fire. When King told the pilot to pull away, the penetrator snagged in the tree and was torn from its mount. An intense search failed to find any trace of Charles King and Thud pilot Charles Brownlee. Both were declared MIA and later KIA.

The on-scene commander of a rescue operation, typically a Sandy pilot, had the awesome responsibility of determining when and if it would be safe enough to commit the Jolly Green helicopter to attempt pickup. Often, the Jolly Green pilot himself faced that difficult decision. Knowing that the enemy preferred to wait for the helicopter when it was in the hover, none of the fliers could be certain that enemy fire was sufficiently suppressed in preparation for the pickup. Seasoned Sandy pilot Randy Jane explained:

> Sometimes waiting is going to hurt you. If you've killed a certain number of the enemy and silenced a certain number of guns, then wait without putting in a continuous stream of ordnance, the bad guys may bring in more stuff. In four hours it may be worse than it is now. It's a hard decision to make, and one that nobody can make but the guy that's down there as on-scene commander.

On November 8, 1967, eight-man Special Forces Recon Team "Massachusetts" engaged in fierce battle on the Laotian border and became surrounded by a large enemy force. After supporting Vietnamese H-34 "Kingbee" and army Huey gunships arrived, two of the choppers got in to rescue survivors, but a Kingbee and a gunship were shot down. Rather than finish off the survivors in a second mass assault, the enemy used them to bait more rescue choppers they knew would come. Jolly Greens "2-9" and "2-6" of the 37th ARRS were scrambled from Da Nang to attempt a night extraction, essentially "to take their turn in the barrel."

While a C-123 flare ship lit the night sky, army Huey gunships raked enemy positions, while the Jolly Green low

Using the hover-in-flight refueling method, an HH-3E of the 37th ARRS refuels from the destroyer USS *Floyd B. Parks* (DD-884). Colors of the Southeast Asia "tritone" color scheme were Dark Green (FS 34079), Medium Green (FS 34102, and Tan (FS 30219) over Camouflage Grey (FS 36622). *Courtesy of Arthur Brand*

bird, piloted by Capt. John McTasney, prepared to attempt a pickup. After confusion and severe battle damage from heavy fire, the Jolly made it out with three survivors. Limping to Khe Sanh with Capt. Gerald Young's HH-3E escorting, McTasney radioed Young, recommending that the mission be terminated in view of the obvious trap and heavy fire. But two survivors remained and Jolly Green 2-6 went back in. Ground fire erupted when Young came to a hover, while gunships worked over enemy ranks. At point-blank range, enemy troops riddled the HH-3E with gunfire, hitting both engines. A rifle grenade slammed into an engine, upending the chopper, which then plunged down a ravine and burst into flame. Held by restraining belts, Captain Young hung upside down, his clothing in flames. Falling through his side window, he rolled about 100 yards down a slope. Severely burned, Young stumbled in the darkness to find an injured man, gave him first aid, and dragged him into underbrush to hide him from searching enemy troops. Young crawled uphill to his burning helicopter but was driven back from intense heat and returned to the unconscious survivor.

At dawn, Young saw the enemy set up heavy machine guns to decimate rescue forces they knew were coming. Despite the realization that his next move would probably cost him his life, Young decided not to let rescue forces again fall prey to the trap. To lure the enemy away from his unconscious survivor and survivors near the crashed helicopters, Young made enough noise to cause the enemy to take chase. Although Young heard Sandys looking for him, he avoided radio contact until he had drawn the enemy far from the battle scene. After making his way painfully through 5 miles of underbrush, certain that the enemy was nowhere near, Young signaled an orbiting army Huey and was picked up uncontested. Later a Special Forces Hatchet Force was inserted near the crash site and engaged in fierce battle. They found that the enemy had dragged two American bodies into the open as bait for rescue

By the end of 1964, seven HU-16Bs were in Southeast Asia: two at Korat RTAFB and five at Da Nang AB, all on rotational duty, primarily from the 31st and 33rd Air Rescue Squadrons. Albatrosses also rotated into the combat theater from the 41st and 48th ARS in the continental US. Serial no. 51-5294, seen here at Osan AB, Korea, for the USS *Pueblo* incident, was one of nine known to have been camouflaged with Glossy Dark Sea Blue (FS 15042) over Camouflage Grey (FS 36622). *Courtesy of Stephen Miller*

forces. Tempers flared among air rescue crews, since a complete SAR task force, which included six heavily armed Sandys, was prohibited by higher authority from leaving orbit to complete the mission.

Capt. Gerald Young was awarded the Medal of Honor, which he would have unhesitatingly traded for the lives of his crew: the copilot, Capt. Ralph Brower; the flight engineer, SSgt. Eugene Clay; and the PJ, Sgt. Larry Maysey.

In February 1969, the Pacific Aerospace Rescue and Recovery Center was redesignated the 41st Aerospace Rescue and Recovery Wing (ARRWg), and the Atlantic ARRC was redesignated the 40th ARRWg, with both under the parent Military Airlift Command. The 3rd Aerospace Rescue and Recovery Group (ARRGp) of the 41st ARRWg at its operational peak governed four squadrons in Southeast Asia: the 37th at Da Nang, 38th at Tan Son Nhut, 39th at Tuy Hoa, and 40th at Udorn. Also subordinate to the 41st ARRWg were six squadrons outside the combat theater: they were the 36th at Yokota AB, Japan; 31st at Clark AB, Philippines; 76th at Hickam AFB, Hawaii; 33rd at Naha AB, Okinawa; 79th at Andersen AB, Guam; and 47th at Fuchu AS, Japan. The 41st ARRWg also governed fourteen detachments throughout the Pacific. When these detachments became the 47th ARRS in June 1970, eight were inactivated. At the 3rd ARRGp command level was the Joint Rescue Coordination Center (JRCC), call sign "Joker," at Tan Son Nhut AB; the Rescue Coordination Center (RCC), call sign "Queen," at Son Tra / Da Nang AB, South Vietnam, with Operating Location Alpha (OL-A); and the RCC, call sign "Jack," at Udorn RTAFB with OL-B. The Tactical Air Control Center ("Agate") was at Tan Son Nhut AB, along with the Seventh Air Force Command Center ("Blue Chip").

The 3rd ARRGp determined the forces necessary to conduct a rescue, which included air, sea, and land resources from all services. The HC-130P "King" provided the communications link between rescue coordination centers and the SAR operation. King also coordinated requests by the on-scene commander for ordnance and various aircraft types. The HC-130P included two pilots, navigator, radio operator, two flight engineers, loadmaster, and PJs.

When the moment came to snatch survivors from enemy clutches, the spotlight shined on the PJs—the vital link between rescue aircraft and the survivor. For example, pararescueman Sgt. Joseph Duffy of Detachment 1, 37th ARRS, made possible Air Rescue's one thousandth combat save. On February 28, 1968, after F-105 Thunderchief pilot Capt. Gene Basel was shot down over Laos, Duffy was lowered from an HH-3E hovering 150 feet over the jungle to rescue Basel. Duffy found the Thud pilot helplessly snagged high up in a tree, with both legs broken. Duffy got him up into the hovering Jolly Green amid enemy fire; it was his twenty-first save. Since December 1964, the 3rd ARRGp had accomplished more than 1,400 successful rescues, both combat and noncombat.

Training for the Jolly Greens was conducted by the Aerospace Rescue and Recovery Training Center at Eglin AFB, Florida.

The HH-43 training was done at Sheppard AFB, Texas. An important adjunct of the Air Rescue organization in Southeast Asia was the PACAF Jungle Survival School at Clark AB in the Philippines. Beginning in mid-1967, all aircrew members slated for combat assignments in Southeast Asia were required to receive intensive training in survival, evasion, resistance, and escape. Students gained an understanding of SAR procedures and learned how they could best assist in their rescue. Home-based at Clark, the 31st ARRS supported the school with five HH-3E helicopters. Eventually, demonstrations of the Fulton Surface-to-Air Recovery System (STARS) were a regular occurrence at the school. These "Gabriel Demos," however, were conducted by C-130s modified for special operations, foretelling diminished use of the system by Air Rescue.

DIMMING STARS

Installation of the Fulton STARS in HC-130H/Ps contributed to the aircraft's multirole capability. Early in the C-130's career, during the war in Southeast Asia, nearly sixty C-130s were equipped with the system, which was termed "Skyhook." Although rescue variants of the Hercules were Skyhook capable, and crews maintained proficiency with its use, the system found a home in the shadowy world of special operations. Fourteen Model C-130Es were developed during the war, eight of which were Fulton-equipped. Camouflaged black and green and typically devoid of markings, these "Blackbirds" saw regular use with the 14th Special Operations Wing (SOW). Declassified documents reveal that the mission of the 15th Special Operations Squadron (SOS) of the 14th SOW included "rescue and recovery operations using the Fulton Surface-to-Air Recovery System; and to carry out a program of unconventional warfare operations assigned under '7th Air Force Order 460-70 "Combat Spear,"' classified Top Secret." In

Celebrating the 1,500th rescue in Southeast Asia on December 21, 1968, are, *left to right*: Maj. Forrest Fenn, Lt. Col. John Carlson, and Lt. Cmdr. Lance Eagan, USCG. Eagan was flying the HH-3E named "Candy Ann" of Det 1, 37th ARRS, when Fenn's F-100D was shot down. Carlson was flying cover in a "Sandy" Skyraider. *Courtesy of USAF*

October 1966, the 15th SOS at Nha Trang AB, South Vietnam, took delivery of four C-130Es mainly for support of MACV's secret Studies and Observation Group (SOG).

Special operations leaders came to the realization that Skyhook was best suited for clandestine snatches, not for extractions under heavy antiaircraft fire or with enemy ground forces nearby. There were several instances when SOG Blackbird crews went after downed airmen in North Vietnam. The first attempt occurred after one of the darkest days for naval aviation, with the loss of six aircraft and ten airmen over North Vietnam. After his A-6A Intruder was shot down on May 19, 1967, Lt. Cmdr. Eugene McDaniel remained hidden from the enemy until the twenty-first, when a Skyhook extraction kit was dropped to him. The Blackbird crew en route to McDaniel had to abort because radio contact was lost. The enemy reached the kit before McDaniel, and he was taken prisoner. Blackbird crewman told of two other cases where downed pilots were captured while preparing the system for extraction. Later in the war, several occasions arose when Skyhook was considered for rescuing downed airmen, including Lt. Col. Hambleton, "Bat 2-1," but in each case a critical factor or the pilot's capture ruled out pickup. Thus, the practical use of Skyhook for in-country rescue was eliminated since helicopters were more effective. Long-range recovery by Skyhook-equipped special operations C-130Es, however, retained its importance, even long after the war.

David Preston provides insight to his experience with the STARS:

I'm an ex-HC-130 "King" pilot and was stationed at Pease AFB, Can Ranh Bay AB, Korat, Udorn, and Hamilton AFB—all in rescue squadrons. While at Pease AFB in 1970–71, we trained in the Fulton system, using sandbags instead of live bodies. Although we never practiced with live bodies, the system was initially tested using some brave volunteers—including then rescue commander Gen. Frank "Speedy" Everest. We never used the system operationally because of its inherent risk and the more practical method of utilizing helicopters for pickups. After I returned to the states following my SEA tour, I learned that some use of the system was made in SEA by clandestine "Blackbird" C-130s.

THE ALBATROSS BOWS OUT

Difficult as it was to find a replacement for the Grumman Albatross amphibian, it took the ability of the Jolly Green to land on water and air-refuel to end the HU-16B's dual combat role of airborne controller and open-sea rescue. After eighteen years of service in the Pacific, including combat tours in Korea and Vietnam, the last Albatross combat mission was flown over the Gulf of Tonkin on September 30, 1967. During five years of service in Southeast Asia, the HU-16B recorded sixty-two combat and noncombat saves. Four HU-16Bs were lost during the war: S/N 51-071 was blown out of the water off North Vietnam in March 1966, with two crewmen KIA;

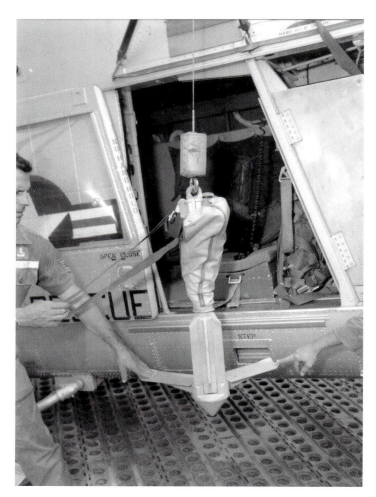

Pararescueman TSgt. Charles Walthers demonstrates use of Kaman's forest penetrator hoist of an HH-43F. Two of the three paddles are lowered to form a seat, and the strap, stored in a zippered pouch, supports the survivor. Credit for development of the device goes to US Navy Helicopter Utility Squadron 2 (HU-2) during the late 1950s. In 1964, Kaman rushed its version into use for HH-43s in the combat theater. Improvements in 1968 included a flotation collar and overhead protective shield. *Courtesy of USAF*

no. 51-7145, with a crew of seven, disappeared in October 1966; and two were lost to operational causes in 1967.

Outside the combat zone, the Albatross soldiered on in Air Rescue; early in 1968, Pacific ARRC HU-16Bs were on hand in Korea following the capture of USS *Pueblo* and its crew. The 33rd ARRS, which in 1962 had flown the first HU-16B sortie of the war, flew the last HU-16B out of Vietnam in October 1968.

A BIGGER AND BETTER JOLLY GREEN

Early in 1962, the navy began a search for a heavy-lift, multirole, ship-based helicopter. Sikorsky's Model S-65 design proposal fit the bill and led to the first flight of the prototype CH-53A in October 1964. Sikorsky engineers based the design on its Model S-61R (the air force H-3) and the S-64 (the army's CH-54 "Tarhe," better known as the "Skycrane"). In late 1966, the Marine Corps took delivery of its first operational CH-53A.

In spring 1966, air force officials chose the Model S-65 over the CH-47 Chinook as the ideal helicopter to recover Apollo spacecraft, and to further adapt the design to meet the demands of combat rescue in Southeast Asia. The rotary-wing behemoth, which was intended to first augment and then replace the Jolly Green, was designated HH-53 and called "Super Jolly Green Giant." To airmen, it was known as the "BUFF," or "Big Ugly Fat Fellow." To the chagrin of air force officials, airmen replaced "Fellow" with a less polite word.

First flown in March 1967, the Super Jolly weighed in at 16 tons, twice that of the H-3. Two powerful T64-GE-3 turboshaft engines rated at 3,080 shp allowed it to lift over 13,000 pounds and fly nearly 200 mph. Like its little brother, the HH-53B could land on water, was equipped for in-flight refueling, and mounted jettisonable fuel tanks on sponsons. Titanium armor surrounded the cockpit and floor to protect the five-man crew of pilot, copilot, flight engineer, and two PJs. Self-sealing fuel tanks, a rescue hoist with 240 feet of cable, and all-weather capability completed the Super Jolly configuration. Armament consisted of two GAU-2B/A 7.62 mm miniguns mounted in the forward doorways, with another mounted on the rear ramp.

When the air force contracted for HH-53Bs, Sikorsky loaned a pair of CH-53As built for the USMC to USAF. They went to the 48th ARRS at Eglin AFB for operational evaluation and to train the first crews. The air force ordered eight HH-53Bs, the first of which, serial no. 66-14428, was delivered to ARRS personnel at the Sikorsky plant in June 1967. Following training at the plant, crewmen of Detachment 2, 37th ARRS, underwent two months of training with the 4401st Helicopter Squadron at Eglin AFB. It was on to San Francisco, where the first two HH-53Bs were loaded aboard the aircraft transport USNS *Card*, destination Vung Tau, South Vietnam, for assignment to Det 2, 37th ARRS, at Udorn RTAFB. Detachment 2's complete assignment of six HH-53Bs was in place at Udorn in January 1968. On March 18, Detachment 2 was upped to

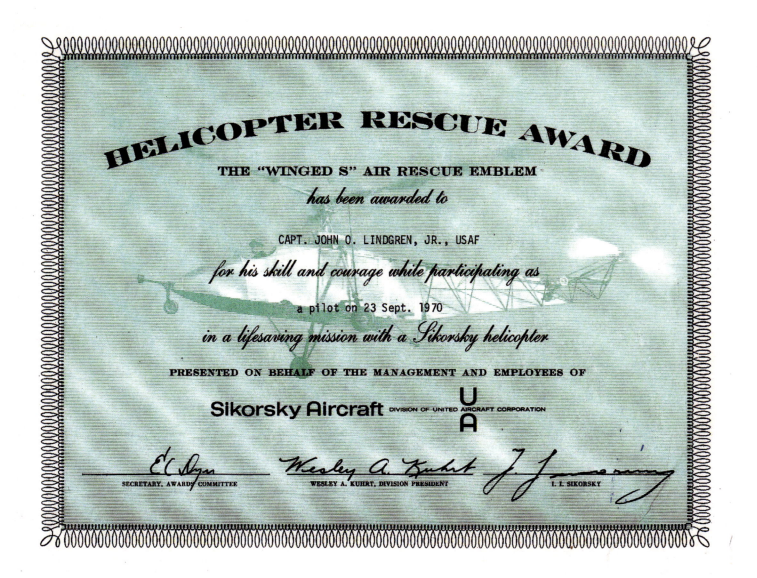

HELICOPTER RESCUE AWARD

THE "WINGED S" AIR RESCUE EMBLEM

has been awarded to

CAPT. JOHN O. LINDGREN, JR., USAF

for his skill and courage while participating as

a pilot on 23 Sept. 1970

in a lifesaving mission with a Sikorsky helicopter

PRESENTED ON BEHALF OF THE MANAGEMENT AND EMPLOYEES OF

Sikorsky Aircraft DIVISION OF UNITED AIRCRAFT CORPORATION

SECRETARY, AWARDS COMMITTEE   WESLEY A. KUHRT, DIVISION PRESIDENT   I. I. SIKORSKY

squadron status, becoming the 40th ARRS. The remaining two HH-53Bs were retained at Eglin AFB to train pilots in air refueling.

Ron Loftis, who was in the first HH-53B maintenance class, reflects on the HH-53B's arrival:

When we started training on BUFFs, there was a great deal of opposition to the HH-53Bs being called BUFFs; ARRS wanted them called "Super Jollys," and that became their official air force designation. But we that flew and crewed them would not be denied our BUFF moniker. After they had made their sea voyage, we were ferried out to *Card* on army Hueys. We reassembled them and readied them for a one-time flight to Vung Tau for further prep to Udorn. I took up a collection from our crew and had a local tailor make flags with crossed refueling probes. These were the first two HH-53Bs in Southeast Asia, and they drew a lot of attention when we first landed at Udorn. With the flags on the refueling probes, we taxied right up to the unit with all of the brass waiting to welcome us. Thereafter, the HH-53Bs were known as BUFFs and our call sign was "BUFF." This changed in later years; however, the people of the first deployment were very proud of our "Big Ugly Fat Fuckers."

Limited ramp space at Udorn required that the resident HH-3E contingent be relocated to NKP, where they formed Detachment 1, 37th ARRS. These helicopters typically stood alert at forward sites in Laos until the detachment was deactivated in February 1968. Detachment 1, 40th ARRS, then assumed the assignment with HH-3Es until they were replaced by HH-53Cs.

For all its capabilities, the HH-53 had drawbacks. Its massive size limited its maneuverability and, coupled with its relatively slow speed, made it a fat target. Due to the position of the rotor mast, the pilot had to maintain a 5-degree

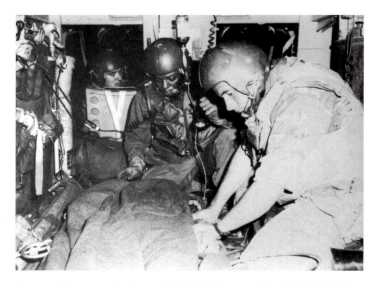

Concern shows on the faces of this HH-43F crew of Det 10, 38th ARRS, as PJ A1C Larry D. Nicholson treats a sailor wounded during a rocket attack on a river patrol boat. Flight engineer A1C Archelous Whitehead and copilot Capt. Leslie Johnson look on. *Courtesy of USAF*

nose-up attitude in a hover, which limited his downward view. The BUFF's cyclonic downdraft confounded the pickup in a hover by flinging debris and injuring survivors. Case in point: after "Jackal 3-3," an F-111A, was shot down near Hanoi on December 22, 1972, the WSO, after four days of evading, came within inches of the penetrator, lowered from an HH-53C, but was blown down a slope by the rotor downwash when Jolly Green 7-3 came under heavy fire. The damaged chopper had to leave, and the survivor was captured. When asked how adequate he thought the HH-53 was in performing the SAR mission, Col. Frederick V. Sohle Jr., commander of the 3rd ARRGp, replied in a 1972 interview:

The HH-53 is good for heavy lift and fairly durable against small arms, but it is too big and produces too much downwash. We need an all-weather capability to locate and recover downed airmen. We need improved radar to fly low-level, and we need a warning system for the missile threat. I think a small, fast, easily maneuvered helicopter with an in-flight refueling capability would be best.

On a typical SAR mission, HH-53s began orbiting prior to a strike mission, refueling from an HC-130 and remaining on station for several hours. When Skyraider pilots located survivors, they suppressed enemy fire, while another pair of A-1s trailed the HH-53 on the run-in. The first flier to be rescued by an HH-53B had ejected from his F-105 after two Thuds collided near Udorn on October 23, 1967. The BUFF's first combat rescue occurred on November 25, when an Air America pilot was rescued. Two HH-53Bs of the 40th ARRS were combat losses. Serial no. 66-14430 ("Jolly Green 6-7") was shot down during the intensive SAR effort for an F-4D "Stormy FAC" in January 1969. The PJ, Sgt. Thomas Pope, was severely wounded and the crashed BUFF was destroyed by strike aircraft. On January 28, 1970, serial no. 66-14434 ("Jolly Green 7-1") was hit and destroyed by an air-to-air missile fired from a MiG-21 while orbiting on a SAR for an F-105G downed in North Vietnam. All aboard were killed.

The aforementioned SAR for the Stormy FAC signaled the beginning of the busiest three days in the history of SAR in Southeast Asia. In the search for the FAC back-seater, a Sandy A-1 was hit and the pilot bailed out, pushing the rescue effort into a second day. Another Sandy went down. Meanwhile, "Stormy 0-2B" was rescued, but while egressing, "Jolly 6-7" was downed and all aboard were rescued. To complicate matters, an O-2 "Covey" FAC with a crew of two was shot down, creating a new mission. One FAC crewman was rescued, but darkness precluded rescue of the other. The next morning, under a blanket of tear gas laid down by Sandy A-1s to stall approaching enemy, the Covey crewman was rescued. The scope of the three-day activity involved an impressive 284 aircraft of numerous types. During the seventy-two-hour period, 3rd ARRGp resources were involved in twenty-one separate incidents throughout Southeast Asia, during which thirty-seven lives were saved.

From the war's onset, Cessna's O-1 "Bird Dog" served as the premier forward air controller (FAC) aircraft. Either alone or with a skilled observer, the FAC pilot, usually armed only with target-marking rockets, flew in harm's way to locate and mark survivors and then remain in the area to control rescue forces and strike aircraft. *Courtesy of USAF*

UPDATING BUFF

The HH-53B was quickly updated, resulting in the HH-53C model, with more-powerful T64-GE-7 power plants producing nearly 800 more shaft horsepower than the T64-GE-3 engines. The 650-gallon-capacity external fuel tanks mounted outboard of the HH-53B's sponsons were found to be too large, which affected performance. Therefore, on the HH-53C, these were changed to 450-gallon tanks on cantilevered "gull wing" mounts. Deliveries of the HH-53C to the air force began in June 1968, with initial assignment to the 48th ARRS at Eglin AFB to support the Apollo space program. Four were slated to join the HH-53Bs at Udorn RTAFB in early 1969 but did not arrive until later that year. BUFF pilot John Lindgren recalls:

My squadron commander knew I was a mechanical engineer, so in April 1970 he sent me and my roommate, Jerry Brown, down to Sattahip, Thailand, with a maintenance crew. Sattahip is the deepwater port serving southern Thailand and is adjacent to Utapao RTAFB. Three new HH-53Cs had arrived in the port aboard a Sea Train Lines ship. Our job was to unload them, pull the rubber coatings off, put the rotor blades on, install the equipment, and test-fly them. After we got each of them assembled, we did engine and hover checks right there on the dock and put just enough fuel in them to get them over to Utapao one by one. When we got the first one there, we finished installing all the equipment, including the guns, and did a couple of check flights. We called "Joker" in Saigon and told them the first aircraft was ready. They sent two PJs from Udorn to make a full crew and two Sandys as escort. We flew the aircraft across Laos, into Vietnam, and then to Da Nang. We got shot at with 23 mm and 37 mm crossing the Trail, but the Sandys peeled off and shut them down. An HC-130 took us back to Utapao and we repeated the process with the other two, except the last flight, which we flew over Cambodia because we were tired of being shot at over the Trail. We never told anyone about that Cambodia journey. When we got the last aircraft to Da Nang, we were met by the squadron commander, who presented Jerry and me with orders transferring us to the 37th ARRS.

Lindgren's new assignment had him flying as copilot for the first rescue by an HH-53 of the 37th ARRS. The following are the details of that mission:

On 5 May, orbiting HC-130P "King 3-6" picked up a mayday that the two crewmen of an RF-4C of the 12th TRS, call sign "Strobe 5-2," had ejected after their aircraft was hit by AAA over the A Shau Valley. Assisted by a Covey FAC, six Skyraiders, and four army Cobra gunships, the low-bird HH-53C, Jolly Green 6-5, picked up both survivors. Flying the high bird, Jolly Green 6-4, was Lindgren's cohort, Captain Jerald Brown.

On August 24, 1970, two HH-53Cs completed the first transpacific flight from Eglin AFB, Florida, to Da Nang AB. The nine-day, 9,000-mile journey trimmed the delivery time by seventy-five percent and again demonstrated the long-range capability of in-flight refueling. Both ferry flights and ship transit were used to fill out the HH-53C requirement in theater. As sufficient numbers of HH-53Cs arrived in theater, the four surviving HH-53Bs were returned to the States. After replacement by an HH-53C, the last HH-3E in theater, which was assigned to the Bien Hoa alert force of the 37th ARRS, was ferried to Kadena AB, Okinawa, on December 29, 1970. More than a year later, however, the HH-3E would be back.

During the summer of 1969, the 3rd Aerospace Rescue and Recovery Group reached peak strength in Southeast Asia, with more than seventy aircraft assigned to four squadrons: the 37th ARRS at Da Nang AB with HH-3Es, the 38th ARRS with HH-43B/F detachments at fourteen bases, the 39th ARRS at Tuy Hoa AB with eleven HC-130Ps, and the 40th ARRS at Udorn RTAFB with HH-3Es and HH-53B/Cs. Since the beginning of air operations in Southeast Asia, rescue crews of the 3rd ARRGp by mid-1969 had amassed over two thousand saves, more than 1,500 of which were combat saves. US Army personnel topped the list of the number of those rescued, followed by US Air Force, US Navy and Marines, and then Vietnamese, Thai, Korean, and Australian. Crews of the HH-3E held the lead in the number of saves, followed by HH-43B/Fs.

SEMPER FI

Two of the Marine "customers" of the Jolly Greens of the 37th ARRS were 1Lt. Gary Bain and his radar intercept officer (RIO), Lt. William Ryan—the officer who occupied the seat behind the pilot in jet fighters in military aviation jargon was simply termed the "guy in back," or the "back-seater." Twice in 1969, the F-4 Phantom duo met trouble in the unfriendly skies over Laos. Bain recounts the first occurrence:

It was a dark and stormy night. The date was January 12, 1969, and we were just off the coast of South Vietnam, over the South China Sea. I had flown well over a hundred combat missions with Marine Fighter Attack Squadron (VMFA) 323, and on this particular night we were attempting to get rid of our ten 500-pound bombs that had malfunctioned and wouldn't come off while conducting a Steel Tiger mission in Laos. After diverting to the jettison area out over the water, I hit the pickle button to drop the bombs, and when I did, the instrument panel started lighting up like a Christmas tree. It is theorized that one of the bombs hung up on the aft lug and drove the fins through the underbelly of the aircraft and into the fuel lines, causing an immediate and catastrophic fire. I stated rather emphatically, "Bill, we're going to have to get out of here!" I then started to make my mayday call and only got one mayday uttered when an explosion rocked the

Pararescueman Duane D. Hackney was a legend in the rescue world, becoming the most decorated enlisted man in US Air Force history. With more than two hundred missions under his belt, PJ Hackney was the first living, and then youngest, recipient of the Air Force Cross. He would be awarded three more and rise to the rank of chief master sergeant. *Courtesy of USAF*

Courage beyond measure. Pararescueman William H. Pitsenbarger of Det 6, 38th ARRS, was killed in April 1966 while aiding and defending soldiers under severe attack. "Pits" had flown nearly three hundred rescue missions. He was awarded the Air Force Cross and, too many years later, the Medal of Honor. *Courtesy of USAF*

ill-fated Phantom. I hardly got the word "EJECT" out of my mouth and Bill was gone in a flurry of noise and smoke as the canopy was blown off and his ejection seat rockets fired. I followed shortly thereafter, and we both floated slowly down into a dark void, punctuated only by the violent impact the pilotless Phantom made as the sea swallowed its flaming mass. The sudden departure from the sanctity of the cockpit to hanging in a parachute, especially at night, is, to say the least, a humiliating as well as frightening experience. A really heads-up air traffic controller at Da Nang heard my "mayday" and alerted the Jolly Greens of the 37th ARRS.

Under a sky lit by a flare ship code-named "Basketball," Capt. Gerald Moore (Jolly 2-8) landed his HH-3E in the water—Moore silently thanked God and Sikorsky for the HH-3E's radar altimeter. Moore steered the refueling probe to the raft, allowing Bain and Williams to hand-walk down the probe to the helicopter's door. Bain continues:

Bill and I were back in the air again in a couple of days, and we continued flying as a team until I went on R&R a few months later. I had to spend two days in Da Nang waiting for my flight, so I decided to look up my Jolly Green rescuers. It just so happened they were in a festive mood, so for two days we consumed massive amounts of booze, told war stories, and I reveled in the camaraderie of my heroes. I got to know one of the pilots real good. His name was "Pete." Little did I know the importance of our meeting, for we were to meet again in a few days, but under much-different circumstances.

Arriving back at Chu Lai a week later, I once again set about winning the war. By this time I had well over two hundred missions under my belt, and Bill and I had flown almost a hundred of those together as a team. Our call sign was "Boomslang," and when we checked in with the FAC, he knew the job was going to get done. We had both been recently transferred to VMFA-115 but were still flying out of Chu Lai. When I found out Bill was scheduled to go on R&R, I insisted he cancel two missions he was scheduled to fly with me the next day. He wouldn't hear of it, but we compromised; he would fly the morning mission. This was a truly bad decision on both our parts. Bill, or "Rhino" as we called him, would not return from the mission.

We launched on May 11 as a flight of two, destination Laos, another Steel Tiger mission. Over the target area, the FAC, "Nail 1-6," designated the enemy position, and I rolled in hot. I let loose the full complement of rockets. Just as I was getting a heavy load of g's on the airplane in the pull-up and started the jinking turn, a tremendous explosion rocked the big Phantom. The aircraft rolled over and was heading for the ground, all controls lost. At 500-plus knots, impact was imminent, and I told Bill three times to eject. Hearing no response, I braced myself and reached for the alternate ejection handle, nestled between my legs. No one saw a second chute, and most concur that we took a 37 mm AAA shell in the rear cockpit area.

With a leg and an arm broken during the ejection, Bain hid from the nearby enemy and called in airstrikes, while Jolly Greens 1-5 and 2-8 of the 37th ARRS were en route. Word was passed to the Jollies that a Marine pilot who had recently visited them was down. The pair of HH-3Es waited in a holding area for the all-clear from the A-1 on-scene commander. Weather was deteriorating, and the Jolly Greens were getting low on fuel, so Capt. Joseph "Pete" Hall decided

it was then or never. The A-1s gassed the area, Bain popped a smoke flare, and, with machine guns blazing, the HH-3E came in and hovered over Bain. He picks up the story:

What an incredible sight, forever etched in my memory: the chopper swooping in, PJ A1C Dennis Palmer coming down the hoist with a gas mask on, the copilot laying down suppressive fire from his window with an automatic rifle, and the flight mechanic hosing the area down with machine gun fire. They took small-arms fire through their approach and hover. As the chopper stabilized over me, I hobbled over to the hoist, and PJ Palmer strapped me on and away we went. The crew pulled me inside, started tending my needs, and administered morphine. From that point on, my memory became a little fuzzy, but one of them traded me a cigarette lighter for my pistol. That was simply a diplomatic way of taking a weapon from someone whose state of mind they were unsure of. Halfway back to Da Nang, the pilot got out of his seat and came back to where I was. I looked up, and there, standing before me, was "Pete," which is Captain Joseph Hall's nickname. Forty-eight years would pass before Lt. Ryan was interred with military honors at Arlington.

Before his Marine flying career ended, Gary Bain ejected a third time. As one of the first marine pilots selected to fly the AV-8A Harrier, in 1977 he punched out of a Harrier, which flamed out and wouldn't relight. Bain adds: "I was over downtown Wilmington, North Carolina, when it quit, and pointed it out to sea. Three relight attempts failed, so I left it and landed in the Atlantic and was picked up an hour later by a marine chopper."

Often, even in a combat theater, operational losses outnumbered combat losses. This HH-3E (serial no. 66-13278) of the 37th ARRS lies forlornly in Da Nang Harbor after being dropped by a US Army CH-54 Skycrane. On April 14, 1969, the Jolly Green crew was practicing hover maneuvers over a sandbar when an engine failed and the Skycrane was summoned to sling-load it out. The HH-3E began to oscillate severely, requiring that it be jettisoned 100 feet above the harbor. *Courtesy of USAF*

The armed and armored HH-3A prototype for the navy (BuNo 149896) featured 175-gallon fuel tanks inboard of the sponsons, door guns, and remote-controlled minigun barbette. The heavy barbette posed too many problems for use and was removed before the HH-3A became operational. *Courtesy of US Navy*

Painted across this HH-3A's door and fuselage in 1968 are the words "JOLLY GREEN," either imitating their air force counterparts or applied as a "zap" by air force air rescue personnel. The .50 cal. machine gun of this HH-3A of HC-7 "Big Mothers" was rare weaponry for H-3s due to its heavy recoil, which damaged the airframe. A small white stencil at far right reads, "MADE IN HANOI." *Author's collection*

COASTIES AT WAR

During 1965, as the Air Rescue Service struggled to transition from peacetime search and rescue to combat rescue, the commitment of US forces to the combat theater created a severe shortage of Albatross and helicopter pilots. Transferring fixed-wing pilots to rotary-wing operations helped fill the gap, but more was needed, especially since new helicopter pilots were short on experience. USAF Air Rescue officials turned to their coast guard counterparts for assistance, specifically suggesting a pilot exchange program. The thrust of the exchange was the benefit that could be derived from coast guard pilots' SAR experience. The program called for each service to trade five pilots—three helicopter and two fixed-wing; the chopper pilots went to the 37th ARRS at Da Nang, and the fixed-wing pilots to HC-130 assignments. Air force pilots in the trade would then take stateside assignments. Coast Guard Headquarters officially agreed to the arrangement in March 1967.

Beginning in July, the pair of fixed-wing pilots—Lieutenants Thomas Frischmann and James Casey Quinn, both HU-16E qualified, were diverted to extensive C-130 training since

USAF Air Rescue's HU-16Bs were being phased out. The three helicopter pilots—Lt. Cmdr. Lonnie Mixon, Lt. Lance Eagan, and Lt. Jack Rittichier—after survival schools and training in the HH-3E—arrived at Da Nang in early April 1968. All had been selected from more than eighty volunteers. Just days after their arrival, the Coastie pilots were flying combat rescue missions, where their experience quickly became evident.

Two months after his arrival in Vietnam on June 9, 1968, having already been awarded two Distinguished Flying Crosses for rescues under fire, Lt. Jack Rittichier was the rescue crew commander of HH-3E serial no. 67-14710, call sign "Jolly Green 2-3." A marine A-4, "Hellborne 2-1-5," had been shot down, and the injured pilot, who had parachuted into an enemy encampment, was being used as bait for rescue forces. Despite suppressive fire laid down by Sandys and marine helicopter gunships, the low-bird Jolly Green was driven off by heavy ground fire on three pickup attempts. Now critically low on fuel, "Jolly Green 2-2" had to depart. Rittichier and crew in the high bird went in for the pickup, but they too were driven off. With Sandys and gunships covering, Rittichier

Pararescueman SSgt. John F. Tobey of the 37th ARRS in mid-1967 demonstrates the HH-3E's horse collar sling, which was later replaced by the forest penetrator. Tobey would fly 240 combat rescue missions. Later, assigned to the 41st ARRS at Hamilton AFB, he was instrumental in the development of new parachute techniques involving the HC-130H. *Courtesy of USAF*

Crew chief SSgt. Ron Loftis poses with "Big Bertha," which displays eight save markings while assigned to Det 2, 37th ARRS, in 1967. Later named "Big Bertha's Cherry," serial no. 66-14434 was destroyed on January 28, 1970, on a SAR for an F-105G crew when a MiG-21 attacked the SAR task force. An Atoll missile fired from the MiG flew into the BUFF's open rear ramp area. The chopper exploded, killing all six crewmen. *Courtesy of Ron Loftis collection*

Ron Loftis, HH-53B crew chief, poses with the first "BUFF" to arrive in Southeast Asia, which displayed a flag with crossed refueling booms. The flag represented crew opposition to officially naming the HH-53B "Super Jolly." *Courtesy of Ron Loftis collection*

The HH-53 was a huge helicopter, measuring 92 feet in length with the refueling boom extended. "NIKKI D," seen here taking on fuel from an HC-130H, was an HH-53B of Det 2, 37th ARRS, based at Udorn RTAFB in 1967. *Courtesy of Ron Loftis*

came around for another attempt. Robert Dubois, one of two FAC pilots on scene, reported:

> Jolly Green 2-3 went into a hover over the A-4 pilot and turned to the west. The PJ was on the wire being lowered when Jolly Green 2-3 reported he was taking heavy fire. I saw fire coming out of the left side near the engine, and I told him he was on fire and to get out of there. He started to pull out, and I advised him that there was a clearing 1,000 meters north if he had to set down. He said he was going for the clearing. He was in descent but still above the height of the trees along the edge of the clearing when the main rotor stopped turning. Jolly Green 2-3 hit the ground and burst into flames that consumed anything that looked like an aircraft.

Rittichier and his USAF crew of copilot, flight engineer, and PJ were listed as MIA, which would revert to KIA/BNR (killed in action / body not recovered). Rittichier was one of seven coast guard combat deaths during the war.

Later in 1968, on December 20, coast guard lieutenant commander Lance Eagan was at the controls of the HH-3E of Det 1, 37th ARRS, that snatched Maj. Forrest Fenn the morning after his F-100D was shot down in Laos. Fenn, call sign "Litter 8-1," ejected from his Super Saber, his parachute dragging alongside a 1,000-foot karst bluff before he became snagged in high trees. Eagan expertly fit the helicopter down into the trees without striking them and stayed clear of the karst wall, while the entire cable was paid out for Fenn's ride up. Not only was this the 1,500th combat save of the war, but by the same HH-3E of the 37th ARRS that made the 1,000th save ten months earlier. Forrest Fenn adds:

> It was my pleasure to have been the 1,500th aircrew to be rescued by SAR in Southeast Asia. It was worth a few free beers for me and gave me a great appreciation of those guys. Sandy lead James Jamerson was a student of mine in pilot training, and he later was the one who found me in the Laotian jungle. I taught him well.

A search-and-rescue task force (SARTF) in 1968, comprising HC-130H "Crown" Hercules, two A-1H "Sandy" Skyraiders of the 1st SOS, and an HH-53C Super Jolly Green Giant. *Courtesy of USAF*

PORTRAIT OF A PARARESCUEMAN

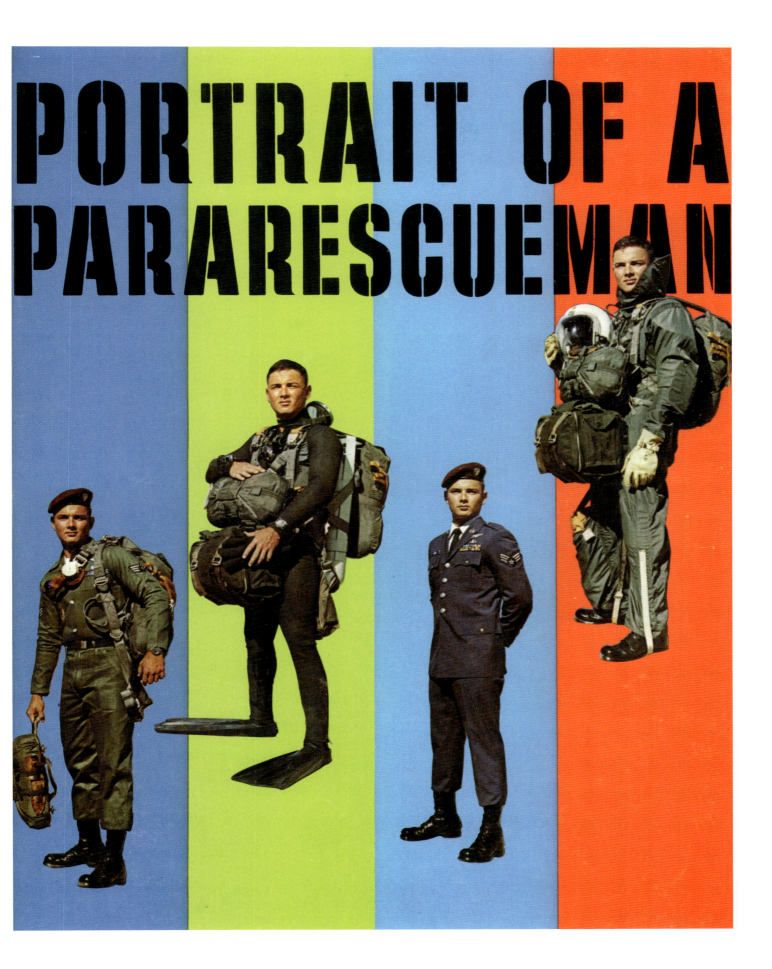

The skill of Coastie fixed-wing pilots also became obvious. A coast guard pilot, Lt. Casey Quinn, had requested assignment to the 39th ARRS at Tuy Hoa to fly HC-130Ps. With four thousand hours under his belt flying prop-driven aircraft during a navy career, plus service as a USCG Albatross pilot, Casey easily adapted to the world of USAF Air Rescue. On January 28, 1970, Casey would demonstrate his skill at the controls of the mighty Hercules. Casey and crew launched from Udorn as "King 0-3" after "Seabird 0-2," a two-seat F-105G Wild Weasel, was shot down over North Vietnam. King met up with the rescue force, comprising HC-130P "King 0-2," two HH-3Es, four HH-53s, and a flight of four Sandys.

While in a holding pattern awaiting the contact from survivors, necessary to initiate the rescue attempt, the helicopters were air-refueled. While the HH-53s trailed King, which had its refueling drogues deployed, one of the Sandy pilots saw a missile fired from a MiG-21 explode against a mountainside. Radios came alive with shouted warnings—"MiGs! MiGs!—Take it down!" A second missile disappeared into the open rear ramp section of HH-53 "Jolly 7-1," which exploded and disintegrated. A second MiG flew into the scattering, diving formation, heading for the biggest target, Casey's HC-130. Gunners on the HH-53 "Jolly 7-2" fired at the MiG as it passed. After its drop tanks were released, the Hercules exceeded redline on the way down to the weeds, tearing off both refueling drogues. Casey flew into a canyon, doing erratic maneuvers between the walls at treetop level. He saw bursts against the canyon walls, which probably were cannon fire from the MiG. Moments later, the HC-130 emerged from the canyon, alone. The MiG didn't make it. Perhaps Casey's skillful jinking, or minigun fire from Jolly 7-2's gunners had hit their mark, or both combined to end the MiG's chase against a mountainside. Regardless, Casey never got confirmation for the kill. And what a bar tale that would have been.

The Wild Weasel's crew, who were seen captured, and the six rescue men of Jolly 7-1 added to the long list of dead warriors and angels. Jolly 7-1, serial no. 66-14434, was an HH-53B of the 40th ARRS. One of the crewmen aboard ill-fated Jolly 7-2 was Gregory L. Anderson, a combat photographer assigned to Detachment 9, 601st Photo Flight. Combat photographers regularly flew aboard Jolly Greens, doubling as qualified gunners. Every two-ship team of the 40th ARRS at Udorn flew with a cameraman on the low bird. During the pickup of the survivor, the photographer swung the minigun out of the doorway, the flight engineer ran the hoist, and the photographer filmed, or fired his M-16.

After 247 combat missions, Casey Quinn returned to a coast guard air station to fly C-130s. Having flown 10,000 accident-free flight hours in three branches of the US military, he ended his military career flying the HH-52A "Seaguard" helicopter.

By 1972, ten Coastie helicopter pilots would rotate assignments to the 37th ARRS. They arrived as fully qualified aircraft commanders, and all had a wealth of experience, mainly in the HH-52 Seaguard, which was similar to the

Pararescueman Kenneth Musnicki mans the ramp-mounted rear minigun of an HH-53C of the 40th ARRS. The mission, on November 18, 1972, was to rescue the crew of "Bobbin 0-5," the last F-105 shot down in the war. Strakes, known as "elephant ears," were added to each side of the HH-53's fuselage at the ramp to reduce drag caused by the design's sharp break in the fuselage. *Courtesy of James Cockerill*

With rocket, phosphorus, and cluster bomb munitions spread across its wings, A-1E serial no. 52-132643 of the 1st SOS taxies at Nakhon Phanom RTAFB. Ordnance configured for combat SAR and ground support were called "Sandy loads." The Skyraider's undersides were left painted black from its role as the first test aircraft for night attack project "TROPIC MOON." The 1st SOS was the last USAF A-1 unit in Southeast Asia, having turned over its A-1s to the VNAF at Bien Hoa AB by 1973. *Courtesy of USAF*

HH-3E. Courageous and dedicated, they were praised for training new pilots and developing highly proficient crews. The Coasties were fiercely proud to be part of the Jolly Greens, which treated them as their own.

THE SON TAY RAID

The line between air rescue and special operations often was crossed, depending on the mission, and special crew skills and aircraft were required. Most indicative of the partnership was the Son Tay prison raid on November 21, 1970. Elaborate plans had begun months prior to an attempt to rescue more than seventy-five POWs believed to be held at the Son Tay prison camp deep in North Vietnam. Seven Air Rescue aircraft manned by specially selected crews were among twenty-nine aircraft directly involved with the operation. First, an HH-3E, serial no. 65-12785 (call sign "Banana 1"), flown by Lt. Col. Herbert Zehnder and Maj. Herbert Kalen, was to crash-land inside the prison compound with a fourteen-man assault team aboard. Five HH-53Cs were key participants, two of which, serial numbers 68-10357 ("Apple 1") and 68-10361 ("Apple 2"), each carried twenty-one raiders. It fell upon the crew of "Apple 3," serial number 68-8286, to take out the guard towers with miniguns. "Apple 4," serial no. 68-8285, and "Apple 5," serial no. 68-10359, were empty in anticipation of carrying freed prisoners. All HH-53Cs, including two spares, were from the 40th ARRS at Udorn RTAFB. The HH-3E, along with a spare, was from the 37th ARRS at Da Nang. Completing the Air Rescue contingent was an HC-130P, call sign "Lime 0-1." A pair of Bell UH-1 Huey helicopters were included in plans and in training but stood by as spares. Little is known of the service or unit to which they were assigned.

The mission was vexed by communication problems and other issues not unusual for a high-risk, nighttime assault in the enemy's backyard; however, they could not compare with the disappointing discovery that the prisoners had been moved to another camp. Two of the HH-53C crews reverted instantly to rescue mode when an F-105G, call sign "Firebird 0-5," was hit by one of countless SAMs fired at the air armada. The battered Thud made it to Laos, where both crewmen ejected. Apple 4, which actually was Jolly Green 5-4, picked up the pilot, while Apple 5 (Jolly Green 6-1) rescued the back-seater. Despite the absence of POWs, the raid was successful in a number of ways, mainly in focusing on the plight of American prisoners and conveying to them the strong message that they had not been forgotten. That message and their consolidation by the enemy into central complexes bolstered their morale.

WINS AND LOSSES

Stories abound and books have been written recounting and detailing air rescue work during the war in Southeast Asia. Prominent among the thousands of rescue missions flown are those that lasted the longest or involved special circumstances. Some were glorious "saves," while others were agonizing losses. Combat search-and-rescue missions usually were complicated affairs, often tinged with controversy over the amount of effort given a CSAR mission. Immense CSAR efforts involving many organizations and a wide variety of resources drew criticism that battlefield operations were compromised, giving advantage to the enemy. Part of the controversy suggested that survivors accept additional burdens during extended SAR missions, especially if downed in enemy territory. Airmen played a crucial role in their recovery, requiring that they rely on techniques taught in survival training. Brig. Gen. R. G. Cross Jr., deputy director of air operations, MACV, stated:

> I believe that it is a definite morale factor that every person that flew over here felt that if he was to go down that there was some chance he would be rescued. However, I feel also that there was a tendency on the part of aircrews to expect that they must be rescued above the requirements of the battle situation. As airmen or soldiers or sailors we should expect that there are times when as one person we must be sacrificed for the overall.

The question of whether the life of one man was worth the effort first came into focus in the December 1969 attempt to rescue Lt. Woodrow Bergeron, the navigator of "Boxer 2-2," an F-4 shot down over Laos. During the fifty-one-hour mission, one of the largest rescue efforts of the war, a total of 366 sorties had been flown and twelve helicopters had been damaged, five severely, along with five A-1s. The ultimate loss was that of PJ A1C David Davison.

Success of some missions in making the rescue was tempered by loss of life, diverting resources, and establishing no-fire zones that gave the enemy distinct advantage. Variations in perspective came from other high-ranking officers. When the MiG-killing team of Maj. Robert Lodge and Capt. Roger Locher was downed in May 1972, Gen. John Vogt, commander of Seventh Air Force, canceled all planned missions over North Vietnam and ordered all forces (about 120 aircraft) diverted to Locher's rescue; Lodge had died in the crash. MiG ace Gen. Steve Ritchie later stated: "Fully understand the effort to which we will go, the resources we will commit, the risks that we will take to rescue one crew member, one American, one ally. Isn't it a powerful statement about what kind of people we are, about the value that we place on life, on freedom, and on the individual?" The much-publicized rescue of EB-66 navigator Lt. Col. Iceal Hambleton ("Bat 2-1") raised many questions about suffering and morality; mainly, "How much was one man's life worth?" The immense CSAR effort lasted eleven days in April 1972 and brought into play about ninety aircraft each day. As four army helicopters converged on the site, a Huey and a Cobra were shot down, killing three, with one taken captive. Enemy missiles scored two OV-10 FACs, with two crewmen missing and later declared dead. The only HH-53C that attempted a rescue—Jolly Green 6-7 of the 37th ARRS—was shot down, killing all six aboard. Although Hambleton was down amid a major troop concentration, a no-fire zone was established, encompassing the area of operation of an ARVN division struggling to blunt the spring invasion. Thus, the ARVN soldiers were unable to call for air support or use artillery, which cost them dearly

HH-53Cs of the 37th ARRS at Da Nang AB in 1970. Da Nang AB, which was called "Rocket City," used high-wall revetments made of sand-filled steel panels for protection from ground attacks. *Courtesy of Don Jay*

and allowed the enemy to advance. As the largest sustained rescue operation of the war, over eight hundred airstrikes, including the use of B-52s, were made. No guidelines existed that defined when a survivor could not, or should not, be rescued because the cost was too high. Because the humanitarian aspect of American rescue was based on commitment to the individual and the value of human life, the question of how much was too much was never adequately answered. Despite the political and ethical fallout that hung over some missions, the selflessness and dedication of those aboard the rescue aircraft were never questioned.

The vastness and complexity of other SAR efforts are apparent in rescues such as that of US Navy lieutenant Kenneth Fields, call sign "Streetcar 3-0-4." Fields's A-7A Corsair succumbed to enemy fire over Laos on May 31, 1968. During the forty-hour period that ended with Fields's rescue, more than a hundred aircraft had been committed to the mission, one of the largest rescue efforts of the war. Records indicate that forty-four F-4 Phantoms, forty-two F-105 Thunderchiefs, six O-2 FACs, six helicopters, three HC-130Ps, and numerous A-1 Skyraiders were committed to the effort. Before it ended,

four pilots had ejected, seven aircraft were lost or badly damaged, seven airmen awaited rescue in enemy territory, and A-1 pilot Capt. Edward Leonard of the 602nd ACS was shot down and captured.

Evidence of the varied nature of rescues occurred on November 18, 1968, when an F-4 of the 497th Tactical Fighter Squadron was hit by antiaircraft fire. Occupying the back seat of the "Night Owl" Phantom was 1Lt. Robert "Kenny" Boone (call sign "Wolf 0-2R"), a weapons system operator (WSO), receiving his orientation flight over the Ho Chi Minh Trail. The pilot thought the F-4C was going to crash but, after ordering Boone to eject, found the damaged aircraft flyable and recovered at Ubon. Boone meanwhile landed in high trees in Laos. Hearing gunfire and feeling safer in the trees, Boone spent the night in the trees in his parachute harness. The next morning, a Jolly Green HH-3E, serial no. 65-12783 of Detachment 1, 40th ARRS, lowered the forest penetrator to lift Boone to safety. Boone later reflected: "Of all the wonderful sights that I had seen in many countries all over the world, there had never been one quite so beautiful as the underside of a Jolly Green Giant helicopter. And I'll never forget it!"

The unenviable record for the war's longest duration between shoot-down and rescue is held by Roger Locher, call sign "Oyster 0-2B," whose F-4D was downed by a MiG-19 on May 10, 1972. The pilot, Maj. Robert Lodge, was killed in the crash. Locher parachuted into the enemy stronghold, escaping and evading the enemy, while living off the land for twenty-three days. After finally making radio contact with a passing F-4, a massive two-day SAR effort got underway involving nearly 120 aircraft. On June 2, an HH-53C of the 40th ARRS, equipped with the new electronic location finder (ELF), pinpointed Locher in the jungle and snatched him with the penetrator in a hail of gunfire. Installation of the ELF system, along with the radar homing and warning (RHAW) system on HH-53Cs, had begun just weeks prior to Locher's rescue.

The RHAW gave HH-53s warning against the enemy's ever-increasing use of radar-controlled antiaircraft artillery and surface-to-air missiles. The system could identify the specific threat, allowing the pilot to take evasive action. To counter the enemy's introduction of the Russian-built SA-7 "Strela" ("Grail") surface-to-air missile during the 1972 Spring Offensive, flare launchers were installed aboard HH-53s to decoy the missile. The device, which could be fired by any crewman, proved effective when several Jolly Greens were fired on, with none lost. Concurrently, an ALE-20 flare system was installed on each HC-130P.

Over time, and through lessons learned, improvements were made in rescue techniques and equipment to broaden the margin of success for the SAR task force (SARTF). The most important element in rescue was communication with the survivor. Without it, the SARTF often could not locate the survivor with enough precision to safely "sanitize" the area and make the recovery. New and more-reliable radios, plus the ELF system, offered dramatic improvement in this area. Not receiving contact from the survivor usually ruled out rescue attempts, since it was then assumed that he was dead or captured. Although conditions under which the SARTF had no control—night and weather—hampered or delayed rescue efforts, rescue under these conditions was under continual study. Until a system was developed, rescues had to occur in daylight and with the ground in sight. If that was not possible, missions then stretched into the next day, which increased the likelihood of the survivor's capture or death from wounds, allowed the enemy to establish a stronghold, and expanded the mission and subsequent numbers of support aircraft.

The determination and premeditation of the enemy to establish a flak trap for rescue attempts were evident in the downing of an F-4D "Wolf 0-6" on March 19, 1970. At first light, two Jolly Greens of Detachment 1, 40th ARRS, launched from "Channel 89," which identified Nakhon Phanom RTAFB—"Channel" was a reference to location based on a TACAN channel programmed into navigation equipment, giving a radial and distance from the station. Two days of repeated attempts to rescue the pair resulted in four HH-53Cs receiving battle damage, along with thirteen A-1s of the 22nd SOS, two of which were shot down, killing one of the pilots. A Jolly Green copilot and a PJ were wounded. The Phantom WSO, 1Lt. Dennis Pugh, "Wolf 0-6B," radioed that the enemy surrounded him within 10 meters. He then requested that the A-1s place whatever ordnance they had left on his position, keeping his transmit button keyed. Horrified listeners heard Vietnamese voices and numerous gunshots, then silence. The A-1s then bombed his position.

This HH-53C (serial no. 68-10361) was one of twelve aircraft destroyed or damaged during rocket attacks on Da Nang AB on August 18–19, 1972. No. 361 had participated in the 1970 Son Tay prison raid as "Apple Two." *Courtesy of USAF*

Floating over the desert near El Centro, California, in July 1970, this combination parachute and hot air balloon, called a pilot airborne recovery device (PARD), was devised by the air force and Goodyear to enable a flier to stay aloft, or even ascend, to over 10,000 feet, while awaiting air rescue. To provide lift, a small burner with propane tank was carried on the flier's back. Deemed impractical and dangerous, the concept was shelved. *Courtesy of USAF*

To rescue the pilot, "Wolf 0-6A," A-1 Skyraiders expended a variety of ordnance, including smoke to screen rescue attempts and CBU-19 tear gas, code-named "Apeman," which required the crew of the low-bird Jolly Green to wear gas masks. John Lindgren, the copilot of Jolly Green 8-1 on a last-light effort, recalls:

The Sandy lead aircraft had found a narrow canyon that led down into the main valley where the survivor was located. We entered the narrow canyon at our maximum airspeed of 170 knots about 10 feet above the trees, jinking left and right every few seconds. We had a Sandy with us on our right side about 20 yards away. The A-1 used his 20 mm cannons and fired rockets to suppress ground fire. We received several small-arms hits during the run-in; the most serious was a hole in the fuel line that ran from the refueling probe to the fuel tank.

When we entered the main river valley from our narrow canyon, all hell broke loose. We were now flying in the trees,

dodging the treetops, and I could feel the branches hitting the bottom of our aircraft. From the caves above us, every gun opened up, and I could see the tracers from the 23 mm, single, dual, and quad mounted, as well as the 37 mm rounds flying by in groups of five. We tried to stay near the base of the cliffs, and the guns could not depress down far enough to hit us. The Sandys had now formed a daisy chain on our right side, and one of them would roll in behind us, strafe and fire rockets, then pull up as another was rolling in behind us. These guys had to pull up and dive down through the wall of fire coming from the caves above us. Our run down the river valley to the survivor was just over a mile, and we told the survivor to pop his orange smoke flare. We spotted him standing in tall grass, and pulled the nose of the helicopter up and used maximum power to come to a stop over his head. We had flown into a trap! Just as we had come to a stop, with the nose still up about 15 degrees and the hoist cable started down, we got hit with withering small-arms fire, 7.62 mm and 12.7 mm. Pieces of "stuff" were flying around the cockpit, holes appeared in the windshield, the standby compass disappeared from the glare shield, and I could feel the rounds hitting the armored cockpit floor. Then the fire-warning light on the left engine came on, and the engine instruments started to unwind. Sandy lead called on the radio, "Jolly, your left engine exploded and you are on fire. Get out, get out, get out!" The HH-53 cannot hover on one engine, and we had to get flying speed immediately. We rolled the nose over and pulled maximum power on the good engine while hitting the jettison switch for our two 650-gallon drop tanks. A 7.62 mm round came through my windshield and hit me dead center in my ceramic-armored vest. The round bounced off the vest and hit me in the left arm. I did not realize I had been hit. There was no pain, and my fingers went numb. I was not even thinking about anything other than surviving the upcoming crash. We hit the

An HH-43F rescued a wounded crewman of a river patrol boat. Small boats usually remained under power to maintain stability under the Pedro's rotor wash. By war's end, Pedros were credited with more than 1,100 saves. *Courtesy of US Navy*

treeline on the riverbank and watched the rotor blades chop off branches. Our good engine was 20 degrees over max temperature, and our rotor rpm was down to 94 percent. We staggered into the smoke cloud laid down by our fighters, and could see nothing. Once again the Sandy lead came to our rescue, calling on the radio, "Jolly, turn right. Jolly turn right." Being in the smoke cloud saved us, because the small-arms fire stopped and we were able to pick up a few more knots of airspeed. When we exited the smoke, we ducked down to the river and got our airspeed up to about 65 knots and got the power reduced on the overheated engine. Sandy lead guided us to the little canyon we had come down, and we exited the river valley. Now we had 65 miles to fly to get to the nearest friendly base, Nakhon Phanom. We had over eighty holes in the aircraft, a smoking hole where our left engine had been, and fuel on the floor of the cargo compartment. It was then that I discovered that I had been hit, when I noticed that there was blood on my sleeve and it was leaking down into my glove. Our PJs wrapped my arm for the one-hour flight to safety.

The next day, Sandy 0-5 controlled the mission, calling for smoke and CBU-19 tear gas, and led Jolly Green 7-6 down to less than 100 feet, where one of three PJs aboard rode the hoist down amid gunfire to rescue the F-4 pilot, Capt. William Rash, Wolf 0-6A. Rash later said of the flak trap:

Enemy activity was astonishing! The minute we were down, the enemy started bringing in guns all around our position. They had 37 mm, 23 mm, ZPU, and small arms. It was obvious what they were doing, and it made me furious. They had set their pattern in a cross fire, knowing that the SAR effort would begin in the morning. They fired about 1,200 rounds throughout the evening to make sure their cross-fire pattern would cover the area where the Jolly Greens and Sandys would be coming in. The first night was spent to the tempo of many rounds of triple A going off all around me.

The main obstacle that prevented the HH-53C from snatching survivors at night or in bad weather was its lack of instruments to indicate when the chopper was hovering motionlessly over the ground; the pilot needed a visual reference to the ground to hold the hover.

The need for a night/low-visibility recovery system was first detailed in "Southeast Asia Operational Requirement # 114," dated April 3, 1967. Sikorsky Aircraft Corporation was tasked with development intended for its HH-53B. The Night Recovery System (NRS) basically comprised low-light-level television (LLLTV), a door-mounted night observation device, night vision goggles, and an automatic approach-and-hover capability. Sikorsky announced that modification would begin on HH-53Cs in mid-1969, but it was not declared complete until May 1971. Emerging more restrictive than had been originally envisioned, the NRS could be used only under limited conditions, mainly a permissive environment, flat terrain, and good weather. Thus, it was redesignated Limited Night Recovery System (LNRS), or "PAVE IMP," which a commander insisted be renamed "PAVE LOW I." PAVE, which stood for precision avionics vectoring equipment, would identify a number of USAF air rescue and special-operations aircraft. Seventh Air Force wanted the system withdrawn due to the absence of terrain avoidance capability, while Air Rescue desired to keep it, citing that it was better than nothing. The seven HH-53Bs—five in the combat theater and two at the Eglin training center—were slated for the forty-five-day modification program during late 1969 and early 1970. Eight HH-53Cs were placed on the schedule for 1971. In September 1971, an agreement was reached to keep the LNRS. Due to its limitations, it was not used until December 21, 1972, in the rescue of crewmen of "Spectre 1-7," an AC-130A gunship of the 16th SOS that had been downed over Laos. Of sixteen men aboard, fourteen perished in the fiery crash, while two who managed to bail out were saved by LNRS-equipped HH-53 "Jolly 3-2" of the 40th ARRS. Jolly 3-2's LLLTV and the systems of an accompanying Spectre gunship were instrumental in locating the two survivors. Their combined effort foreshadowed the union of rescue and special-operations forces after the war.

BIG MOTHERS

During the long wait for development of the ultimate CSAR Sea King to equip the navy's specialized SAR force, reliance on navy CSAR assets came at the hands of shipboard SH-2s and SH-3s of HC-1, HS-2, HS-4, HS-6, and HS-8. Helicopter Anti-Submarine Squadron 6 (HS-6, "Raunchy Indians"), which had arrived on station in July 1966, in February 1968 turned over the job of CSAR to Helicopter Combat Support Squadron 7 (HC-7, the "SeaDevils"). The Indians' Sea Kings were nicknamed "Big Muthas," which HC-7 changed to "Big Mothers." Detachment 110 of HC-7 flew the new HH-3A, which arrived in 1971, while assuming responsibility for Detachments 104 through 109, flying H-2 "Clementines." The HH-3A featured uprated T58-GE-8F engines, self-sealing fuel tanks, external 175-gallon fuel tanks, a high-speed rescue hoist, armor protection in vital areas, and a high-speed fuel-dumping system to quickly lighten the aircraft. In 1970, dual-pod GE TAT-102 7.62 mm miniguns rated at 4,000 rounds per minute were experimentally fit to HH-3A Bureau Number (BuNo) 149896. Their benefit in firepower could not compensate for their excessive weight, which imposed a range penalty, and the inability to service them in the air. Armament continued to be crew-served M60 machine guns and miniguns mounted in doorways. In 1968, Sikorsky had completed the first conversion to HH-3A and supplied the navy with nine conversion kits. The job of installing the kits into SH-3As went to HC-7 Det Cubi, Philippines.

Accolades regarding the H-3 in battle configuration seldom were heard in the navy's rotary-wing community. Capt. William

Wirt of HS-4 "Black Knights" noted, "When we started to weigh them down like tanks, we lost range, endurance, and performance for the dash mission. They were heavy, lumbering things compared to the ASW aircraft." Flying SH-3s, the Black Knights during its five-month 1966 Vietnam deployment rescued twenty-four downed airmen under fire, a record for an ASW squadron. Blue-water aviators shared the opinion of their air force counterparts that the ideal rescue helicopter was small, fast, and uncomplicated.

A total of thirteen HH-3As would be built, five of which equipped HC-7's Det 110, Big Mothers. The helicopters and all personnel began shipboard rotation of about fifteen days, which earned the unit the name "Orphans of the Seventh Fleet."

Often, they flew pre-positioned along the Tonkin Gulf coastline while airstrikes were conducted inland. By the end of 1971, HC-7 had shed all of its original missions, becoming the navy's only dedicated combat SAR squadron. Big Mothers became an all-H-3 squadron in December 1971, when the last H-2 detachment (Det 107) was disestablished. While other air squadrons and ships cycled through Vietnam waters, HC-7 flew combat search and rescue continuously from September 1967 through September 1973, cross-decking every two to three weeks among destroyers, cruisers, and carriers. When HC-7 SeaDevils was disestablished on June 30, 1975, its personnel were credited with rescuing 150 persons.

After the city of Quang Tri fell to the enemy on May 1, 1972, four HH-53s of the 37th ARRS carried out a daring emergency evacuation of 132 American and South Vietnamese troops from Quang Tri's Citadel. Here, Jolly Green 7-1 (serial no. 69-5784) unloads soldiers at Da Nang AB. The O-2A FAC and an A-1H were shot down during the battle, the pilots of which were rescued. *Courtesy of Jack Stoop / David Stoop*

THE FAC

Since the early days of rescue in Southeast Asia, the forward air controller—called simply "the FAC"—had been a key element of the SAR team. Flying a small, light aircraft, often he was in or near the survivor's area. Since their primary mission was visual reconnaissance, FACs were intimately familiar with their area, making them the ideal director of operations during a SAR effort. During the early stages of a SAR mission, the FAC often pinpointed the survivor's location as well as enemy positions, controlled airstrikes, acted as a communications link with survivors, and briefed the arriving Sandy pilot designated the on-scene commander. Flying low and slow in light aircraft with little armor or armament, FAC operations were high risk, and losses were high; more than 220 FACs were killed during the course of the war. The FAC pilot's saving grace was reluctance of the enemy to shoot at him, which revealed their position; the enemy knew the destruction a FAC could summon.

While the FAC mission was flown mainly by the US Air Force, FACs also were vital reconnaissance elements of all other services in theater. Typical FAC aircraft were Cessna's O-1 Bird Dog, O-2 Super Skymaster, and North American's OV-10 Bronco. Although a throwback to the Korean War, the Cessna Bird Dog—in USAF models O-1E, F, and G—with its high wings and all-around visibility, initially was the best available FAC platform. In 1967 it was joined by Cessna's push-pull engine O-2A, which was nicknamed "Oscar-Deuce," "the Duck," and a host of unsavory terms. Both types were fit with underwing hardpoints for launching flares or 2.75-inch white phosphorous target-marking rockets. By the end of 1971, the OV-10A Bronco was proving to be a worthy addition to the SAR task force. Intended to replace the O-1 and O-2, the Bronco was a light-strike platform well suited for FAC

With twin engine safety, superior visibility, multiple munitions racks, and ejection seats, the North American Rockwell OV-10A Bronco proved the ultimate FAC platform in Southeast Asia, essentially replacing O-1 and O-2 aircraft. This Bronco (serial no. 68-3795) was assigned to the 23rd TASS at Korat RTAFB in 1974. *Courtesy of Don Jay*

duty. Powered by twin turboprop engines, the two-place OV-10 could fly on one engine. Other advantages included armor, ejection seats, and provisions for mounting four external stores as well as four M60C machine guns in sponsons. A centerline mount allowed mounting a 150- or 230-gallon fuel tank or an additional store. "PAVE NAIL" designated eighteen USAF Broncos modified with sophisticated electronic equipment, which enabled them to pinpoint a survivor's position and direct very accurate fire against targets.

Air force FACs typically were assigned to five tactical air support squadrons (TASS) numbered 19 through 23, along with the low-profile "Rustic" and "Raven" units. More than a hundred call signs were used, depending on specific secondary unit assignments and operating locations.

By 1972, the A-1 inventory was being depleted due to combat and operational loss, and transfer to the VNAF. Since there was no substitute for the A-1 Sandy, to protect the remaining A-1s, it was suggested at a SAR conference that in extremely high-threat areas, the OV-10 Broncos maintain longer periods as on-scene commander prior to committing Sandys.

VIETNAMIZATION

Vietnamization identified President Nixon's plan to gradually disengage US forces from Vietnam, while turning over responsibility for waging war to the South Vietnamese government. Nixon announced his Vietnamization strategy on November 3, 1969. North Vietnam would exploit fully the US drawdown and the poor performance of the South Vietnamese army and its heavy reliance on US airpower. North Vietnamese leaders had only to watch and wait as American forces thinned.

In anticipation of the changeover, as some units and personnel were withdrawn, some movement took place among the air rescue organization to maintain maximum coverage. In mid-September the 39th ARRS with its eleven HC-130Ps

A "day FAC" (night FACs were painted all black) O-2A (serial no. 68-11037) of the 21st Tactical Air Support Squadron (TASS) at Phu Cat AB in November 1970. The Cessna wears the name "TIGER PAUSE," possibly in reference to participation in the "Steel Tiger" bombing campaign. *Courtesy of Norm Taylor*

relocated from Tuy Hoa AB to Cam Ranh Bay AB. Three aircraft were kept on rotational alert, with three standing alert at Udorn RTAFB; by year's end, only one HC-130P stood TDY alert at Udorn. Helicopter assets were five HH-3Es of the 37th ARRS, and eleven HH-53s distributed among the 37th ARRS and Det 1, 40th ARRS. The 37th had a TDY element at Bien Hoa AB consisting of two each HH-3Es and HH-53s, plus an A-1 element of the 56th SOW. The 38th ARRS had twenty-five HH-43s dispersed among twelve detachments. The ever-important A-1 Sandy force also was affected. Of the four Skyraider squadrons active during the war, only the 1st SOS was left at the end of 1970. Although numerous A-1s had been consistently passed to the VNAF throughout the war, the aircraft never reached its potential, much less as a SAR platform, in the gargantuan air arm. Nor were the large and expensive aircraft that formed the SAR Task Force made available to the VNAF. In addition, the

massive amount of tactical air support and the vast, sophisticated command-and-control system was beyond the scope of the VNAF structure.

The next major change occurred on July 1, 1971, with the 38th ARRS inactivated; the squadron's eleven remaining HH-43 detachments then were placed under control of 3rd ARRGp. Throughout the year, air rescue units shifted locations while the enemy prepared for an all-out offensive. The dawning of the new year saw a reduction in the number of rescue helicopters, with the HH-53 force ordered trimmed from twenty to thirteen aircraft. In March 1972, the HC-130-equipped 39th ARRS moved to Korat RTAFB, only to be dissolved the following month, with its assets becoming part of Detachment 4, 3rd ARRGp, which became the 56th ARRS in July. The 56th then kept one King HC-130P on airborne alert, one on ground alert, and a third on standby. Alerts at Udorn and Cam Ranh Bay were discontinued.

During the final months of America's involvement in the war, four A-7Ds routinely stood alert at Korat RTAFB, loaded with four LAU-60/61 2.75-inch rocket launchers and two SUU-13 cluster bomb units (CBUs) with either antipersonnel, antimaterial, or tear gas (CS) ordnance. If the four were scrambled, another four A-7Ds were prepared for takeoff. Pictured here in August 1973 is A-7D serial no. 70-0987 of the 3rd TFS at Korat. *Courtesy of Don Jay*

THE EASTER INVASION

When North Vietnam sprang its Easter Invasion—also called the Spring Offensive—rolling into South Vietnam on March 31, it was opposed mainly by the South Vietnamese army, backed by US airpower. Within hours, US air units flooded back into the combat theater. The order to reduce the number of HH-53s—which by then numbered seventeen—was suspended, and the 3rd ARRGp was reinforced with six HH-3Es, two each from Okinawa, Korea, and the Philippines. The six operated from Tan Son Nhut AB, where they were attached to Detachment 14. The navy added four carriers to the two already in the Gulf of Tonkin. With the dramatic increase in combat sorties came the correspondingly increased number of downed aircraft and crews. First to go down was an AC-130E gunship on the night of the invasion. During the massive SAR operation, all fifteen crewmen of "Spectre 2-2" were rescued by four HH-53s of the 40th ARRS and Air America H-34s. Unfortunately, the success of the well-orchestrated mission was overshadowed by the downing two days later of "Bat 2-1."

The true reason for the six HH-3Es hurriedly gathered, it turned out, was for possible evacuation of the US embassy in Phnom Penh, Cambodia. Two of the six USAF A-1s remaining in country for CSAR joined the HH-3E contingent. The half-dozen Jolly Greens came with crews with no combat experience, but air force officials didn't have to look far to find their combat-seasoned mentors. Joe Ballinger recalls:

In 1972, with a little more than a year to go to retire with twenty years in the air force, I figured that the Vietnam War was behind me. But one of the unplanned things about the military is the needs of the service.

As the Heavy-Lift Training Squadron standardization officer for H-3s, I was sitting in a classroom at Hill AFB, Utah, when the deputy chief of operations waved me out to the hall. He told me that he wanted me to volunteer for a "classified assignment, destination unknown." It was the end of April 1972, and I knew that things were not going well in Vietnam, so I shook my head and said, "Hell no! I can read the papers, and I'm going to retire next year." He went on with "Your old squadron in the Philippines, along with Korea and Okinawa, is sending two H-3s each, and none of them have had any combat training." Knowing that, having just come from there, and you don't say no to Col. Jack Allison, Son Tay raider, I told him, "Oh hell, Jack! I'm still in the air force; just cut the orders and send me. But you'd better tell my wife I didn't volunteer!" He grinned and said, "Good. Let's go find the other volunteer." Now curious, I followed him down the hall to the office of Major Wally Barnes, Group H-3 standardization officer, where Jack asked him the same as he did me.

So Wally and I, with sixty-day TDY orders, headed off the next day for Tan Son Nhut AB, Saigon, to combat-train six helicopter aircrews to augment air rescue forces in South Vietnam. After the six helicopters arrived, we set up training

at Vung Tau, which was the safest area to train them. With concentrated flying, Wally and I had the crews combat-qualified in two weeks and ready to stand alert.

When Ballinger and Barnes asked to return to Hill AFB, they were briefed on the main reason they were summoned back to Vietnam. At the "Little Pentagon," the pair was told that MACV, very concerned about the war in Cambodia, was planning to evacuate the American embassy in Phnom Penh by helicopter. Using Marine CH-53s and the half-dozen HH-3Es, eight hundred people would be flown to Saigon along the Mekong River, which was a hotbed of North Vietnamese attacks against Tay Ninh and An Loc. It was known that the attackers had been issued Strela shoulder-launched antiaircraft missiles. Ballinger continues:

At the conclusion of the briefing, my opening comment was bluntly, "It's a fucking suicide mission!" We would be better trying to evacuate north into Thailand. Wally, always cooler than me, pulled me back down into my chair and suggested that they get some baby flattops down in the gulf for us. When asked if we had any shipboard landing experience, I said I had and could train our crews if needed. The generals agreed to consider our input, and we left, hoping it didn't happen.

Ballinger describes yet another need for his services before his return to Utah:

On May 2, an aircraft was shot down over An Loc, about 60 miles away, on the Cambodian border. With two tours in Vietnam behind me, I was the most experienced combat pilot and was selected to be the lead pilot. So we scrambled two HH-3E Jolly Green helicopters to see if we could find any survivors. Due to the recent use of Strela missiles being used in the area, I climbed rapidly to above 10,000 [feet], over a cloud layer, to hide us. The only other countermeasures we had was a crewman sitting on the aft ramp with a Very pistol loaded with a thermite flare to possibly decoy the heat-seeking missile, or shutting down both engines, eliminating the infrared signature.

As I led the two birds toward An Loc, I got the word that the aircraft shot down was a Stinger AC-119 gunship with ten crewmen. Legendary army general James Hollingsworth, while overseeing the bitter siege of An Loc, rescued one survivor in his Huey helicopter before being driven off by ground fire. This was not looking like a simple mission! Looking down through the clouds, I could see An Loc, and it was nearly totally destroyed. After contacting our cover A-1, I left the other HH-3E at 10,000 feet for backup and descended through the clouds to join up with the A-1. I spotted an A-1 strafing the area, and fell into loose formation behind him. Then I got a call, "Hey, Jolly. Over here!" as he pulled up and fired a 20 mm tracer into the air. Seeing his airburst, I then fell into formation behind him. So much for being the most experienced combat pilot, as I had been following a Vietnamese air force A-1, which did not perform the SAR function.

Leading me to a survivor, I lowered my landing gear and went into a 150-foot hover with my helicopter belly in the treetops as my crewman lowered the hoist and picked up the survivor with the jungle penetrator. As I was waiting for the call that the survivor was aboard, I heard the A-1 Spad direct the other H-3 over another survivor. Usually the backup helicopter stayed away and came in only if needed, but the Spad driver was on-scene commander, and it was faster this way. As we hopscotched around each other, picking up three survivors each, the A-1 protected us from ground fire. It was over in less than ten minutes. After completing our third pickup, I remained in a hover with my belly in the trees for cover until the other helicopter had his last man on board. It was then that I directed him to follow me, keeping in the trees until max airspeed of 150 mph, then climb out to above cloud cover, using jinking techniques. Jinking is like the flight of a dove, which is the hardest bird to hit when hunting.

Seven of the ten aircrew got out of the Stinger that day, and I gave a lot of thanks for that being my last combat mission and not taking a hit or being injured. And we never had to evacuate the US embassy in Cambodia by helicopter, though when they evacuated Saigon in 1975, I always suspected they dusted off Wally's plan for Phnom Penh.

RETIRE THE A-1?

Most old-timers shared the belief that there was no suitable replacement for the venerable A-1. "Only an A-1 could replace an A-1," they said. Officials even considered reviving A-1 Skyraider production, but that proved cost prohibitive. A number of possibilities were bandied about and scrutinized at high-level meetings during 1971, with focus on the performance of the Ling-Temco-Vought (LTV) A-7D, a relative newcomer to the air force. Since all A-1 Skyraiders, including those in the Sandy role, were to be turned over to the South Vietnamese air force, the A-7D had been selected among a variety of aircraft as the A-1's replacement. Plans for a six-month training program to replace the A-1, however, were scrapped in view of the strong possibility of a ceasefire, which necessitated the rapid transfer of A-1s to the VNAF by the end of 1972. An abbreviated but intense training period begun on November 2 included placing seasoned A-1 pilots aboard Jolly Green helicopters to critique A-7D pilots. The A-7Ds of the newly formed 3rd Tactical Fighter Squadron at Korat RTAFB immediately were assigned the Sandy mission. The 3rd TFS evolved from the 355th TFS of the 354th TFW at Korat. Initially, the squadron kept two flights of three A-7Ds each on alert to escort Jolly Greens.

Lessons came quickly for Sandy pilots in the cockpits of A-7Ds, but they and their aircraft quickly adapted to the vital role. In its intended role as an attack platform, the A-7D was a star performer, known for its ability to place massive ordnance loads with pinpoint accuracy. To fit the Sandy role, some tactics required revision to compensate for the A-7D's two major drawbacks: speed and thirst for fuel. Especially missed would be the A-1's slower speed for maneuvering and visual search, plus keeping the helicopters in sight. To stay with the slower HH-53 helicopters, two A-7Ds flew an elliptical pattern to maintain continual protection. The large amounts of fuel they consumed often meant multiple trips to the tanker, which, in turn, called for more A-7Ds. On the plus side, speed meant survivability in lethal antiaircraft saturations, and reaching survivors faster. It was armored, had self-sealing fuel tanks, and could be refueled in flight. Relatively new to the air force, the A-7D featured a host of electronic equipment to aid navigation, communication, and locating downed airmen.

Just two weeks after training had begun, on November 16–18, 1972, the first rescue mission supported by A-7Ds as A-1 replacements resulted in the successful rescue of two F-105G crewmen downed over North Vietnam. The Thunderchief, call sign "Bobbin 0-5," was the last F-105 shot down.

The last SAR mission for the A-1 Sandy occurred on November 7, 1972. The day prior, a US Army Huey helicopter with crew and three officers spotting for naval gunfire ran short on fuel trying to escape a fast-approaching typhoon and landed in enemy territory. Captain Donald Screws of the 1st SOS, flying an A-1 that was being processed for transfer to the VNAF, picked up a beeper signal from the Huey pilots. Screws, who himself had been shot down and rescued by a Jolly Green six months earlier, laid down covering fire, enabling a pair of Jolly Greens to rescue the seven survivors. Screws and his wingman then flew their A-1s to Bien Hoa to complete their transfer to the VNAF. The pair of Skyraiders was among the last seven of the 1st SOS turned over to the VNAF.

Strangely, despite the high level of air activity to counter North Vietnam's Spring Offensive, inactivation and realignment of air rescue units continued. On November 30, 1972, the 37th ARRS was inactivated, leaving the 40th ARRS to go it alone. The squadron's HH-43F element was designated Detachment 7 and remained at Da Nang. Operating from Nakhon Phanom RTAFB, the 40th ARRS possessed three HH-43 Pedros and ten HH-53s. The squadron also assumed responsibility for all HH-43 LBR detachments in theater. On December 15, three days prior to the kickoff of an intense bombing campaign, two HH-53s were pulled from the 40th's inventory because the unit was deemed "over-strength."

President Nixon ordered the all-out bombing campaign against the North when peace negotiations fizzled. Called Linebacker II, the bombing began on December 18, driving enemy leaders back to the peace table, but at the cost of more than twenty aircraft, fifteen of which were the mighty B-52.

CEASEFIRE AND OTHER FALLACIES

A ceasefire in South and North Vietnam was signed on January 27, 1973, supposedly heralding the end of US involvement in

Members of the 56th ARRS at Korat gather with HC-130P "King 2-1" to commemorate the last mission flown over Cambodia on August 15, 1973. The crew of the rescue Hercules consisted of pilot, copilot, flight engineer, navigator, radio operator, and loadmaster. *Courtesy of David Saville collection*

the war in Southeast Asia. References differ as to the last shoot-downs, last Jolly Green rescue, last combat mission flown, etc. Air rescue assets in theater during late January totaled eleven HH-53Cs, fourteen HH-43Fs, and six HC-130Ps. In conjunction with the ceasefire, the US withdrew forces from Vietnam soil; however, they continued operations from Thailand. War continued in Laos and Cambodia. The last recorded Jolly Green rescue took place on May 26, 1973, when a Udorn-based HH-53 rescued the two crewmen of an F-4D shot down in Cambodia. The 56th ARRS flew the last HC-130P mission of the war on August 15, 1973, the last day of bombing in Cambodia. Although the shooting war for the US basically ended on that day, four A-7Ds stood fifteen-minute alert at Korat for coverage of aircraft still in theater, along with reconnaissance flights being flown over the expanse of Southeast Asia.

Before the final curtain for Air Rescue aircraft and crews in Southeast Asia, they dutifully protected US concerns to the bitter end, as they had throughout the conflict. Commensurate with the withdrawal of USAF units in Thailand, the number of ARRS aircraft thinned. By January 1975, there were eight HH-53Cs, four HH-43Fs, and five HC-130Ps in theater. The 3rd

ARRGp by that time had six AC-130 gunships under its control, along with twenty-four A-7Ds, and twenty OV-10s.

To prepare for the inevitable takeover of Cambodia's Phnom Penh by the Communist Khmer Rouge, Operation Eagle Pull was formulated in mid-1973. When the plan was executed on April 12, 1975, two HC-130Ps controlled the skies over the capital. A trio of HH-53Cs of the 56th ARRS—which had staged at Ubon RTAFB—orbited the city while Marine helicopters evacuated nearly three hundred people. The last two HH-53Cs in the LZ extracting the command element were hit by small-arms fire, but there were no injuries, and Eagle Pull was a success.

The sixteen-year period during which the Kaman HH-43 stood as vanguard of the local base rescue mission ended on September 30, 1975, when Detachment 5's HH-43F serial no. 64-17559 flew the last operational Pedro flight in support of the 432nd TFW. Conversion of the Pedros of the 40th ARRS to Bell's UH-1N helicopter had been nearly completed, and Detachment 5 at Udorn was inactivated. When the 56th deactivated in October 1975, its four remaining HC-130Ps went to the 40th ARRS, which itself was inactivated three months later.

In mid-March 1975, the North Vietnamese violated all aspects of the peace accords by launching a massive offensive against South Vietnam. When the order came on April 29 to execute Operation Frequent Wind—the air evacuation of all US personnel and allies remaining in South Vietnam—air force and marine H-53s lifted from *Midway*'s deck in the South China Sea and headed for Saigon. Simultaneously, three HC-130s of the 56th ARRS maintained orbits overhead. During history's largest helicopter evacuation, over a hundred marine, air force, and Air America helicopters evacuated an estimated seven thousand Americans and South Vietnamese in less than twenty-four hours.

CAMBODIA TESTS AMERICAN RESOLVE

With the long war in Southeast Asia presumably over, the Communist regime dealt American forces another hand less than two weeks after the fall of South Vietnam. On May 12, 1975, Cambodian Khmer Rouge forces seized the US-flagged container ship SS *Mayaguez* in international waters. The following day the ship was anchored at the small island of Koh Tang off Cambodia's coast. The US acted decisively, placing heavy demands upon US Marine ground troops and aircrews of the 40th ARRS and the 21st SOS, both of which remained based at Nakhon Phanom RTAFB.

Six HH-53C Jolly Greens and five CH-53 Knife special-operations helicopters carrying a raiding force of more than 230 marines bore the brunt of intense battle that took place on Koh Tang Island to recover *Mayaguez* and its crew. Although the ship's crew had been moved, the assault force met fierce resistance by a fortified, heavily armed enemy. After fourteen hours of intense battle, only three of the eleven helicopters remained flyable; US casualties were fifteen killed, three missing, and fifty wounded. Despite almost fanatical resistance by the enemy, the skill and determination of the helicopter crews, with superior air support, persevered in recovering the marines from the island. *Mayaguez* and its crew had been recovered elsewhere by naval forces.

During the war, USAF Air Rescue units recorded 4,170 souls recovered, 2,780 of which were combat saves. The cost in lives of air rescue personnel reached 107 KIA, twenty-four of whom are MIA. Seven were taken prisoner, with six released and one killed. Aerospace Rescue and Recovery Service aircraft losses during the war totaled sixty-one, depending on the source: combined combat and theater operational loss totals include twenty-four CH-3/HH-3, seventeen HH-53B/C, fourteen HH-43B/F, two HC-130P, and four HU-16B.

Veteran Jolly Green pilot and president of the Jolly Green Association Barry Kamhoot said in 2019, "Our Jolly Green call sign became more than a call sign; it became a mission, a capability, an expectation, a hope, a part of a combat rescue team, and a special camaraderie." Fifty-two years earlier, in 1967, Secretary of the Air Force Harold Brown foretold of the air rescue man's legacy: "When the history of this war is finally written, I feel that the story of Air Rescue may well become one of the most outstanding human dramas in the entire history of the Air Force" . . . and that it became.

POSTWAR

As air operations decreased during the final months of US involvement in Southeast Asia, the Aerospace Rescue and Recovery Service reorganized to absorb and realign assets returning from the war zone, thus maximizing its peacetime operations. In May 1974 the air force consolidated the three rescue centers into which the continental US had been divided. The result was the Air Force Rescue Coordination Center, established at Scott AFB, Illinois, which would more efficiently coordinate rescue resources across the nation. On a global scale, the ARRS had retained its regimen of conducting peacetime rescues despite wartime commitments.

The effectiveness of combat SAR after the war depended on extensive training to retain the skills and knowledge gained during search-and-rescue operations in Southeast Asia. Therefore, tapping the experience of SAR veterans proved vital to long-range development of SAR equipment and procedures. High on the priority list were development and procurement of aircraft ideally suited for combat search and rescue; no aircraft had been designed specifically for that mission. Typically, in-service aircraft types were altered for CSAR. The two main objections to the HH-53 were its large size and slow speed. Postwar reviews with leaders of the 3rd Air Rescue and Recovery Group pointed to the need for a helicopter able to hover at 7,000 feet in an air temperature of 90 degrees Fahrenheit and have a forward speed of 350 knots. It was to be equipped with a night recovery system, terrain-following/avoidance radar, and electronic safeguards for survivability in high-AAA environments. In the fixed-wing arena, the C-130 held its own, having proven to be a stable, reliable multirole platform. For the rescue escort (RESCORT, or RESCAP) role, there was no denying the record of the venerable A-1 Skyraider. For all its glowing capabilities in the CSAR role, the A-1 lacked the desired speed envelope, which ranged from low speed to stay with helicopters, to high speed to reach a scene quickly and survive in heavily defended areas. The A-1's replacement, the A-7D, proved satisfactory in the RESCORT role, but the Republic Fairchild A-10 "Thunderbolt II" close-air-support aircraft then under development showed greater promise.

Typical of the "Sandy" mission for support of SAR missions was this A-1H Skyraider (S/N 52-135257) named "Sopwith Camel" of the 1st SOS. Standing alert at NKP in Thailand, the Spad carries a symmetrical load of 750-pound napalm bombs, M18 minigun pods, nineteen-round 2.75-inch rocket pods, and cluster bomb units (CBUs). *Courtesy of Tom Hansen collection*

Grumman HU-16B Albatrosses were among the few USAF aircraft in Southeast Asia whose camouflaged livery diverted from the standard tritone scheme. The Sea Blue and Camouflaged Gray scheme gave Albatross crews an edge when on the water in the South China Sea. *Courtesy of Kelly McLarney collection*

While war ravaged in Southeast Asia, disasters in the continental US warranted the attention of air rescue assets. Civil Air Patrol Air Rescue used this military surplus DUKW to search Minnesota's Lake Roosevelt after a series of tornadoes struck the area in August 1969. *Courtesy of Kelly McLarney collection*

Outside the nation's spotlight on the war in Southeast Asia, prior to 1974 consolidation, search-and-rescue operations within the continental US remained coordinated and controlled through the three air rescue centers, although their operations had expanded. Under the Eastern ARRC, Detachment 17 at Albrook AFB, Canal Zone, served as the joint SAR center for the region. The same function applied to Western ARRC's Detachment 1 at Elmendorf AFB, Alaska, for the Alaskan Air Command. Overseas SAR operations were coordinated by the Atlantic ARRC at Ramstein AB, Germany (later the 40th ARRWg), and the Pacific ARRC at Hickam AFB, Hawaii (later the 41st ARRWg). These five centers controlled seventy detachments. Globally, through the 1960s, fourteen squadrons were under command and control of ARRS Headquarters at Orlando AFB, Florida.

Reorganization of the local base rescue (LBR) mission included the 1970 deactivation of fifteen detachments of the 44th ARRS under the Eastern ARRC. The remaining Detachment 1 at Homestead AFB, Florida; Detachment 8 at Myrtle Beach, South Carolina; and Detachment 14 at MacDill AFB, Florida, converted to twin-engine UH-1N helicopters in 1972 and 1973. Among thirteen LBR detachments of the 42nd ARRS, Western ARC was the 1550th Aircrew Training and Test Wing (ATTW), which had sixteen HH-43Bs on the inventory by 1972. In 1970, six of the eighteen detachments of the 43rd ARRS under the Central ARC converted to Bell HH-1H helicopters. Three of the squadron's detachments converted to UH-1Ns in 1973.

HUEY UPGRADES

Satisfied with its UH-1F helicopter of the 1960s, and keenly aware of the Huey's battle record during the Vietnam War, the air force went to Bell Helicopter for the Kaman HH-43's replacement. On November 4, 1970, the air force submitted a contract for thirty HH-1H crash-rescue Hueys. Based on the army's UH-1H, the "stretched" Huey was distinguished by a roof-mounted rescue hoist rated at 600 pounds on a 250-foot cable. The HH-1H was equipped with all-weather instrumentation housed in a belly-mounted radome. Included was a radio suite specially designed for rescue work, allowing direct communication not only with USAF ground vehicles and rescue teams, but with the Civil Air Patrol and civilian law enforcement. Tail rotors were switched to the right side to improve directional control and to better counter main rotor torque. Deliveries began in October 1971 and were completed in 1973. Like the UH-1Fs and TH-1Fs of the early 1960s, about two-thirds of the HH-1Hs were assigned to various detachments of the 37th ARRS, with the remainder assigned to the Reserve 304th ARRS.

Since the Huey's single rotor was not nearly as effective as the Huskie's contrarotating rotors in clearing a path through flames, few units flying the HH-1H carried the fire suppression kit. The solution, therefore, lay in testing single-rotor helicopters with onboard firefighting agents. The navy tried its hand at crash rescue and fire suppression using a Kaman UH-2B Seasprite carrying newly developed "aqueous film-forming foam" (AFFF), called "Light Water" or "A Triple F." Tests conducted by the Naval Research Laboratory at NAS Miramar, Florida, in 1965 had the Seasprite clearing a path with AFFF spray boom, enabling two firefighters to advance through flames. The army, using its UH-1H helicopters, conducted tests with AFFF fire suppression systems from the late 1960s through the early 1970s.

Despite the Huskie's superior rotor system in the crash-rescue role, Military Airlift Command deemed the HH-43 underpowered to carry the FSK and crash-rescue crew. That led to field tests during the late 1960s of piston-powered navy SH-34s believed to have been supplied by HS-1 at NAS Key West.

In view of the difficulty in finding a helicopter that could come close to the HH-43's firefighting ability, in the early 1970s a CH-3C was evaluated in fire suppression at MacDill AFB with the assistance of Detachment 14 of the 44th ARRS. Although the CH-3C's higher-velocity rotor wash was found to have merit in the firefighting role, and its overall performance was equal to or exceeded that of the HH-43, its major drawback was the amount of time needed to become airborne due to its complexity.

Possibly lending support to the idea of using the H-3 for crash rescue was an actual rescue accomplished with an HH-3E using fire suppression techniques. On October 29, 1968, seasoned pioneer Huskie pilot Lt. Col. William Lyell of the 58th ARRS was copilot of an HH-3E on a training flight over Wheelus AB, Libya. Spotting two F-100 jets collide during landing, Lyell assumed command of the helicopter, arriving over the scene before the F-100s came to a stop. One pilot escaped but the other was trapped in the burning wreckage. Not missing a beat, Lyell hovered over the pilot, using his rotor wash to blow away smoke and flame from the cockpit. The pilot jettisoned his canopy and escaped through the corridor created by Lyell's downwash. Lyell picked up the pilot and flew him to safety. In correspondence to this author, "Wild Bill" Lyell related:

I had done rotor blast fire suppression with the H-21, H-19, and H-3 helicopters, and although these aircraft did not utilize the foam bottle and firemen like the H-43, the rotor blast from any helicopter kept flames close to the ground, dissipated smoke, and blew a breath of fresh air to whoever needed it. We positioned ourselves as needed and the pilot was able to get out but suffered facial and hand burns. He later told us he was using his last breath until the cold air from our rotor blast hit. I was squadron commander of the 58th ARRS and had three H-43s and three H-3s, but we were just lucky to be airborne in an H-3.

To give the popular Huey more power and twin-engine safety, Bell Helicopter designed the UH-1N model for the Canadian and US military. While based on the proven UH-1H, the N model featured a Pratt & Whitney PT6T Turbo "Twin-Pac" power plant delivering 1,800 hp. Although both models shared the same speed envelope, the UH-1N had a longer range at 357

The eight HH-53Bs were easily identified by diagonal sponson braces that supported external fuel tanks. The second-built HH-53B (serial no. 66-14429) is seen here at Hill AFB, Utah, in September 1974. It was assigned to the 1550th ATTW at Hill AFB, home of the 1550th from its inception in 1971 to early 1976. *Courtesy of Stephen Miller*

The HH-53C (serial no. 69-5796) at Andrews AFB in September 1972. The 44 HH-53Cs built were powered by two T64-GE-7 turboshaft engines rated at 3,925 hp each. *Courtesy of Stephen Miller*

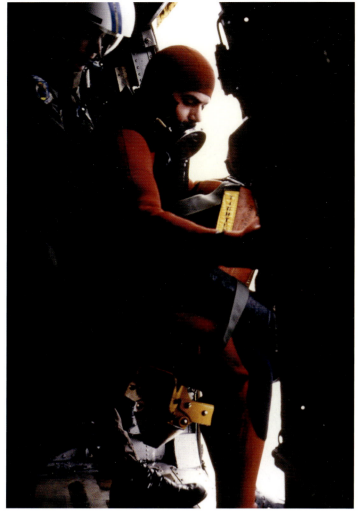

A pararescueman prepares to be lowered by the hoist of an HH-3 helicopter in 1978. His destination likely is very cold water, since he wears a unisuit, which differs from a traditional wetsuit in that it is a dry suit, which prevents water from skin contact. It is completely sealed and is donned by means of a long waterproof zipper. *Courtesy of Charles Isackson*

miles, and a service ceiling of 17,400 feet. Deliveries to the air force to fill an order for twenty-two machines began in October 1970. It was intended that most UH-1Ns would replace UH-1Fs providing missile site support; however, as the missile program was downsized, many of the twin Hueys assumed the air rescue role. A follow-on order for thirty UH-1Ns not only added to the air rescue inventory but supplied twin Hueys for pilot training, VIP transport, and special operations. Like the HH-1H, not all UH-1Ns committed to rescue duty carried the FSK, although an internal rescue hoist was commonly installed. Units such as Det 22 at Mountain Home AFB, Idaho, were kept busy learning the different helicopters during successive transition. Det 22 swapped their HH-43s for HH-1Hs, only to lose them to the Reserves one year later when they inherited UH-1Ns of the 20th SOS in Vietnam.

First to get the Air Rescue twin Hueys was Southeast Asia–based 40th ARRS in 1970, followed in 1971 by the 1550th ATTW. The many detachments of the 37th ARRS became UH-1N equipped beginning in 1973. Two months prior to converting to UH-1Ns, on May 1, 1973, Detachment 14 transferred from MacDill AFB to Richards-Gebaur AFB, the same date that the air force terminated the positions of airborne rescue man / firefighter and aeromedical technician. Next to receive UH-1Ns was the 67th ARRS at RAF Woodbridge, beginning in 1975. USAF procurement of the UH-1N would total seventy-nine helicopters, with nearly half from initial orders assigned to Air Rescue.

In December 1973, SAC's missile site support mission was handed over to Military Airlift Command's Aerospace Rescue and Recovery Service, which reactivated the 37th ARRS to handle the job. The 37th was assigned more than fifty UH-1Fs in ten detachments to support numerous missile sites across the western US; only Detachment 8 at Vandenberg AFB was equipped with UH-1Ns. The secondary mission of these detachments was search and rescue and medical evacuation. Regardless of mission of stateside USAF helicopter units, many were tasked during the early 1970s with an additional mission called "Military Assistance to Safety and Traffic (MAST)" to provide rapid air transport of accident victims. As predicted, the military was unable to maintain the MAST commitment, and by the late 1990s, states in which the service was available declined from twenty-nine to fourteen. In 1974, MAC reorganized air rescue units in Europe, placing HH-1Hs at Aviano AB, in Italy, and Zaragoza AB, in Spain.

To draw from the pages that were written daily in Southeast Asia for the book on combat SAR, Air Mobility Command on April 1, 1971, activated the 1550th Aircrew Training and Test Wing at Hill AFB, Utah. The installation would serve as a test center and training site both for fixed-wing and rotary-wing air rescue crews and technology. The aircraft inventory of the 1550th ATTW included a mix of ten HC-130H, P, and N models; HH-43s until 1975; UH-1Fs until 1982; HH-53s; HH-1Hs; and UH-1Ns. When the wing was relocated to Kirtland AFB in February 1976, it possessed four HH-3Es. The wing's syllabus included advanced pararescue training. Assigned to the 1550th ATTW was the 1551st Flying Training Squadron (FTS), which managed both helicopter and HC-130 crew training. All HC-130 crewmen underwent a thirty-day training program covering intercepts, escorts, search patterns over water and mountains, aerial recovery, delivery of emergency equipment, and use of air rescue electronics gear. On May 15, 1984, the 1550th ATTW became the 1550th Combat Crew Training Wing (CCTW).

Search-and-rescue operations during the war in Southeast Asia had emphasized the need for aircrew survival training so profoundly that it ranked high on the air force priority list. During the nearly two decades between establishment of the first survival school and the peak of the Vietnam War, more than a hundred survival schools existed throughout the air force. The first aircrew survival school opened its doors in August 1947, at Marks Army Airfield near Nome, Alaska. Called the Arctic Indoctrination School and nicknamed "Cool School," the facility merged in November 1948 with Land Survival School at Alaska's Ladd AFB. The large number of schools led to their consolidation in March 1966 as the 336th Combat Crew Training Group. Then the sole manager of USAF survival training, the 336th CCTG began operations in June at Fairchild AFB, Washington. By the time that the unit was redesignated the 3636th Combat Crew Training Wing (Survival) on April 1, 1971, it managed subunits at NAS Pensacola and Eielson AFB, Alaska, along with jungle survival training in the Philippines and tropic survival in Panama.

Organizational changes included activation in January 1970 of the 39th Aerospace Rescue and Recovery Wing, located at Richards-Gebaur AFB, Missouri, and beginning in June 1971, Eglin AFB. The 39th ARRWg coordinated all inland SAR operations by federal agencies, including military units, the Civil Air Patrol, and volunteer organizations. The three regional SAR centers also worked with state and local governments, law enforcement and emergency services, and special-skill groups, such as SCUBA and mountain-climbing organizations. Most active and vital to USAF Air Rescue was the Civil Air Patrol. Brig. Gen. Allison C. Brooks, ARRS commander, stated in 1967:

In prosecution of inland SAR missions, the Civil Air Patrol has consistently performed in an outstanding manner. These pilots make their service and aircraft available on very short notice, often leaving their places of employment for several days during the course of a mission. While they are reimbursed for gas and oil, they bear all other expenses themselves. Over the years their services have been invaluable on literally thousands of missions.

Under a USAF national commander, the CAP was assigned to Air Force Headquarters from 1968 to 1978, when it was transferred to the Air Training Command., and thereafter

An HC-130N (serial no. 69-5824) refuels an HH-3E (serial no. 69-5803) of the 5040th Helicopter Squadron over Alaska in 1970. The 5040th, which flew both CH-3Es and HH-3Es, was deactivated in September 1975, and its assets were absorbed into the 71st ARRS to form a composite unit flying HH-3Es and HC-130Ns. *Courtesy of Kyron Hall*

Equipped with a cargo sling and wearing high-visibility markings, the HH-3E (serial no. 69-5807) of the 5040th HS, Alaska Air Command stands by at a gunnery range in 1973. The helicopter crashed in 1974, when it went rearward in a whiteout while hovering over a crash site. The pilot was killed. *Courtesy of James Burns collection*

An HH-53B undergoes early testing to determine the flight characteristics of a space capsule when slung beneath the helicopter while midair refueling from an HC-130H. *Courtesy of USAF*

The first of eight HH-53Cs modified with PAVE LOW III systems and redesignated HH-53H, delivered in March 1979. A forward-looking infrared radar imager and terrain-following radar were housed in distinctive chin mounts. Serial no. 69-5791 is seen here at the Naval Air Rework Facility, NAS Pensacola, in April 1979. *Courtesy of Rob Mignard*

Although assigned to the 1st Special Operations Wing for most of its air force life, this UH-1N (serial no. 69-6642) flew rescue missions when necessary. The twin Huey is seen here in 1974, finished in Aircraft Gray (FS 16473), also called "ADC Gray," In 2012, it was transferred to the 512th Rescue Squadron, which was part of the Air Education and Training Command that operated both UH-1N and HH-60G helicopters at Kirtland AFB. *Author's collection*

This "White Top" UH-1F (serial no. 63-13153) from the initial delivery batch, along with the first-built UH-1F (serial no. 63-13141), replaced two HH-43B Huskies of Det 18, 43rd ARRS, at Little Rock AFB about 1965. Soon afterward, Det 18 was deactivated and the pair of Hueys and personnel transferred to Det 5 42nd ARRS, at Edwards AFB. A crewman laments: "The UH-1F was not a suitable platform for dragging the FSK around, and the rotor wash was nothing close to that of the H-43." *Courtesy of USAF*

the Air University. During the 1970s, most of CAP's eight regional liaison offices operated permanently assigned C-45 aircraft. Besides numerous L-19, T-34, L-20, and T-41 aircraft transferred to CAP from the air force and army since the 1950s, CAP purchased government-funded aircraft, mainly Cessna model 172s and 182s.

Besides aircraft passed to the CAP, other outmoded types that were mistakenly thought to have been "put out to pasture" in fact continued to serve. John Grasser explains:

When I returned from Vietnam in early 1969, where I had been flying UH-1Fs with the 20th Special Operations Squadron, I was assigned to Homestead AFB, a Tactical Air Command base. I was placed in charge of a small detachment comprising two ancient H-21 helicopters, providing support for the Air Training Command's Sea Survival School. In addition, we were tasked to provide backup for the LBR detachment, which flew HH-43Bs, and to support the base in any other rotary-wing missions. Our main task was to provide hoist pickup training for survival school students. The Vietnam War was still in full swing, and we often flew seven days a week. One-half of each day was devoted to water pickups, and the second half to pickups from a mangrove swamp. While the H-21s managed to provide outstanding service, these machines were quite old, and the saltwater environment proved hard on them. They were kept in the air only through the extraordinary efforts of our maintenance personnel. Our two machines were two of the last three still in service with the air force, the third being stationed at Langley AFB, Virginia.

Sometime in early 1971, rumor had it that we would soon receive H-3s to replace our old birds, and naturally we were looking forward to newer and better equipment. In late summer I returned from leave and found two Air Rescue H-3s parked on the ramp. Furthermore, our small detachment had been disbanded, and we became part of Rescue. Never having flown the H-3, I soon found myself at Sheppard AFB for a checkout in the machine. In addition to having taken over the mission of supporting the Water Survival School, the rescue unit was to support the Presidential Office and assist in supporting the series of missile-tracking stations located throughout the Bahama chain.

Former navy H-34s equipped three Reserve aerospace rescue and recovery squadrons during the early 1970s, replacing HU-16Bs and HC-97Gs. This HH-34J (BuNo 148013) was assigned to the 304th ARRS at Portland (Oregon) International Airport. *Courtesy of David Wendt*

An HH-3E of the 31st ARRS at Clark AB, Philippines, rescues a crewman of the Chinese tanker *Tong Lam* on October 27, 1970. After the ship ran aground on Scarborough Reef in the South China Sea, two HH-3Es of the 31st, along with a navy helicopter, rescued all thirty-nine crewmen. *Courtesy of USAF*

Under command of ARRS Headquarters were the 1550th ATTW, the 39th ARRWg, and the 41st ARRWg. Originally the Pacific Aerospace Rescue and Recovery Center, which controlled fourteen detachments in Southeast Asia, the 41st became the 41st Rescue and Weather Reconnaissance Wing (RWRWg) when it was transferred to McClellan AFB, California, on September 1, 1975. The designation change reflected the wing's new twofold mission of rescue and global weather monitoring, with three squadrons flying WC-130 and WC-135 aircraft. Both the 41st RWRW and the 40th ARRWg took on various squadrons and aircraft types until inactivated during the late 1980s. On February 8, 1969, when the PARRC became the 41st ARRWg, the Atlantic Aerospace Rescue and Recovery Center, based at Ramstein, Germany, became the 40th ARRWg. The wing encompassed the 58th and 67th ARRS, plus fifteen detachments spread among twenty-one air bases in seven European countries.

ICELAND

The early air rescue contingent at Keflavik comprised SA-16As, SH-19s, and L-20s of the 53rd Air Rescue Squadron, which had been formed in 1958 specifically for Iceland but was deactivated in 1960. When Russian bombers became a steady nuisance over the North Atlantic during 1968, flying schedules of the Iceland-based F-102s of the 57th FIS increased dramatically. That brought Air Rescue into the picture to provide its first steady presence at Keflavik in eight years. The Reserve 305th ARRS, which already had been mobilized for the *Pueblo* incident, provided a detachment of two HC-97Gs. Beginning in May 1969, they were replaced by two-week rotations of HC-130s of the 54th, 55th, 57th, and 67th ARRS. To manage these aircraft at what came to be known as "Operating Location One (OL-1)" at Keflavik, a shadow detachment was approved in mid-1969, which became Detachment 14, 40th ARRWg, in July 1970. As of November 1971, Detachment 14, with three HH-3Es and two HC-130s, represented the rescue element of the Icelandic defense force.

Bruce Ware provides insight to the "Sub" mission:

The HH-3E unit at Keflavik NATO base in Iceland had a combat rescue mission; however, we were also responsible for the search and recovery in the entire North Sea region, under the direction of the commander of the Icelandic defense force, a US Navy rear admiral. There were many US Navy submarines operating in that area, and when someone on one of those had to be airlifted in an emergency, our HH-3E unit was called upon. The HH-3E crew was supported by an HC-130 tanker which was TDY to Keflavik. The HC-130 crew provided the navigation and aerial refueling for the HH-3E on every mission which was out over the water.

The actual coordinates of the submarine at the time of pickup were classified "Secret" until the actual launch of the recovery force, and then it was only known by the two crews. Generally, the HC-130 arrived over the area first, guided the HH-3E to the area, and the submarine then surfaced. Many times however, the sub was on the surface when the HC-130 arrived. Most of the recoveries were "radio out" to keep anyone else from locating the submarine. The normal recovery was off the aft deck of the sub, but if the sea state was too high for that, the recovery was from the diving plane, which was really tricky. The sub was to stay underway at 3 to 5 knots and head about 30 degrees to starboard of the wind for the HH-3E to make the pickup.

RESERVE RESCUERS

Since their inception, the five Reserve Air Rescue squadrons have served with distinction around the world, both in peacetime and in combat settings. Despite the fact that reservists do not maintain an alert posture, their response has always been remarkable. The peacetime mission of Reserve units was to train personnel to achieve and sustain a combat rescue capability. They are responsible for global search and rescue of military and government personnel, and they are charged with providing humanitarian and disaster relief.

Activation of the five squadrons began with the 301st and 302nd in August 1956, followed by the 303rd in October, the 304th in November 1957, and the 305th in February 1958. All began service flying Grumman Albatrosses.

When the 301st ARS outgrew its original base at Miami International Airport, it relocated to Homestead AFB, Florida, in 1960. The squadron's legacy includes the first Reserve rescue in January 1957, and participation in NASA's rescue contingency operations beginning with the first Mercury launch in 1961. When the Dominican Republic crisis flared in 1965, the 301st flew 130 hours evacuating Americans from the beleaguered island. The 302nd ARRS, which was based at Luke AFB, Arizona, in late 1966 took delivery from the 33rd ARRS of the last three HU-16Bs to serve in the Pacific. After operating UH-1 and HH-34J helicopters, in 1974 the 302nd converted to CH-3Es in conjunction with a new designation, the 302nd Special Operations Squadron. Three of the 302nd's

CH-3E crews performed in exemplary fashion on November 21, 1980, at the MGM Grand Hotel fire in Las Vegas, which claimed eighty-five lives and injured 650. The crews and aircraft were at nearby Nellis AFB when they were alerted to the disaster. They, along with UH-1N crews of the 57th FWW and 20th SOS, rescued ninety-three people, many in daring hoist rescues. The 303rd Air Rescue Squadron at California's Long Beach Municipal Airport, although organized in late 1956, first reached operational status in mid-1957, when it received its four SA-16As, trading them for four HU-16Bs the following year. As military operations gradually were closed out at the airport in 1960, the 303rd ARS moved to March AFB. During 1965 and 1966, the Albatrosses were replaced by nine HC-97Gs. One example of the variety of missions flown by the squadron was a "Presidential Duckbutt Support" mission using HC-97G serial no. 53-0122. Using call sign "Rescue Mike," the Rescue Strat flew support for "Air Force One" during President Nixon's 1972 "Journey for Peace" to China. Among Rescue Mike's crew of eighteen were three pilots, three navigators, two flight engineers, two radio operators, two PJs, and five crew chiefs. The 304th ARRS acts like a security blanket for southwestern Washington's and Oregon's forests, deserts, and mountains. The squadron flew the HU-16B Albatross until 1971, when it converted to the Sikorsky HH-34J helicopter. Having switched to the HH-1H in 1974, the squadron in 1976 achieved a one-year record when credited with fifty-three saves. That year, the 304th's stellar performance at the "Red Flag" exercises prompted a reevaluation of the light helicopter's role in combat. Five UH-1Ns joined the squadron's five HH-1Hs in 1979, all of which were put to the test when Mount St. Helens erupted in May 1980.

The 304th was in the midst of training when the volcano blew. Within minutes, its Hueys were en route to the mountain. Huey crewmen rescued fifty-one persons that day, and during ten days they flew 111 sorties and saved another ten persons. Two PJs, TSgts. Garvin Williams and David Ward, were aboard the first Huey that flew into the red zone and became the first to set foot on the volcano. While snatching their first trapped person, the PJs outran a wall of mud sliding down the mountain. After the trio dashed aboard their Huey, it was aloft only briefly when the wall of mud buried the survivor's car. The 304th was assisted by the 303rd and 305th ARRS, along with the 129th ARRGp of the California Air National Guard. In all, thirteen USAF, Air and Army National Guard, Air Force Reserve, Civil Air Patrol, and coast guard units participated in the disaster relief.

The motto of the 305th ARRS was "Anytime-Anywhere." Based at Selfridge AFB, Michigan, the squadron's four Albatrosses provided coverage for fighters ferried to Europe for the Berlin Crisis (1961), and in 1965 during the Dominican Crisis. Aircrews were called to active duty in response to the seizure of USS *Pueblo* in January 1966, remaining on active duty for eighteen months. During that time, the 305th exchanged their Albatrosses for Boeing HC-97Gs.

Only a few H-3s were modified for heavy lifting with retrofit of Sikorsky's S-61 fixed landing gear for a 400-pound weight reduction. Serial no. 69-5811 of the Alaska-based 5040th Helicopter Squadron is seen here in 1972 with the retrofit. In 1965, in preparation for the Gemini program, the CH-3E serial no. 63-9688 had been retrofit with the kit, along with serial no. 69-5808. The engine intake FOD shield and rear loading ramp could also be removed to allow heavier lifts. *Author's collection*

Beginning in 1972, HC-130 aircraft joined a mix of HH-1H, UH-1N, and HH-3 helicopters in the Reserve Air Rescue force. The rescue Hercules increased mission ranges, while the helicopters increased the number of lives saved due to their ability to hover and operate in confined areas. The 304th ARRS, for example, based in Portland, Oregon, besides flying ten Huey helicopters, operated six HC-130s. These allowed flights 200 miles west, where any number of the squadron's twenty-six pararescuemen could parachute into the Pacific to aid sailors.

To create a more balanced fleet of fixed- and rotary-wing aircraft in Reserve Air Rescue, in January 1970 the air force acquired thirty-two ex-navy Sikorsky SH-34J helicopters as interim aircraft, pending arrival of new Bell HH-1H Hueys and HH-3Es returning from the war zone. The SH-34Js, which were late-production H-34s powered by 1,525 hp R-182084 Wright Cyclones, were removed from storage and stripped of ASW gear at the Naval Air Rework Facility, NAS Pensacola. Their auto-hover system was retained to enhance hover performance during hoist rescues. The helicopters were designated HH-34Js, and their navy bureau numbers became air force

USAF Bell HH-1Hs wore this attractive color scheme prior to the switch to camouflage. This HH-1H (serial no. 70-2469) was assigned to the 301st ARRS at Homestead AFB, Florida, in 1975. The Air Force Reserve emblem is worn on the tail boom. Although based on the UH-1H Huey, the HH-1H had the tail rotor mounted on the right side of the vertical fin to aid directional control, as proven on the AH-1G Cobra gunship and twin Hueys. *Courtesy of USAF*

The HU-16B serial no. 51-5305 of the 301st ARRS sank on landing near Ramey AFB, Puerto Rico, on August 4, 1970. *Courtesy of Edward Brunner*

Not all missions were rescue. During nine days in November 1978, the 55th ARRS sent to Guyana three HH-53s, one WC-130, and two HC-130s for the grim task of recovering 914 victims of the mass death at Jonestown. Thirty sorties were flown to evacuate the dead. Serial no. 73-1651, seen here, was accompanied by HH-53s 73-1649 and -1652. *Courtesy of USAF*

serial numbers simply by deleting the first number "1." As the last US military unit to fly the H-34, service proved problematic, with parts difficult to obtain and trained aircrew and mechanics in short supply; training was conducted at the army's Ft. Rucker Aviation Center in Alabama. The HH-34Js were assigned to the 301st, 302nd, and 304th ARRS, serving from June 1971 to early 1974, when twenty-five were returned to storage. Remaining examples found extended service in commercial aviation or as museum displays.

Important to the operation of the Reserve Air Rescue was the "Air Reserve technician" (ART), which was the name given to a program begun in 1957 that employed full-time federal civilian workers to staff reserve units. As reserve members, ARTs freed up active-duty personnel who conducted training and numerous daily activities. The ART program especially proved its worth during the buildup for the war in Southeast Asia, when support activities exceeded the active strength.

ON GUARD

Air National Guard rescue squadrons, like those of the Air Force Reserve, are vital to the US Air Force Rescue structure. Air Rescue squadrons within the Air National Guard (ANG) are the 102nd Rescue Squadron, 106th Rescue Group, New York ANG; 129th Rescue Squadron, 129th Rescue Group, California ANG; and 210th Rescue Squadron, 176th Group, Alaska ANG. These units respond to state emergencies under direction of the governor, as well as other federal directives.

The 102nd Rescue Squadron (RS), which began life as the 1st Aero Company in 1915, is the first federally recognized aviation unit in the National Guard. To provide the only Air Force Air Rescue presence in the northeastern US, the unit switched from air defense to air rescue in mid-June 1975, becoming the 102nd ARRS under Military Airlift Command (MAC). Aircraft assigned to the 102nd RS were HH-3E helicopters teamed with HC-130Ps at Long Island's Suffolk County Airport (now Francis S. Gabreski Airport). The squadron's parent unit, the 106th ARRGp, came into existence with the 102nd ARRS. In early May 1975, the 129th converted from its long history of special operations to become the 129th ARRS under MAC. Like the 102nd, the 129th was equipped with HH-3Es and HC-130s, which meant relocation from California's Hayward Air Terminal to more spacious Moffett Field.

First constituted as the 10th Air Rescue Squadron in April 1946, Alaska's air rescue presence has undergone a variety of unit designations and parent commands. The tradition would continue when on April 4, 1990, federal recognition from the National Guard Bureau was granted the 210th ARS. When officially activated in August, the unit was redesignated the 210th Rescue Squadron. The squadron traces its lineage back to World War II to the 10th Emergency Rescue Boat Squadron of the 11th Army Air Force, which patrolled the Aleutian chain and Alaska's coastal waters. As tribute to these forbears, the designation 210th was chosen to signify the Second 10th Rescue Squadron. The 210th and two sister squadrons, the 211th and 212th, form the 176th Operations Group, one of four groups that form the 176th Wing. Like all Air Force Reserve and Air National Guard rescue units, the 210th's civilian SAR mission is secondary to combat SAR. In 1990, the 210th began operations at Kulis Air National Guard Base equipped with Sikorsky HH-60G helicopters, receiving its companion HC-130 aircraft in November and December.

PEACETIME MISSIONS

While space does not permit recounting innumerable activities outside the Southeast Asia theater, in which the Air Rescue and Recovery Service was involved, many are notable and worth mention. For example, reminiscent of Air Rescue coverage during extensive nuclear testing conducted a decade earlier, from August through October 1968, three HU-16Bs were assigned to Eniwetok, Marshall Islands, to participate in Project 68-50, which identified tests with F-4E Phantom jets dispersing a biological agent intended to incapacitate enemy forces. Specific details, such as units involved, remain classified. Also in 1968, ARRS Headquarters relocated to Scott AFB, Illinois, after Orlando AFB, Florida, was turned over to the navy for use as a training center.

An announcement by the US in May 1967 stating that 35,000 military personnel would be withdrawn from Europe triggered a flurry of proposals by various commands over changes in air rescue units, base assignments, and aircraft. Dialogue between the various authorities between 1967 and 1969 reads like Abbott and Costello's "Who's on First" comedy routine. Among the few certainties one is able to discern from

the confusing exchange is the return of Cigli Air Base to the Turkish government, and placement of the 67th ARRS at RAF Woodbridge, UK. In November 1971, when the first two HH-53Cs of four arrived to begin service with the 67th, the squadron's three HH-3Es were transferred to Detachment 14, 40th ARRWg, at NS Keflavik, Iceland. The detachment's workload centered mainly on evacuating seriously ill persons from ships and from isolated Icelandic communities. When the Eldfell volcano on the island of Vestmannaeyjar erupted on January 23, 1973, Det 14 crews saved thirty-three persons and 275 sheep. In May 1973, the detachment came under the 39th ARRWg, and on May 1, 1988, it was elevated to squadron status, becoming the 56th ARRS. One year later, the 56th fell under the 41st RWRW and was redesignated 56th ARS in June 1989.

Taking their cue from the air force H-43, the army and navy tested helicopters for firefighting. In 1968 the army evaluated its UH-1 Huey as a Heliborne Fire Suppression System. Fit with a 25-gallon "light water" tank and 16-foot swing-out boom, UH-1H serial no. 66-6746 goes to work on a fuel fire. The navy tested the Kaman UH-2 Seasprite for aerial firefighting. *Courtesy of US Army*

Impressive study in 1976 of the mighty Hercules, this aircraft (serial no. 69-5832) being an HC-130N of the 41st ARRS at Hamilton AFB. The 41st called Hamilton AFB, California, home from 1962 to 1973 and began flying the HC-130 in 1966. The HC-130N could be identified by its round nose and outer-wing fuel tanks. *Author's collection*

THE DRONE MISSION

Prior to committing Sikorsky's H-3 helicopters to search and rescue, the air force put them to work fulfilling a priority requirement for recovering drones from the water. In response to the requirement, in 1961 a competition for the job was held at Wright-Patterson AFB, Ohio, between the H-3 and the tandem-rotor Vertol 107. Although Vertol was announced the winner, production snags resulted in selection of the H-3. In 1963, three CH-3Bs among six loaned from the navy were put to work with the 4756th Drone Squadron recovering drones from the Gulf of Mexico. In February 1964, shortly after the first of three CH-3Cs arrived at Tyndall AFB to replace the B models, it first rescued two stranded boaters and a few days later made its first drone recovery. Air force leaders could not have been more pleased with its new helicopter, which would go on to serve in numerous capacities.

In conjunction with activation of the 1st Test Squadron at Clark Air Base, Philippines, in September 1969, the 31st

ARRS at Clark received its first of three HH-3 helicopters to take over the drone recovery mission. Since 1967, the program, called "Combat Sage," had been managed by the 6400th Test Squadron. Combat Sage was developed to provide live-fire training and evaluate the F-4 Phantom's air-to-air weapon systems. Beginning in the early 1980s, F-15 and F-16 fighters took their turn against the drones. Veteran HH-3 pilot Bruce Ware provides insight to the drone mission:

The drone recovery mission at Clark AB was basically a backup to the 80-foot drone recovery boat that was assigned to complete the recovery mission on a daily basis. The BQM 34A drones were launched from Wallace Air Station, Poro Point on the Lingayen Gulf, approximately 90 miles north of Clark. The GCI site was colocated and the controllers guided the fighters—mostly F-4s TDY to Clark from Vietnam—to the drone and cleared them to fire after the drone had been put into a tight turn. The drones had either reflectors or flares mounted on each wingtip, and the expected outcome was that the F-4's missile would pass just beyond the drone and not hit it. Often the fighter pilot would anticipate the drone maneuver and fire before cleared, or the missile would catch the drone on either wingtip or rudder. When that happened, the drone would automatically deploy a drag chute [and] simultaneously shut itself down, and the drag chute would then pull out a large chute. If the mission was a success, and the drone made it back to the recovery area without being hit, the recovery boat would retrieve it. If, however, the drone was hit and went down on the range, we launched the HH-3E to recover it. If we could get the drone out of the sea within a couple hours, they could restore it to service and save the USAF approximately $390,000 per drone. If the drone was in the water too long, saltwater corrosion made it unusable for further flights. If the sea state was above 3, then it was too risky for us to attempt recovery.

The recovery required us to get right down on the water with the drone. As we hovered over it, the rotor wash would weather-vane the tail so that the nose of the drone was pointed toward us. We then maneuvered the helicopter so that the refueling probe ran right along the top of the tail. As the tail went past our window, the drone was in position for the hookup. The flight engineer was lying in the doorway with a long pole that was attached to a hook, with which he "caught" the drone. The hook was fastened to a cable that was attached to the slow-response sling beneath the HH-3E. He guided us to a final position directly over the drone so that he could make the hookup. After catching the drone, the flight engineer released the pole from the hook, and we recentered the HH-3E over the drone and slowly lifted it out of the water.

The big parachute was supposed to automatically release from the drone when the drone landed in the water, and usually it did. When it did not, we had pararescuemen on

In July 1979, HH-1N (serial no. 69-6630) of Det 9, 67th ARRS, at Zaragoza AB, Spain, lowers a firefighter to a building on fire. *Courtesy of USAF*

board who would jump into the water and untangle the chute from around the drone.

Then the fun started! Unless the drone ran out of fuel while on the range, it went down because of damage. Many times the damage would cause the drone to twist and turn as we were flying back to Poro Point. There were several occasions which required us to release the drone as it was "flying up" and getting dangerously close to the rotors. Other times it would not stop spinning and would actually twist the cable enough that the cable broke. After a number of those occurrences, we attached a swivel to one end of the cable, thus preventing twist of the cable.

We sent an HH-3E and crew up to the launch area three times a week to stand by for recoveries. It was a very satisfying and fun mission, and one that was entirely suited to the HH-3E. We had to be cognizant of the amount of time we spent in the salt spray created by the rotors; however, we washed the engines with fresh water after every encounter and then washed them with solvent at the end of every day.

In July 1972, an HH-34J of the 304th ARRS practices rescue techniques in the Columbia River by guiding a rescue sling to pararescueman SSgt. John Pierson. *Courtesy of USAF*

TROUBLE IN LIBYA

In 1968, the 58th Aerospace Rescue and Recovery Squadron at Wheelus Air Base, Libya, was equipped with three HU-16Bs and four HH-43Bs. The squadron's long-range capability had been withdrawn in 1967, when its four HC-130Hs were transferred as part of reorganization. The aging Albatrosses, which were overdue for retirement and slated for replacement by new HH-3Es, left in mid-1968. Since delivery of the HH-3Es was delayed, two HC-97Gs of the Reserve 305th ARRS were sent to Wheelus to fill the coverage gap.

The Libyan population saw the prosperous relationship between America and Libyan king Idris as pretense. Resentment peaked on September 1, 1969, with a coup that installed the anti-Western Revolutionary Council, led by Muammar al-Qaddafi. The USAF immediately pulled out aircraft detached to Wheelus for weapons training, and, except for perimeter patrols flown by the Huskies, all flying ceased. Eventually, Libyan authorities allowed flying only during daylight, and aircraft were forbidden to fly over Libyan soil, meaning all flights were to head out to sea. Adding to the restrictions, Libyan officials insisted on examining every landing aircraft. The time had come for the US and Libya to act on a preplanned timetable for withdrawal of US forces.

The following account, told by then Lt. Col. William Lyell, commander of the 58th Aerospace Rescue and Recovery Squadron at Wheelus Air Base, Libya, is a prime example of the extent to which rescue men went to save lives:

When Qaddafi took over, sixty Jewish people, mindful that many Jewish people were executed during the 1967 Arab-Israeli war, made a mad dash for Wheelus Air Base and were hid on base. The USAF Office of Special Investigations (OSI) agent at Wheelus got caught smuggling the Volkswagen dealer to Germany in an air force major's uniform. Then, the principal of the school for dependents got caught smuggling three Jewish people out of Libya in a box of band instruments.

A month or so later, when things cooled a bit, the 58th Rescue Squadron smuggled fifty-six Jewish people—ten at a time—to Malta by practicing water hoist pickup from a boat 5 miles offshore, using practice hoist dummies, plus a live Jewish person every now and then until we got them all out. It took about three weeks because we had been practicing water pickup about three times a week, and we didn't want to arouse suspicion. Our heroic state department said, "If you get caught, we don't know anything about it." Typical.

Both HH-1H and HH-43 helicopters were based at Zaragoza Air Base, Spain, during the early 1970s. *Courtesy of USAF*

During an open-sea rescue exercise in 1979, PJs of the 55th ARRS at Florida's Eglin AFB signal a Huey helicopter to lower a litter. *Courtesy of USAF*

Five weeks after the coup began, the 58th ARRS became involved in the most-massive rescue efforts ever conducted in the European–North African region. Tunisia was deluged with torrential rain during the latter part of September, sweeping away entire villages, roads, and bridges; within a few days, an estimated five hundred persons were dead and nearly 100,000 were homeless. Shortly after the Tunisian government requested international aid, a USAF C-130 brought medical supplies and clothing, while an HC-130 of the 67th ARRS at Moron AB, Spain, flew low-level flights to assess damage. It became quickly obvious that helicopters were the best means of aiding flood victims. The 58th ARRS was alerted by its parent, 40th ARRWg, at Ramstein AB, Germany, and on October 8 the squadron's three HH-3Es departed for Tunis, Tunisia. By midday, the three Jolly Greens were headed for isolated villages to deliver emergency medical supplies and to evacuate others.

One week later, conditions had improved to the extent that the US ambassador released the aircrews. When the rains returned, even more severely than before, so did the three HH-3Es and crews, returning on the twenty-fifth. The pace for crewmen was even more intense than before and included engine changes on two of the helicopters. The weather improved and on November 4, the aircrews flew back to Wheelus, having tallied 2,516 "saves" and 111 tons of supplies delivered during 202 flying hours.

The three HH-3Es (serial nos. 67-14715, -14716, and -14717) were among the first aircraft to leave Wheelus. Escorted by an HC-130P of the 67th ARRS at Moron AB, Spain, the Jolly Greens left in December, arriving at RAF Lakenheath to await assignment to the 67th, also under the 40th ARRWg. Inactivation of the 58th ARRS was completed on February 15, 1970. In its place, Det 15, 40th ARRWg, equipped with HH-43s, operated from Wheelus AB to provide cover during the final weeks of US occupation.

THE DOOMSDAY SQUADRON

One of the most unusual duties entrusted USAF Air Rescue personnel was known as the "Outpost Mission"—one of the Cold War's most closely guarded secrets. Beginning in the mid-1950s, an elite unit of helicopter pilots and crew, under the cover designation 2857th Test Squadron, was stationed at Olmsted AFB, Pennsylvania, posing as a rescue unit. Their real mission, so sensitive that only the pilots and base commander knew, was to rescue President Eisenhower, and all later presidents, in the event of a nuclear attack. Standing alert outside the blast range of a nuclear attack on Washington, DC, they were to land on the White House lawn when an attack seemed imminent, and fly the president to one of several hollowed-out mountain fortresses or to the heavily fortified command and communications ship USS *Northampton* (CC-1) off the Atlantic Coast; *Northampton*'s sister ship was the light carrier USS *Wright* (CC-2), stationed off Norfolk.

The helicopter crews were prepared to effect rescue after a nuclear attack, their aircraft equipped with decontamination gear, along with heavy tools to force entry through the presidential bunker beneath the White House. They flew practice runs with dark visors lowered to shield their eyes from an atomic blast, and wore 20 pounds of protective clothing, including rubber bodysuits impregnated with lead against radiation.

The 2857th TS officially was the "Continuity of Government (COG) Helicopter Squadron." COG procedures, which enable the government to operate in the event of a catastrophic event such as nuclear war, were activated for the first time during the 9/11 attacks in 2001.

US Air Force colonel William A. Lyell, who retired with a wealth of USAF helicopter experience, provides these fascinating details of the Doomsday Mission:

From the 58th ARRS at Wheelus, Tripoli, I volunteered for Vietnam because I had not had a combat tour since World War II, but I was restricted from combat for three years because I had the "Doomsday" helicopter squadron in support of the White House. A *Time* magazine article from August 1992 tells all, although at the time that I was commander, it was top secret. Frankly, I honestly thought the concept was ridiculous, but I kept those thoughts to myself.

Bernard T. "Bud" Gallagher was commander of the 2857th since 1958. Bud was at the Pentagon in 1965 when I got a call while at Goodfellow AFB to report to the Pentagon for "something." The generals checked my credentials, but I told Bud I didn't give a damn about heading the squadron and for them to keep looking. Bud said they looked and I was it. It was a good deal, unlimited budget, controlled effective reports, meaning promotion when eligible if you kept your nose clean.

The alert crews were checked through the White House by the Secret Service once each quarter. The Pentagon and Secret Service conducted "no notice" evaluations of the squadron, with detailed briefings, but we always passed and together we were able to improve on the idea of White House

An HC-130N (serial no. 69-5833) of the 1550th Aircrew Training and Test Wing at Hill AFB in September 1974. *Courtesy of Stephen Miller*

rescue. Those people really took this concept seriously, so it was prudent to do the same. We learned where the emergency entrances to the White House basement were located on the South Lawn, and had blueprints of the entire White House at our disposal to study. The Doomsday Helicopter Squadron was capable of gaining entry into the White House, using cutting torches and other sophisticated gear. There are man-hole covers on the South Lawn that cover entrances to the basement of the White House. Also, you can get from the basement of the Treasury Department to the White House through a tunnel that runs under the street, passing under the guard shack where visitors enter the grounds. The Secret Service scheduled quarterly training in ways to gain access to our target. This necessitated a detailed study of the real estate involved. Secrecy was tight. Roles and missions guarded.

Olmsted AFB was scheduled to close in summer of 1967, so the squadron was moved to Dover AFB, Delaware. We were a tenant of the Military Airlift Command. At both locations our supervision came directly from the Pentagon office that handled presidential movement. At Dover the unit was redesignated the 1042nd Test Squadron. We flew H-3s with no in-flight refueling capability.

The naval unit designated "White House Afloat" cruised off Chesapeake Bay, and we practiced night landings in the bay. The "White House Aloft" could be used by the president and his staff to conduct business while airborne.

Subsequent to my departure from the unit in July 1968 (it was a controlled three-year assignment), the 1042nd joined the 1001st Helicopter Squadron at Andrews AFB and was redesignated the 1st Helicopter Squadron. The unit had been at Olmsted and Dover for survivability of a nuclear exchange, since they wanted the unit 50 miles from Washington; later this didn't seem to matter. As to emergency locations, the Air Force Emergency Operation Center is located underground at an old abandoned coal mine near Fort Meade. We visited there, and those people took their jobs seriously. Camp David, operated by the navy, believed they would be the emergency White House. The Doomsday location in the mountains just above Thurmond, Maryland, was the largest affair. It was the one we worked closely with. Regardless of which location was to be used in an emergency, helicopters of the Doomsday Squadron would move the man.

Once when the president was gone and the Secret Service man was showing us the Oval Office, he let every one of us sit

THE US AIR FORCE AIR RESCUE SERVICE

Dressed for work in 1974, PJs William Lees and Wayne Walls of the 33rd ARRS pose with an unofficial emblem at Kadena AB, Okinawa. Lees, in tree jumpsuit, wears the main parachute, while on his front are a reserve parachute and medical kit. Walls wears the two chutes and medical kit, along with SCUBA tanks, and knife and flare marker strapped to his leg. *Courtesy of Gary Bryant*

in the president's chair—crew chiefs, pilots, sergeants—everyone for a few seconds. That's something I'll never forget, because in 1941 I worked at the Washington, DC, Post Office Department. In January 1942, when the war was on, I took a picture of the White House through the metal fence and, of course, had my film confiscated. All the pictures were returned except the White House photo. Then, twenty-four years later, I've got blueprints of the whole damn thing and have sat in the president's chair. Time and circumstances do wonderful things.

THE RESCUE OF CHARLES LINDBERGH

In April 1972, famed aviation pioneer Charles A. Lindbergh, brigadier general, US Air Force Reserve; a news crew; and a research team investigating a "lost tribe" in the Tasaday mountains of Mindanao, Philippine Islands, became stranded on a 3,000-foot jungle ridge when their support helicopter developed mechanical trouble. Since Lindbergh and his team faced a three-day trek through rugged terrain, the US ambassador to the Philippines requested that the 31st ARRS at Clark AB recover Lindbergh's expedition.

With the HH-3E serial no. 66-13289 in the background at Mactan AB, the crew of "Jolly 3-6" and the HC-130N crew pose with General Lindbergh under the tail of the "King." *Standing left to right:* A1C Smith, Capt. Kent Tatum, Lindbergh, Mactan AB commander, Capt. Mark Sherrill, Lt. Col. Richard Smith, 1Lt. Richard Johnstone, and Maj. Bruce Ware. Kneeling are TSgt. Walden, SSgt. Robert Baldwin, TSgt. Dodson, A1C Zarnowski, MSgt. Taylor, SSgt. Robinson, and TSgt. Wlibur. Sitting are A1C Kim Robinson and a Mactan AB executive officer. *Courtesy of USAF*

Maj. Bruce Ware was selected as aircraft commander of the HH-3E crew, call sign "Jolly 3-6," that would attempt the recovery, which meant operating at 3,000-foot elevation in temperatures nearing 100 degrees. To take advantage of cooler temperature, Maj. Ware and crew lifted off from Clark at 3:20 a.m. on Easter Sunday morning, the second of April, for the 600-mile flight to southern Mindanao. An HC-130N was launched one hour later to provide aerial refueling and navigational assistance to the HH-3E.

Although trees had been cut for clearance, the small landing pad ruled out any chance of landing the big Sikorsky. Ware and his copilot decided to dump fuel to lighten the aircraft and still have enough for power reserve. Hovering out of ground effect with the nose gear on one side of the sharp ridge and the main gear on the other side brought the boarding ladder within inches of the ground. The PJ exited the helicopter to organize loading. Lindbergh's entourage numbered more than forty people, and only a few could be taken out at one time in the risky high-density altitude. Since the minimum fuel load was becoming a concern, passengers were dropped off at a clearing a few miles distant. With the second load of passengers aboard, Lindbergh included, the HC-130 partially refueled the Jolly Green; the process fascinated Lindbergh, despite his broad aviation experience. Eight trips were necessary to recover Lindbergh's research team and news crew—a total of forty-six persons. A second partial air refuel was needed, and after nearly twelve hours of flying, the two rescue aircraft landed at Mactan Air Base, Cebu, Philippines. The rescued later boarded the HC-130 and were flown to Manila. Maj. Ware was awarded the Distinguished Flying Cross, and all other crewmen received the Air Medal.

An HH-3E of the 106th ARRG at Westhampton Beach, New York, comes perilously close to swaying masts of a boat caught in stormy seas, as its crew attempts to rescue the boaters east of Shinnecock Canal, Long Island. The HH-3E is serial no. 65-12783. *Courtesy of USAF*

THE ONGOING NASA COMMITMENT

By the early 1970s, USAF Air Rescue aircraft were an integral element of the airborne recovery force for spacecraft. Flying orbits at both uprange and downrange peripheries of primary recovery areas were HC-130s designated "Rescue 1" and "Rescue 2." Each was equipped with an AN/ARD-17 Cook Tracker, plus a three-man pararescue team and recovery equipment. Flying a racetrack pattern just north of the launch-pad were three HH-53C helicopters of Detachment 15, 44th ARRS, at Patrick AFB. Aboard each were PJs and a flight surgeon. Suspended from one of the HH-53Cs was a fire suppression kit modified from the original HH-43 type to carry 83 gallons of water to control hypergolic or surface fires. The PJs on that aircraft wore Nomex firefighting clothing, versus wetsuits.

NASA's primary safety feature was a 33-foot long "Launch Escape System" (LES) perched atop the command module. The LES could blast the module free of the rocket in prelaunch or separate the module from the rocket should a problem occur during the first few minutes of flight. Recovering the module, rescuing astronauts, and medically treating them fell upon the air rescue crews. Tom Green Sr., who amassed a wealth of USAF helicopter experience, recalls:

> One HH-53 was for beach/surf recovery, one for deepwater recovery, and one for "beach boss" that also carried the launch air boss and a NASA flight surgeon. In training we maintained a space capsule mockup painted battleship gray. Training was extensive. We would pick up the boiler plate steel module on land, take it to the gulf or bay, deposit it, then fly circles around it, deploying three PJs, a raft, and a collar for flotation, though the capsule did remain afloat. We would then practice hoist recoveries, using the NASA-required Billy Pugh rescue net and NASA-approved Stokes litter, used only for astronaut recoveries. NASA also required that we have all of our aircraft soundproofing installed, which was a problem.
>
> When done with training, we'd pick up the capsule, hovering while draining it a bit, then return it to where it was kept. In the training area at Ford's Island, Hawaii, we even lost the capsule once off Oahu in the international shipping lanes, and it had to be declared a hazard to sea navigation until the navy found and recovered it, floating far from where we put it in.

Depending on splashdown location, the airborne force could include HC-130s of the 55th ARRS at Eglin AFB, the 54th ARRS at Pease AFB, the 57th ARRS at Lajes AB, and Hawaii-based 76th ARRS.

NORTH TO ALASKA

Aviation, to a substantial degree, grew up in Alaska. Merciless weather and often-impassable geography are notorious in the forty-ninth state, where the partnership of necessity between

Alaskans and aircraft demands some of the largest and most active peacetime SAR efforts on the planet. Lt. Col. Frank Cardile, commander of the 71st ARRS in Alaska during the late 1970s, reiterated: "Our primary mission is to provide combat rescue. But barring a war and military exercises, we fall back on our capability to help the public."

While the coast guard covers the Aleutian Islands chain and coastal waters, the air force has long relied heavily on the Civil Air Patrol to search Alaska's massive interior. Formed in 1948, Alaska Wing CAP initially was equipped with a Beech C-45 and Stinson L-5s transferred from Alaska Air Command (AAC). Post–Korean War transfers included Ryan L-17 Navions and Piper L-21s. With inactivation of the USAF 10th Air Rescue Group, AAC bolstered CAP's capabilities with the transfer in 1960 of ten de Havilland U-6A Beavers. The wing grew from a modest beginning at Merrill Field to eighteen squadrons, with headquarters at Elmendorf AFB. Eventually, many CAP aircraft were equipped with direction-finding equipment to home in on emergency locator transmitters (ELTs) of downed aircraft, thereby reducing search hours.

Kyron V. Hall provides the following insight:

I flew HH-3Es with the 5040th Helicopter Squadron, Elmendorf, Alaska, from 1970 to 1972. We were not assigned to ARRS but fulfilled a rescue mission as well as support missions for the Alaskan Air Command. In 1970, the 5040th picked up thirteen brand-new HH-3Es, serial numbers 69-5800 through 69-5812, direct from the Sikorsky factory in Bridgeport, Connecticut, and flew them to Alaska.

Stanton Nelson began his air force helicopter career in 1960 as a CH-21 flight mechanic at Goodfellow AFB, Texas. After assignments to an LBR unit in Spain, extensive work with HH-53s, and HH-3E flight engineer training, in 1974 Stanton reported for duty at Elmendorf AFB. Stanton explains: "The mission of the 5040th HS was statewide rescue, remote site support, military exercises, bomb/gunnery range support, search and recovery of high-altitude research rocket nose cones from the Brooks Range north of the Arctic Circle, and aerial firefighting. Flying those Alaskan missions in the HH-3E convinced me that the H-3 was the overall best rescue helicopter ever, due to its capability, reliability, and versatility."

Following a ten-year absence, the 71st ARRS was reactivated on March 8, 1970, equipped with four HC-130s. An air force effort to consolidate all rescue helicopters into the ARRS had the HH-3Es of the 5040th HS transferred to the 71st ARRS in 1975; the 5040th was then deactivated. The Jolly Greens replaced HH-21s, which were phased out of AAC's inventory. The value of the HC-130/HH-3E team was proven the following summer. Kyron Hall picks up the story:

On 25 July 1971, I was called by the squadron commander, Lt. Col. Grady Fisher, to be the aircraft commander to attempt the rescue of a Korean seaman with acute appendicitis on a

merchant ship 600 miles south of Anchorage, Alaska. The time required to fly the mission would require three pilots, and Majors William Dodd and Robert Robinson were selected as the other pilots. We left Elmendorf early in the morning to rendezvous with an ARRS HC-130 that would provide air refueling and navigational assistance. The weather en route to Kodiak Island deteriorated to a point that we had to make an instrument approach into Kodiak NAS and wait for a couple of hours for the weather to improve. We took off later and, with two air refuelings en route, reached the Korean ship 450 miles at sea. Hovering over the fantail of the ship, a doctor and pararescueman were lowered to the deck. The seriously ill seaman, along with our crewmen, was hoisted back on board, and the return flight to Kodiak [was] with another en route refueling. This was the longest overwater rescue mission accomplished by a land-based helicopter.

Having logged thousands of hours in helicopters in a span of forty-four years, Kyron Hall reflects: "The H-3 was the most pleasurable helicopter I ever flew. It was a dream to fly, and with twin engines and water-landing capability, it could perform about any mission you asked of it."

As part of the proud history of the 71st ARRS, on October 4, 1980, an HC-130 and an HH-3E were dispatched to the Gulf of Alaska to join rescue forces when the Holland-American cruise ship *Prinsendam* caught fire. While the rescue Hercules orbited overhead, the Jolly Green crew—Captains John Walters and William Gillian, and two PJs, SSgt. John Cassidy and Sgt. Jose Rios—rescued passengers from lifeboats. After repeated trips flying survivors to the nearby oil tanker *Williamsburgh*, the HH-3E's hoist cable broke, but not before the crew had rescued seventy-four persons. An HC-130, piloted by Capt. David Briski, located and escorted a Canadian rescue helicopter that had lost its instruments. In the confusion of the massive rescue effort and an approaching typhoon, the lifeboat with Sergeants Cassidy and Rios, tending eighteen survivors, went adrift. Twelve hours later, they were rescued by coast guard cutter.

Most worrisome for rescue personnel, then and now, is the polar ice cap rescue if a commercial airliner passing over the North Pole went down. Although a rescue mission of such proportion would be difficult due to extreme cold and reaction time, air force units plan and practice for that possibility.

PAVE LOW AND BLACK KNIGHTS

The HH-53 Limited Night Recovery System, evaluated in Southeast Asia in 1969, left much to be desired, leaving some combat-seasoned aircrew in the H-53 community convinced that systems could be developed to create a night/all-weather SAR helicopter. Such capabilities, they lamented, had they been available during the war, would have greatly reduced the number of aircrew killed or captured. Their motivation was clear.

HH-53B serial no. 66-14433 was the 1969 test platform and would spend most of its existence in test mode. In 1975, it was outfitted with a much-improved "PAVE LOW II" system, resulting in the prototype designation YHH-53H. Improvements mainly were in electronics, including the addition of FLIR (borrowed from the A-7), terrain-following radar, radar navigation, internal guidance system, moving map display, and radar-warning receiver. Chaff-flare dispensers were added, and the rear ramp minigun was replaced by the time-honored Browning .50-caliber machine gun. The weapons in both forward doorways remained 7.62 mm GAU-2B/A miniguns.

Robert Jones, who was assigned to the 1550th ATTW from 1972 to 1979 and maintained early PAVE LOW systems, remembers:

That first bird was something. It came to us from Wright-Patterson. It was integrated parts from, I believe, the B-52,

A-6, F-111, and Minuteman. Everything was analog, so we had big racks behind the cockpit bulkhead with all the boxes mounted in them. Halfway back on the cabin left side was another console that was a copy of the cockpit's primary instruments and screens, so an evaluator could see what the pilots were seeing and doing. The ground mapping looked pretty funny by today's standards, and we had to load the FLIR with liquid nitrogen. They also put a laser box under the nose and never really told us what it was for. I think they were testing a laser designator for use from the H-53 platform.

One of the first attempts to use the PAVE LOW system in a recovery effort was to try to find a single-engine airplane. A sergeant from the base and his wife had gone out of state to pick up the airplane for the flying club. He got caught in bad weather on the way back. After the weather broke, we went to the last reported position near Taos, New Mexico. I sat in the back and watched the IR screen to spot the aircraft

During the late 1970s, a Bell UH-1F of the 37th ARRS searches a flooded region of the US for victims stranded by rising floodwaters. *Courtesy of USAF*

under the snow. We never found it. It turned out that his last reported position by radar was more than 20 miles from where they actually went in. The first successful rescue with the system occurred in early 1980 on Sandia Mountain. It was great to be a very small part of that program and then see it in action. The informal name of the program was "Colonel Pehr's Flying Circus." He was chief test pilot, and some say that if Col. Pehr hadn't stood up for the program, it might not have been accepted.

Frank Pehr was considered the driving force behind the development of PAVE LOW. After he was wounded in a combat rescue mission in Vietnam while with the 37th ARRS, Pehr became an instructor, and then lead instructor for the LNRS program. Not only did skeptics not want to believe in the system, they did not want to fly extremely low level at night with Pehr.

Thanks to Pehr and his fellow believers, the PAVE LOW II proved satisfactory, and eight HH-53Cs were scheduled for modification to HH-53H. The Naval Air Rework Facility (NARF) at NAS Pensacola did the honors since its personnel were old hands at high-level maintenance of marine and navy H-53s. Painted all black and equipped with see-in-the-dark systems, the first and succeeding machines were appropriately labeled "Black Knight." The first HH-53C slated for conversion, serial no. 69-5791, arrived at the NARF on August 23, 1977, and was rolled out as an HH-3H on March 13, 1979. The remainder of HH-53Hs, now named "PAVE LOW III," was completed during early 1980. The prototype also was brought up to production HH-53H standards. Although PAVE LOW referred to specialized systems, the term became synonymous with the aircraft. The unofficial Black Knight moniker and emblem were never adopted by the air force.

US Air Force acquisitions of Sikorsky Model S-65 H-53s ultimately would total eighty-one airframes. Besides eight HH-53Bs and forty-four HH-53Cs, the air force purchased twenty CH-53Cs for general transport, covert operations, and drone recovery. These aircraft differed from HH-53Cs in not having aerial-refueling booms; only one example is known to have been assigned to an air rescue squadron. Serial numbers of CH-53Cs were 68-10922 through -10933, and 70-1625 through -1632. In 1989, seven low-time TH-53As were transferred from the marines to the air force for use as trainers. Some, and possibly all, were up-engined with T64-GE-14 power plants, and some eventually were fit with aerial-refueling booms. Serial numbers were 70-14468 through -14473 and 67-30046. In addition, two ex-USMC NCH-53As, serial nos. 63-13693 and -13694, initially modified for testing satellite capsule retrieval, were later remodified to trainer configuration when the 6594th TS was inactivated.

At inactivation in 1986, the 6594th inventory counted thirteen C-130s, three of which were HC-130P tanker aircraft, and five HH-53Cs that had arrived in 1974. During the twelve years the HH-53Cs served the unit, sixty rescues were accomplished, with the loss of an HH-53C occurring on January 15, 1985. When the coast guard notified the unit that the ship *Asian Beauty*, 540 miles off Oahu, had a gravely ill sailor aboard, HH-53Cs 68-10355 and -10357, plus an HC-130P, responded. As 10355 lowered a PJ, rotor blade failure severed the tail of the helicopter, and the out-of-control aircraft crashed onto the ship's deck and exploded, killing all seven crewmen.

What was considered the modernization of Air Force Air Rescue, begun during the early 1980s, changed not only the organizational structure but the very concept of air rescue. What was thought would be a hallmark in the history of air rescue, ironically, did not include ARRS helicopter units or aircraft, yet it changed the face of Air Rescue. The aborted mission to rescue fifty-two American embassy hostages in Tehran, Iran, in the spring of 1980 resulted in the deaths of eight US servicemen, with four wounded, and the loss of large aircraft. An official investigation of the failed mission cited deficiencies in mission planning, command, and control, and the shortfall in coordination and communication between the services involved. Other factors combined to doom the mission, not the least of which included helicopter mechanical problems and inadequate pilot training.

There was little doubt that Air Force Air Rescue's new Pave Low III helicopters were better suited to the mission than the modified minesweeper RH-53Ds flown by marine pilots. Pave Low aircrews, who were trained in combat search and rescue and routinely teamed with HC-130s, were the logical choice for Operation Eagle Claw. Whatever the case, it remains clear that the entire operation was critically dependent on helicopters. And on that premise, less than three weeks later, the air force vice chief of staff, Gen. Robert C. Mathis, ordered reassignment of nine Pave Lows from Air Rescue to the 1st Special Operations Wing at Hurlburt Field. On May 17, eight were flown from Kirtland AFB to Hurlburt; the ninth aircraft was still undergoing Pave Low modification at NAS Pensacola. The hurried transfer spelled the end of Air Rescue's role in CSAR, or so it seemed, and in the process helped clear the clouded distinction between Air Rescue and Special Operations.

Although special-operations aviation was afforded a low priority after Vietnam and up until the failure of Eagle Claw, transition already had begun within Air Force Air Rescue that pulled both aircraft and aircrew further into the shadow world of special operations. For example, on April 10, 1974, the Reserve 302nd ARRS at Luke AFB became the 302nd

Special Operations Squadron (SOS). With its seven CH-3Es upgraded for night and adverse-weather operations, the squadron relocated to Davis-Monthan AFB in 1987 to become the 71st SOS. Soon the "Super CH-3Es" morphed into MH-3Es, dubbed "Pave Pigs," with FLIR imagers, global positioning, and 1,500 shp T58-GE100 engines for sustained power. The "M" would become the standard prefix designator for special-operations aircraft.

The three major aircraft types in the Air Rescue inventory during the decade were Bell's UH-1 Huey, Sikorsky's H-3 and HH-53 derivatives, and Lockheed's HC-130 Hercules. The mighty Hercules—called "the Herk" by generations of those who flew and maintained it—has the longest continuous production run of any military aircraft in history. The Herk's adaptability ensured it a lasting home in Air Rescue. Damon Blair, a retired C-130 mechanic, says he was fortunate to have worked on C-130 aircraft for his entire twenty-year air force career, as well as in several civilian overhaul jobs after retirement. Here, Blair provides an inside look at what it was like working with the Herk:

My career field was called APG, which stands for airplane general, but we were commonly called "crew chiefs" or "all-purpose grunts." A crew chief is a mechanic for the airframe, while a "dedicated crew chief" is the person responsible for maintaining and controlling all the maintenance activities on one airplane. I worked on HC-130H-, N-, and P-model aircraft at Kirtland AFB. Kirtland was my first duty station, and I was fortunate to spend eight years there as a C-130 crew chief. It was home of the Air Force Rescue schoolhouse, where pilots trained in T/UH-1H, UH-1N, HH-3, HH-53, and HC-130 aircraft. One of the most important things that the helicopter and HC-130 crews practiced was air-to-air refueling.

In the early 1980s, the air force came out with an outer-wing replacement program for the C-130s. This time compliance technical order (TCTO) involved replacing outer wings with new, stronger, and redesigned outer wings. The

TCTO directed replacement of the outer wings of all C-130 airplanes from the first C-130B aircraft up to C-130E aircraft that have fiscal year 1972 serial numbers.

Each C-130 was equipped with four twenty-man life rafts, each contained in its own compartment (two to a wing) just outboard of the fuselage, and on the trailing edge of the wings right above the flaps. The rafts were intended for crew and passengers in the event of a ditching. They were a bear to remove and install. I removed and replaced many life rafts in my career and never had a problem. However, I have seen the life rafts deploy on two occasions while they were being removed. The rafts are inflated with CO_2. There is a short

Wearing high visibility markings that were standard for Alaska-based rescue aircraft, an HC-130H (serial no. 65-0986) of the 71st ARRS at Elmendorf AFB in 1980. A sign in the observer's window reads, "ALERT AIRCRAFT." The 71st flew HC-130Hs from 1970 to 1987. The rescue Hercules returned to the squadron inventory in 1991, when the 71st relocated to Patrick AFB, Florida. *Courtesy of Marty Isham*

An air rescue milestone was reached on December 29, 1980, when three PJs of the 71st ARRS parachuted from an HC-130H into the North Pacific to save a gravely ill crewman of Panamanian tanker *Chi Yung*. The three PJs were SrA Jeffrey Hill, SSgt. Donald Humphreys, and MSgt. Rick Garley. *Courtesy of USAF*

cable with a loop on the end that comes out of the CO_2 bottle's valve, and you had to be damn careful that little piece of cable was tucked up somewhere out of the way. Both times, the crew chiefs removing the life rafts got that little cable snagged on the aircraft, and "BOOM" . . . the huge life raft inflated in about twenty seconds. The crew chiefs jumped clear of the maintenance stands as soon as they heard the boom, and a few seconds later, the fully inflated raft slid down onto the floor. Scary as hell. One-person life rafts stowed in the cargo compartment could be dropped to survivors.

HC-130H, N, and P aircraft can be equipped with two extra fuel tanks, called Benson tanks, inside the cargo compartment. Plumbing was installed permanently on the aircraft; all we had to do was install and hook up the tanks to the fuel plumbing via hose. There were three configurations possible: no tanks installed, one tank installed (usually on the left side of the aircraft), and both tanks installed. They are time-consuming, pain-in-the-butt things to install and remove. For a time our crew chiefs kept changing the configuration of the

On September 21, 1981, pararescuemen treat injured survivors of the capsized Philippines destroyer escort *Datu Kalantiaw* after a typhoon drove it aground on the rocky shore of Calayan Island in the Philippines, killing seventy-nine crewmen. *Courtesy of USAF*

SSgt. Carlton Johnson of the 31st ARRS preflights an HH-3E when a major rescue operation began in response to the capsizing of the Philippines destroyer escort *Datu Kalantiaw*. The HH-3Es landed aboard USS *Mount Hood* with injured and took others ashore. *Courtesy of USAF*

Rescue equipment aboard this HC-130 of the 41st ARRS in the 1980s included ten tubes that ejected flares, smoke markers, and sea dye cartridges. Five bundles composed the MA-1 rescue kit, consisting of two seven-person life rafts (large bags) and three bundles of survival equipment, all connected with 120 feet of buoyant rope; LUU-4 flares were kept in two large red cases with placards that read, "SPECIAL FIREWORKS–FIRE AWAY." *Courtesy of Fred Zayas*

Freshly painted in 1981, the HC-130H (serial no. 65-974) of the 102nd ARRS of the New York Air National Guard. *Courtesy of USAF*

Modified from the original Sikorsky UH-60A Blackhawk, serial no. 82-23718 underwent a number of development and designation changes. Here, in 1984, it flies near Edwards AFB as the sole example of the HH-60D. Later it became the prototype HH-60A. Two external 117-gallon fuel tanks were not used on US versions since they interfered with the rescue hoist. *Courtesy of USAF*

aircraft for each mission, and we were moving around a lot of Benson tanks. Finally, our maintenance and operations chiefs agreed that we would configure two birds with one tank installed, one bird with both tanks installed, and two birds with clean cargo compartments.

Installing or removing a Benson tank is a heavy-duty "grunt" affair with all the manhandling needed to move these big tanks Each Benson tank was approximately 6 feet in diameter and approximately 15 feet in length. They are mounted on a cradle structure that was bolted to the floor. Each tank weighed approximately 300 pounds empty. We moved the tanks in and out using the Overhead Delivery System (ODS), which had a crane and was mounted on top of the cargo compartment. After the air force removed the ODS, it was pure-grunt sweat and blood to remove the damned things. And let's not forget that the cargo

compartment floor had antiskid material applied, which is like working on 50-grit sandpaper that can cut flesh to ribbons.

Each HC-130N/P had two in-flight refueling pods (IFRs) just outboard of the outboard engines. Each pod contained a reel with 110 feet of hose and a mechanism that controlled the refuel hose. Since the system had been developed by Lockheed for the US Navy's KC-130 aircraft, the hose reels were overhauled at a navy facility. The hose reels were tricky and prone to numerous malfunctions. One of the worst malfunctions was what we called a "spaghettied hose," which meant the hose didn't rewind properly onto the reel's drum and had come off the drum. It literally looked like spaghetti when it was a bad malfunction. If we (and the aircrew) were lucky, the hose came back intact, and we could work the hose out of the pod and off the reel in one piece. Most of the time, however, the hose would spaghetti bad enough that we would have to cut the hose into pieces to remove it, resulting in quite a mess, since the hose was full of fuel, and we were always aware of the danger of sparks with fuel fumes. We used a hacksaw to cut through the thick hose, and there was limited access to some parts of the reel and hose. Sometimes, when the hose would spaghetti, there was a length of hose hanging out the end of the refuel pod. If that segment was 10 feet or less, the crew could bring it home, landing quite gently. Beyond 10 feet, the crew had to fire the guillotines that cut the hose off.

In 1987, HC-130H 65-0975 returned from programmed depot maintenance (PDM) with green-painted prop blades as a test. The idea behind the green props was to reduce glare from the silver props, especially when the aircraft was flying low level. The basic idea was sound, and all of us crew chiefs thought it was cool. We quickly realized that it was impossible to see the spinning props at night, and they were hard to see during the day, both of which created hazards because crew chiefs needed to see the props as we launched aircraft. Within a month or two, the paint on the props began to get blasted away, and after three months they were interesting to see half green, half silver. The idea was considered a failure, mainly because the props would have to be painted every two months or so. The old paint would have to be stripped off before new paint was applied, to maintain prop balance. It wasn't cost effective, but while it lasted it was cool!

The failure of aircraft systems was not always mechanical in nature, but the result of human error—that, in turn, sometimes led to insufferable loss. Damon Blair talks about the loss of the HC-130P, serial no. 66-0211:

I have seen some misconceptions and inaccuracies of the loss of 211 and the eleven souls on board.

April 2, 1986, was a typical New Mexico spring day, with snow flurries and wind gusts up to 30 mph or so. We launched two HC-130s, 66-0211 (P model) and 65-0975 (H model). About 11 a.m., we got the first call that there was trouble. Then we were brought into our office and the door was locked.

After a thirty-three-year period of inactivation, the 66th Air Rescue Squadron was back in business in March 1991 with HH-60G helicopters. In the Nevada desert, PJs practice boarding UH-60A serial no. 82-23689, originally assigned to the 55th ARS. Equipped with a fleet of HH-60Gs, the 66th flew a hectic schedule of deployments. *Courtesy of USAF*

That's when we were told that we had just lost an aircraft. I remember all of us rushing out to the flight line to see which aircraft had returned. The bird taxiing in was 975.

The two aircraft were flying in trail formation, with 211 in the lead and 975 trailing by 2 miles or so. The crew of 975 saw the whole thing happen. The right wing separated from 211 in flight; 975's crew reported there was turbulence at the low-level route they were following, but the crew commented that it was moderate at the accident site. Since the right wing had separated, the accident investigation centered on that right wing.

The wreckage was hauled back to Kirtland and laid out in one of our hangars. When I saw the remnants laid out, it really hit home just how bad it was. I'll never forget the image of 211's remains laid out and the stench of the wreck. For about a week, the entire C-130 fleet was grounded because of the accident. When the accident board found that 211 had the old-style wing, C-130s with the new outer wings were cleared to fly. Those with the old-style wings were grounded for an outer-wing inspection. This involved stripping the outer wing top and bottom, from the wing to the outboard engines. This turned up a lot of cracked wings that needed replacement. Three color codes were assigned to the aircraft:

green meant that the aircraft could fly without restrictions, yellow meant there were limits on flying in turbulence, and red aircraft were grounded immediately and awaited a one-time flight to a repair facility to have their outer wings replaced.

As the investigation continued, they began finding extra metal in the right wing, and that raised a lot of eyebrows among us. Number 211 had undergone a PDM a few months prior to my assignment to Kirtland. The company performing the depot maintenance had discovered a crack in a wing panel. Rather than replacing the wing, the company decided to repair the wing. The company never told anyone on the government side that the crack existed. The wing should have been replaced instead of repaired, and the government would have told the company to replace the wings. No 211's right-wing strength was reduced to 60 percent because of the repair. When 211 encountered turbulence, the wing, already weakened, came off.

Fred Zayas was an HC-130 loadmaster with the 41st ARRS at McClellan AFB from 1981 to 1986. A primary mission of the 41st was cross-ocean rescue support for tactical aircraft. In case of an ejection, the Hercules rushed to the ditching

A replacement tail boom resulted in this unusual scheme of HH-1H serial no. 70-2471 of the 37th ARRS in August 1982. *Courtesy of Johan Ragay collection*

THE US AIR FORCE AIR RESCUE SERVICE

A pair of PJs of the 55th ARRS are recovered from the Gulf of Mexico during an exercise in 1988. The Pave Hawk (serial no. 82-23728) began life as an army UH-60A, which was to be the second HH-60D prototype but was canceled. *Courtesy of USAF*

point to drop MA-1 sea rescue kits and PJs. Emphasizing the danger of ocean jumps, Zayas points out that in 1983, PJ SSgt. Jeffrey Jones was lost on a jump into rough seas of the Pacific to rescue a navy pilot that had ejected. Zayas reflects:

We HC-130 crews were never in the limelight of rescues. We were regarded as "support" for the helicopters and PJs. We came into our own in rescues way out at sea where some poor soul needed to be found and then got a raft with survival gear, and/or a PJ parachuting into his lap. In combat, there were a few instances where the King element flew unprotected past "the fence" to give gas to a helicopter full of holes that was trying to make it home. The squadron commander was always a helicopter-rated officer, the executive officer, a C-130 guy.

PAVE HAWK

An aging fleet of Huey and Jolly Green helicopters inhibited Air Rescue from accomplishing the combat search-and-rescue (CSAR) mission in the threat environment of the 1980s and 1990s. Huey avionics were outdated; however, the HH-3E remained useful due to its air-refueling capability and the use of night vision goggles. Training, therefore, continued in night CSAR, but the inactivation of Huey CSAR units in 1987 thinned the ranks of CSAR-trained crews and limited CSAR to four overseas units equipped with HH-3Es; they were the 31st, 33rd, 38th, and 56th Air Rescue Squadrons. In the US, both Air National Guard squadrons—the New York–based 102nd ARRS and California-based 129th ARRS—had received HH-3Es in 1975, along with HC-130 tanker aircraft to form composite groups. These units then specialized in long-range overwater search and rescue. With regard to the Hueys, it is important to note that their retirement from pure rescue work did not prevent their assignment to units, which, despite their main mission, also flew rescue when necessary. A number of UH-1Ns, in fact, reclaimed their rescue identity when rescue flights were formed. Concurrent with major organizational changes in 1983, the Air Staff's original intent was to replace the HH-3 and remaining HH-53 helicopters with new UH-60 Black Hawk helicopters. Congress had other ideas.

On April 12, 1989, a Japanese salvage ship hoists an HH-3E from its 1,800-foot-deep watery grave nearly 6 miles off the coast of Okinawa. Serial no. 67-14719 of the 33rd ARRS crashed during a night hoist training mission on March 14, 1989, when its tail rotor struck the water. The pilot, copilot, and flight engineer were killed. *Courtesy of USAF*

After monitoring the US Army's selection of Sikorsky's Model S-70 UH-60A Black Hawk to replace its Huey fleet, air force planners, in their search for a replacement for both the H-3 and UH-1N helicopters, also teamed with Sikorsky. To say that the early history of the H-60 helicopter in air force service was problematic is an understatement.

Hopeful for congressional approval for a large order of the new helicopter, in 1982 the air force purchased eleven UH-60A helicopters diverted from the army production line at Stratford, Connecticut. Assigned to the 55th ARRS at Eglin AFB, Florida, beginning in late 1982, these were intended mainly for pilot and maintenance familiarization. Two of the Black Hawks—serial numbers 82-23718 and -23728—were slated for conversion to HH-60D "Night Hawks." Since funding already indicated a shortfall in production goals, conversion was begun only on serial no. 82-23718. The plan to gradually convert the balance of the "Plain Janes" to HH-60D CSAR platforms, however, was canceled. A new approach had Capt. Donald C. Wurster of MAC's acquisition branch charged with developing a cheaper yet capable Black Hawk derivative with

An HH-60 Pave Hawk of the 210th RSQ and HC-130 (serial no. 93-2105) of the 211th RSQ in a refueling operation over Knik Arm, Alaska, in 2008. The 176th Rescue Wing of the Alaska ANG received their first HC-130Ns in 1990. Six that served the wing bore within their sequential serial numbers "210," denoting assignment to the 210th ARS. Serial nos. were 88-2101 and -2102, and 90-2103 through -2106. In 2004, the unit was restructured, dividing the HC-130s, HH-60G helicopters, and pararescue component into separate squadrons. *Courtesy of USAF*

The Air Staff's procurement plan, which was to purchase 243 HH-60D CSAR helicopters, was scrapped by Congress in 1984. An air force officer at congressional hearings stated emphatically, "If you kill the plan, you kill air rescue." The nonsensical political response was "If we spend all the money on HH-60s, we can't buy fighters and there won't be any pilots to rescue." After the purse strings were loosened for a second Credible Hawk contract, the air force began a gradual, limited-upgrade program with sixteen airframes. At the 1986 Department of Defense Appropriations hearings for fiscal year 1987, USAF representation stated:

> The current Army production UH-60A represents a utility helicopter which is not equipped to satisfy US Air Force combat rescue requirements due to a lack of range, navigation, and defensive systems capabilities. To provide a minimum capability to conduct extended[-]range combat rescue operations in a night, clear[-]weather threat environment, a derivative of the basic UH-60A is required and should be equipped as a minimum with the following upgrades: aerial refueling and auxiliary fuel tanks; growth engine, transmission, and hoist developed for the SH-60B; self-contained precision navigation system such as Doppler and INS combination; night vision goggle-compatible lighting and displays; secure communication, radar warning receiver, flare/chaff dispensers, IR jammer, and defensive weapons.

Addressed first was range extension, NVG (night vision goggle) lighting, and wire strike protection; folding stabilators followed in 1985, and special avionics in 1986 resulted in the MH-60G Pave Hawk for special operations.

A second upgrade program had an additional eighty-two Credible Hawks converted to HH-60Gs, which were based on the more powerful UH-60L model Black Hawk, with two 1,857 shp T700-GE-701C turboshaft engines. This ultimately gave the air force 112 HH-60Gs, also called Pave Hawks, beginning in 1990. Eventually, all HH-60Gs incorporated enhancements that included automatic flight control, color weather radar, engine/rotor blade anti-icing, folding rotor blades, IR jammer, flare/chaff dispenser, and 600-pound-capacity hoist. Two crew-served weapons were either 7.62 mm miniguns or GAU-18/A .50 cal. machine guns. The majority of upgrades were completed at NAS Pensacola's NARF and Sikorsky's Troy, Alabama, facility. Defensive weapons aside, the HH-60G and MH-60G were nearly identical in design and function. The HH-60G's main mission is CSAR, with a secondary mission of peacetime SAR and counterdrug operations. Special-operations MH-60Gs flew in Operation Just Cause in Panama in 1989 and provided CSAR coverage in Operation Desert Storm in 1991.

SURVIVORS

Some USAF officials lamented that HH-60 variants never achieved technological parity with Pave Low HH-53s. The sheer

On February 11, 1985, Pararescueman John Harkness of the 304th ARRS rescued a man whose canoe capsized near the top of Willamette Falls at Oregon City, Oregon. The man's companion drowned when she was swept over the falls. *Courtesy of Donald R. Herd*

off-the-shelf avionics. The result, which used the Inertial Navigation System (INS) borrowed from the C-141 and color weather radar from VIP jets, prompted the name "Credible Hawk." The convoluted course the H-60 took through its introduction to the air force continued.

While the 55th ARRS was gaining experience with its UH-60A Credible Hawks, the HH-60D made its maiden flight on February 4, 1984, at Sikorsky's West Palm Beach, Florida, Development Flight Center. After its shakedown period, it went to Edwards AFB for additional testing. Although a test platform, in September the Night Hawk was credited with a save when it rescued two hikers in the High Sierra. The first save credited to a Black Hawk crew of the 55th ARRS occurred during the summer of 1983, when an air force wife in premature labor was rushed from Eglin to the Keesler AFB hospital.

A PJ of the 83rd Expeditionary Rescue Squadron "Guardian Angel" unit at Bagram Airfield, Afghanistan, on a high-altitude/high-opening free-fall jump in March 2018. His parachute is a CPS SOV 3-HH (HAHO/HALO) Military Silhouette series. *Courtesy of USAF*

Seen from inside an MH-53, another MH-53 flies over devastated New Orleans in the aftermath of Hurricane Katrina in 2005. Disaster response teams of US military forces saved thousands of lives. *Courtesy of Sean Borland*

immensity of the helicopter that began air force life named BUFF made any attempt at such parity improbable. Success of the Pave Low program led to all USAF HH-53Hs being modified in 1986 with cockpits compatible with night vision goggles, resulting in the designation MH-53H. A mix of thirty-one HH-53 airframes, after being fit with 4,380 shp engines, more armor, and avionics upgrades, became MH-53Js, which began service with Special Operations Command in 1987. A series of upgrades extended their service lives, increased load capacity, and made them more transportable. Improved defense avionics and a data-link terminal added to twenty-five MH-53Js created MH-53M Pave Low IVs. Eventually, all MH-53H and MH-53J airframes were brought up to Pave Low IV standards as special-operations platforms, which operated worldwide until their retirement in 2008. A number of HH-3Es and CH-3s soldiered on through the 1980s and into the early 1990s. Air National Guard rescue squadrons exchanged their H-3s for HH-60Gs during late 1990. By late 1991, H-3s could be found only at Kirtland and Patrick Air Force Bases in the US, and at Kadena Air Base, Okinawa, and NAS Keflavik, Iceland.

THE HUEY LIVES

Often heard in the air rescue helicopter community is the satirical comment "When the last Pave Hawk is flown to the boneyard, a Huey will fly the crew back home." How true that becomes years from now is anyone's guess, since new Pave Hawk models are in the works to replace overworked HH-60Gs, and new life is being breathed into a fleet of Hueys converted to trainers.

The service of the versatile twin-engine air force UH-1N Huey helicopter spans five decades. Until 1988, Hueys remained operational with the 67th ARRS in Europe and the 48th ARRS at Homestead AFB. During the 1990s, they remained operational with the 1550th ATTW, the 37th ARRS, the 40th ARRS, the 36th Rescue Squadron, the 54th Helicopter Flight, and the 512th Rescue Squadron, plus the 459th Airlift Squadron in Japan. While the missions of the UH-1N had changed during its first forty years of service, the helicopter had not. To catch up with technology and survive on the modern battlefield, upgrades were required and, in most cases, applied. In the second decade of the twenty-first century, the

TSgt. Lem Torres, PJ with the 38th RSQ at Moody AFB, Georgia, rescues a child during Hurricane Katrina. *Courtesy of USAF*

Said to be the air force equivalent of elite US Army Special Forces and navy SEALs, PJs are highly trained and motivated specialists who endure an incredibly grueling training regimen to earn the Pararescue flash on their hard-earned maroon beret. *Courtesy of USAF*

air force Huey is alive and well. By mid-2013, the USAF possessed sixty-two UH-1Ns: nineteen at Joint Base Andrews, Maryland, for the Continuity of Government (COG) mission (the emergency evacuation of government officials), eighteen for training and testing, and twenty-five for nuclear security support. While the HH-60G serves the core purpose of personnel recovery, UH-1Ns assigned to seven states and Japan are tasked with search and rescue as a secondary mission. The nineteen Hueys assigned the COG mission fell far short of the twenty-seven required by the Air Force District of Washington to stand around-the-clock alert, while addressing maintenance, SAR missions, training, and VIP airlift. A program to replace UH-1Ns with ninety-three off-the-shelf helicopters was canceled in 2013, forcing the Air Staff to reexamine Huey upgrades and operational strategies. Deliberations continued, which included the planned transfer of twenty-six UH-1Ns from the US Marine Corps to the air force. Finally, in September 2018, the Dark Horse Boeing/Leonardo beat out Bell's UH-1Y Venom, Sikorsky's HH-60U, and Eurocopter's UH-72 Lakota to secure the contract for the air force UH-1N's replacement, the MH-139A, named "Grey Wolf." The MH-139A is a spin-off of the AW139 developed by Bell and Italy's Augusta during the late 1990s. At Eglin's Duke Field on December 18, 2019, the day prior to the unveiling-and-naming ceremony, Test Detachment 7 was established to put four test Grey Wolfs through their paces. Plans call for eighty-four HW-139s, with delivery to begin in 2021.

Since rotary-wing aviation has become a major entity in the US Air Force, an undergraduate program for helicopter pilot training got underway in 1994. Conducting the training was the 23rd Flying Training Flight, which in 1999 was reactivated as the 23rd Flying Training Squadron at Ft, Rucker, Alabama, the long-established home of US Army aviation. The program began with 1970s-era UH-1H Hueys transferred from the army. After amassing an inventory approaching forty Hueys, some of which received interim upgrades, the Air Staff contracted with Lockheed Martin in 2004 to convert UH-1Hs into a modernized version based on the Huey II configuration. Labeled the TH-1H, deliveries began in July 2005, with twenty-eight completed by 2007. Features of the TH-1H include the more powerful T53-L-703 engine, a beefier transmission and rotor system, new nose and tail boom, crashworthy seats,

Finished in Gunship Gray (FS 36118) over Light Ghost Gray (FS 36375), this C-130E (serial no. 63-9810) served the 71st RQS as a training and cargo aircraft. It wears the "FT" tail code and time-honored shark mouth of the 23rd Wing at Pope AFB, North Carolina. *Courtesy of Erik Roelof*

Artwork that was painted on the forward bulkhead of an HC-130P of the 71st RQS, 347th RQG. *Courtesy of Stephen Miller*

and digital, NVG-compatible cockpit. The TH-1H fleet is expected to provide twenty years of cost-effective preparation for pilots slated for all rotary-wing operations.

Overseeing Huey training at Ft. Rucker is the 58th Special Operations Wing, which serves as the premier training organization for air force special operations and combat search-and-rescue aircrews. The 58th SOW evolved from the 542nd Crew Training Wing at Kirtland AFB in April 1994. The 542nd had been formed from the 1991 merger of the 1550th CCTW and the 1606th Air Base Wing. In 2004, the air force assumed ownership from the army for USAF helicopter pilot training, graduating the first "All-Blue" class in 2005. Training in the new tilt-rotor CV-22 "Osprey" began in early 2007. Although training is the main mission of the 58th SOW, wing members typically engage in search-and-rescue missions.

IDENTITY LOST

In 1983, when the Air Staff had devised a plan to standardize the Air Rescue helicopter fleet with Sikorsky Black Hawks, leadership reorganized air rescue and special operations under

Fairchild Republic's A-10 Thunderbolt II served as the CSAR attack aircraft into the twenty-first century. This modern "Sandy" (serial no. 80-178) was flown by the 74th Fighter Squadron "Flying Tiger," 23rd Fighter Group. In 2008, the 23rd FG relocated from Pope AFB to its former home of Moody AFB, Georgia. Unique to the A-10 is the GAU-8 20 mm Gatling gun, which allows the pilot to fire with precision "danger close" to friendly forces. *Courtesy of Erik Roelof*

Rescue specialists of the Reserve 920th Rescue Wing secure a flotation collar around a mockup of the Orion crew module at Port Canaveral, Florida, in 2009. *Courtesy of USAF*

Twenty-Third Air Force at Scott AFB, Illinois. The change meant realignment of the 39th ARRW, 41st RWRW, and 1550th ATTW under 23rd AF, which, in turn, changed the ARRS Headquarters function to that of a coordinating agency. Air rescue and special operations operated separately under 23rd AF, with the 2nd Air Division established at Hurlburt Field to focus on special operations. Next came the transfer of HC-130s and remaining HH-53s from air rescue to special operations to bolster overseas special-operations wings. By 1987, the consolidation of special-operations forces had been completed. In 1989, the Twenty-Third Air Force was replaced by Air Force Special Operations Command (AFSOC) at Hurlburt. The Aerospace Rescue and Recovery Service then reverted to Air Rescue Service and again reported to Military Airlift Command. Its headquarters was transferred to McClellan AFB, while the Air Force Rescue Coordination Center remained at Scott AFB. Despite mutterings heard among air rescue personnel about being the lost children of rescue that nobody wanted, reorganization was far from ending. More importantly, Air Rescue faced the arduous task of rebuilding its combat-ready status. New combat rescue squadrons were planned, with the 39th ARS at Misawa AB, Japan; the 66th ARS at Nellis AFB; and the 48th ARS at Holloman AFB all scheduled to receive

HH-60G Pave Hawks. In June 1991, the 71st Rescue Squadron turned over its aircraft and mission to the Alaska Air National Guard and set up shop at Patrick AFB, Florida, with seven HC-130 tanker aircraft. In taking over responsibility for rescue in Alaska, the Alaska ANG created the 210th Rescue Squadron, tracing its lineage back to the 10th Emergency Rescue Boat Squadron, which protected Alaskan waters during World War II. In tribute to these forebears, the designation 210th stood for "the second Tenth Rescue Squadron."

In March 1993, the seven helicopter detachments of the 37th ARRS, all of which had the dual mission of missile site support and CSAR/SAR in the western US, were redesignated rescue flights (RQFs) under operational groups; they were the 37th, 44th, 79th, 40th, 54th, 76th, and 47th. The 36th RQF supported the USAF Survival School at Fairchild AFB, Washington. Concurrently, Air Rescue squadrons were redesignated rescue squadrons (RQS). By 1995, the 41st and 33rd Rescue Squadrons had traded their aging HH-3Es for HH-60G Pave Hawks. During the rebuilding process, ARS units responded to numerous peacetime efforts, including the 1989 San Francisco earthquake and Hurricane Andrew in 1992.

After Operation Desert Storm in 1991, the Military Airlift Command was relegated to history, giving way to the newly created Air Mobility Command. Since Special Operations Command then relinquished MH-60Gs to rescue, and to eliminate confusion caused by similarities in Pave Hawk helicopters, in January 1992, eighty-two MH-60Gs were re-designated HH-60Gs. In 1993 Air Rescue was again dises-tablished, with the majority of its assets transferred to Air Combat Command (ACC) under USAF Combat Rescue School at Nellis AFB. A short-lived merger of these assets under AFSOC led to all air rescue forces, including Reserve and Air National Guard rescue units, transferred back to Air Combat Command in 2005. By late 2011, ACC rescue units consisted of Guardian Angel Pararescue squadrons and glob-ally dispersed rescue units. In the US were two rescue groups—the 347th RQG at Moody AFB, Georgia, and the 563rd RQG at Davis-Monthan AFB, Arizona. The 347th consisted of the 71st Rescue Squadron (RQS) with HC-130P/Ns, the 41st RQS with HH-60Gs, and the Pararescue 38th RQS. Reporting to the 563rd RQG was the 79th RQS, with HC-130P/Ns; two

HH-60G squadrons (the 55th RQS at Davis-Monthan AFB and the 66th RQS at Nellis AFB); and the 48th and 58th Pararescue squadrons. Covering the Pacific were the 31st Pararescue Squadron and 33rd RQS with HH-60Gs. Providing rescue in Europe were the HH-60G-equipped 56th RQS and 57th Pararescue Squadron at RAF Lakenheath.

THE RESCUE ELITE

In the twenty-first century, eight rescue squadrons formed abroad in Africa, Turkey, and Afghanistan were appropriately labeled "expeditionary rescue squadrons" (ERQS). Two were pararescue components, with the remainder assigned HC-130s or HH-60Gs. Missions typically involved a pair of HH-60Gs with PJs aboard, supported by an AH-64 Apache gunship or available support aircraft. Unusual among these units was the 83rd ERQS, which flew Guardian Angel Pararescue teams in Pave Hawk helicopters until late 2017. After the drawdown of troops in Afghanistan permitted removal of ERQS units, the 83rd not only remained but created a new dimension in combat search and rescue. Based at Bagram Air Field, Afghanistan, the

In September 2005, crewmen of a UH-1N (serial no. 69-6619) of the 54th Helicopter Flight at Minot AFB, South Dakota, prepare to depart for Columbus AFB, Mississippi, to assist with Hurricane Katrina disaster relief. One month later, the 54th was redesignated 54th Helicopter Squadron, joining the 582nd Helicopter Group, which governs missile wing support. On the FLIR-equipped Huey's tail fin are the code "MT" and a red band with the words "Rough Riders." *Courtesy of USAF*

The UH-1N-equipped 36th Rescue Flight at Fairchild AFB, Washington, supports the USAF Survival School. Of note in this 2015 view are the various systems mounted to the aircraft: forest penetrator, FLIR units, and fast-rope insertion/extraction system. *Courtesy of Skip Robinson*

83rd's PJs and army CH-47F Chinook aircraft and crews merged to form an elite, one-of-a-kind rescue unit. The Chinook's size advantage over the HH-60G helicopter was but one of the factors that gave rise to the unique partnership. The Chinook can carry a team of PJs and combat rescue officers, numerous survivors, and advanced medical gear, including surgical equipment . . and the CH-47F can carry it faster, higher, and farther than the Pave Hawk. The Chinook's armored floor greatly increases the margin of safety for crew and PJs as they treat wounded. Both Chinook crew and pararescue teams learn each other's responsibilities, and both must work together to determine mission risk and conduct mission planning. As of this writing, the unique, highly successful arrangement continues. Time will tell if the army–air force rescue team concept holds promise for the future of CSAR. Although contractual controversy in 2007 denied the air force the HH-47F Chinook as a rescue platform, the achievements of the 83rd ERQS could one day swing the pendulum the other way. In the meantime, the air rescue triad comprises the HH-60G "Pave Hawk," the HC-130P/N "Combat King," and the A-10 "Thunderbolt II." The A-10, like its A-1 "Skyraider" and LTV A-7D predecessors, continued the proud tradition of the "Sandy" call sign for close support of rescue forces.

Combat search-and-rescue forces also exist in the Air Force Reserve Command (AFRC) and the Air National Guard. As in the active air force, major organizational changes occurred in Reserve Air Rescue. The 303rd ARRS was the first of the five Reserve rescue squadrons to undergo revision, when in spring 1984 the squadron traded its six HC-130H aircraft for six C-130Bs, becoming the 303rd Tactical Airlift Squadron. The 939th ARRGp, which had been activated in 1985, was expanded in 1990 to "wing" status with the 301st, 304th, and 305th squadrons; in 2003 the group reverted to the air-refueling role, causing dispersal of the three squadrons under the AFRC's 920th Rescue Wing, which then came under the Air Combat Command. Structured for both combat SAR and peacetime SAR, as well as spaceflight support, the wing, which is located at Patrick AFB, operates six HC-130P/Ns in the 39th RS, fifteen HH-60G Pave Hawks of the 301st RS, and pararescuemen of the 308th RS. During duty in Iraq following the tragic events of 9/11, crews of the 920th recovered twenty-six survivors. The humanitarian side of the wing included support of rescue efforts in the wake of Hurricane Katrina in 2005. The 920th also manages three geographically separated units (GSUs) of the 943rd RQG at Davis-Monthan AFB: the 305th RQS, flying HH-60Gs, and the 304th and 306th.

PARARESCUE SQUADRONS

Air Combat Command also gained the New York Air National Guard's 106th Rescue Wing, under which was centered the 102nd Rescue Squadron, which combined five HC-130P/N and six HH-60G aircraft, plus pararescue assets. Primary duties of the 102nd included rotational deployment of HC-130s to support the 56th RQS at NAS Keflavik, presidential

Pararescuemen often entered the water to secure drones for recovery. A PJ prepares a BQM-167A aerial target system for recovery by helicopter off Tyndall AFB, Florida. *Courtesy of USAF*

of squadron HH-60G ("Jolly 110") and Pararescueman Arden "Rick" Smith in 1991 was immortalized in the film *The Perfect Storm*. Also in the Air National Guard are California's 129th Rescue Wing and Alaska Air National Guard's 176th Wing.

As part of reorganization of ANG rescue wings by Special Operations Command in 2004, separate squadrons were created for fixed-wing aircraft, helicopters, and pararescuemen. Under the 106th RQW, the 101st Rescue Squadron was equipped with HH-60Gs, the 102nd flew HC-130Ps, and the 103rd became home to pararescue specialists. The California Air National Guard's 129th RQW followed the same pattern, with the 129th RQS operating HH-60Gs, while the 130th RQS operates HC-130Ps, and the 131st is the pararescue squadron. Although the 130th RQS comes under the Rescue heading, its HC-130Ps are "Combat Shadow" special-operations variants. The Alaska Air National Guard's 176th Wing follows suit, with its 210th RQS flying HH-60Gs, the 211th RQS flying HC-130P/Ns, and the 212th RQS comprising pararescue specialists. The scope of reorganization reverted from a vertical to horizontal chain of command, giving control of twenty-seven rescue squadrons to seven wing commanders.

support, coverage of space shuttle launches, and counterdrug operations. Attesting to the squadron's long-range rescue ability, on December 10, 1994, two 102nd Pave Hawk helicopters set an overwater rescue record by flying 784 miles out to sea following the sinking of a Salvadorian freighter. Three in-flight refuelings made the flight possible. The loss

A NEW CROWN FOR THE KING

On June 1, 2017, members of the Alaska ANG 176th RQW were at Lockheed Martin's Greenville, South Carolina, facility to accept

In the combat search-and-rescue role, armament of the HH-69G Pave Hawk consisted of two 7.62 mm miniguns or two .50 cal. machine guns. Armed with miniguns, this Pave Hawk of the 301st Rescue Squadron carries special-operations troops in southern Iraq in April 2003. *Courtesy of USAF*

An Alaska ANG HH-60G (serial no. 92-26467) conducts a hoist mission from coast guard cutter *Long Island* in March 2012. *Courtesy of USAF*

the first HC-130J Combat King II assigned to the Air National Guard. Each of the three ANG wings took delivery of four Combat King IIs as they completed postproduction testing. The first of an air force order for nearly eighty HC-130Js was delivered in October 2010. After developmental testing, the aircraft became operational with the 79th RQS, 563rd RQG, at Davis-Monthan AFB in November 2012; two additional HC-130Js earmarked for the squadron followed. Powering the stretched, highly advanced rescue Hercules are 4,591 pshp Rolls-Royce AE2100DS engines, driving six-bladed Dowty props. Besides the ability to refuel partner Pave Hawk helicopters, the Combat King II itself is air-refuelable, giving it limitless range. Features of the HC-130J include improved navigation, threat detection and countermeasure systems, night vision–compatible interior and exterior lighting, FLIR, and satellite communication. Intense crew and maintenance training with the new airframe and myriad systems is conducted by the Air Education and Training Command (AETC), which is a major tenant at four US air force bases and NAS Pensacola. The HC-130J crew comprises a pilot, a copilot, a combat systems officer (formerly the navigator position), two

loadmasters, and a pararescue component consisting of three PJs and a combat rescue officer (CRO). The CRO position, which is heavy on leadership and planning, plus all PJ skills, was created in late 2000. The flight engineer position was eliminated from the HC-130J crew. Operators of the Combat King II are the 71st and 79th RQS, the 550th SOS of the AETC, Air Force Reserve 920th RQG, and the three ANG rescue wings.

SALVATION FOR THE PAVE HAWK

After more than a decade of service, the Pave Hawk began experiencing declining readiness rates, which prompted Air Staff to begin a search for a medium-lift CSAR helicopter that was faster, longer ranged, and more survivable, and with all-weather capability and more cabin space; it would have to accommodate three PJs in addition to flight crew, and four litters. The decade-long search ended in April 2009, when Defense Secretary Gates canceled the helicopter replacement program. To make matters worse, Gates called into question the need for a single-service combat search-and-rescue force, and its single-purpose helicopter. Apparently what escaped

This HH-60G (serial no. 82-23680), converted from a UH-60A, was one of eleven Pave Hawks originally assigned to the 55th ARRS. Protective systems included flare/chaff dispensers at four positions, plume detectors atop the nose, and a radar-warning receiver on the tail fin trailing edge. *Courtesy of USAF*

The popular, time-honored shark mouth was worn by this CH-3E (serial no. 63-9676) of the 302nd ARRS at Luke AFB, Arizona, during the 1980s. *Courtesy of Larry Wielgosz*

Wearing nonstandard camouflage, an HH-3E (serial no. 67-14703) of the 302nd ARRS practices hoist operations in 1986. The 302nd used tail code "LH."
Courtesy of Larry Wielgosz

By the 1980s, rescue Hueys traded their high-visibility paint schemes for the European 1 camouflage scheme seen here on UH-1F (serial no. 65-7922) of the 37th ARRS. *Courtesy of USAF*

Gates was the unique global aspect of the air force rescue mission, which drives a high level of training and specialized hardware for such high-risk challenges. Also noteworthy is the air force ability to apply the complete CSAR/SAR network containing all the elements necessary to support the mission—HC-130s to refuel helicopters and deploy PJs and equipment such as Zodiac boats, all-terrain vehicles, etc., as well as tactical air support, intelligence—the list goes on. Only the navy comes close to having a CSAR capability, flying the MH-60S Knighthawk helicopter, some of which are equipped for CSAR and carry crew members specially trained in CSAR operations. The army considers combat rescue part of its overall mission, fielding medevac units flying Black Hawk helicopters. Thankfully, Gates decided not to make CSAR a multiservice mission, which would have severely taxed other services to attain USAF Air Rescue's operational level. With that off the table, the air force resumed its search for the HH-60G's replacement.

The HH-60G Pave Hawk is a low-supply/high-demand asset that quickly attained a high utilization rate to conduct personnel recovery and humanitarian relief operations across the globe. Of the original 112 airframes procured, only about ninety are flyable, due to unscheduled maintenance. After twenty years of being overworked, major structural cracks were found in more than half the fleet, and many sustained battle damage. Ongoing modifications in avionics, defensive systems, and safety features kept the Pave Hawk a viable CSAR platform pending a replacement. The years-long saga of the on-again/off-again search for a replacement finally ended in September 2019, when Sikorsky gained approval to begin production of the HH-60W derivative of the original Black Hawk helicopter. Based on the army UH-60M, the HH-60W is powered by two 1,716 shp GE-T-700-GE-701D turboshaft engines. The "Whiskey" model includes a new 660-gallon fuel system, nearly doubling the HH-60G's 360-gallon capacity, along with improved hover performance, avionics, and weapons. The air force signed on for 113 HH-60Ws, four of which arrived on November 6, 2019, at Eglin's Duke Field for the 413th Flight Test Squadron; they are serial numbers 14-4480 to -4483. The Whiskey's first operational assignment is expected to be the 347th Rescue Group in 2021.

GUARDIAN ANGELS

You're injured, thirsty, alone. The fear that grips you makes it difficult to swallow. You expect to hear animal sounds in the jungle, but the silence is deafening. You listen for an approaching enemy, but the only sound you hear is the sure destruction of your crashed aircraft as it burns in the distance, or maybe the drone of an airplane searching high overhead. Is that your heart pounding through your flight suit? You'd give anything now for the security of your cockpit, up there, with them. If your emergency radio works, you hear a tinny voice a million miles away imploring, "Come up voice." And a glimmer of hope washes over you. Eventually, you hear it before you see it. A deep pulsation. Then you make out the shape that matches

An HH-1N of the 304th ARRS investigates an automobile among the devastation left by the eruption of Mount Saint Helens, Washington, in May 1980. The 304th at its peak operated twelve UH-1Ns. *Courtesy of USAF*

the sound of rotor blades beating the air. Your heart skips a beat as salvation looms nearer. The hulking machine slows. It's over you, roaring, hanging there. Suddenly a figure emerges from the aircraft, looming quickly larger as he descends near you. You were never so thrilled to see someone. It's your guardian angel and you vow never to take that term lightly. Skilled hands work over you, a calming voice, and in no time you're stabilized and riding the cable with him up to your hovering, waiting chariot. Strong hands pull you in, more medical attention among a dizzying cacophony of shouts over the turbine's whine, and maybe gunfire. Soon, you're in a medical facility. And you'll never forget that your life was in the hands of a pararescueman.

Similar scenes were, and are, repeated thousands of times, in oceans, in deserts, on mountainsides, and in Arctic conditions. Although no two rescues are alike, in each case the pararescueman has prepared mentally and physically to accept the challenge and the risk involved. Since the beginning of space flights, PJs have constantly trained to support NASA missions.

A1C Natasha Libby, then the only female gunner with the 66th RS at Nellis AFB, in 2013 poses with her flight gear and the HH-60G's minigun. *Courtesy of USAF*

When medical corpsmen voluntarily parachuted into uncharted jungle near the China-Burma border in 1943 to aid survivors of a C-46 crash, pararescue was born. Since then, countless airmen, soldiers, and civilians across the globe have discovered firsthand the skills, dedication, and bravery of friends in high places who had come to help. Some of the most dramatic, inspiring stories about the men, known simply as PJs, originated in Southeast Asia, where they voluntarily rode the hoist cable down into enemy territory to aid their fellow man. The vital link between rescue aircraft and survivors is the pararescueman. The PJ's "ride to work" might be a C-130 from which he parachutes, or a helicopter from which he descends via rope or cable, or even a specially built vehicle. Most of the PJ's skills are learned for one purpose: to get him to the survivor, where he will use the most important of his skills: his medical ability.

A career as a PJ is not for the faint of heart. The weeding-out process is grueling, physically tormenting, and designed to quickly determine who has the right combination of stamina, intelligence, independence, fortitude, and desire. Strapped with their own weight in equipment, PJs can parachute day or night onto surfaces ranging from forest to oceans. More than a jack-of-all-trades, they are masters of all trades: parachutist, diver, mountain climber, survival specialist, paramedic, combatant—they are all of them. Tenacity and mental stability are helpful attributes to be among the mere 10 percent who make it through all phases of PJ training and earn the maroon beret. It is no small wonder that the two-year pararescue training program is dubbed "Superman School." And that is only the beginning. PJs then move on to advanced training in parachuting, SCUBA, survival, weapons, combat tactics, mountain rescue, aerial operations, and medicine, to name a few. So extensive is the range of required skills that it can take a PJ a few years to become a fully productive team member. They then are the most highly trained specialists in the US armed forces. Training is never ending, as PJs train constantly to hone skills and devise new techniques. That obligation is even more demanding for pararescuemen of the Air National Guard and Air Force Reserves. In the modern air force, PJs might be assigned to a special-operations unit.

Over time, the more they come in contact with human suffering and save lives, the stronger the urge to help others.

Throughout the war in Southeast Asia, the elite ranks of PJs numbered fewer than three hundred. In the modern air force, that number does not exceed five hundred. Throughout the history of the air force, aircrews have held PJs in high esteem, and it is not lost on the guardian angels that they are the heirs of a priceless heritage.

Today's air force categorizes search and rescue into combat search and rescue, which identifies the recovery of isolated personnel during combat, and civil search and rescue, which is the search for and rescue of distressed persons on land or at sea in a permissive environment. Air Rescue is the arm that stretches across the world to perform that duty, and air rescue aircrews and pararescuemen are the helping hand of that arm. The importance of personnel recovery lies in the value that America places on the sanctity of human life. Despite fiscal constraints, the air force commitment to aircraft modernization remains as strong as its commitment to personnel recovery, which is rooted in its resolve to bring home from combat every man and woman, regardless of service.

Responding to the tragic fire at the Las Vegas MGM Grand on November 21, 1980, were air force UH-1N and CH-3E helicopters. The Hueys were based at Nellis AFB, Nevada, while the CH-3Es of the 1st Special Operations Wing happened to be in Nevada for Exercise Red Flag. This CH-3E of the 1st SOW rescued numerous persons from the roof of the burning structure. *Courtesy of USAF*

Rows of ribbons and tiered rank stripes on Senior Master Sergeant Wayne Fisk's uniform, along with master aircrew and parachutist's wings, are the mark of a seasoned pararescueman, or "PJ." Fisk poses with members of the CAP at the 2009 dedication of HH-53C serial no. 69-5785, displayed at Maxwell AFB, Alabama. No. 5785 had an equally distinguished career, having served rescue units in Southeast Asia and participated in the evacuation of Phnom Penh, Cambodia, the Mayaguez battle, Operation Just Cause in Panama, the Persian Gulf War, and combat in Afghanistan and Iraq. Her hard-earned retirement came in 2008. Fisk was awarded Silver Stars for action during the Son Tay prison raid and SS *Mayaguez* incident. *Courtesy of US Air Force*

PJs see themselves as competitive, highly motivated, rugged individualists who challenge themselves—sometimes against all odds—doing what most people would shrink from. Pararescue is a profession in which the glory of elitism is tempered by the physical and mental strain endured during training, the loss of those they couldn't help, and the loss of their own in a brotherhood that knows no bounds.

Used for USAF helicopter pilot training, this revamped Bell UH-1H (serial no. 72-21549) was nicknamed "Tony the Tiger." The Huey is seen here at Cairns Army Air Field, Ft. Rucker, Alabama, in 2011, painted a nonstandard camouflage scheme that was not popular with the brass. *Courtesy of Erik Roelof*

TSgt. Jewel Steamer, HH-60G flight engineer with the 33rd RQS, fires an upgraded version of the time-honored .50 cal. machine gun from her Pave Hawk in 2014. *Courtesy of USAF*

The new look in Pave Hawks, the HH-60W (serial no 14481), in May 2019. *Courtesy of USAF*

More technologically advanced and able to fly higher, faster, and farther than previous models, Lockheed's HC-130J Combat King II is the combat search-and-rescue version of the modern C-130J. The first example was rolled out in April 2010. This Combat King II (serial no. 16-5863) departs Lockheed's Marietta, Georgia, plant in March 2019, for delivery to the New York Air National Guard's 106th Rescue Wing. *Courtesy of USAF*

A ski-equipped HH—60G (serial no. 92-26467) of the Alaska Air National Guard. *Courtesy of Emiel Sloot*

One of two PJs of the 38th Rescue Squadron at Moody AFB follows an inflatable boat dropped from an HC-130 over the Atlantic to treat an injured Chinese fisherman 350 miles northeast of Caribbean Island St. Martin. *Courtesy of USAF*

ABBREVIATIONS AND TERMINOLOGY

AAA	All American Aviation, or antiaircraft artillery (a.k.a. "triple A")	ATC	Air Transport Command /Air Training Command
AAB	US Army air base	ATTW	Aircrew training and test wing
AAC	Alaskan Air Command	beeper	Repetitive tone broadcast by an emergency radio, usually activated by parachute deployment
AAE	All American Engineering		
AAF	US Army airfield		
AAFBU	Army Air Force base unit	BUFF	Nickname for CH/HH-53 helicopter, "Big Ugly Fat Fellow" (last word often changed to a less savory name)
AARRC	Atlantic Aerospace Rescue and Recovery Center		
AB	Air base	BuNo	US Navy Bureau Number
ABG	Air base group	Bluie	Used to reference Greenland bases (e.g., "Bluie West" or "BW 1")
ABU	Air base unit		
AC	Aircraft commander	CAP	Civil Air Patrol
ACRU	Aircrew rescue unit	CBI	China-Burma-India
ACS	Air Commando squadron	CBU	Cluster bomb unit
ADC	Air Defense Command	CCTW	Combat crew training wing
ADCC	Air Defense Control Center	CIA	Central Intelligence Agency
AF	US Air Force, numbered air forces	COD	Carrier onboard delivery
AFB	US Air Force base	COG	Continuity of Government
AFSOC	Air Force Special Operations Command	CRFB	Crash rescue boat flight
ANG	Air National Guard	CSAR	Combat search and rescue
ARB	Aircraft rescue boat, a.k.a. "crash boat"	Det	Detachment
ARC	Air rescue center	DoD	Department of Defense
ARCS	Air Resupply and Communications Service	EARRC	Eastern Aerospace Rescue and Recovery Center
ARCW	Air resupply and communications wing	ELF	Electronic location finder
ARG/ARGp	Air Rescue group	ELT	Emergency locator transmitter
ARK	Air rescue kit	ERBS	Emergency rescue boat squadron
ARRC	Air Rescue coordination center	ERS	Emergency rescue squadron
ARRG/ARRGp	Aerospace rescue and recovery group	FAC	Forward air controller
ARRS	Aerospace Rescue and Recovery Service	FE	Flight engineer
ARRW/ARRWg	Aerospace rescue and recovery wing	FEAF	Far East Air Force
ARS	Air Rescue Service	feet wet	Overwater
ART	Air Reserve technician	FLIR	Forward-looking infrared radar
ARU	Aircraft repair unit (WWII) / Air Rescue unit	Flt	Flight
ASW	Antisubmarine warfare	FM	Frequency modulation, radio voice communication

FSK	Fire suppression kit	NAS	Naval air station
FTD	Field training detachment	NASA	National Aeronautics and Space Administration
FTS	Flying training squadron		
GCI	Ground-controlled interception	NCO	Noncommissioned officer
HA	Hauling, auxiliary-aircraft recovery ship	NKP	Military slang for Nakhon Phanom Royal Thai Air Force Base, also called "Naked Fanny"
HC	US Navy helicopter combat support squadron		
HF	High frequency	NVG	Night vision goggles
HIFR	Hover in-flight refueling	OD	Olive Drab (color)
HQ	Headquarters	OL	Operating location
HS	US Navy helicopter antisubmarine squadron	OSS	Office of Strategic Services, World War II predecessor to the CIA
HSL	High-speed launch	PACAF	Pacific Air Force
ICD	India-China Division	PARC	Pacific Air Rescue Center
INS	Inertial navigation system	PARRC	Pacific Aerospace Rescue and Recovery Center
IP	Instructor pilot		
JATO	Jet-assisted takeoff, also termed RATO for rocket-assisted takeoff	PAVE	Precision avionics vectoring equipment
Jolly Green Giant	Sikorsky CH/HH-3 helicopter	PJ	Pararescue jumper, the symbol for pararescuemen entered in early flight records
JRCC	Joint rescue coordination center		
KIA	Killed in action		
LBR	Local base rescue	POW	Prisoner of war
LS	Lima site	RAF	Royal Air Force
LLLTV	Low-light-level television	RCC	Rescue coordination center
LNRS	Limited Night Recovery System, Night Recovery System, when perfected	RESCAP	Rescue combat air patrol, heavily armed aircraft that supported rescue aircraft
MAC	Military Airlift Command	RESCORT	Rescue escort, akin to RESCAP
MACV	Military Assistance Command, Vietnam	RHAW	Radar homing and warning
MARS	Mid-Air Retrieval System	RIO	Radar intercept officer, often simplified in slang to "back-seater" or "guy in back"
MASH	Mobile army surgical hospital		
MATS	Military Air Transport Service	RN	Royal Navy (Great Britain)
METO	Maximum except takeoff	RO	Radio operator
MIA	Missing in action	RPG	Rifle-propelled grenade
Mk.	Mark, used in systems nomenclature, including avionics, ordnance, etc.	RPV	Remotely piloted vehicle
		RS	Rescue squadron
MLR	Main line of resistance	RQS	Rescue squadron (late)
NARF	Naval air rework facility	RTAFB	Royal Thai Air Force Base

RU	Rescue unit
RWRW	Rescue weather and reconnaissance wing
SAC	Strategic Air Command
SAM	Surface-to-air missile
SAR	Search and rescue
SARTF	Search-and-rescue task force
SEA	Southeast Asia
SHP	Shaft horsepower
SOG	Studies and observation group, US Army special force
SOS	Special-operations squadron
SOW	Special-operations wing
STAR	Surface-to-air recovery
STOL	Short takeoff and landing
Super Jolly Green	Sikorsky CH/HH-53 helicopter
TAC	Tactical Air Command
TACAN	Tactical air navigation
TASS	Tactical air support squadron
TAWC	Tactical Air Warfare Center
TDY	Temporary duty
TF	Task force
TFS	Tactical fighter squadron
TFW	Tactical fighter wing
Thud	Nickname for Republic F-105 "Thunderchief," said to be derived from the sound the aircraft made when it crashed
TIC	Troops in contact
TRS	Tactical reconnaissance squadron
TS	Test squadron
TTU	Tactical training unit
UDT	Underwater demolition team of the US Navy
UHF	Ultra high frequency
USAAF	US Army Air Force
USAF	US Air Force
USAFE	US Air Forces Europe
USFS	US Forest Service
USNS	US naval ship
VA	US Navy attack squadron designation
VNAF	Vietnamese air force
WADC	Wright Air Development Center
WARRC	Western Aerospace Rescue and Recovery Center
WIA	Wounded in action
WSO	Weapons system operator
ZI	Zone of the Interior (continental US)

APPENDIX A
WORLD WAR II AIR RESCUE BOAT MODEL DESIGNATIONS

"P" Boats

Design No.	Length
127	63 feet
168	63 feet
195	72 feet
203	83 feet
221	42 feet
235	104 feet
314	63 feet
379	85 feet
385	45 feet
416	63 feet

"J" Boats

200	40 feet
292	16 feet
311	27 feet
326	22 feet
387	32 feet
390	18 feet
415	19 feet

APPENDIX B
AIRCRAFT RESCUE BOAT UNITS DURING WORLD WAR II

Squadron 5, 3rd AF Bomber Command (Gulfport AAF) at Ocean Springs

1st through 15th Emergency Rescue Boat Squadrons

921st Quartermaster Boat Company (Aviation); activated May 1942 at Langley Field, VA, with a detachment activated at Washington, DC, in September; platoons at Baltimore, MD, Training Center; Bolling Field, Anacostia, DC; Bradley Field, Windsor Locks, CT; Dow Field, Bangor, ME; Midland Airport, TX; Mitchell Field, Hempstead, Long Island, NY; and Stewart Field, West Point, NY; deactivated April 1944

922nd Quartermaster Boat Company (Aviation); activated July 1942 at MacDill Field, FL; platoons at Dale Mabrey Field, Tallahassee, FL; Lake Charles AAF, LA; Key Field, Meridian, MS; Drew Field, Tampa, FL; Hunter Field, Savannah, GA; Columbia AAB, SC; Cuyahoga Falls, OH; Harding Field, Baton Rouge, LA; Morris Field, Charlotte, NC; Orlando AB, FL; Selfridge Field, MI; and Avon Park Bombing Range, FL

923rd Quartermaster Boat Company (Aviation); activated 1943 at Hamilton Field, CA; platoons at Gray Field, Ft. Lewis, WA; Portland AAB, OR; and Salt Lake AAB, UT

924th Quartermaster Boat Company (Aviation); began as Air Corps Marine Rescue Service; activated January 1942 and sent to Elmendorf Field, AK; at least ten detachments throughout Alaska; relocated to Adak and redesignated 10th ERBS July 1944; inactivated February 1946

925th Quartermaster Boat Company (Aviation); activated 1943 at Borinquen Field, Puerto Rico; redesignated 11th ERBS in 1944 with detachments at Atkinson Field, British Guiana; Barbados, British West Indies; Batista Field, Cuba; Beane Field, St. Lucia; Coolidge Field, Antigua; Vernam Field, Jamaica; and Zandery Field, Suriname

926th Quartermaster Boat Company (Aviation); activated July 1942 at Howard Field, Canal Zone, and sent to Albrook Field, CZ; redesignated 12th ERBS in June 1944; inactivated October 1946

927th Quartermaster Boat Company (Aviation); activated July 1942 at Hickam Field, Hawaii; redesignated 13th ERBS in July 1944

791st Quartermaster Boat Company (Aviation) at Kindley Field, Bermuda, in 1944; became detachment of 1st ERS

1000th Quartermaster Boat Company (Aviation); platoons

at Eglin Field, FL, and Phillips Field, Aberdeen Proving Ground, MD; redesignated 4th ERBS

1001st Quartermaster Boat Company (Aviation); activated December 1942; redesignated 14th ERBS June 1944 with detachments at Biak Island, Morotai, and Oro Bay, New Guinea; inactivated March 1946 at Yokohama, Japan

1002nd Quartermaster Boat Company (Aviation); activated January 1944 at Keesler Field, MS, and later transferred to Miami Beach, FL, Training Base; platoon at Boca Raton, FL; redesignated 5th ERBS

1003rd Quartermaster Boat Company (Aviation); platoon at Tyndall Field, Panama City, FL; redesignated 6th ERBS

1004th Quartermaster Boat Company (Aviation); activated March 1943 at Matagorda Island Bombing and Gunnery Range, Port O'Connor, TX; platoons at Ellington Field, TX, and Ft. Worth AAF, Harlingen, TX; redesignated 7th ERBS 1944 but disbanded

1005th Quartermaster Boat Company (Aviation); formed 1941 at Morrison Field, FL; acquired by Air Transport Command Caribbean Division February 1943; deactivated May 1944

1006th Quartermaster Boat Company (Aviation); platoons at Brookley Field, AL; Hensley Field, Grand Prairie, TX; Olmsted Field, Middletown, PA; Homestead Field, FL; and New Orleans AAF, LA

1007th Quartermaster Rescue Boat Operational Training Unit (Aviation) at New Orleans, LA

1008th Quartermaster Boat Company (Aviation); platoon at Miami, FL

1525th Quartermaster Rescue Boat Crew (Aviation); platoon at Rome AAF, NY

1526th Quartermaster Rescue Boat Crew (Aviation) at Keesler Field, MS

1527th Quartermaster Rescue Boat Crew (Aviation) at Langley Field, VA

1530th Quartermaster Rescue Boat Crew (Aviation) at New Orleans, LA

1531st Quartermaster Rescue Boat Crew (Aviation) at Mitchell Field, Hempstead, Long Island, NY

1532nd Quartermaster Rescue Boat Crew (Aviation) at Langley Field, VA

1534th Quartermaster Rescue Boat Crew (Aviation) at Mitchell Field, Hempstead, Long Island, NY

Note: New Orleans Army Air Base was home to thirty-nine quartermaster rescue boat crews numbered 1535 through 1573

APPENDIX C
KNOWN AIRCRAFT OF USAAF/USAF AIR RESCUE

OA-10 (PBY-5As TRANSFERRED FROM USN)
42-10741
42-107402
42-107403

42-107404
42-107405
42-109022: 1st ERS
42-109024: went missing on ferry flight; interned in Spain, July 1943
43-3259
43-3260
43-3261
43-3262: went missing in New Guinea, October 1943
43-3264
43-3265
43-3266
43-3267
43-3269
43-3270
43-43839
43-43840
43-43841
43-43842
43-43844
43-43845
43-43846
43-43847
43-43849
43-43850: 1st ERS, Flt. C
43-43851
43-43852
43-43854
43-43855: 1st ERS, Flt. C
43-43856: 1st RS; "LAZY DAISY," "PICK-UP"
43-43857: 10th ARS; crashed in Cheyenne, WY, on August 8, 1949
43-43858: 1st ERS
43-43859: 1st ERS; crashed in India on September 12, 1944
43-43860
43-43861: 1st ERS
43-43862
43-43863
43-43863
43-47839: 1st ERS, Flt. C
43-47850: 1st ERS, Flt. C
43-47956: 1st ERS, Flt. A
43-47957: 1st ERS, Flt. B; lost on rescue mission in Mediterranean, November 16, 1944
43-47958: 1st ERS, Flt. B
43-47959: 1st ERS, Flt. B; crashed on takeoff in Albania, on September 12, 1944
43-47960: written off on June 2, 1945
43-47961: 1st ERS

OA-10A/SA-10A
44-33868
44-33869
44-33870

44-33871

44-33873

44-33874: 2nd ERS; written off at Mindanao following beaching, on January 26, 1945

44-33875: 2nd ERS, destroyed during air raid on Morotai on November 25, 1944

44-33876: 2nd ERS

44-33877: 2nd ERS; crashed at sea on October 26, 1944

44-33878: 2nd ERS

44-33879: 2nd ERS

44-33880: 2nd ERS; written off following damage from open-sea landing on May 18, 1945

44-33881: 2nd ERS; destroyed at Palawan by air attack on April 28, 1945

44-33882: 2nd ERS

44-33883: 2nd ERS, written off after damaged by ground fire on April 8, 1945

44-33884: 2nd ERS; written off following damage during landing on December 18, 1944

44-33885: 2nd ERS; lost at sea following rescue at Borneo on June 23, 1945

44-33886

44-33888

44-33889

44-33890

44-33891

44-33893

44-33894

44-33895

44-33896

44-33898

44-33899: 9th ARS, Flt. C

44-33900

44-33901

44-33903

44-33903

44-33904

44-33905

44-33906

44-33908: 4th ERS; damaged on takeoff with rescued B-29 crew on May 29, 1945; all rescued by sub USS *Tigrone*, which sank aircraft with gunfire

44-33909

44-33910

44-33911: 5th ERS

44-33912

44-33913: 5th ERS

44-33914: "PICK-UP"

44-33915: 5th ERS, "MISS PICK UP"; strafed on water during rescue and sunk on March 30, 1945

44-33916: 5th ERS, "SOPHISTACAT"

44-33917: 5th ERS, "GOING MY WAY"; sunk in North Sea after damage from landing on March 30, 1945

44-33919

44-33920: 5th ERS

44-33921

44-33922: 5th ERS

44-33923: 5th ERS

44-33924: 4th ERS

44-33925

44-33926

44-33927

44-33928: 2nd ERS, "NURSE MAID"

44-33929: 2nd ERS, "JUNIE"

44-33930: 2nd ERS

44-33931

44-33932: 2nd ERS

44-33933: 2nd ERS

44-33934

44-33935

44-33936

44-33937: 10th ERS

44-33939: 4th RS, Flt. B

44-33940: 2nd ERS

44-33941: 2nd ERS

44-33942

44-33943: 2nd ERS

44-33944: 2nd ERS

44-33945

44-33946

44-33947

44-33949

44-33950

44-33951: 2nd ERS

44-33952

44-33954

44-33955

44-33956: Keesler Amphibious School / 4th RS, Flights C and B

44-33957

44-33958: 5th RS /4th RS, Flights B and C

44-33959

44-33960

44-33961

44-33962

44-33963: 7th ERS

44-33964

44-33965

44-33966

44-33967

44-33969

44-33970

44-33971

44-33972

44-33974: 7th ERS

44-33975: 7th ERS

44-33976: 7th ERS, "OLD IRONSIDES" / 6th ERS; lost during open-sea takeoff off Okinawa on July 31, 1946

44-33977
44-33979
44-33980
44-33981
44-33982: 7th ERS
44-33984
44-33985
44-33986: 7th ERS
44-33987: 5th ERS
44-33988
44-33989
44-33990: 7th ERS, "BOUNCING BETTE"
44-33991: 5th ERS
44-33992
44-33994: 1st ERS
44-33995: 5th ERS
44-33996
44-33997: 3rd ERS
44-33999
44-34000: 10th RS, "LAME DUCK"; went missing in Pacific on
    August 13, 1945
44-34001
44-34002
44-34003: 5th ERS
44-34004
44-34005: 5th ERS
44-34006
44-34007
44-34009
44-34010
44-34011
44-34012
44-34013: 5th ERS
44-34014: 1st ERS, Flt. C
44-34015
44-34016
44-34017: 5th ERS
44-34019
44-34020
44-34021
44-34022
44-34024
44-34025
44-34026
44-34027
44-34028: 5th ERS
44-34029
44-34030
44-34032
44-34033: 4th RS
44-34034
44-34035
44-34036
44-34037

44-34038: 1st RS
44-34039
44-34040
44-34041
44-34042
44-34043: 2nd ERS
44-34044
44-34045
44-34046
44-34047
44-34048: 6th RS, Flt. C
44-34049
44-34050
44-34051
44-34052: 2nd ERS
44-34054: 2nd ERS
44-34055
44-34056: 3rd ERS, "I'LL BE SEEING YOU"
44-34-57
44-34059
44-34060
44-34061
44-34062: Headquarters, ERS
44-34064
44-34065
44-34066
44-34067: 5th ERS
44-34068 1st Arctic SAR Squadron; crashed in Greenland,
    summer 1945
44-34069
44-34070
44-34071: 2nd ERS
44-34072
44-34074: 2nd ERS
44-34075: 4th ERS
44-34076
44-34077: 2nd ERS
44-34079
44-34080: 4th ERS; shot down after rescuing F6F pilot from
    Tokyo Bay on August 13, 1945; all KIA
44-34081
44-34082: 4th ERS
44-34083: 2nd ERS
44-34084
44-34085
44-34086
44-34087
44-34088: 2nd ERS
44-34089
44-34090
44-34091
44-34092
44-34094
44-34095

44-34096
44-34097

OA-10B
45-57833
45-57834
45-57837
45-57839
45-57840

A-10A (EX-USN PBY-5A)
47-638
47-639
49-2894
49-2895
49-2896 (A-10B)
PBY-5A BuNo **48393**: 2nd ERS; sank March 17, 1945
PBY-5A BuNo **48401**: 2nd ERS
Royal Australian Air Force A-24-109: loaned to 2nd ERS with RAAF crew

REPUBLIC P-47DS OF 5TH EMERGENCY RESCUE SQUADRON
42-22472: destroyed on takeoff from RAF Boxted on May 27, 1944
42-22476: 5F-V, "HELEN"
42-22547: destroyed on takeoff from RAF Ashford on July 15, 1944
42-22784: 5F-N
42-25711: 5F-D, "BUBBLES"; combat loss over North Sea on July 31, 1944
42-74622: 5F-R, "TERRY"; lost in landing accident at RAF Halesworth on November 6, 1943
42-74664: 5F-U; destroyed colliding with 42-8402 during landing at RAF Boxted on August 7, 1944
42-74690 5F-J, "LADY JANE"
42-74705: 5F-O, "LADY LORELEI"; lost in midair with 42-76175 on April 8, 1945
42-74724: "ICE COLD KATTIE"
42-74744: 5F-P, "BLIND DATE"
42-75154: 5F-I, "SAD SAM"
42-75228: 5F-G, "HARRIET"
42-75528: 5F-H, "DIANE III"
42-75855: 5F-A, "TONY"
42-76143: 5F-X, "MAN MADE MONSTER"
42-76175: 5F-D, "BIG DICK II"; lost in midair with 4274705 on April 8, 1945
42-7899: 5F-M, "EL BANGO"
42-7910: 5F-Q
42-7914
42-7922: 5F-Z
42-8375: 5F-C
42-8401: 5F-K, "CHRIS"
42-8402: 5F-F

42-8410: 5F-L
42-8485: 5F-T
42-8490: 5F-L, "BUNDLE OF JOY"
42-8496: 5F-X, "GALLOPING CATASTROPHE"; lost in midair with B-24H of 448th BG on March 13, 1945
42-8554: 5F-W
42-8586: 5F-S
42-8646: 5F-Y, "PRIMROSE PEGGY"
42-8693: 5F-E, "MISS MARGARET" / "PEE WEE"
43-25534: 5F-B, "VICIOUS VIRGIN" / "INVINCIBLE FAY"
43-25565: 5F-K, "KATIE" / "CHRIS'S FAVORITE"; crashed-destroyed on landing in England on December 15, 1944

BOEING SB-17G
42-3465 (B-17F): 6th ERS, "WEE BONNIE II"
42-97825
42-102588
42-102720: 5th RS
42-102723: 5th RS
42-102753: 5th RS
42-102827: 5th RS
42-30108: Keesler AB airborne lifeboat training aircraft
43-37652: 4th RS, Flt. A
43-37765: 5th ERS / 8th ERS, first at RAF Halesworth fit with airborne lifeboat
43-38882 5th ERS / 4th ERS, "WATER WITCH"; shot down over Japan during search for P-51 pilot on July 25, 1945; nine KIA
43-39074: 2nd ERS / 13th ARS
43-39112: 8th AF SAR radar platform / 53rd ARS
43-39262: 4th ERS
43-39264: 3rd ERS / 5th ERS
43-39266: 3rd ERS / 6th ERS, "PRETTY BABY"
43-39272: 2nd RS
43-39274: 2nd ERS
43-39361: 3rd ERS
43-39362: 3rd ARS / 6th ARS, Flts. A and B / 51st ARS
43-39364: 3rd RS; written off after ground collision with 43-39365 at Ashiya AB, Japan, on November 8, 1950
43-39365: 4th ERS / 3rd RS, Flt. A; written off after hydraulic failure caused ground collision with 43-39364 at Ashiya AB on November 8, 1950
43-39367: 2nd ERS
43-39374: 4th ARS
43-39376: 2nd ERS
43-39457: 10th ARS
43-39473: 10th RS; crashed at Cold Bay, AK, on August 15, 1947; eight killed
43-39478: 4th ERS
43-39482: 10th ARG
43-39488: 3rd ERS
43-39491: 4th RS / 2nd ERS
43-39492: 10th ARS
43-39493: 3rd ERS

43-39494: 3rd ERS

43-39496: 3rd ERS

43-39498: 6th RS / 9th RS

43-39499: 2nd ERS

43-39500: 9th ARG

43-39501: 6th RS

43-39502: 2nd ERS "JULIE MAE" / 4th ARS, "ONE MORE TIME"

43-39503: 2nd ERS

43-39504: 2nd ERS

43-39505: 10th RS

43-39507: 6th ERS

43-39508: 2nd ERS / 54th ARS

43-49565: 74th ARS

44-63722

44-82780: 5th RS

44-83301: 6th ARS / 54th ARS / 55th ARS; crashed at Thule AB on April 7, 1953

44-83342: 3rd RS, Flt. B

44-83345: 2nd RS, Flt. C; destroyed by fire during refueling on October 31, 1951

44-83470: 10th ARS; ditched 3 miles from takeoff from Davis AFB, AK, into Kulak Bay on July 5, 1950; four killed

44-83474: 6th RS

44-83504: 2nd ERS

44-83508: 2nd ERS / 3rd ARS, Flt. A

44-83509: 2nd ERS / 3rd ARS

44-83511: 3rd ARS; crashed at Johnson AB, Japan, on January 5, 1951

44-83512

44-83518: 2nd ERS

44-83521: 2nd ERS

44-83522: 9th ARS

44-83527: 2nd RS, Flt. D; crashed near Haneda, Japan, on November 18, 1950

44-83539: 2nd RS

44-83550: HQ Co., Hill AFB

44-83565: 4th ARG

44-83567: 2151st RU / 9th RS

44-83570: 4th RS; crashed off coast of Brazil

44-83573

44-83575: 1st RS, Flt. C

44-83578: 2152nd RU

44-83581: 2nd ERS; crashed at sea following takeoff from Morotai on September 1, 1945; nine killed

44-83585

44-83595: 10th RS

44-83642: 54th ARS

44-83692

44-83700: 62nd AAFBU, AR 9, Luke Field / 4th RS, Flt. A / 10th RS

44-83701: 2152nd RU

44-83703: 6th RS

44-83705: 6th ARS, Flt. A (51st ARS)

44-83706: 72nd ARS

44-83708: 4th RS/2nd RS

44-83710: 2151st RU / 9th RS

44-83711: 5th ARS

44-83713: 2152nd RU /6th RS / 7th RS

44-83714: 4th RS, Flt. C

44-83717: 54th ARS

44-83718: 73rd ARS / 10th ARS

44-83719: 7th ARS / 10th ARS

44-83722: 2nd ERS

44-83723: 3rd ARS, Flt. A

44-83724: 2152nd RU; snowbound after landing to rescue C-47 crew, abandoned on Greenland ice cap in December 1948

44-83725: 4th RS, Flt. C

44-83754: 5th RS, Flt. A

44-83756: 53rd ARS

44-83761: 2nd RS / 4th RS

44-83763: 2nd RS, "READY TEDDY"

44-83764

44-83770: 7th ERS

44-83771: 1386th ABU, Keflavik based; lost and low on fuel, crew of five bailed out over Shetland, Scotland; aircraft crashed into sea on January 2, 1947

44-83772: 3rd ARS, Flt. A / 54th ARS

44-83773

44-83777

44-83780: 6th ARS, Flt. B (51st ARS); crashed at Ernest Harmon AFB, NL, on March 6, 1951

44-83781: 4th RS

44-83783: 4th ERS; went missing near Kwajalein on May 27, 1946

44-83784: 1st RS

44-83785: converted to TB-17G, then CIA Intermountain Aviation for Fulton System

44-83786: 3rd RS

44-83787: 10th RS

44-83788: 4th ERS

44-83791

44-83793: 5th ERS

44-83794: 4th RS, Flt. D / 5th RS, Flt. D / 6th RS; crashed on takeoff from Ernest Harmon AFB on May 21, 1951

44-83795: 4th RS/2nd RS

44-83796: 4th ERS

44-83798: 10th ARS

44-83799: 4th RS / 10th ARS

44-83800: 3rd ARS

44-83802: 2nd RS, "PACIFIC TRAMP"

44-83824: 3rd RS, Flt. D / 7th ARS; first A-1 lifeboat drop of Korean War

44-83885: 3rd ARS, Flts. A and C; flew first SAR mission of Korean War on June 25, 1950

44-85497: 55th RS

44-85505: 6th RS; written off after accident near Talkeetna, AK, on September 10, 1951

44-85531: HQ 2nd ARS

44-85577: 10th RS

44-85581: 10th RS, Flt. C; written off following crash on takeoff from Shemya, Japan, on October 23, 1950

44-85594: 6th RS, Flt. A (51st ARS)

44-85604: 4th RS / 2nd RS

44-85654: 5th RS / 9th RS

44-85673: 1st ARS

44-85746: 7th ARS, Flt. D / 4th RS; crashed on Olympic Peninsula, WA, en route to McChord AFB from British Columbia on January 19, 1952; three killed

44-8821: 2nd RS

NORTH AMERICAN B-25C

41-13179: 1st ERS

41-30362 (B-25D): Eastern Sector Headquarters CBI / 1333rd AAFBU / 1352nd AAFBU, "Blackie's Gang"

42-53373: 1st ERS

42-64519: 1st ERS Headquarters, "KENTUCKY DERBY"

MARTIN B-26

3rd ARS, Flt. A (Korea 1950)

NOORDUYN UC-64A NORSEMAN

43-35444

44-70369: 10th RS

WACO CG-15A GLIDER

45-5502: 10th RS

45-5451: 10th RS

CURTISS C-46D

44-78420: 2nd RS

44-78542: 3rd RS

DOUGLAS SC-47

41-15667

42-15894 (C-53): 10th ARS "JATO BRONC"/54th ARS/to USN as BuNo. 06994

42-24057 (SC-47A): 8th ARS

42-92813 (SC-47A): 2nd ERS

42-92816 (SC-47A): 2nd ERS

42-93086 (SC-47A): 8th ARS

42-93513 (SC-47A): crashed at Thule AB on March 26, 1952

42-100629 (SC-47A): 2nd ERS; written off at Tacloban, 1946

42-101000 (SC-47A): 61st ARS

42-108944 (SC-47A): 8th ARG

43-15195 (SC-47A)

43-15270 (HC-47A)

43-15277 (SC-47A): 64th ARS; crashed shortly after takeoff from Wiesbaden AB on May 19, 1961; two killed

43-15345 (SC-47A): 8th ARS; crashed on takeoff from Elmendorf AFB on September 9, 1958; thirteen killed

43-15524 (SC-47A)

43-15537 (SC-47A): 61st ARS

43-15540 (SC-47A)

43-15541 (SC-47D)

43-15548 (SC-47A): crashed at Ft. Bridger, WY, on October 9, 1954

43-15558 (SC-47A)

43-15561 (SC-47A): 48th ARS / 62nd ARS

43-15574 (SC-47A/HC-47A)

43-15665 (SC-47D): 10th ARS / 1st RS, Flt. C; first US landing at T-3 Ice Island North Pole, May 3, 1952

43-15689 (SC-47A): ditched at sea 62 miles off Libya on June 7, 1959

43-15732 (SC-47A): 48th ARS / 4400th CCTS; crashed in Vietnam on February 11, 1962

43-15764 (SC-47A): 6612th ABG

43-15991 (SC-47A)

43-16097 (SC-117A): converted from VC-117C

43-16145 (SC-47D): crashed in Wyoming on September 24, 1955; seven killed

43-16157 (SC-47B/HC-47D): 9th RU, Det 6, Biggs Field, TX / 61st ARS

43-16160 (SC-47D): 60th ARS

43-16161 (SC-47D)

43-16250 (SC-47D)

43-16252 (SC-47D)

43-16256 (SC-47D): Squadron B

43-16277 (SC-47D): 6th ARS, Flt. B / 51st ARS / 53rd ARS / 54th ARS / 55th ARS

43-16367 (SC-47D): 52nd ARS / 87th ARS

43-16400 (SC-47D/HC-47D): 60th ARS

43-16411 (SC-47D): 64th ARS

43-45883 (SC-47D): 60th ARS

43-47994 (C-47A): 2nd ERS

43-47995 (SC-47B): 2nd ERS; shot down in Manila and ditched in Pacific on April 17, 1945

43-48074 (SC-47B)

43-48398 (SC-47D): 2nd RS, Flt. C / 33rd ARS

43-48575 (SC-47B): 84th ARS

43-48765 (SC-47B): 52nd ARS / 51st ARS

43-48911 (SC-47B)

43-48957 (SC-47D): 1st ARS, Flt. C / 2157th ARS

43-48963 (SC-47J): USN R4D-6S ASW trainer

43-49144 (SC-47B)

43-49220 (SC-47B): 63rd ARS

43-49353 (SC-47D)

43-49368 (SC-47D/HC-47D): 60th ARS

43-49431 (SC-47D)

43-49508 (SC-47B/SC-47D/HC-47D): 8th ARS / 61st ARS

43-49511 (SC-47D): damaged in accident in February 1955 and written off in October 1956

43-49517 (SC-47B): 51st ARS

43-49523 (SC-47B): 53rd ARS / 51st ARS

43-49565 (SC-47B): 60th ARS / 10th RS

43-49638 (SC-47B): 8th ARS

43-49656 (SC-47D)

43-49784 (SC-47B)

43-49681 (SC-47D): 3rd ARS, Flt. C; written off following damage on takeoff from Misawa AB, Japan, on November 4, 1950

43-49810 (SC-47B): 2nd ERS

44-76306 (SC-47D, later HC-47D): 61st ARS

44-76330 (SC-47B): 60th ARS (modified for electronic surveillance over Laos with 315th Air Division; shot down in Laos on March 23, 1961, to become the first combat loss and first US casualties in Southeast Asia since World War II; pilot captured, seven KIA)

44-76447 (SC-47D): 61st ARS

44-76558 (SC-47B): 47th ARS

45-1012 (SC-47B): Det 6, Biggs Field, TX

45-1013 (SC-47B): 6th RS, Flt. D, "JOKULL"; abandoned on Iceland glacier in 1950 after ski-landing to rescue survivors of crashed DC-4; damaged during JATO takeoff attempts while frozen to ice and written off; recovered 1951 by Icelandic airline Loftleidir and made airworthy

45-1015 (SC-47B): damaged beyond repair during search for C-54 in Yukon Territory, Canada, January 30, 1950

45-1019 (SC-47D): 60th ARS

45-1040 (SC-47B): 6th ARS

45-1090 (SC-47D): 81st ARS

45-1091 (SC-47B): 3rd ARS

45-1123 (SC-47D/HC-47D): 8th ARS

GRUMMAN OA-9 "GOOSE"
38-556 through -581

Five former US Navy JRF-6Bs redesignated A-9s were serial nos. 42-106979 through -106983

GRUMMAN OA-12A "DUCK"
Five aircraft with serial nos. 48-563 through -567: all assigned to 10th RS

PIPER L-4
43-1037

43-1198

43-1234

STINSON L-5
42-14945: 475th AAFBU, Sect. 9, Reno Municipal Airport

42-89023

42-98187: 303rd AAFBU, MacDill Field

42-98475: 8th ARU, Flt. A

42-98479: 62nd AAFBU, Det 5, Memphis Municipal Airport

42-98481: 5th RS

42-98572 (L-5A): 8th ARU, Flt. A

42-98578: 2nd ARS

42-98633 (L-5A)

42-98730 (L-5A)

42-98731: Sect. 5, Hamilton Field

42-98770: 209th AAFBU, Biggs Field

42-98780: 2nd ERS, "LIL LES"

42-99022:\ (L-5A): 2nd ERS

42-99023 (L-5A): 2nd ERS

42-99024 (L-5A): 2nd ERS

42-99441: 2nd ERS

42-99442: Hawaii ARS

44-16876 (L-5B): 10th AJR Det, 1st Air Commando Group

44-17096 (L-5G): 2nd ARS, Flt. L

44-17157 (L-5B)

44-17677 (L-5E): 62nd AAFBU Biggs Field

44-17701

44-17706 (L-5E): 3rd ARS, Flt. F; crashed in Korea on October 11, 1950

44-17874 (L-5C): 2nd RS

44-17875 (L-5E): 2nd ERS

44-17898: 3rd RS, Flt. D

44-17943 (L-5E): 2nd ERS

44-18029: 475th AAFBU, Reno Municipal Airport

44-18034: 3rd ARS, Flt. F

44-18147 (L-5E) 2nd ERS

44-18190 (L-5E)

45-34912 (L-5E): 10th ERS

45-34913 (L-5G): to Alaska Wing CAP

45-34914 (L-5G): 10th ERS

45-34926 (L-5G): 10th RS

L-17B
48-0952: 1st ARS; destroyed in Japan

BEECH AT-7A
41-21160: 10th RS

41-21161: 10th RS

BEECH AT-11
41-21158: 10th RS

42-37386: 62nd AAFBU, AR 9, Luke Field

BEECH C-45
42-7030 (C-45G): 48th ARS

44-47687 (C-45F): 10th RS

51-11785 (C-45G): 5th ARG

DE HAVILLAND L-20A "BEAVER"
51-16490: 52nd ARS

51-5111: 6th ARS

52-6102: CARC, Det 15

52-6119

52-6122: 52nd ARS; attached to 6605th ABW at Ernest Harmon AFB

DOUGLAS HC/SC-54D "RESCUEMASTER"
42-72440: 48th ARRS (first-built C-54D model)

42-72454

42-72456: 1604th ABG Bermuda / 74th ARS

42-72459: 57th ARS

42-72464: 67th ARS
42-72475: 48th ARRS
42-72477
42-72507
42-72512: 79th ARS / 36th ARS
42-72517: 36th ARS / 79th ARS
42-72518: 54th ARS / 10th ARS
42-72521: 79th ARS
42-72524: ADC 4683rd ABW, Thule AB, "THULE KNOT" / "ARCTIC RAVEN"
42-72527: 54th ARS
42-72529
42-72536: 54th ARS
42-72540: 79th ARS
42-72541
42-72547: 53rd ARS
42-72555: 2157th ARS / 74th ARS / 72nd ARS / 58th ARRS / 48th ARRS
42-72559
42-72564: 5th ARG / 48th ARS / 76th ARS / 79th ARRS
42-72566: 53rd ARS / 67th ARS; written off after running off runway in Spain on January 23, 1961
42-72567: 79th ARRS
42-72568
42-72569
42-72575
42-72586
42-72590: 57th ARS; midair collision with HC-97G 52-2773 of 55th ARS on June 29, 1964, near Kindley AB, Bermuda, on NASA training mission; seventeen killed
42-72601: 67th ARRS
42-72603
42-72609: 48th ARS / 67th ARS / 79th ARRS
42-72615: 57th ARS
42-72622
42-72624: 67th ARS
42-72647: 36th ARS / 58th ARRS / 67th ARRS
42-72654: 76th ARRS
42-72658: 79th ARS
42-72665: 36th ARS / 54th ARS
42-72666: 36th ARS
42-72668
42-72671: 36th ARS
42-72696: 67th ARS
42-72702: 36th ARRS
42-72703: 54th ARS
42-72708
42-72713: Kwajalein
42-72725
42-72726
42-72734: 10th ARS
42-72743: 48th ARS
42-72747: 48th ARS / 55th ARS / 4683rd ABG, Thule AB
42-72749

42-72756: 48th ARS / 76th ARS
43-17204
43-17205
44-9033 (SC-54E): 58th ARS
44-9073 (SC-54E): 54th ARS / 48th ARS
44-9125
45 484 (SC-54G): sold to Pan American Airways
45-556 (SC-54G) 9th ARG
45-578 (SC-54G)
45-608 (SC-54G): 67th ARS / 57th ARS
45-632 (SC-54G): 74th ARS / 52nd ARS / 48th ARS
45-637 (SC-54G): last C-54 built

BOEING SB-29A/B
42-63750: 9th ARS
44-27308: 3rd ARS
44-61671: 400th ABU Wright Patterson AFB
44-62190: 52nd ARS
44-62210: 52nd ARS
44-62212: 5th RS / 48th ARS
44-69957
44-69971
44-69982: 52nd ARS; disappeared into St. George's Bay, NFLD, during search for RB-26H on March 18, 1953
44-70089: 34th ARS / 79th ARS
44-70101: 2nd ARS / 37th ARS
44-70104: 29th ARS
44-70117: 37th ARS
44-70127: 52nd ARS
44-70128: 3rd ARS
44-70129: 52nd ARS / 29th ARS
44-84030
44-84054: 5th RS, Flt. C
44-84078: 3rd ARS, Flt. C / 52nd ARS
44-84084: 5th ARS, Flt. C / 37th ARS
44-84086: 3rd ARS
44-84088
44-84094: 5th ARS, Flt. C / 37th ARS
44-84096: 52nd ARS
44-84112
44-84124: 3rd ARS, Flt. B; crashed shortly after takeoff from Yokota AB on January 31, 1951; three killed
44-84303
44-84308
44-86355: 3rd ARS
44-87644
44-87665: 52nd ARS
44-87768: 3rd ARS

FAIRCHILD SC-82A "PACKET"
44-22963: 5th ARS, Flt. D / 6th ARS
44-22966: 5th ARS, Flt. D / 1st ARS
44-22971: 5th ARS / 9th ARS / 2151st ARU
44-22972: 4th ARS, Flt. B / 2150th ARU

44-22973: 5th ARS, Flt. D
44-22976: 5th ARS, Flt. D / 2151st ARU
44-22978: 5th ARS / 4th ARS, Flights A and B / 2150th ARU
44-22979: 2150th ARU
44-22982: 1st ARS/5th ARS, Flt. D
44-22983 4th ARS, Flt. B / 2150th ARU
44-22984: 5th ARS, Flt. D / 2151st ARU
44-22986: 2151st ARU / 5th ARS; damaged beyond repair landing at Selfridge AFB following search for USAF transport in Yukon Territory on February 1, 1950
44-22990: 4th ARS, Flt. B / 2150th ARU
44-23011: 5th ARS / 8th ARS / 6th ARS / 2152nd ARU
44-23015: 5th ARS, Flt. D / 47th ARS / 2156th ARU
44-23019: 5th ARS / 4th ARS, Flt. B / 2150th ARU
44-23021: 5th ARS; written off following crash at Tallahassee, FL, on July 31, 1950
44-23027: 58th ARS
44-23029: 7th ARS / 66th ARS / 67th ARS
44-23030: 5th ARS, Flt. D / 48th ARS
44-23031
44-23033: 4th ARS, Flt. B / 41st ARS / 84th ARS
44-23036: 6th ARS, Flt. D / 5th ARS, Flt. D / 46th ARS
44-23041: 1st ARS / 28th ARS
44-23057: 4th ARS, Flt. B / 6th ARS, Flt. D / 43rd ARS
44-23058: 1st ARS / 27th ARS
45-57733: 5th ARS, Flt. D / 46th ARS
45-57734: 1st ARS / 46th ARS / 2156th ARU
45-57736: 4th ARS, Flt. B / 44th ARS / 2156th ARU
45-57737: 5th ARS, Flt. D / 49th ARS
45-57762 (C-82A): 7th ARS
45-57798
45-57799: 4th ARS, Flt. B
45-57827: 1st ARS / 2156th ARU
45-57828: 4th ARS, Flt. B / 42nd ARS
45-57829: 7th ARS / 69th ARS
45-57830: Alaskan Air Command 1st RS / 10th ARS
45-57831: Alaskan Air Command 1st RS / 10th ARS
48-568: 7th ARS / 67th ARS
48-575: 6th ARS, Flt. D / 52nd ARS / 2152nd ARU / 51st ARS
Note: Not all SC-82As assigned to rescue units were listed in official records as such, but they retained their original C-82A designations.

CONVAIR L-13B
46-73
46-110
46-111
46-139: 5th ARS, Flt. A
47-395
47-396
47-397
47-398
47-399
47-400

47-401
47-402
47-403
47-404
47-405
47-406
47-407
47-408
47-409
47-410
47-411
47-412
47-413
47-414
47-415
47-416
47-418
47-419
47-420

CESSNA LC-126A
49-1948: 10th RS
49-1949: 10th RS
49-1951: 10th RS; written off following landing accident at Elmendorf AFB on June 25, 1951
49-1952: 10th RS, Det B
49-1953: 10th ARG
49-1954: 10th ARS; crashed at Lake Hood, AK, on December 9, 1951
49-1955: 10th ARS, Flt. A
49-1956: 10th ARS, Flt. A; crashed at Sheep Mountain, AK, on August 4, 1951
49-1957: 10th ARG
49-1958: 10th ARS; written off following landing accident at Ladd AFB on April 19, 1951

GRUMMAN SA-16A/SA-16B/HU-16B "ALBATROSS"
48-588: ARS Headquarters, "Arctic Albatross"; 6th ARS / 49th ARS / 54th ARS
48-590
48-596: 5th ARS, Flt. A
48-600: 5th ARS, Flt. A; crashed-destroyed at Quabbin Reservoir, MA, on October 2, 1951
48-601: 5th ARS
48-602: 3rd ARS / 5th ARS, Flt. D; crashed-destroyed at Mt. Clemens, MI, when it lost engine on approach to Selfridge AFB on April 6, 1956
48-603: 3rd ARS
48-604: 3rd ARS
48-605: 3rd ARS
48-606: 12th ARS
49-069: 6th ARS, Flt. A; crashed on takeoff from NAS Argentia into Placentia Bay on March 12, 1956; six killed
49-071: 6th RS, Flt. A / 5th RS, Flt. A

49-072: 7th ARS, Flt. C; on July 27, 1952, landed in heavy seas to rescue thirty-two survivors of Dakota airliner ditched in Mediterranean Sea; after arriving to take survivors, whale-boats heaved against aircraft, making it nonflyable; it was towed by Royal Navy frigate to Benghazi, but aircraft collided with frigate during tow, causing more damage, and it was written off.

49-074: 7th ARS, Flt. D

49-075: 7th ARS, Flt. D

49-079

49-080: 3rd ARS

49-082: 3rd ARS, Flt. A

49-083: 3rd ARS; written off after crashed on landing at Tsu Shima, Japan, on January 20, 1951

49-084: 3rd ARS; fuel exhaustion, lost at Okinawa on June 5, 1953

49-085: 2nd ARS / 38th ARS

49-086: 2nd ARS / 3rd ARS

49-089: 28th ARS

49-090: 2nd ARS

49-091: 3rd ARS, "My Wild Irish Rose"

49-094: destroyed in crash landing at Subic Bay on August 21, 1951

49-095: 2nd ARS / 3rd ARS

49-096

49-097: 2156th ARS; crashed-destroyed at St. Petersburg, FL, on November 15, 1951

50-173: 2nd ARS

50-177: 43rd ARS

50-178: crashed into sea near Nassau on October 18, 1951; five killed

50-180

50-181: 2nd ARS

51-004: 5th ARS

51-006: 2nd RS / 3rd RS / 33rd ARS

51-008: 3rd ARS / 48th ARS; during SAR for C-119 in South Korea on January 16, 1952, crashed into mountain; crew of five found alive four days later

51-009: 31st ARS

51-010: written off after damage on February 8, 1956

51-012: 2nd ARS

51-014: 36th ARS

51-015: 33rd ARS

51-016: 11th ARS, Flt. C / 31st ARS

51-018: 33rd ARS / 31st ARS

51-019: 33rd ARS

51-020: 33rd ARS

51-022: 47th ARS / 54th ARS

51-024: 3rd ARS / 66th ARS, "Body Snatchers" / 6th ARS

51-025: 33rd ARS

51-026: 1st ARS, Flt. C

51-027: 32nd ARS; stalled on takeoff and crashed at Clark AB, PI, on January 16, 1953

51-029: 38th ARS

51-030: lost in Italy on November 4, 1952

51-034: 9th ARS, Flt. C

51-035: 9th ARG, 53rd ARS; crashed in Iceland on September 20, 1955

51-036: 6th ARS, Flt. D; crashed into Atlantic between Iceland and Greenland on November 15, 1953; five killed

51-037: 39th ARS

51-038: 52nd ARS

51-039: written off after damage near Wheelus AB on April 18, 1956

51-040

51-041: 84th ARS

51-042: 54th ARS

51-043: 6th ARS, Flt. D (51st ARS) / 52nd ARS / 54th ARS / 56th ARS / 301st ARRS; after 52nd ARS 10th ARS

51-044: 6th ARS, Flt. D / 52nd ARS / 54th ARS

51-045: 46th ARS / 71st ARS / 302nd ARRS; 10th ARS

51-046: 74th ARS / 301st ARRS; cut adrift after open-sea landing off Bermuda on July 15, 1967; after plasma delivery to ship, couldn't take off or water-taxi in rough seas

51-047: 302nd ARRS

51-048: 53rd ARS / 48th ARS

51-050: 53rd ARS; crashed in Iceland on October 5, 1953

51-051: lost in Alaska on August 28, 1952

51-052: 52nd ARS / 54th ARS / 51st ARS / 67th ARS / 302nd ARRS

51-053: 67th ARS / 302nd ARRS / 10th ARS

51-054: 301st ARRS

51-055: 6th ARS, Flt. C; crashed on Iceland glacier due to icing on May 16, 1952; five killed

51-056: 301st ARRS; before 301st ARRS 10th ARS

51-057: 54th ARS / 53rd ARS / 52nd ARS / 51st ARS; during month of July 1952, remained stranded on ice cap 200 miles east of Thule AB

51-058: 39th ARS / 53rd ARS; crashed into Pacific 120 miles off North Vietnam on July 3, 1965

51-059: 10th ARS / 71st ARS / 51st ARS / 67th ARS

51-060

51-061: 3rd ARS; sank in rough seas off Korea on January 13, 1953

51-062: 3rd ARS / 39th ARS; crashed into mountain in Japan on February 13, 1953; six crew and two passengers killed

51-063: 55th ARS / 6th ARS, Flt. A / 51st ARS; blown by high winds into fjord and sank; written off at BW 1 on January 1, 1954

51-064: crashed on water takeoff in Japan on October 30, 1953

51-065: 54th ARS; crashed at Narsarssauk AB, Greenland, on August 19, 1954

51-066: 52nd ARS; crashed onto land attempting water takeoff at Saint Anthony, Newfoundland, on July 30, 1954; one civilian killed

51-067: 6th RS

51-071: 12th ARG / 304th ARRS / 31st ARRS; combat loss off North Vietnam on March 14, 1966; two KIA

51-471: 304th ARRS / 74th ARS

51-473: 302nd ARRS / 304th ARRS

51-474: 54th ARS

51-475: crashed in France on July 22, 1953, due to fuel exhaustion; crew bailed out

51-476: 5th ARG / 46th ARS

51-5278: 304th ARRS / 302nd ARRS (camo)

51-5279: 84th ARS / 48th ARS / 31st ARRS / 67th ARRS / 37th ARRS / 302nd ARRS (camo)

51-5282: 51st ARS / 301st ARRS; set altitude record prior to final USAF HU-16B flight

51-5284: 302nd ARRS

51-5286: 49th ARS

51-5287: 53rd ARS / 58th ARRS; damaged in heavy seas on takeoff 120 miles off North Vietnam after rescuing four survivors of B-52 midair collision on June 18, 1965; all aboard rescued by Norwegian freighter; aircraft taken in tow by navy destroyer but quickly sank

51-5288: 51st ARS

51-5289: 46th ARS

51-5290: 44th ARS / 51st ARS / 58th ARS; stranded on ice cap on January 7, 1954; retrieved on February 22

51-5291: 49th ARS / 302nd ARRS / 58th ARRS

51-5292: 302nd ARRS

51-5293: 38th ARS / 41st ARS / 304th ARRS

51-5294: 302nd ARRS (camo)

51-5295: 58th ARS / 31st ARRS / 304th ARRS / 302nd ARRS (camo)

51-5297: 51st ARS / 54th ARS

51-5298: 51st ARS; transferred to US following wind damage at Narsarssauk AB on January 1, 1954

51-5299: 47th ARS / 55th ARS

51-5300: 49th ARS

51-5301: 47th ARS / 46th ARS / 53rd ARS

51-5302: 41st ARS / 55th ARS / 54th ARS / 301st ARRS

51-5303: 46th ARS / 54th ARS / 51st ARS / 301st ARRS

51-5304: 36th ARS / 31st ARS

51-5305: 58th ARS / 301st ARRS; sank on landing near Ramey AFB, PR, on August 4, 1970

51-5306: 55th ARS / 67th ARS / 41st ARS / 71st ARS / 301st ARRS

51-5311: 54th ARS

51-7140: crashed in Saudi Arabia on September 27, 1953

51-7142: 302nd ARRS

51-7143: 4th ARS / 41st ARRS (camo)

51-7144: 37th ARRS / 33rd ARRS / 304th ARRS / 301st ARRS (camo)

51-7145: 31st ARS / 37th ARRS; went missing in bad weather returning to Da Nang AB on October 18, 1966; seven killed

51-7146: crashed due to engine failure in Tunisia on June 6, 1953; one killed

51-7147: 46th ARS / 47th ARS

51-7148: 1707th Flying Training Squadron (Amphib) / 42nd ARS

51-7149: crashed in Gulf of Oman on September 25, 1953; four killed

51-7151: 36th ARS / 304th ARRS

51-7152: 47th ARS / 67th ARS

51-7153: 48th ARS

51-7155: 46th ARS / 304th ARRS

51-7158: crashed on landing in Saudi Arabia on July 5, 1953

51-7159: 46th ARS; crashed in Azores on August 25, 1955; five killed

51-7161: 33rd ARRS

51-7162: 46th ARS; crashed at Grenier AFB, NH, on March 22, 1954

51-7163: 31st ARRS

51-7164: 48th ARS

51-7165: 304th ARRS

51-7166: 5th ARG, 46th ARS / 47th ARS / 67th ARS / 31st ARRS

51-7167: 49th ARS / 54th ARS

51-7168: 41st ARS; crashed at Westover AFB, MA, on July 30, 1953

51-7169: 305th ARRS

51-7171: 46th ARS; on SAR for WB-29 on September 19, 1953, damaged during unauthorized open-water landing off Bermuda and sunk by USCG gunfire

51-7172: 28th ARS

51-7173: 41st ARS; crashed due to engine failure while searching for missing private Bonanza in Kings Canyon National Park, CA, on May 25, 1953; crew bailed out

51-7175: 46th ARS / 38th ARS

51-7176: 47th ARS

51-7177: 304th ARRS

51-7178: 51st ARS / 55th ARS / 48th ARS; crashed in Greenland on June 20, 1953

51-7179: 54th ARS

51-7180: 48th ARS / 304th ARRS

51-7182: 41st ARS / 39th ARS

51-7183: 36th ARS

51-7184: 49th ARS

51-7185: 43rd ARS / 304th ARRS (camo)

51-7186: 41st ARS / 88th ARS

51-7187: 304th ARRS

51-7189: 48th ARS / 58th ARS / 301st ARRS

51-7191: 5th ARG

51-7194: 31st ARS

51-7195: 304th ARRS

51-7196: 28th ARS

51-7197: crashed on SAR at Jardín, Colombia, on January 18, 1955; three killed

51-7199: 41st ARS / 38th ARS / 37th ARRS / 305th ARRS (camo)

51-7200: 48th ARS / 302nd ARRS

51-7201: 38th ARS

51-7202: 58th ARS

51-7203: 39th ARS / 41st ARS

51-7204: 38th ARS

51-7205: 46th ARS / 39th ARS / 301st ARRS / 304th ARRS

51-7207: 48th ARS

51-7208: sank in Lake Fergusson, Greenland

51-7211: 1707th Flying Training Squadron (Amphib) / 41st ARS / 48th ARS

51-7217: 38th ARS / 304th ARRS (camo)

51-7218: 46th ARS / 66th ARS / 48th ARS

51-7219: 46th ARS / 48th ARS / 304th ARRS

51-7224: 33rd ARS; on SAR for F-100 pilot, damaged in open-sea landing; sank in East China Sea

51-7244: 5th ARG / 47th ARS / 304th ARRS / 302nd ARRS

51-7252: crashed in Libya on July 5, 1955

51-7253: 301st ARRS

Note: Two SA-16As (serial numbers unknown), along with a helicopter, were destroyed by fire in a USAF hangar at Goose Bay Air Base, Labrador, on October 14, 1954.

BOEING HC-97G "STRATO-RESCUER"

52-0916: 55th ARS / 303rd ARRS

52-2617: 76th ARS / 303rd ARRS

52-2618: 58th ARS

52-2651: 76th ARS

52-2665: 76th ARS

52-2713: 58th ARS / 305th ARRS / 33rd ARS

52-2714: 55th ARS / 303rd ARRS

52-2716: 58th ARS / 305th ARRS

52-2739: 58th ARS / 303rd ARRS

52-2754: 55th ARS / 305th ARRS

52-2773: 55th ARS; written off on June 29, 1964, due to accident

52-2782: 55th ARS / 305th ARRS

52-2783: 58th ARS

52-2791: 55th ARS / 303rd ARRS

52-2797: 76th ARS / 303rd ARRS

52-2806: 76th ARS

53-0115: 76th ARS / 303rd ARRS

53-0117: 58th ARS / 305th ARRS

53-0122: 76th ARS / 303rd ARRS

53-0126: 76th ARS / 36th ARRS

53-0131: 76th ARS / 303rd ARRS

53-0134: 58th ARS

53-0147: 76th ARS

53-0161: 76th ARS

53-0165: 55th ARS / 305th ARRS

53-0170: 55th ARS / 305th ARRS

53-0173: 55th ARS / 305th ARRS

53-0174: 58th ARS / 305th ARRS

Note: Of eight KC-97s used by Air Rescue for transition training, s/n 53-0216 and -0217 were not fully converted to HC-97G, having only their in-flight refueling equipment removed, and then designated C-97Gs.

SIKORSKY R-4

42-107237 (YR-4B): 10th Jungle Rescue Unit; crashed in Burma on July 26, 1945

43-28223 (YR-4B): 1st Air Command Group

43-28230: 1st Air Commando Group; crashed in India during test flight immediately following assembly

43-28247 (YR-4B)

43-46531: 2nd ARU(F)

43-46532: 2nd ERS

43-46546 (R-4B): 4th ARU (F) / 6th ERS

43-46549 (R-4B)

43-46571 (R-4B): 4th ARU (F) / 6th ERS

43-46573 (R-4B)

SIKORSKY/NASH-KELVINATOR R-6A

43-28240 (XR-6A): 8th ERS

43-45321 (YR-6A)

43-45322 (YR-6A): 8th ERS

43-45324 (YR-6A): 8th ERS

43-45328 (YR-6A): 8th ERS

43-45329 (YR-6A): 8th ERS

43-45330 (YR-6A): 8th ERS

43-45342: 5th ARU(F) / 2nd ERS

43-45343: 6th ARU(F), "Quick Match" / 2nd ERS

43-45345: 6th ARU(F) / 2nd ERS

43-45346: 7th ERS (spare for 8th ERS)

43-45347: 7th ERS (spare for 8th ERS)

43-45348: 2nd ERS

43-45349: 7th ERS (spare for 8th ERS)

43-45351: 3rd ERS Hawaii

43-45352: 2nd ERS

43-45353: 2nd ERS

43-45354: 3rd ERS

43-45355: 2nd ERS

43-45356: 2nd ERS

43-45357: 3rd ERS

43-45358: 7th ERS (spare for 8th ERS)

43-45359: 7th ERS (spare for 8th ERS)

43-45360: 7th ERS (spare for 8th ERS)

43-45361: 3rd ERS

43-45363: 3rd ERS

43-45364: 3rd ERS

43-45365: 3rd ERS

43-45369: 3rd ERS

43-45370: 4th ERS Guam / 2nd ERS

43-45372: 4th ERS / 6th ERS

43-45374: 4th ERS

43-45378: 6th ERS Okinawa

43-45381: 4th ERS

43-45387: 2nd ERS

43-45388: 6th ERS

43-45389: 4th ERS

43-45391: 6th ERS

43-45393: 4th ERS / 2nd ERS

43-45396: 4th ERS; crashed in Hawaii on October 7, 1948
43-45397: 6th ERS
43-45398: 2nd ERS / 6th ERS
43-45399: 4th ERS
43-45400: 6th ERS
43-45402: 6th ERS
43-45403: 6th ERS
43-45408: 2nd ERS
43-45409: 2nd ERS
43-45410: 2nd ERS
43-45412: 2nd ERS
43-45414: 2nd ERS

SIKORSKY R/H-5
43-28237 (XR-5)
43-46600 (YR-5A): 10th RS; written off in Alaska on May 20, 1950
43-46614 (YR-5A): 47th ARS
43-46616 (YR-5A): 10th RS / 60th ARS; crashed at Ladd AFB, AK, on July 8, 1951
43-46620 (YR-5A): 5th RS
43-46623 (YR-5A): 10th RS, Flt. D
43-46630 (YR-5A): 47th ABG; ditched at Grand Beach, VA, after engine failure on March 31, 1951
43-46631 (YR-5A)
43-46632 (YR-5A): 10th RS
43-46633 (YR-5A): 10th RS
43-46635 (YR-5A): 62nd AAFBU SAR, MacDill Field
43-46636 (YR-5A): 4th RS, Flt. A
43-46640 (R-5D)
43-46642 (R-5D)
43-46647 (H-5D): 47th ARS
43-46648 (H-5D): 3rd ARS; crashed in Okinawa on April 26, 1952
43-46649 (YR-5A)
43-46651 (YR-5A): written off at Connally AFB, TX, on February 16, 1951
47-480 (H-5F): 3rd ARS, Flt. F
47-481 (H-5F): crashed at Lakeland, FL, on December 21, 1949
47-482 (H-5F): 3rd ARS; crashed at MASH in Korea on August 20, 1951
47-484 (H-5F)
47-485 (H-5F): crashed at Connally AFB, TX, on February 17, 1950
47-486 (H-5F): 3rd ARS, Flt. F; destroyed in crash landing in Korea on November 30, 1950
47-487 (H-5F): 10th ARS, Det B; crashed in Alaska on July 25, 1950
47-488 (H-5F): 10th ARS
47-489 (H-5F): 10th ARS
47-490 (H-5F): 10th ARS / 74th ARS
47-786 (H-5F): 3rd ARS
48-524 (H-5G): 6th ARS, Flt. A; written off following crash at Westover AFB on February 25, 1950

48-525 (H-5G): crashed in Washington on October 5, 1948
48-526 (H-5G): 8063rd MASH, Korea / 4th ARS, Flt. A; written off at Hamilton AFB, CA, on May 27, 1950
48-527 (H-5G): crashed in Canada on November 24, 1948
48-528 (H-5G)
48-529 (H-5G): 3rd ARS, Flt. F / 2157th ARS; operational loss in Korea on May 12, 1953
48-530 (H-5G): 3rd ARS, Flt. F
48-531 (H-5G)
48-532 (H-5G)
48-533 (H-5G): crashed in British Guiana on November 5, 1948
48-536 (H-5G)
48-537 (H-5G)
48-538 (H-5G): 3rd ARS, Det 1; crashed in Korea on March 25, 1952
48-540 (H-5G): 3rd ARS, Flt. F
48-541 (H-5G): 3rd ARS
48-542 (H-5G): 3rd ARS; crashed in Korea on March 17, 1952
48-543 (H-5G): 6519th ARU
48-544 (H-5G)
48-545 (H-5G): 3rd ARS; crashed in Korea on March 9, 1951
48-548 (H-5G): 3rd ARS; crashed on takeoff in Korea on June 25, 1952
48-549 (H-5G): 3rd ARS
48-550 (H-5G)
48-551 (H-5G): 10th ARS, Flt. D; crashed en route to C-47 crash site in Alaska on September 8, 1951; two killed
48-552 (H-5G): 10th ARG; destroyed on takeoff near Palmer, AK, on August 27, 1951
48-553 (H-5G): 52nd ARS
48-554 (H-5G): 51st ARS; crashed at Narsarssauk AB on March 3, 1954
48-555: shot down in Korea when attempting rescue of T-6 crew; first combat loss of 3rd ARS personnel; pilot and medic KIA
48-556 (H-5G): 3rd ARS; shot down in Korea on October 25, 1951; destroyed by allied airstrike
48-557 (H-5G): 5th ARS, Flt. B; written off following crash at Walker AFB, TX, on May 27, 1950
48-558 (H-5G): 3rd ARS; written off after damage on takeoff on September 8, 1951
48-559 (H-5G): 3rd ARS; crashed into sea off Korea on November 21, 1951
48-560 (H-5G): written off after damage on takeoff in Korea on April 25, 1951
48-561 (H-5G)
48-562 (H-5G): 5th ARS; written off following crash at Hartsville, SC, on April 26, 1950
49-1996 H-5H)
49-1997 (H-5H): 3rd ARS, Flt. F; crashed due to power loss on August 22, 1950
49-1998 (H-5H)
49-1999 (H-5H)
49-2000 (H-5H): 2nd ARS / 3rd ARS; shot down in Korea on June 25, 1952; two crewmen and rescued, USN pilot POW

49-2001 (H-5H): 7th ARS, Flt. D (float-equipped)
49-2002 (H-5H)
49-2003 (H-5H): 54th ARS
49-2004 (H-5H): 3rd ARS, Flt. F; written off in Korea following takeoff accident on November 29, 1951
49-2005 (H-5H): 3rd ARS, Flt. C
49-2006 (H-5H): 3rd ARS, Flt. F; destroyed on ground in Korea by USN after fuel exhaustion on ferry flight on August 4, 1950
49-2007 (H-5H)
49-2008 (H-5H)
49-2009: 3rd ARS, Flt. F; crashed into mountain in bad weather after rescuing F4U pilot in North Korea on November 28, 1950; three killed
49-2010 (H-5H): 10th ARS; written off at Ladd AFB, AK, on May 28, 1950
49-2011 (H-5H): 3rd ARS; written off following damage during landing in Korea on March 9, 1951

SIKORSKY H-19

49-2014 (YH-19): 3rd ARS
49-2016 (YH-19): 3rd ARS; crashed due to engine failure in Korea on May 2, 1952

H-19A

51-3846: "RUDOLPH," WADC
51-3847
51-3849: 46th ARS
51-3850: 57th ARS
51-3851
51-3852: 3rd ARS; crashed into water and lost off Korea on July 31, 1952
51-3853: 3rd ARS, Det 1 / 36th ARS / 33rd ARS / 3rd ARS
51-3854: 3rd ARS
51-3856: 55th ARS
51-3858: 3rd ARS; written off due to battle damage in Korea on May 1, 1952
51-3860: 49th ARS
51-3862: 55th ARS / 49th ARS
51-3863: 47th ARS
51-3867: float-equipped
51-3868
51-3870
51-3871: 36th ARS / 2157th RS
51-3873: 2157th RS
51-3875: 47th ARS
51-3876: crashed at San Marcos, TX, on August 20, 1952; two killed
51-3878: 36th ARS / 69th ARS
51-3879
51-3883: 3rd ARS
51-3884: 2157th RS
51-3886: 2157th RS
51-3888

51-3890: "WHIRL O WAY" / 9th ARS
51-3893: "HOP A LONG" / 66th ARS
51-3894: 68th ARS / 53rd ARS
51-3895

SH/HH-19B

51-3908
51-3915
51-3917
51-3920
51-3922: crashed at Sheppard AFB
51-3935
51-3942
51-3950
51-3952
51-3955
51-3964: 5th ARG
52-7480: 58th ARS / 36th ARS; film *Flight from Ashiya* / 38th ARS
52-7481: 2157th RS
52-7483: 2157th RS
52-7484: 38th ARS
52-7485: 38th ARS
52-7486: 38th ARS
52-7487: 39th ARS
52-7488: 36th ARS
52-7489: 10th ERS
52-7493: 84th ARS
52-7494: 36th ARS / 917th FTD
52-7495: 36th ARS
52-7496
52-7497: 2157th RS / 38th ARS
52-7498: 58th ARS
52-7499: 54th ARS
52-7504: transferred to USN as BuNo 150193 in July 1961
52-7505: 58th ARS / 917th FTD
52-7507
52-7511: 83rd ARS / 84th ARS
52-7513
52-7514: 33rd ARS
52-7515
52-7516
52-7517: 33rd ARS
52-7518: 46th ARS
52-7519: 5th ARG
52-7521: Tropical Survival School, Panama
52-7523
52-7525: 46th ARS
52-7526: film *Battle Taxi*
52-7527: 55th ARS
52-7528: 55th ARS; lost in Greenland on November 7, 1955
52-7529: 51st ARS / 67th ARS
52-7532
52-7535: 47th ARS

52-7536: 5th ARG

52-7537

52-7538: transferred to USN as BuNo 150194 in July 1961

52-7539: 41st ARS

52-7540: 5th ARG

52-7551: 55th ARS

52-7552: 52nd ARS

52-7553: 51st ARS / 67th ARS

52-7554: 54th ARS / 7th AF / 81st ARS / Jungle Survival School, Philippines

52-7555: 52nd ARS

52-7556: 41st ARS

52-7605 (SH-19D): 7th RS

53-4415: 74th ARS

53-4454: 917th FTD; crashed at Tan Son Nhut AB, South Vietnam, on June 16, 1964

53-4455

53-4458

53-4462: 36th ARS; film *Flight from Ashiya*

53-4463: 2157th RS / 917th FTD

53-4464: 2157th RS

57-5937 (HH-19D)

PIASECKI H-21

50-1236 (YH-21): 55th ARS

50-1238 (YH-21)

50-1239 (YH-21)

50-1240 (YH-21): 55th ARS; crashed at Thule AB on November 17, 1953; four killed

50-1244 (YH-21)

50-1246 (YH-21)

50-1247 (YH-21): 55th ARS

50-1248 (YH-21): 54th ARS

51-15260 (SH-21A)

SH-21B

51-15854

51-15855

51-15859

52-8666: 58th ARS

53-4341: CARRC, Det 15

53-4343

53-4354: 54th ARS

53-4357: 54th ARS

53-4359

53-4362: 71st ARS

53-4363

53-4366

53-4372

53-4379: crashed-destroyed during SAR in mountains northwest of Denver in July 1961

BELL H-1 "HUEY"

UH-1F

63-13141: 43rd ARRS

63-13142: 37th ARRS

63-13147: 37th ARRS

63-13148: 37th ARRS

63-13153: 40th ARRW, Det 5 / 43rd ARRS

65-7911: 37th ARRS, Det 5

65-7914: 37th ARRS, Det 9

65-7915: 37th ARRS, Det 5 / Det 9

65-7916: 37th ARRS

65-7918: 37th ARRS, Det 5

65-7922: 37th ARRS / GUH-1F ground trainer

65-7933: 37th ARRS

65-7946: 37th ARRS, Det 3

65-7951: 37th ARRS

65-7953: 37th ARRS

65-7954: 37th ARRS

65-7959: 37th ARRS, Det 2

65-7965: 37th ARRS, Det 10

66-1214: 37th ARRS, Det 2

66-1215: 37th ARRS, Det 7

66-1219: 37th ARRS

66-1223: 37th ARRS, Det 10

66-1224: 37th ARRS, Det 5

TH-1F

66-1227: 37th ARRS, Det 5

66-1228: 1550th ATTW

66-1230: 37th ARRS, Det 2

66-1232: 37th ARRS, Det 5

66-1237: 37th ARRS

66-1238: 37th ARRS

66-1243: 37th ARRS

66-1246: 37th ARRS, Det 5

HH-1H

70-2457: 37th ARRS, Det 1

70-2458: 37th ARRS, Det 1 / Det 3

70-2459

70-2460: 37th ARRS, Det 4

70-2461: 304th ARRS / 37th ARRS, Det 3; crashed-destroyed at Grand Forks AFB on October 25, 1991; four killed

70-2462: 37th ARRS, Det 3 / 304th ARRS

70-2463: 37th ARRS, Det 3 / 79th RQF

70-2464

70-2465: 37th ARRS, Det 3

70-2466: 37th ARRS, Det 7 / 304th ARRS / 54th RQF

70-2467: 37th ARRS, Det 6

70-2468: 304th ARRS

70-2469 37th ARRS, Det 3 and Det 6 / 301st ARRS / 304th ARRS

70-2470: 1550th ATTW / 37th ARRS, Det 4

70-2471: 37th ARRS, Det 1 / Det 3

70-2472: 37th ARRS, Det 1
70-2473: 37th ARRS, Det 6
70-2474: 37th ARRS, Det 6
70-2475: 37th ARRS, Det 6
70-2476: 37th ARRS, Det 7 / 304th ARRS
70-2477: 304th ARRS / 37th ARRS, Det 7
70-2478: 304th ARRS
70-2479: 304th ARRS
70-2480: 304th ARRS
70-2481: 304th ARRS
70-2482: 304th ARRS
70-2483: 37th ARRS, Det 7 / 301st ARRS
70-2484: 37th ARRS, Det 4
70-2485: 37th ARRS, Det 4
70-2486: 37th ARRS, Det 7 / 301st ARRS

UH-1N

68-10773 48th ARRS / 512th RQS; crashed at Kirtland AFB on January 31, 1996
68-10775: 41st RWRW, Det 18
69-6600: 40th ARRS, Det 5
69-6601: 37th RQF
69-6602: 37th RQF
69-6606: 67th ARRS, Det 2
69-6607: 67th ARRS, Det 2
69-6608: 67th ARRS, Det 2
69-6609: 67th ARRS, Det 2
69-6611: 67th ARRS
69-6612: 37th ARRS, Det 8 / 304th ARRS / 512th RQS
69-6613: 36th RQF
69-6615: 40th ARRS, Det 6
69-6616: 37th ARRS, Det 11
69-6618: 40th ARRS, Det 4
69-6619: 40th ARRS, Det 6 / 67th ARRS, Det 9 / 54th Hel. Flt.
69-6620: 40th ARRS, Det 4
69-6622: 40th ARRS / 304th ARRS
69-6623: 40th ARRS, Det 4
69-6625: 40th ARRS, Det 5 / 44th ARRS
69-6627: 304th ARRS
69-6628: 40th ARRS, Det 5
69-6629: 40th ARRS, Det 6
69-6630: 67th ARRS, Det 9
69-6632: 304th ARRS
69-6638: 37th ARRS, Det 8
69-6640: 40th ARRS, Det 24 / 37th RQF
69-6641: 40th ARRS, Det 2 / 37th ARRS
69-6642: 512th RQS
69-6646: 40th ARRS, Det 24 / 37th ARRS
69-6648: 40th ARRS, Det 24 / 37th ARRS / 36th RQF
69-6652: 37th ARRS, Det 8
69-6660: 40th ARRS, Det 4
69-6663: 38th ARRS, Det 1 / 40th ARRS
69-6664: 1550th ATTW
69-6665: 1550th ATTW

69-6666: 1550th ATTW
69-6670: 304th ARRS
69-7536: 38th ARRS, Det 1 / 40th ARRS, Det 1
69-7537: 38th ARRS, Det 1

SIKORSKY HH-34J
143855: 304th ARRS
143865: 302nd ARRS
143885: 304th ARRS
143936: 304th ARRS
145678: 304th ARRS / 302nd ARRS
145693: 301st ARRS
145707: 301st ARRS
145710: 301st ARRS / 304th ARRS
147999: 301st ARRS
148008: 304th ARRS
148011: 302nd ARRS
148013: 304th ARRS
148014: 304th ARRS / 302nd ARRS
148019: 302nd ARRS
148021: 301st ARRS
148023: 302nd ARRS / 301st ARRS
148025: 304th ARRS / 302nd ARRS
148027: 304th ARRS
148028: 301st ARRS
148029: 301st ARRS
148934: 304th ARRS
148936: 302nd ARRS / 304th ARRS
148938: 302nd ARRS
148941: 301st ARRS
148942: 304th ARRS / 302nd ARRS
148943: 304th ARRS; from storage to 302nd ARRS for work as Hill AFB display
148944: 301st ARRS
148948: 302nd ARRS / 304th ARRS
148953: 302nd ARRS
148954: 304th ARRS
148957: 302nd ARRS
148958: 304th ARRS
148963: 301st ARRS / 304th ARRS

SIKORSKY H-3 "JOLLY GREEN GIANT"

CH/HH-3C
63-9676: TDY with 63-9685 to 38th ARS, Det 1 NKP, June 1965 / 38th ARS Udorn RTAFB, December 1965
63-9682: 58th ARS
63-9683: first CH-3C in ARS, Det Prov., 1st ARS HQ, Tyndall AFB / EARRC, Det 15 Patrick AFB, first rescue July 8, 1964 / 33rd ARS, Det 15 / 44th ARRS / 39th ARRS, Det 5 / 38th ARRS Osan AB
63-9685: 38th ARS, Det 1 NKP; shot down (some sources state by MiG-17) on November 6, 1965, over North Vietnam on SAR for A-1E "Sandy 1-4"; three crew POW; first Jolly Green loss

63-9686: 41st ARRS / 55th ARRS / 38th ARRS

63-9687: 38th ARRS / 33rd ARRS

63-9688: EARRC, Patrick AFB Gemini program, 39th ARRW / 44th ARRS; written off at Tyndall AFB, 1977

63-9690: 71st ARRS, 1980s

64-14223: 44th ARRS, Det 5 / 39th ARRW, Det 5 / 305th ARRS

64-14224: EARRC, Det 15 / 39th ARRW / 44th ARRS

64-14225: EARRC / 44th ARRS / 33rd ARRS, Det 13 / 38th ARRS / Det 15 / EARRC; used in 1969 film *Marooned*

64-14226: 39th ARRW, Det 5 / 301st ARRS

64-14227: first HH-3E conversion, 38th ARRS, Udorn RTAFB; damaged during crash landing on September 1, 1966, then destroyed when dropped from recovery CH-47 on September 6

64-14228: 71st ARRS / 305th ARRS

64-14229: 38th ARRS / 40th ARRS / 37th ARRS

64-14230: 38th ARRS / 39th ARRW / 44th ARRS / 304th ARRS / 305th ARRS / 301st ARRS

64-14231: 38th ARRS, Det 5; destroyed in crash landing on night mission in North Vietnam on November 29, 1966

64-14232: 38th ARRS / 37th ARRS / 40th ARRS, Det 1 / 44th ARRS / 39th ARRW / 129th ARRS

64-14233: 37th ARRS, "Jolly 2-0"; crashed into mountain in bad weather in North Vietnam on SAR for EB-66C "Preview 0-1" on January 15, 1968

65-5690: 129th ARRS

65-5693: 33rd ARRS / 31st ARRS

65-5698: 305th ARRS / 71st ARRS

65-5699: 39th ARRS, Det 15 / 41st ARRS

65-5700: 301st ARRS / 305th ARRS

CH/HH-3E

65-12777: 48th ARRS / 33rd ARRS / 129th ARRS / 41st ARRS

65-12778: 38th ARRS, "Jolly 0-2"; shot down in Laos on SAR for F-4C crew, made emergency landing and destroyed by friendly artillery on October 20, 1966

65-12779: 38th ARRS, "Jolly 0-5"; shot down in North Vietnam on February 6, 1967, on SAR for O-1F "Nail 6-5"; three crew KIA, FAC pilot rescued by PJ Hackney but KIA

65-12780: 37th ARRS / 39th ARRW / 129th ARRS / 304th ARRS

65-12781: 40th ARRS / 37th ARRS / 31st ARRS / 39th ARRW / 129th ARRS; written off on January 9, 1988

65-12782: 37th ARRS, "Jolly 1-0"; shot down in Laos on October 5, 1968, attempting extraction of SF team; two crew KIA

65-12783: 37th ARRS / 41st ARRW / 102nd ARRS / 304th ARRS / 301st ARRS

65-12784: 37th ARRS / 33rd ARRS / 41st ARRW / 102nd ARRS / 304th ARRS

65-12785: 40th ARRS / 37th ARRS / with 40th ARRS as "Banana One"; intentionally crashed into Son Tay prison compound with fourteen-man assault force on November 21, 1970

65-12786: 37th ARRS, Jolly 2-4"; sank in sea after water landing off North Vietnam following ground fire on October 16, 1968

65-12787: 40th ARRS / 39th ARRW / 305th ARRS / 304th ARRS

65-12794: 55th ARRS, Det 12 and Det 15 / 39th ARRS, Det 5; written off after flying accident, 1984

65-12797: 39th ARRS, Det 11 / 41st ARRW, Det 15

65-12798: 39th ARRW / 31st ARRS / 33rd ARRS

65-12799: 39th ARRW / 33rd ARRS, Det 1

65-12800: 304th ARRS / 39th ARRW

66-13278: 37th ARRS; destroyed when dropped by recovery CH-54 into Da Nang Harbor on April 14, 1969

66-13279: 37th ARRS, "Jolly 2-6"; while attempting takeoff with rescued SOG team in Laos on November 9, 1967, hit by RPG, engine exploded, aircraft burned and rolled down hillside; three crew KIA, pilot Capt. Gerald Young WIA, MOH

66-13280: after record-breaking New York-to-Paris flight in 1967, ferried with 66-13281 to Rhein-main AB, Germany, for C-133 transport to Da Nang AB; assigned to 37th ARRS as "Jolly 2-7"; crashed and burned from ground fire while landing in South Vietnam on April 15, 1970; two killed

66-13281: 48th ARRS; record-breaking flight New York to Paris with 66-13280 / 37th ARRS; as "Jolly 2-8," shot down in Laos during SAR for F-100 "Misty 1-1"; destroyed by allied aircraft on October 24, 1969

66-13282: 37th ARRS, "Jolly 2-9"; while on water off Tiger Island, North Vietnam, after rescuing crew of F-4D "Dover 0-1," hit by mortar round, severing tail boom; taken in tow by naval craft but sank in heavy seas on October 20, 1968

66-13283: 37th ARRS, "Jolly 3-0"; hit in engine by gunfire while hovering during SAR in Laos on October 27, 1967; destroyed by friendly forces

66-13284: 48th ARRS / 39th ARRW / 44th ARRS / 129th ARRS / 304th ARRS

66-13285: 39th ARRW / 67th ARRS, Det 14

66-13286: 48th ARRS / 31st ARRS

66-13289: 37th ARRS / 31st ARRS; landed in South China Sea after pickup from freighter, had mechanical trouble and sank

66-13290: 37th ARRS / 31st ARRS / 55th ARRS / 38th ARRS

66-13292: tested TAT-102 minigun turret in 1967; after 21st SOS, converted to HH-3E, 302nd ARRS / 304th ARRS

66-13296: 301st ARRS

67-14703: converted to HH-3E, 301st ARRS / 302nd ARRS; only H-3 to serve in Southeast Asia and Desert Storm

67-14704: converted to HH-3E, 37th ARRS / 41st ARRW, Det 13 / 38th ARRS, Det 13 / 33rd ARRS

67-14705: converted to HH-3E, 55th ARRS / 39th ARRW, Det 15 / 33rd ARRS

67-14706: converted to HH-3E, 37th ARRS / 40th ARRS / 31st ARRS / 3rd ARRG, Det 14 / 38th ARRS

67-14707: 304th ARRS; written off in March 1973

67-14708: converted to HH-3E, 37th ARRS / 41st ARRW, Det 13; converted to ground trainer after flying accident in 1973

67-14709: converted to HH-3E, 37th ARRS / 41st ARRW / 38th ARRS, Det 13 / 31st ARRS

67-14710: converted to HH-3E, 37th ARRS / 40th ARRS / 37th ARRS, "Jolly 2-3"; shot down while hovering during rescue attempt of USMC A-4E "Hellborne 2-1-5" in South Vietnam on June 9, 1968; USCG exchange pilot Lt. j.g. Jack Rittichier and crew of three KIA

67-14711: converted to HH-3E, 48th ARRS / 38th ARRS, Det 11 / 39th ARRW, Det 15 / 41st ARRS

67-14712: converted to HH-3E, 37th ARRS / 40th ARRS / 44th ARRS / 33rd ARRS

67-14713: converted to HH-3E, 48th ARRS / 41st ARRS

67-14714: converted to HH-3E, 58th ARRS / 48th ARRS / 39th ARRW / 44th ARRS / 41st ARRS, Det 15

67-14715: converted to HH-3E, 58th ARRS / 67th ARRS, Det 12 / 40th ARRW, Det 14

67-14716: 58th ARRS / 67th ARRS / 40th ARRW, Det 14; written off in December 1979

67-14717: 58th ARRS / 67th ARRS / 40th ARRW, Det 14 / 33rd ARRS

67-14718: converted to HH-3E, 305th ARRS; only Southeast Asia–based HH-3E modified with fixed landing gear (while assigned to 21st SOS in 1969); reverted to CH-3E 302nd ARRS / 71st SOS, 1970s

67-14719: converted to HH-3E, 55th ARRS / 33rd ARRS; crashed into sea off Okinawa during night hoist training on March 14, 1989; crew of three killed; wreckage recovered on April 12

67-14720: 305th ARRS

67-14722: 37th ARRS / 31st ARRS / 41st ARRW, Det 1 / 33rd ARRS / 38th ARRS

67-14723: 31st ARRS

67-14724: 31st ARRS / 41st ARRW, Det 1

67-14725: 37th ARRS / 41st ARRW / 33rd ARRS / 129th ARRS

68-8282: 33rd ARRS / 41st ARRW, Det 13 / 38th ARRS, Det 13; crashed in 1987

69-5798: 39th ARRW, Det 4 / 102nd ARRS / 41st ARRS; one of last two USAF H-3s retired, August 1994

69-5799: 39th ARRW, Det 4 / 102nd ARRS

69-5800: 5040th HS / 71st ARRS / 102nd ARRS, "Jolly 8-5"; crashed-destroyed on June 13, 1978, killing all aboard, including three PJs

69-5801: 5040th HS / 71st ARRS / 38th ARRS / 39th ARRW, Det 11 / 56th ARRS

69-5802: 5040th HS / 71st ARRS / 41st ARRS

69-5803: 5040th HS / 71st ARRS / 41st ARRS

69-5804: 5040th HS / 71st ARRS / 305th ARRS

69-5805: 5040th HS / 71st ARRS / 102nd ARRS / 305th ARRS

69-5806: 5040th HS / 71st ARRS, "CHRISTINE"

69-5807: 71st ARRS; written off in December 1974 in Alaska, following crash on rescue mission; pilot killed

69-5808: 5040th HS / 71st ARRS, one of two Alaska-based modified with fixed landing gear / 305th ARRS

69-5809: 5040th HS / 71st ARRS / 33rd ARRS

69-5810: 5040th HS / 71st ARRS / 33rd ARRS / 31st ARRS

69-5811: 5040th HS, one of two Alaska-based modified with fixed landing gear / 71st ARRS / 33rd ARRS / 55th ARRS / 41st ARRS, Det 15; one of last two USAF H-3s retired, August 1994

SIKORSKY H-53 "SUPER JOLLY GREEN GIANT"

HH-53B

66-14428: 37th ARRS, Det 1 / 40th ARRS / 1550th ATTW

66-14429: 37th ARRS, Det 1 / 40th ARRS / 1550th ATTW

66-14430: 40th ARRS, "Jolly 6-7"; shot down in Laos on January 18, 1969, on SAR for F-4D "Stormy" FAC and "Sandy 0-2"; destroyed by friendly forces

66-14431: 37th ARRS / 40th ARRS / 1550th ATTW; crashed on July 18, 1980

66-14432: 40th ARRS / 41st ARRS

66-14433: 37th ARRS, Det 2 / 40th ARRS, LNRS modification December 1969 / prototype YHH-53H-PAVE LOW II, "Black Knight," September 1975

66-14434: 37th ARRS, Det 2, "Big Bertha" / 40th ARRS, "Jolly 7-1'" shot down by MiG-21 on January 28, 1970, on SAR for F-105 "Seabird 0-2"; crew of six KIA

66-14435: 37th ARRS / 1550th ATTW; operational loss at Kirtland AFB on September 23, 1981

HH-53C

67-14993: 6514th Test Squadron MARS

67-14994: 1550th ATTW / 40th ARRS; first MH-53J

67-14995: 55th ARRS / 40th ARRS

67-14996: 55th ARRS; crashed into Gulf of Mexico during aerial refuel in October 1969; all aboard killed

68-8283: 40th ARRS, "Jolly 5-4"; shot down in Laos on June 30, 1970, on SAR for OV-10A "Nail 4-4"; five KIA

68-8284: 40th ARRS / 37th ARRS / 67th ARRS / 55th ARRS / 39th ARRS

68-8285: 37th ARRS / 40th ARRS, Son Tay Raid, "Apple 4"; shot down in Laos on July 21, 1971, on drone recovery; destroyed by friendly forces

68-8286: 40th ARRS; Son Tay Raid, "Apple 3"

68-10354: 6514th Test Squadron MARS; crashed-destroyed on October 30, 1986, during site survey at Swasey Peak, UT

68-10355: 40th ARRS / 6594th Test Group, "Arris 0-1"; crashed onto ship *Asian Beauty* 540 miles off Hawaii on January 15, 1985, while hovering to rescue crewman, main rotor separated; crew of seven killed

68-10356: 440th ARRS / 6594th Test Group

68-10357: 37th ARRS / 41st ARRS / 40th ARRS, Son Tay Raid, "Apple 1" / 6594th Test Group

68-10358: 33rd ARRS / 37th ARRS / 41st ARRS / 40th ARRS

68-10359: 37th ARRS / 40th ARRS, Son Tay Raid, "Apple 5" / as "Jolly 6-1," crashed-destroyed in Cambodia on March 27, 1972; crew of five killed

68-10360: 6594th Test Group / 37th ARRS / 40th ARRS / 67th ARRS

68-10361: 40th ARRS, Son Tay Raid, "Apple 2" / 37th ARRS; destroyed in rocket attack at Da Nang AB on August 18, 1972

68-10362: 37th ARRS / 40th ARRS, "Jolly 6-4"; lost tail rotor and crashed in Cambodia on June 14, 1973; three killed

68-10363: 1550th ATTW / 33rd ARRS / 37th ARRS

68-10364: 37th ARRS / 40th ARRS, "Jolly 1-1"; assault on Koh Tang Island, May 1975

68-10365: 37th ARRS / 40th ARRS, Det Bien Hoa AB, as "Jolly 6-7"; shot down in South Vietnam on April 6, 1972, on SAR for EB-66C, "Bat 2-1"; 5 KIA

68-10366: 37th ARRS, "Jolly 7-0"; shot down in South Vietnam on November 25, 1971; four KIA

68-10367

68-10368: 67th ARRS; crashed-destroyed near Stuttgart AAF, Germany, on June 24, 1977; salvaged as cockpit trainer at Kirtland AFB

68-10369: 37th ARRS, Bien Hoa Det

68-10925: 40th ARRS

69 5784: 37th ARRS / 67th ARRS

69 5785: 37th ARRS / 40th ARRS, "Jolly 4-2"; assault on Koh Tang Island, May 1975

69-5786: 40th ARRS, "Jolly 4-4"; assault on Koh Tang Island, May 1975 / 1550th CCTW; crashed-destroyed July 18, 1980, at Dugway Proving Grounds; one killed

69-5787: 37th ARRS / 40th ARRS / 33rd ARRS; crashed into Pacific during aerial refueling on February 26, 1979; three killed

69-5788: 37th ARRS / 40th ARRS, "Jolly 7-3"; damage from ground fire on December 27, 1972, on SAR for F-111A "Jackal 3-3" prevented aerial refueling; abandoned Laos and destroyed by A-7D "Sandys"

69-5789: 40th ARRS

69-5790: 40th ARRS; converted to HH-53H

69-5791: 40th ARRS / first converted to HH-53H-PAVE LOW III on March 13, 1979, rollout, 1550th ATTW

69-5792: 40th ARRS, "Jolly 4-3"; assault on Koh Tang Island, May 1975 / 1550th ATTW CCTW; operational loss on July 27, 1982, at Kirtland AFB following aerial refuel; four killed

69-5793: 41st ARRS / 40th ARRS, "Jolly 1-2"; assault on Koh Tang Island, May 1975

69-5794: "Jolly 1-3" assault on Koh Tang Island, May 1975

69-5795: "Jolly 4-1" assault on Koh Tang Island, May 1975; last flight from NKP on September 21, 1975

69-5796: 67th ARRS

69-5797: 1550th ATTW / 44th ARRS / 67th ARRS

70-1629: 67th ARRS; converted from CH-3C to replace HH-53H

HH-53H PAVE LOW III

73-1647: 67th ARRS

73-1648: 67th ARRS

73-1649: 55th ARRS

73-1650: 55th ARRS

73-1651: 55th ARRS

73-1652: 55th ARRS

TH-53A

63-13694

66-14468

66-14469

66-14470

66-14471

66-14472

66-14473

67-30043

67-30046

Note: One GCH-53A ground instructional airframe was at Sheppard AFB.

SIKORSKY HH/MH-60G "PAVE HAWK"

81-23643 (converted from UH-60A): 512th RQS

81-23644 (converted from UH-60A): 38th ARRS

81-23645 (converted from UH-60A): 55th RS / 38th RS

81-23646 (converted from UH-60A)

81-23647 (converted from UH-60A)

82-23671 (converted from UH-60A)

82-23680 (converted from UH-60A): 38th RS

82-23689 (converted from UH-60A): 55th RQS

82-23708 (converted from UH-60A)

82-23718 (HH-60D)

82-23728 (converted from UH-60A): 38th RS / 512th RQS, "Ghost 6-9"; crashed-destroyed in New Mexico on May 11, 2005; FE killed

87-26006: 66th RS / 332nd ERQS, "Jolly 1-2"

87-26007: 66th RS

87-26008: 66th RS

87-26009: 66th RS / Weapons Squadron

87-26010: 55th RQS

87-26011: 55th RS, "SAND DEVIL"

87-26012: 66th RS / 55th RQS

87-26013: 55th RS

87-26014: 66th RS; crashed in Afghanistan on October 20, 2004, on medevac; one crewman killed

88-26105: 66th RS; collided with 91-26359 at night on Nellis range on September 4, 1998

88-26106: 129th RQS

88-26107: 129th RQS

88-26108 (MH-60G): 102nd RQS (101st RQS)

88-26109: 56th RS; crashed in Great Britain on January 7, 2014; crew of four killed

88-26110: 102nd RQS, "Jolly 1-1-0"; ditched 250 miles out to sea in "Perfect Storm," unable to air-refuel on October 30, 1991; PJ lost

88-26111: 102nd RQS (101st RQS)

88-26112: 102nd RQS (101st RQS)

88-26113: 102nd RQS (101st RQS)

88-26114: 101st RQS

88-26115: 129th RQS

88-26116: 129th RQS/1st SOW; crashed into Great Salt Lake, UT, on October 29, 1992; twelve killed

88-26117
88-26118: 129th RQS
88-26119: 129th RQS
88-26120: 129th RQS
88-26195: 55th RS / 304th ARRS
88-26196: 55th RS
88-26197: 55th RS / 38th RQS
88-26198: 55th RS / 304th ARRS
88-26199: 55th RS / 304th ARRS
89-26200: 55th RS / 38th RQS
89-26201: 55th RS / 939th RWg, 304th ARRS; named "SNOWBALL" after crash on Mt. Hood to rescue three injured climbers on May 30, 2002
89-26202
89-26203
89-26204: 55th RQS
89-26205
89-26206: 48th RQS
89-26207: 33rd RQS
89-26208
89-26209: 33rd RQS
89-26210: 33rd RQS
89-26211: 33rd RQS
89-26212: 56th ERQS / 101st RQS
90- 26222
90-26223
90-26224: 305th ARRS / 301sr RQS
90-26225: 305th ARRS
90-26226: 305th ARRS / 304th ARRS
90-26227: 301st RQS / 305th RQS
90-26228: 305th ARRS
90-26229: 943rd RGp
90-26230: 301st RQS
90-26231: 301st RQS
90-26232: 301st ARRS
90-26233
90-26234
90-26235
90-26236: 301st RQS
90-26237
90-26238: 301st RQS
90-26239
90-26250
90-26309
90-26310: 66th RS
90-26311: 66th RS
90-26312
91-26352: 66th RS
91-26353: 66th RS
91-26354: 33rd RQS; crashed near Okinawa's Camp Hanson on August 5, 2013; FE killed
91-26355: 210th RQS; written off in September 1993
91-26356: 41st RS
91-26357: 66th RS

91-26358
91-26359: 66th RS; collided with 88-26105 at night on Nellis range on September 4, 1998
91-26401: 33rd RQS / 33rd ERQS
91-26402: 33rd RQS
91-26403: 33rd RQS
91-26404: 33rd RQS; crashed in Korea on October 6, 1994; four killed
91-26405: 33rd RQS
91-26406: 33rd RQS
91-26407: 66th RS
92-26460
92-26461: 66th RS / 33rd RQS
92-26462
92-26463: 66th RS
92-26464
92-26564
92-26466
92-26467
92-26468: 102nd RQS
92-26469
92-26470
92-26471
92-26472
93-26466
97-26772
97-26773
97-26774
97-26775: 66th RS
97-26776: 41st RQS, "Jolly 8-3"; crashed in Florida on October 14, 2001
97-26777
97-26778: 41st RQS, "KOMODO 1-1"; crashed in Afghanistan on March 23, 2004
97-26779: 41st RQS / 41st ERQS

LOCKHEED HC-130 "HERCULES"
62-1863: 23rd Wing; only C-130E converted to HC-130P (other planned conversions canceled)

HC-130H
64-14852: rollout at Lockheed's Marietta, GA, plant on December 8, 1964, configured as first Skyhook; 57th ARRS / 305th ARRS / 301st ARRS / 71st RQS, converted to HC-130P
64-14853: 76th ARRS / 305th ARRS / 71st RQS, converted to HC-130P
64-14854: converted to HC-130P, 1551st FTS, "THE BASTARD"
64-14855: JHC-130H Fulton System test / 67th ARRS / 76th ARRS / 57th ARRS / 48th ARRS / 303rd ARRS / 304th ARRS / 39th RQS
64-14856: 48th ARRS / 55th ARRS / 305th ARRS / 303rd ARRS / 304th ARRS; crashed into sea off California on November 22, 1996; ten killed
64-14857: training aircraft

64-13858: 33rd ARRS

64-14859: 76th ARRS / 305th ARRS / 71st RQS

64-14860: 48th ARRS / 58th ARRS / 303rd ARRS / 304th ARRS / 79th RQS

64-14861: 48th ARRS / 57th ARRS

64-14862: 48th ARRS / 57th ARRS / 303rd ARRS

64-14863: 48th ARRS / 305th ARRS / 301st ARRS / 71st RQS

64-14864: 57th ARRS / 67th ARRS / 303rd ARRS / 304th ARRS / 39th RQS

64-14865: 54th ARRS / 305th ARRS / 303rd ARRS / 304th ARRS / 71st RQS / 39th RQS / 79th RQS

64-14866: 57th ARRS / 55th ARRS

65-0962: 67th ARRS

65-0963: 36th ARRS

65-0964: 67th ARRS / 304th ARRS / 301st ARRS / 39th RQS / 79th RQS

65-0965: 36th ARRS / 48th ARRS / 79th ARRS

65-0966: 54th ARRS / 41st ARRS / 76th ARRS

65-0967: 6th ARRS / 76th ARRS

65-0968: 54th ARRS / 55th ARRS / 76th ARRS

65-0969: 36th ARRS / 76th ARRS / 48th ARRS / 31st ARRS

65-0970: 67th ARRS / 79th ARRS / 57th ARRS / 303rd ARRS / 304th ARRS / 305th ARRS, converted to HC-130P

65-0971: 36th ARRS; converted to HC-130P

65-0972: 57th ARRS / 71st RQS

65-0973: 54th ARRS / 55th ARRS / 41st ARRS / 303rd ARRS, converted to HC-130P / 71st RQS

65-0974: 48th ARRS / 79th ARRS / 36th ARRS / 54th ARRS / 102nd ARRS, converted to HC-130P

65-0975: 67th ARRS / 57th ARRS / 41st ARRS, converted to HC-130P

65-0976: 54th ARRS / 67th ARRS / 48th ARRS / 304th RQS / 303rd RQS, converted to HC-130P

65-0977: 48th ARRS / 58th ARRS / 67th ARRS / 39th RQS

65-0978: 48th ARRS / 79th ARRS / 71st ARRS / 2nd ARRS, converted to HC-130P

65-0979: 36th ARRS / 31st ARRS / 54th ARRS / 41st ARRS

65-0980: 41st ARRS

65-0981: 41st ARRS / 76th ARRS / 303rd ARRS / 129th ARRS, converted to HC-130P / 71st RQS / 39th RQS

65-0982: 41st ARRS / 37th ARRS / 76th ARRS / 305th ARRS / 67th ARRS / 71st RQS, converted to HC-130P

65-0983: 41st ARRS / 37th ARRS / 303rd ARRS / 305th ARRS / 129th ARRS / 71st RQS

65-0984: 41st ARRS / 37th ARRS / 48th ARRS / 57th ARRS / 76th ARRS / 33rd ARRS

65-0985: 79th ARRS / 55th ARRS / 36th ARRS

65-0986: 55th ARRS / 71st ARRS / 33rd ARRS, converted to HC-130P / 71st RQS

65-0987: 55th ARRS / 48th ARRS / 41st ARRS / 33rd ARRS / 1551st FTS, converted to HC-130P / 71st RQS / 79th RQS

65-0988 (HC-130P): 41st ARRS / 31st ARRS / 102nd ARRS / 71st RQS

65-0989: 41st ARRS / 36th ARRS

65-0990: 57th ARRS / 31st ARRS; ditched off Taiwan during search for sunken freighter on February 6, 1969; only one crewman of fourteen, the PJ, survived

65-0991: 41st ARRS, converted to HC-130P / 39th ARRS

65-0992: 48th ARRS, converted to HC-130P / 41st ARRS / 33rd ARRS

65-0993: 48th ARRS, converted to HC-130P / 39th ARRS / 71st ARRS / 41st ARRS / 55th ARRS

65-0994: 55th ARRS, converted to HC-130P / 39th ARRS / 33rd ARRS

HC-130P

66-0211: 39th ARRS / 48th ARRS / 1551st FTS; crashed in low-level turbulence in New Mexico on April 2, 1986

66-0212: 39th ARRS / 48th ARRS / 33rd ARRS / 1551st FTS

66-0213: 39th ARRS / 48th ARRS / 37th ARRS / 41st ARRS

66-0214: 48th ARRS / 39th ARRS; destroyed in ground attack at Tuy Hoa AB, South Vietnam, on July 29, 1968

66-0215: 48th ARRS / 37th ARRS / 39th ARRS / 56th ARRS / 55th ARRS

66-0216: 37th ARRS / 39th ARRS / 56th ARRS / 33rd ARRS

66-0217: 39th ARRS / 41st ARRS / 55th ARRS

66-0218: 39th ARRS; destroyed in ground attack at Tuy Hoa AB, South Vietnam, on July 29, 1968

66-0219: 39th ARRS / 56th ARRS / 41st ARRS / 1551st FTS / 129th RQS

66-0220: 39th ARRS / 56th ARRS / 67th ARRS

66-0221: 55th ARRS/67th ARRS/76th ARRS/129th ARRS

66-0222 76th ARRS / 36th ARRS / 102nd ARRS, "SPIRIT OF LONG ISLAND"

66-0223: 55th ARRS / 1550th ATTW / 41st ARRS

66-0224: 55th ARRS / 1550th ATTW / 303rd ARRS / 129th ARRS, "CITY OF MOUNTAIN VIEW" / 39th RQS / 79th RQS / 71st RQS

66-0225: 1550th CCTW, "Mambo" / 67th ARRS

HC-130N

69-5819: 1550th ATTW / 67th ARRS

69-5820: 31st ARRS / 54th ARRS / 67th ARRS

69-5821: 36th ARRS / 33rd ARRS

69-5822: 36th ARRS / 31st ARRS / 67th ARRS / 33rd ARRS

69-5823: 67th ARRS / 33rd ARRS

69-5824: 71st ARRS / 301st ARRS / 39th RQS

69-5825: 41st ARRS / 71st ARRS / 67th ARRS / 33rd ARRS

69-5826: 67th ARRS / 55th ARRS

69-5827: 67th ARRS, "THE KING"

69-5828: 55th ARRS

69-5829: 55th ARRS / 305th ARRS / 301st ARRS / 39th RQS

69-5830: 36th ARRS / 33rd ARRS / 301st ARRS

69-5831: 71st ARRS / 33rd ARRS / 67th ARRS / 1551st FTS

69-5832: 41st ARRS / 55th ARRS

69-5833: 55th ARRS / 1550th ATTW / 305th ARRS / 301st ARRS / 39th RQS

88-2101: 210th RQS / 102nd RQS

88-2102: 210th RQS / 102nd RQS
90-2103: 210th RQS / 211th RQS
92-2104: 210th RQS / 211th RQS
93-2105: 210th RQS / 211th RQS
93-2106: 210th RQS / 211th RQS

Note: The only aircraft omitted from this listing is the Kaman H-43A/HH-43B/HH-43F helicopter, since it was acquired solely for the local base rescue mission, and both aircraft and units to which they were assigned remained in a state of flux.

APPENDIX D
COLORS

Throughout the history of Air Rescue, color schemes and markings for rescue aircraft, like those of other commands, followed general guidelines. Olive Drab was the rule for aircraft and vehicles in combat theaters. Late in the war, interesting deviations saw Catalina amphibians painted overall white, and rescue aircraft that flew "the Hump" wearing a striking scheme of overall yellow with blue stripes. Air Rescue boats appeared in gray, olive-drab, or two-tone-blue schemes, some of which were enhanced with yellow markings. After World War II, high-visibility schemes and markings were common until war broke out in Korea, marking the return to subdued finishes and minimal markings. Bare-metal finish eventually gave way to overall protective Silver, or "Aluminized Lacquer." During the colorful Cold War period, high-visibility Day-Glo Red, International Orange, and Orange-Yellow were introduced. These shades were substituted by Insignia Red on aircraft operating in Arctic climes. Common to aircraft of the USAF Air Rescue Service was a wraparound fuselage band of Orange-Yellow (also called "Chrome Yellow") with black edging. Similar markings were repeated on wings and vertical tail surfaces. Normally, the word "RESCUE" appeared somewhere on the aircraft.

The official government color system used to identify colors is termed "Federal Standard 595," usually shortened to "FS" followed by a five-digit color number. Federal Standard 595 is not an absolute color system, but a color collection. The first number denotes the level of sheen: 1 for gloss, 2 for semigloss, and 3 for matte. The second number indicates a general color classification, which is as follows:

0: Brown
1: Red
2: Orange
3: Yellow
4: Green
5: Blue
6: Gray
7: Others, such as metallic, white, black, etc.
8: Fluorescent

A camouflage paint scheme for aircraft operating in Southeast Asia introduced during late 1965 used standard patterns for each aircraft type, shown in USAF technical orders labeled T.O. 1-1-4. Often referred to as the "tritone" scheme, its colors were Green FS 34079, Green FS 34102, and Tan FS 30219, with Gray FS 36622 undersides. An exception was a handful of HU-16B Albatross amphibians, which wore Dark Sea Blue FS 15042 over Gray FS 36622. Most HU-16Bs that were not camouflaged had their Orange-Yellow FS 13538 rescue markings painted over. Due to its size, the diminutive HH-43 "Pedro" often was seen wearing an alternate version of the tritone scheme, which used Dark Green and Tan.

Testing for a service-wide aircraft camouflage scheme in 1978 resulted in the "European I" scheme, often referred to as the "Lizard" scheme. European I used Dark (or Gunship) Green FS 34092, Medium Green FS 34102, and Medium Gray FS 36118. Dark Ghost Gray FS 36081 often was substituted for FS 36118. In some circles, this was referred to as "Euro II," but the term faded from use. One deviation of the Euro I scheme was applied to A-7Ds as only two colors: Dark Green FS 34079 and Dark Gray FS 36081, in wraparound pattern.

Basic Federal Standard 595 colors seen on USAAF/USAF Air Rescue aircraft are as follows:

15042: Dark Sea Blue
36622: Camouflage Gray (underside of tritone camouflage)
16473: Aircraft Gray (a.k.a. "ADC Gray"), often used as an overall color
16081: Dark Gunship Gray (Engine Gray in USN), Euro I
26118: Medium Gunship Gray (overall color of Sikorsky HH-60G/W)
36173: AMC Gray
36375: Light Ghost Gray (overall HC-130)
23620: Dark Compass Ghost Gray (overall HC-130)
17178: Silver (Aluminized Lacquer), also called "Aluminum"
13538: Orange-Yellow (also called "Chrome Yellow")
12197: International Orange
31136: Insignia Red
38915: Fluorescent Red (also called "Day-Glo")
18913: Fluorescent Red-Orange
34079: Dark Green (tritone and Euro I)
34102: Medium Green (also called "Gunship Green," tritone and Euro I)
30219: Tan (tritone)
14087: Olive Drab

1

2

83D EXP RESCUE SQUADRON 3

50 COMBAT MISSIONS USAF RESCUE PEDRO S.E.A. 4

SUPER STARS PROJECT 46 5

SKYHOOK 6

TEST TEAM HC-130H 7

ARRS AERIAL RECOVERY 8

41st ARRS THAT OTHERS MAY LIVE 9

301ST RESCUE SQ. GUARDIAN WINGS 10

EVACUATION OF SAIGON PEDRO ALERT 29 APRIL 75 11

1730 WE'RE ALL MAD YOU KNOW PARARESCUE SQUADRON 12

THAT OTHERS MAY LIVE 13

MAYAGUEZ MARAUDER KOH TANG 15, MAY, 1975 14

PHNOM PENH 12 APR 1975 FIRST IN - LAST OUT GOTCHA 15

RESCUE SOLL LOW LIGHT LOW FLIGHT 16

36th RESCUE FLIGHT THAT OTHERS MAY LIVE 17

USS CONSOLATION KOREA AH-15 18

35 AIR RESCUE 19

WESTERN AIR RESCUE CENTER 20

USAF PARARESCUE
THAT OTHERS MAY LIVE

21

THAT OTHERS MAY LIVE
ALASKA
212TH RESCUE SQUADRON

22

CIVIL AIR PATROL
U.S.A.F. AUXILIARY
AIR
SEARCH & RESCUE

23

41st RESCUE SQ
JOLLY GREEN

24

71ST RESCUE SQUADRON

25

23RD WING

26

STRENGTH AND HONOR
38TH RESCUE SQ.

27

1ST RESCUE FLIGHT
MH-1N
PAVE HUEY

28

563RD RESCUE GROUP

29

30

AIR RESCUE SERVICE
LABRADOR NEWFOUNDLAND GREENLAND

31

5040TH HELICOPTER

32

FEET WET OR FUCK EM

33

67TH AIR RESCUE SQ.

34

305 AIR-RESCUE SQUADRON

35

WINGS OF MERCY

36

LAND RESCUE TEAM

37

81 AIR RESCUE SQ
HELP'S-A-COMIN

38

DET. I-3RD ARS
RESCUE
KOREA

39

76TH AIR RESCUE SQDN
SAMARITANS OF THE SKY

40

41

42

43

44

45

46

47

48

49

50

51

52

53

54

55

56

57

58

59

60

61

62 63 64 65

66 67 68 69

70 71 72 73

Key to insignia
1. 1st Air Commando Group, Glider Section
2. 71st ARRS
3. 83rd Expeditionary Rescue Squadron
4. HH-43
5. Project 46, USAF test of Fulton system multilift
6. Skyhook, Fulton system HC-130
7. HC-130 Fulton System
8. ARRS Aerial Recovery, midair snatch
9. 1730th Pararescue Squadron
10. 41st ARRS King HC-130
11. Reserve 301st Air Rescue Squadron
12. Saigon evacuation
13. HH-43 helicopter
14. Battle to rescue Mayaguez crew

15. Phnom Penh evacuation
16. Rescue Special Operations Low Level
17. 36th Rescue Flight
18. Hospital ship USS *Constellation*
19. Civil Air Patrol 35th Rescue Squadron, California San Fernando Airport
20. Western Air Rescue Center
21. Pararescue
22. 212th Rescue Squadron, Alaska
23. Civil Air Patrol
24. 41st Rescue Squadron
25. 71st Rescue Squadron King HC-130
26. 23rd Wing
27. 38th Rescue Squadron
28. 76th Rescue Flight
29. 563rd Rescue Group
30. Air Transport Command

31. Air Transport Command
32. 5040th Helicopter Squadron, big dipper of Alaska state flag
33. Jolly Green implying aircrew to bail out over water
34. 67th Air Rescue Squadron
35. Reserve 305th Air Rescue Squadron, first patch SA-16A
36. 54th Air Rescue Squadron
37. 7th Rescue Squadron Land Rescue Team
38. 81st Air Rescue Squadron
39. Det. 1, 3rd Air Rescue Squadron
40. 76th Air Rescue Squadron
41. 66th Rescue Squadron
42. 943rd Rescue group

43. 12th Air Rescue Squadron
44. 49th Air Rescue Squadron
45. Battle damage Jolly Green
46. Pararescue "zap"
47. 37th ARRS Jolly Green
48. 40th ARRS Jolly Green
49. 56th Rescue Squadron
50. 46th Expeditionary Rescue Squadron
51. 37th ARRS
52. Sikorsky HH-60W first flight
53. LBR HH-43
54. Civil Air Patrol
55. 5th Emergency Rescue Squadron
56. Thule AB, Greenland Ground Rescue
57. Reserve 303rd ARRS
58. 48th Rescue Squadron
59. USAF Helicopter School

60. 40th Helicopter Flight
61. 40th ARRS
62. Reserve 301st Air Rescue Squadron
63. Reserve 304th ARRS
64. Reserve 305th ARRS
65. Air Rescue Service
66. Aerospace Rescue and Recovery Service
67. 7th Rescue Squadron
68. Reserve 304th ARRS
69. 36th Air Rescue Squadron
70. 56th Air Rescue Squadron
71. Sikorsky "Winged S"
72. 3rd Emergency Rescue Squadron
73. 41st Rescue and Weather Reconnaissance Wing

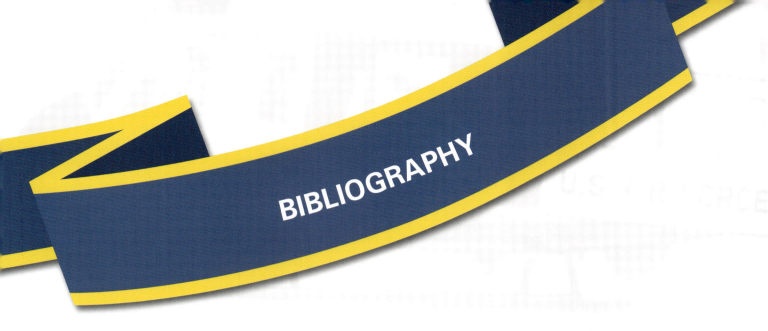

BIBLIOGRAPHY

BOOKS

Air Rescue Association. *USAF Air Rescue*. Paducah, KY: Turner, 1997.

Arnold, Elliott. *Rescue!* New York: Bantam Books, 1956.

Beck, Simon D. *Fairchild C-82 Packet: The Military and Civil History*. Jefferson, NC: McFarland, 2017.

Blair, Don. *Splashdown! NASA, the Navy & Space Flight Recovery*. Nashville: Turner, 2010.

Boyne, Walter J. *Beyond the Horizons: The Lockheed Story*. New York: Thomas Dunne Books, 1998.

Brandt, Robert J., and William J. Davies. *The Piasecki H-21 Helicopter: An Illustrated History of the H-21 Helicopter and Its Designer, Frank N. Piasecki*. Victoria, BC: Trafford, 2007.

Cantwell, Gerald T. *Citizen Airmen: A History of the Air Force Reserve, 1946–1994*. Washington, DC: US Government Printing Office, 1994.

Chinnery, Philip, D. *Stories of Vietnam Air Combat*. London: Blanford, 1988.

Dean, Charles L. *Soldiers & Sled Dogs: A History of Military Dog Mushing*. Lincoln: University of Nebraska Press, 2005.

Dorr, Robert F. *Chopper*. New York: Berkley Books, 2005.

Gradidge, J. M. G. *The Douglas DC-3 and Its Predecessors*. Tonbridge, UK: Air-Britain, 1984.

Harrington, Scott. *They Called It Naked Fanny*. New York: Hellgate, 2016.

Haulman, Daniel L. *The United States Air Force and Humanitarian Airlift Operations, 1947–1994*. Maxwell Air Force Base, AL: Air Force Historical Research Agency, 1998.

Keogan, Joseph. *The Igor I. Sikorsky Aircraft Legacy*. Stratford, CT: Igor I. Sikorsky Historical Archives, 2003.

LaPointe, Robert L., SMSGT, USAF (Ret.). *PJs in Vietnam: The Story of Air Rescue in Vietnam as Seen through the Eyes of Pararescuemen*. Anchorage, AK: Northern PJ, 2000.

Lewis, David W., and William F. Trimble. *The Airway to Everywhere: A History of All American Aviation, 1937–1953*. Pittsburgh, PA: University of Pittsburgh Press, 1988.

Little, Donald D. *Aerospace Rescue and Recovery Service, 1946–1981: An Illustrated Chronology*. Scott Air Force Base, IL: Office of MAC History, USAF, 1983.

Lundh, Lennart. *Sikorsky H-34: An Illustrated History*. Atglen, PA: Schiffer, 1998.

Momyer, William W., Gen., USAF (Ret.). *The Vietnamese Air Force, 1951–1975: An Analysis of Its Role in Combat and Fourteen Hours at Koh Tang*. USAF Southeast Asia Monograph 3. Washington, DC: Superintendent of Documents, September 1975.

Pocock, Charles. *Cleared Hot*. Polson, MT: Forward Air Controllers Association, 2008.

Politella, Dario. *Operation Grasshopper*. Tyler, TX: R. R. Longo, 1958.

Pararescue—Fifty Years, 1943–1993. Woodbridge, VA: Pararescue Association, 1996.

Stafrace, Charles. *Douglas C-54 / RFD Skymaster and DC-4*. Denbigh East, UK: Warpaint/Guideline, 2016.

Taylor, L. B., Jr. *That Others May Live*. New York: E. P. Dutton, 1967.

Tilford, Earl H., Jr. *Search and Rescue in Southeast Asia*. Washington, DC: Center for Air Force History, 1992.

Thigpen, Jerry L., Col., USAF (Ret.). *The Praetorian Starship: The Untold Story of the Combat Talon*. Maxwell Air Force Base, AL: Air University Press, December 2001.

Wendt, Dave. *304th ARRS Portland IAP, OR: 1970 to 1985*. Blurb Books UK, 2011.

Whitcomb, Darrel D., Col., USAF (Ret.). *Combat Search and Rescue in Desert Storm*. Maxwell Air Force Base, AL: Air University Press, September 2006.

Whitcomb, Darrel D. *On a Steel Horse I Ride: A History of the MH-53 Pave Low Helicopters in War and Peace*. Maxwell Air Force Base, AL: Air University Press, September 2012.

Williams, Nicholas M. *Aircraft of the United States Military Air Transport Service*. Leicester, UK: Midland, 1999.

BIBLIOGRAPHY

ARTICLES

"ACC Emblem Flies at Scott." *Combat Edge*, September 1993.

"Airborne Lifeboats." *Flight*, January 18, 1945.

Briscoe, C. H. "Helicopters in Combat: World War II." *Special Warfare*, Summer 2001.

Brooks, Allison C., Brig. Gen. "Aerospace Rescue and Recovery: Southeast Asia to Apollo." *Air University Review*, May–June 1967.

Brown, Harold, Secretary of the Air Force. "Air Rescue in Vietnam: That Others May Live." *Air Force Magazine*, March 1967.

Buhler, Jean E. "Development of the Miami: 63-Foot Aircraft Rescue Boat." *Northern Mariner*, July–October 2008.

Butera, J. L. "Rescue Concepts Before and After." *Aerospace Historian*, March 1974.

Colucci, Frank. "Big Charlie, Jolly Greens and Pave Pigs: The Sikorsky H-3 in US Air Force Service." *Air International*, December 1996.

Colucci, Frank. "Clementine and the Big Mothers." *Air Enthusiast* 20 (December 1982–March 1983).

Conner, Roger. "Medevac from Luzon." *Air & Space Magazine*, July 2010.

Cooling, Franklin B. "A History of US Army Aviation." *Aerospace Historian* 21, no. 2 (Summer 1974).

Correll, John T. "A Habit of Heroism." *Air Force Magazine*, January 2010.

Damonte, Carlton R., Capt. "Caring for Big Charlie." *Aerospace Maintenance Safety Magazine*, September 1965.

Dorr, Robert F. "Combat Rescue: North Vietnam." *Aviation News*, April–May 1986.

Drachlis, David B., MSgt. "A Matter of Life." *Airman*, May 1979.

Epifano, Anthony J., Maj. "Real Heroes." *Citizen Airman*, 1989.

Eppinger, Josh. "The *Prinsendam* Fire: History's Greatest Sea Rescue." *Popular Mechanics*, April 1981.

Fowler, Chuck. "Bill Somers' Military Service: The World War II Crash Rescue Boat Years." *Sea Chest*, December 2002.

George, James A., SMsgt. "One Day at a Time." *The Airman*, January 1969.

Glines, C. V. "The Son Tay Raid." *Air Force Magazine*, November 1995.

Hayes, Karl. "Boeing HC-97G: The 'Rescue Strat.'" *Air-Britain Aeromilitaria*, Summer 2009.

Jacobsen, Allan H., Capt. "Udorn Pedro Unit Last in AF." *Easy Flyer*, September 12, 1975.

Jones, Robert E., Capt. "The Most Highly Decorated Navy Squadron in Vietnam." *Foundation*, n.d.

Kamhoot, Barry. "President's Letter." *Footprints Magazine*, Jolly Green Association, 2019.

Kilbourne, Jimmy W., Maj. "Only One Returned." *The Airman*, March 1969.

Kinney, William A. "The Chopper Comes of Age." *The Airman*, n.d.

Kreisher, Otto. "Is CSAR Really Nothing Special?" *Air Force Magazine*, November 2009.

Leeker, Joe F. "Air America: Douglas C-54s." http//www.ut-dallas.edu/library.collections/speccoll/leeker/c54.pdf.

Marion, Forrest L. "Bombers and Boats: SB-17 and SB-29 Combat Operations in Korea." *Air Power History*, Spring 2004.

Marion, Forrest L. "That Others May Live: USAF Air Rescue in Korea." Air Force History and Museums Program, 2004.

Morris, Ted A., Lt. Col., USAF (Ret.). "Flight D, 7th Rescue Squadron, Dhahran Air Field, Saudi Arabia, 1950–1951."

Nikolaus, Larry D., Lt. j.g. "End of Big Mothers." *Naval Aviation News*, August 1975.

Olmsted, Merle. "Down in the Drink." *Journal of the American Aviation Historical Society*, Fall 1998.

Purvis, Pete, Capt., USNR (Ret.). "Fulton's Skyhook." *Flight Journal*, October 2004.

Robb, Raymond L. "Darkness Falls: A Farewell to the Pave Low." *Vertiflite* 54, no. 4 (Winter 2008).

Smith, Allen D., Col., USAF. "Early Medical Evacuation." *Air University Quarterly Review*, Summer 1953.

Smith, Clyde, Lt. Col., USMC (Ret.). "That Others May Live." *Proceedings*, April 1996.

Sochurek, Howard. "Air Rescue behind Enemy Lines." *National Geographic*, September 1968.

Story, Roger W. "Helicopter Projects at GE's Schenectady Flight Test Center." *Journal of the American Aviation Historical Society*, Summer 2003.

"That Others May Live: Rescue Forces Join ACC." *Combat Edge*, March 1993.

"The Flying Dutchman." *Air Force: The Official Service Journal of the U.S. Army Air Forces*, July 1944.

Tuder, William W., MSgt. "Knight School: A Report on 25 Years of Helicopter Training." *Air Historian*, Autumn 1969.

Vandegrift, John L. "Rescue: Past, Present and Future." *MATS Flyer*, June 1964.

Veazey, Robert G. "Pick-Up!" *Friends Journal* (Air Force Museum Foundation), Summer 1993, Spring 1994, Winter 1994, Fall 1995.

Ware, Bruce. "The Rescue of Charles Lindbergh, Easter Sunday, 1972."

Wartenberg, Steve. "Rescue in Burma." *Vertiflite*, March–April 1987.

Wells, Kristin L., Maj., USAF. "Luck of the Irish." *CAF Dispatch*, November–December 1987.

GOVERNMENT PUBLICATIONS

Air Rescue Service Historical Reports: July–Dec. 1947; July–Dec. 1952; June 1956. Headquarters Air Rescue Service.

The Air Sea Rescue Manual JANP 300, Wash., DC July 1945. Air Sea Rescue Agency.

Air-Sea Rescue, 1941–1952. US Air Force Historical Study No. 95. USAF Historical Division, 1953.

Department of Defense Appropriations for Fiscal Year 1987. United States Congress.

Flight Handbook USAF Series SC-54 Aircraft T.O. IC-54 (S)-1. USAF, 29 March 1957.

Flight Manual: CH-3C, CH-3E, HH-3E Helicopters T.O. 1H-3 © C-1. USAF, 27 Dec. 1967.

Handbook of Instructions for AAF Rescue Boats 42-Foot, 15 April 1945 T.O. No. 19-85AD-1.

Heritage of the Combat Search and Rescue Professionals. AFSOC History Office, 2005.

Historical Report 5th Air Rescue Group. USAF, Westover AFB, MA, 19 February 1954.

Historical Report 62nd AAF Base Unit, Activation to 1 July 1946. Headquarters Air Rescue Service.

History of the 40th Aerospace and Recovery Wing 1 July to 31 December 1972. ARRS/MAC/USAF.

History of the 57th Aerospace and Recovery Squadron 1 July 1972 to 30 September 1972. ARRS/MAC/USAF.

Project CHECO (Contemporary Historical Evaluation of Combat Operations) Report; USAF Search and Rescue, Nov. 1967–June 1969. 30 July 1969.

Project CHECO (Contemporary Historical Evaluation of Combat Operations) Report; Search and Rescue Operations in SEA, 1 April 1972–30 June 1973. 27 November 1974.

TACM.PACAFM 55-1 Sept. 1969. USAF.

Thompson, Walter S., and Raymond E. Wheeler. *Analysis of Combat Damage on CH-53A and HH-53B Helicopters in Southeast Asia, 1967 through June 1969.* US Army, Aberdeen Research and Development Center, June 1971.

USAF Mission Narrative Report # 2-3-020-19 Mar. 70 (U), 24 March 1970.

Weinert, Richard P., Jr. *A History of Army Aviation, 1950–1962.* United States Army Training and Doctrine Command, 1991.

NEWSPAPERS

"2 Boat Builders Win Praise for L.I. Yard's Pace." *New York Herald Tribune*, November 13, 1942

Bauer, Ray, 1Lt. "33rd Pilot Recalls Day of Gemini 8 Recovery Mission." *Outpost*, March 26, 1966.

Holstine, Harry A1C. "ARRS Commander Visits 303rd." *Beacon*, May 20, 1966.

Kirtland, Charles R., Maj. "303rd ARRS Here for Training Period." *Beacon*, Aug. 9, 1968.

"Spacemen Both A-OK." *Pacific Stars and Stripes*, March 19, 1966.

NEWSLETTERS

"ARRS Celebrates 26th Anniversary." *Huskie Happenings* (Kaman), 1972.

HUMP EXPRESS 1, no. 43 (November 15, 1945). ICD/ATC.

"Reservists Tied into Apollo Mission." *Air Reserve West*, August 1, 1971.

SEARCHER: Newsletter of the Pacific Aerospace Rescue and Recovery Center 1, no. 1 (November 1968).

INTERNET

http://www.pedronews.org.

www.rotorheadsrus.us.

http://www.ragay.nl/ Kaman H-43 Huskie Service History.

MISCELLANEOUS

Cole, John Haile. *Top Cover for America: The Air Force in Alaska 1920–1983.* AFA Anchorage Chapter, 1984.

Mosley, John. *US Coast Guard Aviation in Vietnam: Combat Rescue and Recovery.* Pterogram Special Edition, April 2004, Ancient Order of the Pterodactyl.

Olausson, Lars. *Lockheed Hercules Production List, 1954–2008.* 25th Edition.

(Notice) *Wing Sandy Alert Force.* 56th Special Operations Wing, February 15, 1970.

North American B-25C, 11, 12, 14, 15, 44
nuclear testing, 41, 84, 86–87

O

OA-10 Catalina (PBY-5As transferred from USN), 9–10, 22, 25
OA-10A/SA-10A, 10, 11, 12, 14, 17, 19
O'Mara, Oliver, 67
Operation Castle (nuclear tests), 41
Operation Desert Storm, 92, 94
Operation Hardtack (nuclear tests), 41
Operation Hayride (Haylift), 26
Operation Humanity (peacetime rescue operation in Holland), 40
Operation Just Cause (invasion of Panama), 92
Operation Redwing (nuclear tests), 41
Operation Snowbound, 26
Osborn, Earl Dodge, 30

P

P boats, 6–7
Panama Canal Zone, 4, 24, 48, 50, 80
Paradoctors, 32
parajumpers (PJs), 31–32
pararescue and pararescuemen, 11–12. 39, 43–44, 46, 49, 52–53, 57, 65, 66, 67, 67, 84, 85, 88, 94–96
Pardue, Littleton J., 23
Passage, John B., 12
Passey, Richard S., 11
PAVE (precision avionics vectoring equipment), 76, 77, 89
Peerson, James, 62–63
Pehr, Frank, 89
Piasecki, Frank N., 30
Piasecki Helicopter Corporation, 30, 42
    CH-34 "Arctic Rescue," 56
    H-21, 30, 42, 48, 52, 59, 81, 82
    SH-21A/B, 42–43, 48, 51
    YH-16 "Transporter," 30
    YH-21 (PD-22) "Work-Horse," 30
Piper L-4, 26
Pitsenbarger, William H., 66
PJs. *See* parajumpers (PJs)
Pleiman, James, 63
Pogue, Joseph, 45–46
Pope, Thomas, 70
Porter, John L. "Blackie," 11
Pratt & Whitney, 16, 25, 27, 29–30, 41, 53
    PT6T Turbo "Twin-Pac" engine, 81
    R-1340 Wasp engine, 27
    R-2000–11 Twin Wasp engines, 25, 41
    R-4360 Wasp engine, 53
precision avionics vectoring equipment (PAVE), 76, 77, 89
Preston, David, 69
Price, Donald, 63

Prigg Boatworks, 7
Priser, Donald C., 11
programmed depot maintenance (PDM), 91
Pugh, Dennis, 75

Q

Qaddafi, Muammar, 85–86

R

Randall, James Edward Prestle, III, 60
Rash, William, 75–76
redesignated rescue flights (RQFs), 94
Redington, Joe, 21
Rentoul, Norman, 44
Republic P-47D (5th Emergency Rescue Squadron), 9, 29, 44
rescue coordination centers (RCCs), 46, 64, 66, 68
Reserve Air Rescue, 47, 54, 83–84
Rios, Jose, 88
Ritchie, Steve, 74
Rittichier, Jack, 72
Rizon, Robert, 13, 20–21, 40
Roach, Charles David "Charlie," 7
Robb, A. C., 13
Robbins, Les, 49
Robertson, Stamford, 15
Robinson, Rufus, 31
Roosevelt, Franklin D., 4, 6, 14, 18
Royal Thai Air Force Bases
    Korat RTAFB, 57, 58, 61, 69, 77, 78, 79
    Nakhon Phanom RTAFB, 57, 58, 59, 61, 75, 79, 80
    Takhli Royal RTAFB, 56, 57, 58, 61
    Udorn RTAFB, 55, 58, 59–60, 61, 65, 68–71, 73, 77, 79
    U-Tapao RTAFB, 58
Ryan, William, 71, 72

S

SA-10A (ex-USN PBY-5A), 11, 17, 33
Salem, Harold, 66
San Francisco earthquake (1989), 94
SAR task force (SARTF), 74–75
Saud of Saudi Arabia, 22
Saunders, Alan W., 57
Scheib, James A., 33
Scheiner, John George, 8
Schibler, Mark, 66
Schneider, Lee, 49
Schroeder, Charles E., 34–35
Scopinich, Fred, Jr., 6
Scott, David, 49
Scott-Paine, Hubert, 6
SCUBA gear and training, 49, 57, 82, 96
Shepard, Alan, 49
Shumate, John C., 32